Exiles at Home

Exiles at Home

THE STRUGGLE TO BECOME AMERICAN IN CREOLE NEW ORLEANS

Shirley Elizabeth Thompson

HARVARD UNIVERSITY PRESS
Cambridge, Massachusetts, and London, England 2009

Printed in the United States of America

Publication of this book has been aided by a University Co-operative Society Subvention Grant awarded by the University of Texas at Austin.

Library of Congress Cataloging-in-Publication Data

Thompson, Shirley Elizabeth.
Exiles at home: the struggle to become American in Creole New Orleans / Shirley Elizabeth Thompson.
p. cm.
Includes bibliographical references and index.
ISBN 978-0-674-02351-2
1. Creoles—Louisiana—New Orleans—History. 2. Creoles—Louisiana—New Orleans—Social conditions. 3. Creoles—Race identity—Louisiana—New Orleans. 4. Racially mixed people—Louisiana—New Orleans—History. 5. Racially mixed people—Louisiana—New Orleans—Social conditions. 6. Racially mixed people—Race identity—Louisiana—New Orleans. 7. New Orleans (La.)—Race relations. 8. Assimilation (Sociology)—Louisiana—New Orleans—History. 9. New Orleans (La.)—Social conditions. I. Title.
F379.N59C878 2009
305.896'073076335—dc22 2008023696

The worlds within and without the Veil of Color are changing, and changing rapidly, but not at the same rate, not in the same way; and this must produce a peculiar wrenching of the soul, a peculiar sense of doubt and bewilderment. Such a double life, with double thoughts, double duties, and double social classes, must give rise to double words and double ideals, and tempt the mind to pretence or revolt, to hypocrisy or radicalism . . . the Negro faces no enviable dilemma.

W. E. B. Du Bois, *The Souls of Black Folk*

To Stephen and Solomon

Contents

Exiles at Home

Prologue: Passing as American

ON A LATE MAY EVENING in 1858, just as the day's uncommonly oppressive heat was breaking, a "colored young man" named Lucien made his way to Villere Street in the far reaches of the New Orleans neighborhood of Marigny. He was gathering gossip about an upcoming trial that had all of Creole New Orleans astir, and Marguerite Ménard, a free woman of color in her sixties, was sure to have some news. A mutual acquaintance, Anastasie Desarzant, had filed a $10,000 slander suit against Pierre LeBlanc and Eglantine Desmaziliere, both of whom had referred to Desarzant as a woman of color on several public occasions.[1] With the suit, Desarzant hoped once and for all to secure her reputation as a white woman. Charting the development of the pending case, Lucien wanted to know if Ménard had received a citation to testify. A lifelong friend of the woman of color who had raised Desarzant and whom the defendants claimed was actually Desarzant's mother, Ménard would be an important source of information regarding Desarzant's racial identity. She could recall Desarzant's early years as the blue-eyed child whose plump appearance had earned her the nickname "Toucoutou." At Lucien's suggestion that Ménard "had better" testify in favor of Desarzant, though, Ménard answered "No! Eglantine has far more sense than Toucoutou, and moreover when I die, Eglantine I'm sure will come to my funeral, but Toucoutou won't."[2]

As the exchange between Lucien and Ménard suggests, the stakes were high in this case—not only for the litigants, but also for a whole network of people whose loyalties and allegiances would be put to the test. Tellingly, New Orleanians have long referred to the process of racial passing—assuming a white identity—as "losing one's boundaries."[3] In claiming whiteness, Desarzant sought to cross the boundaries of race and legitimate kinship, in effect to lose friends, siblings, extended family, and others who had known her all her life. For tightly knit communities such as those existing in the intimate neighborhoods of New Orleans, each such loss to whiteness would resonate powerfully and personally. Lucien's eagerness to know the lay of the land further hints that the monetary stakes involved were far more extensive than the $10,000 Desarzant stood to recoup. Was he gathering intelligence merely to satisfy his own curiosity? Or were his inquiries an attempt to quantify chance, to translate Desarzant's unknowable outcome into a profitable opportunity for those willing to gamble? Lucien's enthusiasm—almost palpable beneath the words of the trial transcript—attests to the heightened sense of preparation preceding the main event. Were bets being placed? What were the odds of Toucoutou's victory? Who would benefit from her defeat? Many a wager may have rested on Toucoutou's fate.

The days leading up to and during the trial retained a festive air even though late May typically marked the end of the social and business season. During the cooler months, New Orleans was, according to one 1842 visitor, "one vast waltzing and gallopading hall. The commingled sounds of fiddles and piano-fortes could be heard at every corner of the street throughout the livelong night."[4] By day the port of New Orleans—second only to that of New York in the traffic it handled—presented a similarly chaotic scene. One 1850s observer called New Orleans the "Calcutta of America": "Thousands of hogsheads, bales, and bays and packages crowd and jostle and hedge each other in. And down the river-ward streets, flow rapid streams of human heads whose escape from entanglement is quite a disappointment."[5] As the summer approached, though, residents typically settled in for the slow and frequently sickly "off season" or retreated to cooler locations. The summer of 1858 was to be among the most miserable on record. By season's end over four thousand residents had died in one of the worst yellow fever epidemics in the city's history—second only to the 1853 epidemic that took more than twice as many lives.

In late May 1858, unaware of the epidemic's approach, New Orleanians filled the commercial and social void with politics and news of select criminal and civil court proceedings. With the June municipal elections fast approaching, a deeply divided electorate prepared for what New Orleanians expected to be a reprisal of the poll-day violence marking previous city elections. When the court rendered Desarzant's verdict on June 6, political factions were in the midst of a street battle that would last for five days, leaving four people dead and many more wounded. In the heart of the French Quarter, the colonial-era building housing the city courts sat ponderously at the rear of Jackson Square, the scene of a large portion of the violence. At least some judges, jurors, lawyers, and witnesses continued to make their way across the square, perhaps dodging the occasional bullet or brickbat.[6] As the slow season of 1858 commenced, New Orleanians had plenty to keep themselves entertained.

For French-speaking free people of African descent, *Anastasie Desarzant v. P. LeBlanc and E. Desmaziliere, his wife* promised to be one of the more compelling courtroom dramas in recent memory. Pierre LeBlanc—one of the defendants—had, like Lucien, also apparently made the rounds before the trial. According to a few witnesses, he had offered a variety of bribes: "an umbrella, a veil, two dresses, one pair of shoes, and gloves . . . six yards of calico, one handkerchief, and two hair stockings." If he were to win, LeBlanc seemed to have promised that the good times would roll for all who supported him: "he would give everybody plenty of money."[7] Not to be outdone, Desarzant's supporters sought as well to influence the outcome of the trial. Antoine Abat, the man Desarzant lived with and hoped to marry, turned up at Ménard's house the day after Lucien's visit. Finding her absent, he complained to Ménard's daughter of the ribald atmosphere surrounding the case, supposing "they would make [Ménard] take one or two drinks of whiskey and come to court to talk for two hours." Trading on the promise of violence rather than of money or drink, Abat warned Ménard later that "if she dared to testify against his wife, he would cane her in open court."[8]

Despite the threats, Ménard seemed to relish the opportunity to enter her testimony on behalf of the defendants when she took the stand on May 28. The case gave her a chance to ruminate over the series of dislocations and catastrophes that had given contour to her own life and that of many of her friends and neighbors. She and Justine Bacquié, the woman the defendants charged was Desarzant's mother, had been girls together in Saint Marc, Saint Domingue. They had been born in the 1790s in the throes of a series of slave uprisings that would culminate in the creation of the Haitian Republic in 1804. Both women and their families had remained on the island until the last stand of the French against the revolutionary forces of General Jacques Dessalines. Only then did they uproot themselves and relocate to Santiago de Cuba, across a channel directly to the west. In 1809, after a young Bacquié had lost one child and given birth to another, the two girls were again forced to move, this time by Spanish decree expelling all "Frenchmen" from the empire. Joining a motley assembly of refugees—a desperate population with members straddling categories of race, status, and class—they boarded separate vessels bound for New Orleans.

From 1809–1810 successive waves of approaching ships signaled an imminent humanitarian crisis and precipitated controversy and excitement in a newly American New Orleans. Since the Louisiana Purchase of 1803, the city had promised to become a linchpin of the nation's economy: "All the varied product of that [Mississippi] valley," President Jefferson had predicted, "would find their way to New Orleans by a thousand streams, while to the South lay Mexico, Cuba, and the tropics."[9] In the meantime, U.S. officials were having difficulty taming the unruly, indignant, and polyglot population bequeathed to them by successive French and Spanish colonial administrations. Enslaved people, free people of color, and remnants of local Native American populations gathered weekly on a large patch of cleared ground behind the original city grid. The sounds of African-inflected rhythms and the sight of dark bodies in motion titillated and scandalized white officials and visitors, but their market in surplus goods provided an important lifeline for New Orleans—more a "great straggling town than a city." French-speaking privateers—many of them San Dominguans of an earlier migration—congregated in the contiguous Attakapas region. Sailing under a variety of flags, they continually frustrated the interests of the nascent shipping industry in the port of New Orleans. In the city proper, ball-goers rioted when orchestras played English country dances rather than the French contredanse.[10]

Admitting the San Dominguan refugees to the territory would only exacerbate the problems officials encountered in their attempts to enforce

American laws, culture, and racial discipline, and the refugees huddled aboard their ill-provisioned ships while authorities equivocated over their status. The English-speaking residents of New Orleans and U.S. government officials took measures to impose order on the crisis. Those refugees of African descent—free and enslaved—were of particular concern: they had witnessed and perhaps taken part in the largest and most successful slave rebellion in the New World. They might, many feared, "contaminate" local populations of color with revolutionary ideas. The enslaved population languished on the boats for months as the francophone population of the city (along with slave-owning refugees now trying to eke out a living without their valuable slave property) lobbied U.S. officials to sidestep the 1808 congressional ban on the importation of foreign-born slaves. In a vain attempt to prevent "free people of Colour of every description" from relocating to Louisiana, the frantic governor William Claiborne conveyed to the American consul in Santiago de Cuba that "We have already a much greater proportion of that population, than comports with our interest."[11]

In their relief efforts, officials encouraged citizens to adhere to the racist logic that would become a trademark of American culture. For white refugees, New Orleanians raised upwards of $5,000—almost as much money as the city coffers held—set up temporary shelters in warehouses along the riverfront, took up a collection of blankets, and secured gainful employment. Encouraged to care for their own "class," the city's free people of color mobilized similar relief efforts, particularly for those young women of color such as Bacquié "burdened with children of a young age."[12] However, as refugees settled in new neighborhoods (*faubourgs* in local parlance) that had been recently carved from private plantations, the official segregation gave way to friendship and kinship patterns that cut across racial lines. Bacquié and Ménard eventually settled in faubourg Marigny immediately downriver from the French Quarter on territory once belonging to Phillippe Marigny de Mandeville, who at his death in 1800 had been one of the richest men on the continent. According to local lore, when San Dominguans began to arrive in large numbers, his son and heir, Bernard Marigny, subdivided his holdings into small lots in order to settle his mounting gambling debts. During her trial, Desarzant lived on Goodchildren Street in the Marigny, a couple of blocks away from her birth home on Greatmen Street.

As late as 1858, witnesses on both sides in Desarzant's trial described a dense network in which acquaintances took each other into their homes for extended periods of time, assisted each other in childbirth and other times of travail, served as godparents for each other's children, and monitored each other's whereabouts. A diverse assembly of witnesses—white people, people of color, and those who "did not know" their race; those of San Dominguan heritage; natives of New Orleans; and more recent immigrants—testified to a long tradition of locally sanctioned interracial intimacy. As territorial officials had done in the face of the 1809 migration, the courts struggled to fit these inchoate identities into the more easily managed—more American—categories of black and white. When the Louisiana Supreme Court finally ruled against Desarzant on appeal, the court's language sought to clarify racial realities, to "place this matter in its true light": "It can be no more doubted," the final judgment read, "that the plaintiff's real status is that of a person of color and that she has been endeavoring to usurp that of a white person."[13]

Desarzant's quest for a white identity was much more than an isolated event. In failing to pass as white, she demonstrated for other New Orleanians the benefits as well as the perils of passing as American. For Desarzant, as for other "self-made" Americans of the nineteenth century, individual choices coincided with and clashed with corporate and national concerns in provocative ways. Through the sheer force of her will and determination, Desarzant chased the American dream, but her peers and the courts met her with a powerful will of their own, effectively stopping her in her tracks. Desarzant and other New Orleanians of African descent recognized the limitations that the mere hint of impurity placed on their aspirations in their Americanizing city, and they responded to these strictures with a variety of contradictory strategies. They alternatively denied racial reasoning and embraced racial solidarity; they retreated within their isolated communities and mediated among conflicting interests; they espoused national ideals and nurtured skeptical exiles. Through their acts of resistance, accommodation, and resignation, they limned the contours of the dilemmas of race and pluralism and eked out an existence amidst paradoxes that the United States has never been able to face squarely. This book tells the story of their struggles to become American.

What does it ultimately mean, though, to suggest that New Orleans and New Orleanians were undergoing a process of "Americanization" in the nineteenth-century context or in any period since? Hasn't New Orleans always presented the very antithesis of American culture? In the face of American forgetfulness and notions of relentless progress, New Orleanians have embraced their ruins, becoming the nation's premier "city of collective memory."[14] In contrast to the Protestant propriety and racial standardization reigning elsewhere in the United States, New Orleans has exhibited a legacy of impurity, sin, and corruption of all sorts. In a national culture where citizens have proclaimed their "manifest destiny" in terms of an Anglo-Saxon racial purity, New Orleanians—in their linguistic and architectural heritage and cultural practices—have worn their French and Spanish colonial legacy on their sleeves. The local culture—encompassing such performance and gastronomic traditions as Mardi Gras, gumbo, and jazz—exposes the borders of the United States to the influence of a series of overlapping diasporas.[15] For many critics, the Creole culture of New Orleans has served as an antidote to Americanization, calling forth traditions of métissage issuing from the Caribbean and other locales that are decidedly *not* the United States of America, and Americanization has functioned as a "grim reaper," forcing a vibrant (Creole) ethic of irrepressible cultural mixture to retreat within a stultifying Anglo-American racial and moral binarism.[16]

When we scratch the surface of the history of nineteenth-century New Orleans, though, any strict distinction between processes of Americanization and Creolization begins to erode. For one thing, the U.S. national identity itself has incorporated and facilitated powerful narratives of vibrant becoming. Likewise, Creole identities have often masked enduring commitments to racial essentialism and other forms of determinism.[17] The process of Americanization, therefore, is not as limited or limiting as it seems, and Creolization is not as unrestrained or as freeing a concept as it is often taken to be. More importantly, though, the "Creole" city of New Orleans, from the early decades of the nineteenth century on, has functioned as a chief site of Americanization in two respects.[18] From New Orleans, U.S. officials incorporated the vast territory and diverse peoples of Louisiana into the nation and engineered a brand of imperialism that would influence decades of domestic and foreign policy. Also, as a bustling port city, New Orleans acculturated countless immigrants—particularly during the 1840s and 1850s—to the opportunities and strictures of becoming American. In New Orleans, as we will see, processes of Americanization and Creolization have proceeded in a tandem fashion with both progressive and conservative implications for the expansion of freedom, equality, and basic civil rights to all. Making sense of the New Orleans context is crucial not because New Orleans, in being Creole, harbors a special case that the rest of the United States would do well to emulate, but because it demonstrates in microcosm the challenges and contradictions of becoming American.

The symbiotic relationship of Americanization and Creolization is mirrored in the way the term *Creole* itself morphed its way through nineteenth-century New Orleans. A chameleon of a word, *Creole* has, in the most general sense, both masked and exposed anxieties over place, culture, and race. Wherever it is used, the term confronts the challenges posed by a radical pluralism. It attempts to name an ethic of in-between-ness—to connect multiple allegiances and to channel them into a singular identity with deep roots in a particular context. Marked by acts of translation, Creole languages and cultural practices develop from the urgency of communication among people from a variety of places who suddenly find themselves on common ground.[19] Deriving from the Portuguese *crioulo*, the Spanish *criollo*, and the Wolof *kréyol*, the term originally described a person of Old World parentage born in the New World.[20] Those with "Creole" sensibilities constituted a "new people" profoundly distinct from the indigenous peoples of their birthplace but increasingly separate from the political culture and social affectations of their country of heritage. In this most general sense, the United States of America is itself a Creole nation. In the wake of the American Revolution, the French immigrant turned American farmer J. Hector St. John de Crèvecoeur answered the question "What, then, is the American, this new man?" by pointing to the "strange mixture of blood, which you will find in no other country." Prefiguring Ralph Waldo Emerson's "smelting pot" and Israel Zangwill's "melting pot," he named the process by which "individuals of all nations are melted into a new race of men."[21] At the same time, though, Crèvecoeur confirmed emerging ideas about the nature of racial division and erected boundaries that would prevent black and Indian blood from flowing into American veins. Like Creoleness, Americanness implies and demands mixture and thrives in an atmosphere of fluidity and flux; however, these identities—for the Creole as well as for the American—are never as arbitrary as they might seem. Creolization and Americanization are compelling ideas in the abstract, but the potential and dangers attending these processes only realize themselves in particular locales.

On the ground of nineteenth-century Louisiana, the term *Creole* displayed an impressive elasticity, taking on a variety of forms to fit a range of individual and communal needs. When used with a lowercase *c*, as it often was in the antebellum period, the term benignly attributed native birth or origin. When used with an uppercase *C*, the word took on an overtly political cast from the early nineteenth century on. "Creoles," joined by former San Dominguans and others, clashed—often violently—with "Americans," whose numbers and influence grew steadily as the decades progressed. However, Creoles also accommodated themselves to American concerns and prejudices. For example, in 1836, after years of political wrangling, the city government broke down in a schism fueled by these cultural divisions. Sixteen years later, the divided municipality reunited under the terms of a consolidated government bearing all the hallmarks of an American ascendancy. Creoles and their chroniclers would mythologize this concession as a loss. It was a "hare and tortoise race," New Orleanian Grace King would write of the competition for internal improvements, political influence, and economic solvency in the divided city, and "in the United States it is always the hare that wins."[22] Nostalgia aside, some Creoles—particularly wealthy ones who could claim white identities—gained significantly by this practical alliance with Americans. From the middle of the nineteenth century to well into the twentieth, Creole and American elites defended their claims to belonging and priority against a host of "outsiders," including immigrants, Reconstruction-era carpetbaggers, and activists campaigning for black civil and political rights.

Throughout the nineteenth century, Americans as diverse as Emerson, Walt Whitman, Sojourner Truth, Frederick Douglass, and P. T. Barnum and as numerous as the burgeoning population embraced an ethic of self-creation, and New Orleans provided fertile ground for similar acts of personal transformation. Slave traders, slave owners, and those who aspired to wealth and privilege within the U.S. plantation economy descended on New Orleans, the country's most important slave market, to remake themselves from the bodies of the men, women, and children traded there. Sold down the river in larger and larger numbers, enslaved people shed their old affiliations and accumulated new ones on the antebellum New Orleans auction block. The urban anonymity of the city also offered some fortunate slaves their best hope for escape. This was certainly the case for J. Sella Martin who, after fleeing New Orleans on a steamboat, established himself as a leading abolitionist and religious figure. For pro-slavery imperialists, antebellum New Orleans provided a convenient base of operations for filibustering expeditions in Latin America and the Caribbean. To widespread popular acclaim, the adventurer William Walker struck out from New Orleans and transformed himself from a somewhat effete lawyer into the swashbuckling president of Nicaragua. In the midst of Desarzant's trial, the defendants' lawyer, the controversial expansionist Pierre Soulé, also served as chief counsel for Walker, who withstood federal charges in the late spring of 1858 for violating U.S. neutrality laws.[23]

For those seeking to recreate themselves in antebellum New Orleans, as elsewhere in the United States, "whiteness" was a particularly powerful tool.[24] Minimizing distinctions of class, trivializing any particular cultural heritage, and overcoming glitches in individual genealogies, whiteness produced a condition of equality before the law and created opportunities for economic gain and social prestige. Over the course of the antebellum period, New Orleanians of African descent—free and enslaved, francophone or otherwise—faced an accumulating body of laws meant to track and subjugate them.[25] The harshness of these measures was compounded by the arbitrariness of their enforcement, leaving free people of color with no reliable guidelines for how to conduct themselves in their public and private lives. Desarzant was not the first New Orleanian to attempt to evade sanction by passing as white. By 1858 other New Orleanians had established a powerful precedent for achieving personal freedom and equality through whiteness. In a sensational court case of 1845, the enslaved woman Bridget Wilson more than likely assumed the identity of the lost German immigrant Salome Müller. In doing so, Wilson passed for white, gained her freedom, and promptly quit the New Orleans scene, moving perhaps to California.[26] In 1853 the city councilman George

Pandelly weathered charges from a political opponent that he was a man of color. After he filed a slander suit, coverage of his trial filled the columns of the local newspapers for two long weeks, and Pandelly's case for his whiteness held an anxious public in rapt attention. Desarzant would certainly not be the last to attempt to become white. In the mid-twentieth century, Anatole Broyard, a member of a large and influential Creole family of color, embraced whiteness within the bohemian anonymity of Greenwich Village in New York City and became an important cultural arbiter of the mid-twentieth century.[27]

In seeking to prove their white status, Desarzant and other New Orleans Creoles excised questionable genealogies and created narratives of their multivalent racial pasts that conformed to an Anglo-American black-white binary. But these new accounts of white racial purity would prove difficult to substantiate in the face of repeated counterclaims. In particular, mixed-race people labored under a dual stigma of racial impurity and sexual impropriety—a stigma that by the mid-nineteenth century had become ingrained in the fiber of Louisiana law.[28] In Louisiana as elsewhere, families served as a conduit through the act of inheritance of wealth and property. They also provided the context for romantic and filial affection. Situated at the nexus of public concern and private desire, Louisiana laws governing marriage and family relationships sought to secure white wealth for posterity and to confirm white love and morality.[29] For instance, the digest of 1808 expressly prohibited marriage across lines of race and status (slave and free), rectifying what the new regime considered to be a somewhat permissible colonial practice under Spanish law, which had permitted interracial marriage.[30] In 1825 a state legislature trying to integrate American and white Creole interests enacted a civil code that tightened legal loopholes accessed by those involved in interracial commitments. Domestic arrangements and sexual partnerships across color and status lines provoked official outrage and caused all manner of legal wrangling, as *Desarzant v. LeBlanc* and other popular cases would make painfully public.

In large part, Desarzant's claims to whiteness faltered on the reputation of the late Justine Bacquié, the free woman of color the court was increasingly certain had been her mother. As others of her caste had done, Justine Bacquié had entered into a succession of liaisons with white men, much-romanticized arrangements known as *plaçage*.[31] Deriving from the verb *placer* (to place), *plaçage* was at its core a Creole practice inasmuch as it recalled a crucial strategy of Creole existence: securing one's placement in the face of contention. Creating a middle ground between legitimate marriage and mere concubinage, *plaçage* allowed a *femme de couleur* to stake a material, social, and psychic claim to belonging that could reverberate generations into the future. Forgoing the minimal but very real legal protections bestowed on women by legitimate marriage, *plaçage* was also a danger zone that exposed women of color and their children to the harsh consequences of arbitrary affections and loose commitment. As a *placée* (or "placed woman"), Justine Bacquié need not have suffered in the esteem of her peers. One witness referred to a Mr. Bacquié, a white man, as Justine's "first husband."[32] When asked what Justine Bacquié had done after her initial protector had deserted her, Marguerite Ménard replied, "She *married* again as she had done with [Mr.] Bacquié and others," suggesting that *plaçage* and marriage enjoyed the same sanction, at least in some circles.[33]

In the eyes of an Americanizing law, however, *plaçage* was increasingly seen as an outrage. Courts continually referred to interracial relationships as "abominations" and "illicit connexions." Any official endorsement of interracial sexuality would open up the legacies of Creole families to the mechanisms of racial scrutiny, and not many of these families would be able to endure such intense examination. One consequence of *plaçage*, as we shall see in Desarzant's and other cases, was a confusing practice of naming, whereby families of color, according to whim and circumstance, adopted or rejected the names of their white fathers. Thus, family surnames forming the mythology of white Creole aristocracy resound in the genealogies of Creoles of African descent as well.[34] Creole New Orleans continues to teem with these "twin families," and many a white Creole finds himself shadowed in his daily life and in the public records by a "darker brother."

In the late nineteenth century, allegations of impurity prompted those New Orleanians with stakes in the whiteness of their bloodlines to "purify" the definition of *Creole*. Turning the original sense of the term on its head, they argued that a Creole was a native solely "of European extraction, whose origin was known and whose superior Caucasian blood was never to be assimilated to the baser liquid that ran in the veins of the Indian and the African native." In a formulation reiterated over and over again in the late nineteenth and twentieth centuries,

New Orleanians contended further that while the noun *Creole* was to be reserved for whites, the adjective *creole* could be made to modify lesser beings and inanimate objects: "creole horses, creole cattle, creole eggs, creole corn, creole cottonade," and creole "negroes."[35] Conversely, New Orleanians of African descent have long considered a Creole to be a person of mixed racial ancestry and labored to discount the stigma carried by such "base liquid" as "black blood." In a 1910 essay for the *Journal of Negro History*, New Orleanian Alice Dunbar-Nelson attempted to set the record straight: "The Caucasian will shudder with horror at the idea of including a person of color in the definition, and the person of color will retort with his definition that a Creole is a native of Louisiana, in whose blood runs mixed strains of everything un-American, with the African strain slightly apparent."[36] For those of African descent, a Creole identity signaled a struggle against the limits the United States imposed on individuals and groups who had not become white.

In his community memoir, *Nos Hommes et Notre Histoire* (Our People and Our History), published in 1911, the civil rights activist and self-described Creole Rodolphe Desdunes also assumes a more inclusive definition of *Creole*. Born in New Orleans in 1849 of a Haitian father and a Cuban mother—both of Saint Dominguan heritage—Desdunes chronicled the experiences and achievements of his "people": Creoles of decidedly African descent. His tribute honors such courageous and loyal men as Hyppolite Castra, who fought alongside Andrew Jackson in the 1815 Battle of New Orleans, and such virtuous and chaste women as Henriette Delille, who established the Sisters of the Holy Family, an order of nuns of color.[37] In characterizing Armand Lanusse, a free man of color and the editor of the influential poetry anthology *Les Cenelles* (1845), Desdunes remarks that "His pride in being Creole was more dear to him than his being a Louisianan, or than anything else pertaining to his origin. All his preferences and resentments stemmed from this."[38] This curious formulation suggests that for Creoles of African descent, Creoleness is rooted in place but not tied to it. It has something to do with one's origin or heritage, but it competes with other aspects of these. Above all, "being Creole" binds together a group of cultural insiders able to discern a specific meaning from the vagueness of the term and distinguishes them from cultural outsiders who, in having to ask what *Creole* means, will never completely understand. Reclaiming the word *Creole* from white supremacists, Desdunes's composite memoir attempts to make a virtue of indeterminacy and ambiguity and to bind together a community in mutual trust and accountability.

Throughout *Exiles at Home*, I refer to Desdunes's "people" as "Creoles of color," although that is not what many of them would have called themselves—opting instead for *gens de couleur* (people of color) or simply Creoles depending on the circumstance. In the spirit of Desdunes's usage, I wish to disentangle the word *Creole* from racist motives and interests by focusing on the particular travails of Creoles of African descent. *Creole of color* combines the terms *Creole*, which includes enslaved and free people, and *free people of color*, which includes French and English speakers. I use the phrase to encompass a free francophone population and follow people such as Desdunes who distinguish this group from enslaved Creoles on the one hand and anglophone free blacks on the other. More specifically, the group that interests me corresponds with the antebellum group *gens de couleur libre* and their descendants who continued after emancipation to identify as the *ancienne population libre*, or old free population.[39] Not all Creoles of color were light enough to pass as white as Desarzant tried to do, but many of them bore the phenotypic evidence of a mixed racial ancestry. The 1850 census lists 81 percent of all free people of color in New Orleans as "mulattos" and 19 percent as "black." Ten years later, "mulattos" still constituted close to three-fourths of all free people of color.[40] Because masters who emancipated their slaves in the colonial period tended to free their own children, the courts ruled that people of color with discernable white ancestry should be presumed free in the 1810 lawsuit *Adelle v. Beauregard.* An 1845 case cited *Adelle v. Beauregard* as "the settled doctrine here."[41] Many *gens de couleur* "passed as free," and the lightest of them occasionally "passed as white."[42]

Creoles of color sustained themselves in the nebulous realm between free and slave, between black and white, and between French and American. Their in-between-ness often rendered them a disappearing people, making them difficult to track as they moved into and out of the racial, cultural, and national designations that increasingly mattered. In 1840 the free population of color had reached a peak of 20,000. In 1850 the census reported fewer than 10,000 free people of color, a number that by 1860 had rebounded to a little over 10,500.

This general decline defied an upward trend in the overall population of New Orleans, which grew from 102,293 to 170,000 in the same period. After the Civil War left everyone nominally free, a swelling population of African descent subsumed the antebellum *gens de couleur libre*. In 1870 census enumerators counted almost 50,500 "blacks and mulattos."[43] In the face of these demographic trends, Creoles of color—as individuals and as a distinctive group—ran the risk of being forgotten.[44] However, their suspension outside of acceptable classification often meant that they would be highly conspicuous as well. When they attempted—as Desarzant had—to "get out of their class," they could become objects of intense popular fascination.[45]

Throughout the mid-nineteenth century, amidst shifting boundaries of race, culture, and status, Creoles of color moved within and without a "veil" of invisibility and anticipated the pronouncement of W. E. B. Du Bois that the "problem of the Twentieth Century [would be] the problem of the color-line."[46] The experiences and cultural production of New Orleans' Creoles of color demonstrate that Du Bois's formulation was not so much a prognostication of the future as a reiteration of an ongoing challenge confronted by Americans of African descent in New Orleans and elsewhere. Throughout the nineteenth century, they expanded Du Bois's "color line" into a broader field of contestation and addressed the variety of opportunities and frustrations that congregated there. New Orleans' Creoles of color not only pursued limited personal gain—as Desarzant and others had—by passing as white; at key moments, they also underscored their African heritage and chose to pass as black. When they did so, they often risked their lives and reputations, but they also articulated a powerful formulation of civil rights that would only be realized well into the twentieth century. To dwell within the color line rather than squarely on either side of it is, in the U.S. context, to experience a kind of racial and national exile. It is to live—in the appraisal of Du Bois—a "double life" that "must give rise to double words and double ideals, and tempt the mind to pretense or to revolt, to hypocrisy or to radicalism."[47] As exiles, then, Creoles of color have offered understandably conflicted and compromised testimony.[48] In their varied acts of passing for white and passing for black, they articulated a morally ambivalent (and in that sense typically American) dream.

The history of *Plessy vs. Ferguson*, perhaps the most famous eruption of Creole identity in American law, exemplifies this ambivalence. In

1891 activist-minded Creoles of color, including Rodolphe Desdunes, formed the Citizen's Committee to Test the Constitutionality of Louisiana's Separate Car Act. Under its auspices, Homer Plessy, a Creole of color who appeared white, purchased a railroad ticket to travel from New Orleans to Covington, Louisiana. After informing the conductor that he was "colored," he took a seat in a car reserved for "whites." The train had barely left the Marigny terminal when authorities removed Plessy "by force" and prompted a lawsuit that, carefully considered and crafted, would survive the appeal process and make it to the United States Supreme Court.[49] In passing as both white and black—"losing (and finding) his boundaries"—Homer Plessy transformed himself into a trompe l'oeil passageway through the hardening logic of racial classification.[50] As one might expect of trompe l'oeil methods that attempt to make façades seem real, his argument also reinscribed some of the most pernicious aspects of that logic. Plessy and his lawyers argued that segregation laws forced a dark skin color to persist, against the spirit if not the letter of the Thirteenth Amendment, as a "badge of servitude."[51] But they also complained that the railroad company had divested Plessy of valuable property in the reputation of being white. In the Citizen's Committee's vision, would citizens stand equally before the law regardless of skin color, or would white skin continue to convey an advantage?

Plessy demonstrated that, in their search for markers of race, badges of servitude based on skin color went much farther than skin deep. They could penetrate far into a person's genealogy and rest, in Plessy's case, on a great-grandparent of color. For the rest of his life and even after his death, Plessy's own racial badge would take on as many shapes and tints as a hologram. Over the course of the early twentieth century, the U.S. Census would classify Plessy alternatively as black, colored, and white, and various voting registers in the 1920s would list him as a white Democrat. What are we to make of this designation? Had he "given up" on racial justice in his old age? Or was this an indication of his continued activism? Was "white Democrat" merely the cover that would allow him to vote his presumably more radical conscience? His racial boundaries lost to whiteness in some documents, Plessy would nevertheless continue to perform an important function in the black historical and cultural imagination. His efforts and those of the Citizens' Committee served as an impetus for a barrage of legal challenges to segregation, culminating in *Brown v. Board of Education* (1954), the case that effectively struck down the *Plessy* decision. Accordingly, Plessy's gravesite in Saint Louis Cemetery #1 on the edge of New Orleans' Tremé neighborhood has long been an important pilgrimage site for African American history and heritage seekers.[52]

By passing as white and passing as black—navigating the difficult transits of the Du Boisian color line—Creoles of color also demonstrated Du Bois's claim that "we who are dark can see America in a way that white Americans can not."[53] As dark people who have been "neither black nor white yet both," they have been perpetual victims of an American racial binary that could only regard them with shame and derision.[54] However, they have also forged from this binary powerful tools of self-creation and national critique. In passing amid the shaky foundations of racial and national identity, New Orleans' Creoles of color raised questions as necessary as those of Du Bois: "Do we want simply to be Americans? . . . Seeing our country thus, are we satisfied with its present goals and ideals?"[55] As abandoned children and disremembered ancestors, Creoles of color have been "tragic mulattos" caught up in melodramatic narratives over which they have had no control. As those who have often "changed the joke and slipped the yoke" of racial discipline, Creoles of color have also been savvy tricksters, masterful and sardonic manipulators of America's racial script.[56] But they have been more than these. Between the twin limits of the tragic mulatto and the trickster lies a world of human possibility. To pity Creoles of color their predicament—as some have done—or to champion them as America's racial heroes—as have others—is to cheat them of their significance to American and African American culture. The poignant range of their experience compels empathy from those of us who seek to understand their complex legacy. Their acts of self-making in the city of New Orleans—this Creolized middle ground of racial and national possibility—have mirrored and helped to structure the processes by which the rest of us have become American.

For these reasons, it is important to recognize the power and limits of metaphors and memories in forging legitimate legacies, real claims that can be defended on particular grounds. As an in-between people exiled from the comfortable confines of racial solidarity and national citizenship, Creoles of color have served as convenient prisms, refracting and reshaping competing ideas about race and belonging.

As she watched her case unfold, Anastasie Desarzant might have sensed herself entering the more symbolic realm of folklore. When she finally lost her case on appeal to the Louisiana Supreme Court in 1859, her neighbor Joseph Beaumont, a Creole of color musician, wrote a wildly popular song inspired by the courtroom drama and the neighborhood-wide debate it precipitated. "Ah Toucoutou," he taunted Desarzant. "We *know* you!" Later, in his 1911 *Nos Hommes et Notre Histoire*, Rodolphe Desdunes paid tribute to Beaumont, whose song had endured in the repertoire of New Orleans' street poets. Desdunes ridicules Desarzant for denying her African ancestry and praises Beaumont for helping to set the record straight. In 1928, however, the white newcomer to New Orleans Edward Larocque Tinker bristled at the apparent animosity of Beaumont's song. An admirer of New Orleans' Creole culture, Tinker had already placed himself at the service of a racially exclusive definition of *Creole*. Building on his previous research, he sought and found Desarzant's original court records and reconstructed her story in the historical romance *Toucoutou*.

Encountering Toucoutou in Desdunes's entry on Beaumont also awakened my historian's desire to discover the "truth" behind the fiction of Beaumont's song. Suspecting the case to be little more than urban legend, archivists directed me to Tinker's novel. There I was confronted with the stereotype of Toucoutou as "tragic mulatta," her humanity as well as her actual identity concealed beneath the melodrama of abandonment and exposure—the twin perils of Americanization for the racially ambiguous. If Tinker had indeed found the case, he had certainly done his best to obscure it again. Sensing my frustration, archivists reassured me that I was not the first to have searched for Toucoutou, that she had left a long line of seekers in her wake. Louisiana historian Marcus Christian was perhaps among those who searched the hardest. Head of the 1930s Works Progress Administration's Negro Writers Project in Louisiana, Christian and his team of African American researchers had been responsible for compiling a history of Louisianans of African descent. His dog-eared copy of Tinker's *Toucoutou* resembled my own well-thumbed photocopy, and I was certain that he had not read it for pleasure any more than I had.

Meanwhile, Desarzant's story lived on in the cultural imagination of New Orleanians—especially those concerned with the legacy of racial ambiguity and the predicament of exile. A mainstay performer in the brothels of Storyville during the first two decades of the twentieth century, trombonist Edward "Kid" Ory joined the Great Migration of African Americans from the South when he left his Tremé home for Southern California, a favorite refuge for New Orleanians of color. In "New Orleans Revival" (*Decca*, 1945), an attempt to bring jazz—by the 1940s a national and international phenomenon—back to its roots in the Creole city, Kid Ory and his sister, Cecile, recorded a version of Beaumont's "Toucoutou" as a dialogue between two characters—themselves brother and sister—over the culturally fraught issue of racial passing. In alternating stanzas, Cecile denies her "colored relations" and claims the personal freedom of whiteness, "*Ah, es te fou; Mo nom n'est pas Touquatoux!*" (Are you crazy; my name is not Toucoutou!), and Kid Ory warns her that society's retribution will be swift and certain, "*Société venez pour nous; vous ne passez donc en bas . . .*" (Society will come for us; you will no longer pass over there). In an atmosphere in which white bands dominated the lucrative jazz scene and secured the best recording deals, Kid Ory proclaims the futility of his flight from the Jim Crow South. Channeling Toucoutou's antebellum predicament, he decries the persistence of racial hierarchy and white entitlement: "*Eh Blanche,*" he interjects at the beginning of the song. "*C'est la misère!*" (Ah, white woman / whiteness, this is misery!)

In *An American South*, a collection of poems published in 1996, New Orleans poet Sybil Kein also revisits Toucoutou's story. Her collection coincides with the emergence of a new New South, as the region shook off the tarnished image it earned in its violent resistance to the civil rights movement of the 1950s and 1960s. Through the Republican Party of Ronald Reagan and Lee Atwater, Americans had again embraced the voice of the white South as a crucial component of the national chorus, and by 1996 the region rode the crest of an economic revival. Boosters of the South had successfully memorialized their history, creating opportunities for national and international tourism from the bloody legacies of slavery and the struggle for civil rights.[57] For people of African descent, the South was no longer "Hell on Earth" but constituted rather a "Black Mecca." In response to lucrative visions of *the* American South, Kein offers, in New Orleans, a multivalent depiction of *an* American South, one where unpredictable and angry elements still combined in spontaneous eruptions of nature. In New Orleans, it is true, the storms constituting local history and racial memory have left a profound ambivalence in their wake. Kein's American South groans under the weight of moral ambiguity and alerts us to the ravages unleashed by Americanization on francophone culture. Kein's Toucoutou brings us to the mirror where, collectively, we stare at the "rose-bud mouth / small French nose / Indian-brown hair." Just below the surface, our "ghost-grey slave / ancestors cause sudden / puffs of color to cheeks; / blush the eyes / with bitter tears." Toucoutou's own ambiguous "image narrows to vanishing / point," and the seemingly apparent newness of the current southern landscape mocks us readers, forcing us right back to where we have always been, left to "chime, vaunt, proclaim / this infinite untouchable / privilege of being / white."[58]

Ghosts, whether literal or symbolic, are not to be taken lightly, especially those originating in nineteenth-century New Orleans. Death hovered in the atmosphere of the city and pervaded its culture. New Orleans was so sickly that migrants to it understood the near-death experience of yellow fever or another tropical disease to be part of the process of acculturation. Those who did not make it were buried in one of the aboveground cemeteries skirting the edges of the city proper. As New Orleans grew, so too did these "cities of the dead," grim reminders of the stakes involved in living and dying there. New Orleans has a long-standing reputation as a haunted landscape, and dying there increased one's presence in the cultural imagination.[59] Death is the ultimate exile, especially for those banished from the living before they have secured a viable legacy. In New Orleans' literary and legal culture, ghostly figures contend for legacies of property and status that they might pass on to their successive generations. At the very least, they prompt the living to continue to speak their names.

The frequent incantation of Toucoutou's name through decades of New Orleans' cultural expression reminded me of the predicament of Mariquita la Calentura, a woman of indeterminate age, race, origin, and sanity. According to local legend, Mariquita roamed the streets of antebellum New Orleans and picked fights with young boys who taunted her verbally and pelted her with rotten vegetables. In turn, she demanded of them and other passers-by the price of a "picayune" for coffee. Only after her former tormenters found her dead in a vacant lot under an abandoned shed did they realize her value to them. Apparently, the young boys took up a collection among themselves for a pine casket, and hundreds of them dutifully attended her burial. Or perhaps not—they could just as well have left her decomposing where she fell. Nonetheless, the memory of this posthumous charity lived on in the cultural imagination of the city, providing a necessary complement for the blatant neglect and ridicule Mariquita allegedly suffered while alive.[60] In death, she has shifted shape according to the tale and the psychic needs of the teller. In the imagination of Creole of color poet Camille Thierry, Mariquita was a once-noble Castilian princess fallen from grace in the farthest recesses of the faded Spanish empire, and her spiritual destitution echoed his own exile in Bordeaux, France, where he died in 1874. In the memories of privileged whites at the beginning of the twentieth century, Mariquita was merely a "half-crazed . . . negress."[61]

Sorting out the stakes involved in remembering the stories of people like Mariquita and Toucoutou has led me to qualify the authority of the various archives on which I relied. Though many of us have abandoned the notion of biological essentialism and the quest for racial purity, historians generally presume a purity of a different sort: the fantasy that the archive is a shrine and the sense that our own spirit of inquiry is as antiseptic as possible. The traces left by Toucoutou and others have humbled my presumptions and raised my suspicions. As present-day people poking around in a long and complicated past, we are limited in what we can know for certain. We must not pretend that the archive is impartial—that the water in which we swim is clear and untroubled. Traces and evidence of past lives surface in archives, but never as innocently as we would have them. Various perspectives and motives—many of them quite pernicious—have shaped and continue to shape these repositories of historical evidence.[62]

When I searched for Toucoutou in 1999, I was fortunate that the relevant court records were then housed in climate-controlled, open-access public buildings. That had not always been the case. In Tinker's day, individual judges guarded or neglected these precious historical resources at their whim, and Tinker's personal entrée into white Creole society granted him special access to them. Before him, even George Washington Cable, the New Orleans writer whose characterizations of a mongrel New Orleans' culture would provoke local ire, could draw on his Confederate pedigree for research favors. Perseverant research assistance, the "intervention of a friend in the legal profession," and the "courtesy of the court" gained Cable access to the story of Salome Müller, the so-called German slave girl, and others collected in his *Strange True Stories*.[63] By contrast, Marcus Christian and his team of "Negro researchers" encountered quite a different scene in their Jim Crow setting. Committed to preserving white privilege as well as important documents, archivists barred Christian from accessing key source material and forced his team to rely primarily on newspapers and other published sources. As a result, Christian's painstaking work remains consigned to the footnotes of more "thorough" scholars, and we continue to raid his research and his multivolume *Blacks in Louisiana* for leads and frameworks.[64] It was in the Christian Collection that I finally found the citation for *Desarzant v. LeBlanc* on two faded index cards, water-stained from Hurricane Betsy of 1965 and stored in one of the hundreds of shoeboxes containing similar notes.

In New Orleans, public records present a particular challenge to historians seeking objective facts. The locally notorious Naomi Drake, head of New Orleans' Bureau of Vital Statistics from 1949 to 1965, leveraged her public post in a vendetta against "half-breeds" and "adulterous bastards" claiming white status. If she suspected an individual was of African ancestry, Drake changed the person's racial designation on pertinent documents from "white" to "Negro," often without notifying the individual or family members. She also attempted to bring decades of historical records in line with her racial sensibilities, "flagged" those with particularly "black" family names, and failed to issue birth and death certificates to dubious claimants. When she was finally forced from office, she left a backlog of thousands of such certificates. In spite of her infamy, though, her successors took up the mantle of her vigilant defense of white racial purity.[65]

Even the U.S. Census, the cornerstone of many a social history, cannot be taken at face value—especially in New Orleans. In 1850, for example, the federal government added the racial designation "mulatto," reminding enumerators that important scientific research hinged on their precision. However, within the gap between the perceiver—the census taker—and the perceived—the subject at the front door—there existed ample room for interpretation, evasion, and manipulation of racial identity.[66] When George Pandelly, acting as official census taker for the 1850 census, encountered Anastasie Desarzant on her Marigny threshold, her appearance convinced him that she should be listed as "white." However, within the decade not only Desarzant but Pandelly as well would initiate unrelated legal proceedings hoping to convince an anxious public of the purity of their white blood.[67] Sorting among these contingencies reminds us that the archive is—like the men and women whose lives it seeks to order—a "quintessence of dust," a living, breathing thing animated by the motives and actions of both the living and the dead.[68]

Exiles at Home attempts to secure footing in this shifting ground and therefore pursues a Creole methodology of speaking across and within boundaries of race, gender, and culture as well as those of discipline and genre. Echoing the spirit and structure of Du Bois's *The Souls of Black Folk*, I embrace the richness of the historical record but seek in the poetical and imaginative life of Creole folk the means by which I might surmount the clear limitations of the historical method. Through an interlocking series of representative portraits and significant moments, I follow Creoles of color as they attempted to address what Du Bois might have called the "peculiar problems of their inner life—of the status of women, the maintenance of Home, the training of children, the accumulation of wealth, and the prevention of crime."[69] As quotidian as these concerns might seem, they often loomed large and insurmountable for a people caught up in the dilemmas of Americanization. Like Creoles of color themselves, I adopt an ethic of translation, even though I have been continually reminded of both the clear advantages and the potential pitfalls of such a perspective. Though they serve a necessary purpose, translations are always inadequate if their goal is to convey the exact meaning of an original text or experience. Transposing among different languages and genres always produces an excess, a residue of significance that sometimes takes on a life of its own.[70] In this respect, more than one kind of ghost haunts these pages, and I am inclined to let the apparitions speak their piece.

1

Seeking Shelter under White Skin

THE SUMMER OF 1853 IS infamous in the lore of New Orleans. That year, the worst yellow fever epidemic in the history of the city presented a tableau of disease, suffering, and gruesome death. In late May and early June, a smattering of individuals, all recent immigrants to the city, began to exhibit the familiar signs of yellow fever, also known as "Yellow Jack." In its early stages, the disease mimics the symptoms of more benign ailments—a slight fever, chills, a cough. However, in the most severe cases, sufferers suddenly take a turn for the worse. Their skin takes on a jaundiced hue, and they typically experience delirium and a suppression of urine and stools before they begin to bleed from the nose and mouth. A sufferer wealthy enough to procure medical attention might have undergone a range of therapies, including sweet oil and camphor liniments, laxative drinks, opium infusions, orange flower water and syrup of maidenhair, *enemata*, vinegar frictions, and half-baths. If none of these remedies worked, the patient would invariably erupt with spasms of copious black vomit—the telltale sign of heavy gastrointestinal bleeding and a signal that "the doctor's function is at an end, and the undertaker's is to commence."[1]

During the first weeks of the epidemic's visitation, the press, under pressure from business interests eager to project a healthy image of the city, was slow to emphasize the severity of the problem, one paper attributing reports of the disease to "Madam Rumor."[2] Following the course of the disease through the major newspapers reveals its curious absence throughout June and the early part of July. Coroner's inquests divulged causes of death ranging from the ubiquitous "apoplexy" to "*Coup de soleil*" and "congestion of the brain" without much mention of yellow fever. In any case, the idea of recent immigrant laborers' dropping dead in their "feculent shanties" or "filthy, wet yards" did not raise concern among the New Orleans business elite or long-standing residents who believed themselves to be acclimated to the city's usual diseases. After all, these immigrants, an "indolent and disorderly horde," and the city's more established residents rarely crossed paths socially.[3] As late as July 30, the *Daily Picayune* could speak, for example, of "the vast disproportion between the gross number of deaths and the number of sick who are known to our citizens at large."[4]

As the summer progressed, the number of victims mounted rapidly, and the disease began "[attacking] all classes and [preying] upon all with the same gluttonous appetite," taking its toll among long-time New Orleanians, rich and poor, regardless of race.[5] Accordingly, most newspapers began to cover the disease in earnest by midsummer, publishing daily tallies of the newly sick and dead. An 1855 portrayal of the 1853 epidemic recalled crowds of orphaned children roving the streets and the ubiquitous markings covering the doors of the city's houses: "Here, there are four, five, seven, ten dead bodies!"[6] One article commented on the socially leveling scene at the cemeteries. "On the one hand slowly swept the long corteges of the wealthy nodding with plumes and drawn by prancing horses . . . where there again the pauper was trundled to his long home on a rickety cart, with a boy for a driver who whistled as he went."[7] Averaging over one thousand per week during August, the staggering number of interments prompted such morbid headlines as "Food for Worms" and "Down among the Dead Men."[8] Gravediggers frequently fell behind in their race against the epidemic, and the time-honored practice of aboveground entombment, traditionally performed because of the city's high water table, gave way to mass trench burials in which "the coffins have been sunk no lower than level with the surface of the ground, and then covered over in the manner of potato ridges."[9] Hasty burials performed by overwhelmed laborers provoked spectacles such as that occurring in early August at Lafayette Cemetery, where the "Chairman of the Committee on Cemeteries" found "seventy-one bodies laying piled on the ground, swollen and bursting their coffins and enveloped in swarms of flies."[10] Reaching its peak on August 22, when 283 people died—"a fresh victim every five minutes"—the death toll tapered off, finally reaching a more manageable level by late October and evaporating entirely after the November frost.[11] Official reports of the 1853 epidemic counted 7,849 yellow fever deaths, roughly 10 percent of the yearlong population, over 5,000 of them in August alone. Countless deaths and burials went unreported; other victims fell sick and died as they fled the city; and many more people suffered the disease and survived.[12]

In many ways, the worst yellow fever epidemic in the history of the city presents a portal into the fears and anxieties of New Orleans' residents over the cultural health of their city.[13] Yellow fever was hardly unknown to them. Over the course of the nineteenth century, the disease visited the city every summer, taking an especially devastating toll in 1822 and 1847. Despite the regularity with which yellow fever ravaged New Orleans and other tropical and subtropical port cities, its origin and spread remained a mystery throughout this period. General acknowledgement of the *Aedes aegypti* mosquito as the specific vector of the disease would have to wait until the turn of the century.[14] In the meantime, doctors and scientists understood yellow fever to be part of the unique topography of New Orleans, reflective of and produced within the confluence of social, historical, geographical, and environmental conditions.[15] The inexplicable etiology and unpredictable course of yellow fever allowed wide latitude for New Orleanians to exercise their fears and anxieties regarding their cultural climate.

Acting as a cipher, the response to yellow fever gave interpretive shape to concerns over rapid growth and social change.[16] Was yellow fever of local origin, or did it attack the city from outside? For city officials, the theory of local origin provoked concern over pockets of filth that festered in the heat and humidity, giving rise to "miasms" that, according to health experts, harbored the disease. "Whatever their opinions as to the causes of yellow fever," one contributor to the *Daily Picayune* wrote, "the effluvia arising from thousands of these piles of filth and offal all over the city cannot be healthy."[17] Alternatively, ideas about the disease's possible importation fueled anxiety over the port, not only a source of commercial growth and prosperity but also a point of vulnerability and potentially deadly contamination.[18] Was immunity or resistance to the disease a matter of nature or nurture, stemming from biology, culture, or some mixture of both? For white Creoles, this issue had dire implications. If they and blacks shared a biology that rendered both groups immune to yellow fever, as many medical experts believed, then perhaps white Creoles would not be able to distance themselves racially from people of African descent. If, on the other hand, "acclimatization" were simply a matter of adapting to the culture of the place, then in time "Americans," immigrants, and other outsiders could have as much of a claim on their city as they enjoyed. These concerns over the epidemic sharpened racial and cultural tensions. They provided an immediate backdrop for another prominent event, a civil trial that sought to confirm the racial status of a local politician, a member of one of New Orleans' leading families.

During the epidemic of 1853, citizens addressed their anxieties about contamination and death to the Board of Assistant Aldermen, the municipal body assigned to the mundane tasks of city administration. One would appeal to this board if, for example, a cesspool were forming in the lot next door or a dead animal were trapped in one's drainage pipe. In 1852, after five years without a major yellow fever epidemic, the Board of Assistant Aldermen had decided to scale back what it perceived to be an ineffectual Board of Health and, by default, assumed health-related responsibilities.[19] Thus, when yellow fever resurfaced with a vengeance in 1853, it met a largely unprepared city council. The Board of Assistant Aldermen had not been tending adequately to the condition of the streets, much less developing preventive and emergency measures for responding to a potential epidemic. With the residents of New Orleans dropping dead at an alarming rate, the assistant aldermen fielded charges that they were "unable to provide the slightest means of alleviating public distress and can do nothing, except perhaps, take a trip across the Lake, and enjoy a purer and more healthful atmosphere."[20] When their numbers happened to reach a quorum that summer, they devoted precious time and resources addressing "idle questions" and "silly disputes," including the accusation that one of them, George Pandelly, was not a free white person, but a "man of color."[21]

The seeds of the scandal over Pandelly's race had been sowed well before the epidemic surfaced in New Orleans. A member of the large and socially prominent Dimitry family, a Creole family whose members had been extremely influential in building the New Orleans public school system, Pandelly was elected in the spring of 1853 as a representative from the eighth ward in the Third District.[22] Less than two weeks after the elections, another member of the board received an ominous and urgent letter from Victor Wiltz, a concerned citizen, charging "that the maternal ascendants of Mr. G. Pandeli [sic] are not, or were not, *free white* persons." Along with this letter, which expressed a concern of "the highest importance to the country," Wiltz bundled documents "of the highest authenticity" that, he claimed, were sure to make his case. In compiling his dossier of accusatory material, Wiltz had searched the archives of the St. Louis Cathedral and various notaries public. His records ranged widely across both time and type, consisting of slave sales, marriage licenses, baptismal records, and wills dating from 1756 to 1853.[23] This evidence supplemented rumors that Pandelly had been an active member of the Clay Club, an association of free men of color light enough to pass for white who crossed racial lines to vote for Henry Clay in the 1844 presidential election.[24]

Just as the first smattering of yellow fever deaths were beginning to surface in the newspapers, George Pandelly decided to shore up his racial status by legal means. Seeking an injunction against the board's potential scrutiny of his ancestry, he appealed to the court that he was "from his birth to the present moment in the possession and enjoyment of his *status* of a free white citizen of the United States and of the State of Louisiana."[25] Frustrated over this wrangling, his accuser Wiltz went public, filling a whole page of the August 9 *New Orleans Daily Crescent* with his accusations and complaints. The debate over Pandelly, like the debate over yellow fever, continued into the more temperate season. In late October 1853, Pandelly had exhausted the potential of his first lawsuit, and the disruption caused by Wiltz's newspaper article ultimately led him to resign from the board. Three days later, Pandelly brought suit against Wiltz claiming $20,000 as damages for "slanders uttered by defendant to the prejudice of his (Mr. P's) social and political standing."[26] *Pandelly v. Wiltz* was tried, to enormous public interest, during the first two weeks of February 1854.

According to George Washington Cable, "The dreadful scourge of 1853 roused the people of New Orleans for the first time to the necessity of *knowing the proven truth* concerning themselves and the city in which they dwelt."[27] This curiously redundant sentiment held for the Pandelly affair as well. Each in its own way a matter of public health, the epidemic and the trial demonstrated the search for accurate definitions and remedies in the face of the contingency and mystery associated with both yellow fever and racial identity. The yellow fever epidemic and the highly publicized trial both raised the possibility of contamination—by insidious germ or by "black blood." Accounting for the source and spread of disease and interpreting race required for some a certain degree of exposure; particular bodies needed to bare themselves for the benefit of the larger community. Making public that which was intensely private, this exposure promised to reveal falsehoods and, thus, provoked a heightened sense of vulnerability.

It is possible to read the epidemic and the trial as catalysts for Americanization, as moments demonstrating the need for stricter sanitary measures and racial policies.[28] However, reading these events against the grain demonstrates the way the "people of New Orleans" arrived at "knowing the proven truth" and the stakes involved in getting there. Forcing the city to suspend business as usual, the pervasive atmosphere of death and the overwhelming obligations associated with mourning exposed the weaknesses of a city that understood itself to be one of the world's preeminent emporia. The Pandelly affair prompted a similar disruption in business as usual. Potentially dislodging personal, familial, and racial identities, the case threatened to tug at the frayed edges of the social fabric. One newspaper asked, "if one of the oldest families of the state . . . is to be suddenly disfranchised in consequence of a close but legitimate investigation of their origin, it may be that some of the dwellers in other parts of our State would *tremble for their status.*"[29] For the duration of the trial, Pandelly was not, as he claimed, a "free white citizen" wrongfully accused of being a person of color, but someone who attempted before all of New Orleans to "pass" as such.

As he lingered between racial categories, his right to civic belonging suspended, Pandelly's predicament both reflected and precipitated new understandings of race, culture, and belonging. The atmosphere of actual death accompanying yellow fever underscored the specter of cultural death raised by Americanization. How could legitimate and useful members of the community be distinguished from potentially corrosive elements? How might a citizen concerned over proper sanitation and cultural and racial purity begin to detect dangerous pathogens and contaminated blood? How might one distinguish insiders from outsiders? Was it possible to weave an edifying narrative about the history of the community from diverse and competing familial and personal histories? The urgency with which some bodies and genealogies came under suspicion created an environment in which individuals such as Pandelly and their families trembled publicly for their whiteness amidst mounting evidence to the contrary.

Yellow Jack and the Status of Creoles

1853 was to be a banner year for the city. After a sixteen-year schism, the municipal government, reunified in 1852, finally seemed primed to facilitate commercial growth.[30] During the previous winter, the city had handled $130 million of produce shipped downriver from the interior of the southwestern United States.[31] The city's burgeoning population had reached 120,000 by 1853, making it one of the five largest cities in the country. New construction proceeded apace, trying to keep up with the city's enormous growth. Freshly dug drainage ditches traversed the city in an attempt to prepare more acres of swamp for settlement in the rapidly expanding metropolitan area. Economic boosterism became a prime function of much of New Orleans' press. On May 29, the *Daily Picayune* proclaimed: "Nature has placed no limits to her greatness, she must become one of the largest cities in the world, perhaps one day the greatest commercial emporium on the face of the earth."[32]

Characterized only weeks before its appearance as an "obsolete idea," the scourge of yellow fever threatened to stop this industry in its tracks. "We have been thrown back for years in our progress," the editors of the *Daily Picayune* lamented in early August. When public health officials, doctors, and editors assessed the summer's events, they begrudgingly acknowledged that this progress may have even helped to precipitate the epidemic. Haphazardly launched development schemes left behind a potentially dangerous mess: "The gutters are uncleansed and carrion can be scented every block or two. In many places, the unimproved lots have been left to fill up with stagnant water or decaying vegetation, steeped in rotting moisture until they become centers for the generation and diffusion of pestilential vapors."[33] Voicing its suspicion of the port, the editorial staff of the *Picayune* admonished city leaders for failing to implement a quarantine strategy, in effect putting commerce before public health. Occasioning scenes that would become fodder for sensational articles for years, the epidemic posed an extensive public relations problem for New Orleans' boosters.[34]

As cultural geographer Ari Kelman has shown, the yellow fever epidemic of 1853 overwhelmed any attempts made by economic elites and city leaders to distinguish clearly between public and private. The flight path of the mosquito traversed the already precarious spatial boundaries between rich and poor, black and white, immigrant and long-term resident. The sick and the dying, forced to forgo the privacy they may have expected in these conditions, found their bodies, domestic arrangements, and private habits exposed to the care of strangers and to the curiosity of national reportage. After the epidemic petered out, *Harper's New Monthly Magazine* revisited some of the gruesome scenes: "Here, you will see the dead and the dying, this sick and the convalescent, in one and the same bed. Here you will see the living babe sucking death from the yellow breast of its dead mother. Here, father, mother, and child die in one another's arms."[35] Creating such spectacles and demolishing boundaries of decorum, the epidemic emphasized health as a *public* concern rather than a problem indicative of private disorder and treatable primarily within private spaces.[36] Moreover, the chaos created by the epidemic provided an opportunity for social inferiors to eke out more prominent public roles, if only momentarily.[37] African Americans performed overwhelmingly the indispensable task of digging graves, putting white officials at their mercy and commanding much higher pay than usual. Rumor of a subverted slave insurrection in New Orleans during the early stages of the epidemic suggests that enslaved people may have aimed to capitalize on the impending health crisis. Female nurses assumed a high degree of visibility, defying conventional wisdom about their "proper sphere."[38]

For New Orleanians, yellow fever was much more than a disease; it was a measure and test of cultural belonging.[39] The experience of yellow fever had long been an important part of the ritual of belonging in New Orleans, and the response to an epidemic distinguished in the public mind the city's cultural "insiders" from its "outsiders." Newcomers to the city were perceived to be the most vulnerable of all segments of the population. In 1853 Irish-born and German-born residents suffered the brunt of the disease. Of the nearly four thousand victims with a stated birthplace, over eighteen hundred hailed from

Ireland and over twelve hundred from Germany.[40] It was customary for writers to portray the process of social acclimation to New Orleans in terms of the physical experience of yellow fever. A. Oakey Hall, a self-described "Manhattaner in New Orleans," described suffering with the disease as an initiation into New Orleans' culture: "The back is like an unhinged door. You seem infatuated with a desire to immortalize yourself with a discovery of perpetual motion and, influenced thereby, toss from side to side like a rudderless vessel off the banks of Newfoundland."[41] Here Hall brings forth the transitional aspects of the immigrant's trek—discovery, dislocation, disorientation, and hardship in passage. The "unhinged door" is the illusive but attainable passageway. Here, Hall's proverbial newcomer emerges on the other side, fully able to record his experience, this record being the chief evidence of his hard-won belonging.

It is fitting, then, that German immigrant Baron Ludwig von Reizenstein brings the action of his *Die Geheimnisse von New Orleans (Mysteries of New Orleans)* to a climax during the epidemic of 1853 and its aftermath. One of a spate of German-American "urban mysteries" written during the 1850s and published serially during 1854 and 1855 in *Louisiana Staats-Zeitung*, one of the city's more liberal German-language dailies, *Mysteries* portrays a densely layered urban landscape, an underworld of class, status, linguistic, and racial dissonance governed by a host of irreconcilable energies and conspiratorial forces. Like the Paris setting of the genre's most famous practitioner, French author Eugène Sue (*Mysteries of Paris* and *The Wandering Jew*), Reizenstein's New Orleans provides a backdrop for romantic adventure even as it forges a proto-realist reform-minded depiction of the pitfalls of urban life. Effecting a comprehensive portrayal of New Orleans in all its complexity, Reizenstein intends to exercise a kind of mastery over the city to which he had only recently migrated. His account of the yellow fever epidemic gives us a glimpse of how an outsider might achieve an intimate knowledge of his new environment. Perching atop the gray wall of Lafayette cemetery at the height of the epidemic, amid the stench of (a wildly exaggerated) five hundred unburied bodies, the narrator observes: "*The ragpicker will be a rich man if he stays alive.* It embarrasses us to say that it is a German eagerly going over the corpses. The ragpicker is smoking a miserable half-Spanish cigar as he strips clothes from the bloated corpses. Summer trousers, good linen shirt-fronts, and women's dresses— . . . Do you recognize this ragpicker from last year? Oh, to be sure—he is sitting in a lawyer's office, and he's pushing a pen. A man can get rich if he can just stay alive."[42] Epidemics so upset the course of everyday life that an enterprising young stranger might remake himself as a wealthy proprietor.

Or he might at least gain moral stature in the eyes of longtime residents. Having just arrived in New Orleans in 1822, Theodore Clapp, a young Presbyterian minister from Massachusetts, learned an important lesson from one of his predecessors in the ministry. In the midst of the 1822 epidemic, the older minister preached a powerful sermon on the obligation of the clergy in times of crisis, demonstrating the high stakes involved in being a Protestant minister in a Catholic city: "Catholic priests always remain at their posts whatever perils assail them."[43] Even though Clapp's mentor began to display symptoms of yellow fever on the way home from church that day and died a couple of days later, his prescription for cultural inclusion was not lost on the young reverend who, resolving never to leave during a sickly season, earned a reputation as one of the most selfless citizens of New Orleans. In 1853, Theodore Clapp actually cut short his trip to the "salubrious regions of New England" in order to attend to the sick and dying, as he had done valiantly during previous epidemics. New Orleans, "this charnel house, this receptacle of plague and death," overwhelmed even the experienced Clapp's senses. "Whilst waiting to get my baggage, I could smell the offensive effluvium that filled the atmosphere for miles around. . . . As I rode upward towards the heart of the city, I became quite ill, and on reaching my residence was seized with fainting and vomiting."[44]

The stakes involved in demonstrating cultural belonging were exceedingly high in 1853. Some accounts of the epidemic, convinced of the inadequacy of "Yankee blood" in the face of "the pestilential vapors of New Orleans," continued after 1853 to portray a Creole population that remained "even now undisturbed in the midst of the slaking pestilence . . . the wizened-faced old gentlemen who here for twenty years smoked their cigars around the St. Louis Exchange or upon the esplanade by the Cathedral puff bravely on to this day."[45] Drawing on conventional wisdom about the exceptional immunity of blacks, Samuel Cartwright went so far as to propose the installation along the wharves of a "cordon of non-conductors, in the shape of negroes," as a solution to yellow fever.[46] However, most observers of the 1853 epidemic indicated that the trusted rules about acclimatization did not seem to hold: "the pestilence had attacked the Creoles and the blacks." The *New Orleans Bee* seemed dumbfounded at the course of the disease. "We have heard," wrote one of the editors, "of fatal cases among persons who had lived ten, twelve, and fifteen years in New Orleans, and who, having passed unscathed through several visitations fondly imagined themselves secure from an attack."[47] If immunity had been understood as one of the cornerstones of cultural insiderdom in New Orleans, this cornerstone seemingly could no longer support its creaky edifice. If insiders lacked control over their own responses to this supposedly place-specific disease, perhaps they were more vulnerable to other kinds of infiltration than they had previously thought.

If newcomers to New Orleans traditionally entered the public through the "unhinged door" of yellow fever, the events of 1850s threatened to close this and other doors to acculturation and acceptance. Throughout the antebellum period, especially in the late 1840s and early 1850s, New Orleans became more diverse than ever. Between 1820 and 1860, over half a million immigrants passed through the port of New Orleans, with over 350,000 people entering the city from 1847 to 1857 alone. Fleeing famine and revolution, most hailed from Ireland, Germany, and France, and a substantial number remained in the Crescent City. French speakers and German Catholics tended to consolidate in the Creole faubourgs downriver from Marigny, while Irish immigrants clustered upriver from Canal Street in the so-called American sector of the city.[48] In Reizenstein's *Mysteries of New Orleans*, the influx of immigrants to the Creole faubourgs accompanies the cultural changes of Americanization. "What is there about the name 'Frenchman Street' to recall the old *Rue de Français*, where five grenadiers of Emperor Napoleon Bonaparte built their houses next to one another?" Reizenstein's narrator asks. "A German cobbler has been living in [one of these houses] for a good ten years, and on his greasy walls hang neither Napoleon nor Josephine . . . but rather Hecker, Basserman, Kinkel, and Kossuth, the girls of the barricades, and Jenny Lind—these are the heroes and darlings he displays. How times change!"[49] Displacing memories of the colonial period with its particular ethnic preoccupations, the heavily immigrant population wrought changes to Creole New Orleans akin to the Anglicization of French street names. Immigrants and Creoles coexisted uneasily within the faubourgs.

The events of 1853 accelerated and disrupted local and state political alignments. In New Orleans as in other places, the two-party system weakened under tides of immigration, the debates over slavery's expansion, and a more vocal urban labor movement. The spring 1853 municipal election that carried Pandelly into office was a triumph for Democrats and inspired consternation in the press of the collapsing Whig Party; the elections also signaled a growing rift in the Democratic Party between entrenched propertied interests and urban workingmen.[50] By 1854, many elite white Creoles had begun to align themselves with English-speaking New Orleans natives in a coalition that over the next few years would violently suppress the immigrant vote, finding expression in the semi-secretive Know-Nothing movement. Charles Gayarré, the leader of the Louisiana delegation to the 1855 national nativist convention in Philadelphia, was particularly prominent. A state senator, judge, and historian, he would re-define *Creole* as white and come to exemplify that identity in the coming decades.[51]

The French-speaking Catholic Creoles of Louisiana formed an anomalous wing of the anti-Catholic, pro-English-language movement. They resisted what they felt to be the intense clericalism of immigrant Catholics and articulated a qualified nativism.[52] "As an individual, I have many causes to be grateful to foreigners and to our naturalized citizens," Gayarré assured his audience in Philadelphia. "Some of them are among my best friends and others for whom I cherish the warmest esteem and affection have become members of my family." In spite of these individual ties, Gayarré argued for the health of the body politic. "Pauperized Europe is pouring upon us an avalanche of human beings who, shortly after their arrival here, claim the exercise of as much political power as possessed by the children of the soil."[53] Just as ships from foreign ports were likely to be vessels of yellow fever, he claimed in another 1855 speech, immigrants would be vessels of the "German interest, the Irish interest, and God knows what other foreign interest," all potential contaminants of American political ideals.[54]

In the urban South, Know-Nothing-ism took a peculiar shape, distinguishing itself from the American Party in the rural South by its commitment to native-born white workingmen as "free labor" and diverging from its counterpart in the North by its need to accommodate a pro-slavery stance. Thus, in New Orleans the large umbrella of Know-Nothing-ism shaded diverse interests: an urban elite class of planters and merchants who typically had ties to the sugar rather than the cotton industry, evangelical Protestants attracted to the party's moral pronouncements, and native-born white skilled laborers. Posing as disinterested, nonpartisan concerned citizens, members of the American Party in New Orleans gained major political victories in 1854 and 1856 by violently suppressing the immigrant vote in scenes of "bloody saturnalia." Throughout the middle of the decade, voter intimidation and election-day violence were the norm. In the late 1850s, however, tension within the American Party over free labor reform upset its delicate coalition, causing elite slaveholders to defect back into the Democratic Party or into an independent movement. Before the 1858 election, these independents formed a Vigilance Committee, arming twelve hundred citizens in anticipation of an election-day showdown with the police force, newly reinforced with partisans of the American Party.[55] In this Jackson Square showdown, the much larger police force overwhelmed the Vigilance Committee. However, by the end of the decade, the political pendulum had swung back. The reform element was shorn of some of its nativist sentiment, having courted the German immigrant vote and affected an alliance with the Creole wing of the Democratic Party.[56] Marked by interparty and intra-party rivalry and competition, the volatile political landscape of New Orleans seemed rife with corruption, instability, and ill will.

In his remarks as a Know-Nothing leader, Gayarré spoke of "contamination" in the cultural and political sense, but the specter of possible racial contamination lurked in the background.[57] In touting their acclimation to yellow fever, white Creoles attempted to distance themselves socially and politically from the recent immigrants whose bodies appeared to threaten both the public health and the civic identity of New Orleans. However, because blacks were also considered immune, the legendary Creole immunity opened them to possible charges of racial impurity, a claim that rapidly accrued negative implications during this period. In the decade previous to the epidemic of 1853, American ethnologists, drawing on their research in comparative craniology and physiognomy, built a case for a biological and intellectual hierarchy of races, emphasizing Caucasian superiority and African inferiority. Josiah Nott of Mobile, one of the major practitioners of the "American school" of ethnology and a frequent lecturer in New Orleans, advanced his theory of polygenesis, claiming separate origins of the races. He spoke and wrote extensively on the subject of the relative weakness and sterility of the mulatto, augmenting a mere distaste for "amalgamation" to a forecast of race suicide.[58] While this theory in its pure form threatened to drive a rift between religious and scientific defenders of white supremacy, its popularizers, among them Samuel Cartwright of New Orleans, sought to reconcile the biological theories with the Biblical creation story, thus making them more palatable to the general public.[59]

When it flared up in 1859, the debate over race and yellow fever immunity reflected the influence of this ethnological research on New Orleans' francophone medical establishment. Drawing on data from the 1853 and 1858 epidemic seasons, Charles Délery and Charles Faget filled the pages of the slim journal of the *Société médicale de la Louisiane* (Medical Society of Louisiana). Even though these two doctors considered their differences of opinion to be irreconcilable, both sought to traverse what was potentially perceived as a racial divide between "white Creoles" and other whites. Seeking to dispel the romance ascribing immunity to New Orleans' Creole elite, Délery addressed this gap by claiming that no one held immunity, and he cited numerous examples of black and mulatto sufferers of the disease. The increased ability exhibited by some people to withstand the disease, according to Délery, stemmed from prior exposure to the "*principe morbifique*" (agent of morbidity), perhaps during childhood. Echoing ethnological theories, Faget, on the other hand, argued that Creoles, as "whites," indeed fell victim to yellow fever. However, because "yellow fever acts differently upon the human races," white Creoles derived their relative protection against the disease from the "slow and progressive action of climatic factors" on their constitutions, while black immunity was built into black bodies as a racial characteristic.[60] As far as Faget could tell, citing his own experience and several studies from Havana, both the "African race" and the "Mongolian race" were exempt from yellow fever; "this terrible fever was the exclusive domain of the Caucasian race."[61]

In offering an explanation for the legendary Creole immunity, both Délery and Faget sought primarily to align the cultural category "Creole" with the racial category "white." In earlier decades, immunity to yellow fever had distinguished between Creoles who belonged within the cultural context of New Orleans and Americans who were outsiders.

By the end of the 1850s, immunity, if it could be said to exist at all, indicated the existence of inherent biological differences between nonwhites and whites. As the city's most disastrous epidemic season, the summer of 1853 marked a watershed in this shift. It dramatized the extent to which the anxieties about actual death were intimately connected to fears about racial death or the imminent death of culture and history as a way of expressing one's "race." Unfolding within the context of disease and death, the Pandelly affair illuminates the processes accompanying this move away from an emphasis on place and history toward an emphasis on race—or, more appropriately, "blood"—and phenotypic qualities in determining belonging. The Pandelly case suggests that these two modes of classification are not mutually exclusive. The metaphor of blood, after all, refers to the history of one's family.[62] The instability of the metaphor—the elusiveness of the substance's "essence"—also mimics the contested and troubled relationships comprising the pasts of all families, particularly families emerging from such a diverse colonial history as that of Louisiana. In the Pandelly case, family histories would take center stage in making the case for or against Creole whiteness and belonging. In his efforts to facilitate Americanization, Victor Wiltz sought to make Pandelly's family history and community memories about the family prove Pandelly's biological race. In the process, he narrowed the scope of cultural meanings attributable to this genealogy and precipitated a crisis among those who understood this particular family history to be linked to the history of the entire Creole population. Just as the response to yellow fever blurred the distinction between public and private, the interrogation of the private stories and intimate commitments constituting Pandelly's genealogy assumed supreme public relevance.[63]

The Pandelly Affair and Public Genealogy

As his initial charge made clear, Wiltz possessed documents claiming the highest authenticity in the disclosure of Pandelly's ancestry. This documentary evidence, which tracked Pandelly's maternal line over a hundred years, revealed that his ancestors had not been "free white persons."[64] Instead, his lineage proceeded in the following manner: Marianne Lalande (or Delha) gave birth to a daughter named Maria Francesca in 1755. The father was probably a Frenchman named

François Monplaisir Chauvin Beaulieu, and his daughter often went by the shorter name Françoise (or Francesca) Monplaisir.[65] Françoise Monplaisir lived with Michel Dragon, a Greek immigrant and slave trader, whom she eventually "married" in 1815 when he was seventy years old. In 1777 they baptized a daughter, Maria Anna Dragon, who years later became the legitimate wife of her father's friend Andreas Dimitry, also from Greece. George Pandelly's mother, Euphrosine, was born of this union in 1801.

Consisting of marriage certificates, baptismal records, notarized slave sales, and wills, Wiltz's evidence clearly shows that the Monplaisir-Dragon-Dimitry women were commonly referred to as "mulatresses" or "quateroons." The oldest document, a baptismal certificate from 1756, records the ceremonial rites given to "Maria Francesca, mulatress daughter, aged about eight months, of Marianne Lalande, slave of Mr. Lalande le Conseiller." When Maria Francesca baptized her own daughter in 1777, the official record identified her as a "free mulatto woman." In various transactions from 1785 to 1795, including a debt recovery and a number of slave sales, Françoise appears as a "free quadroon woman of this city." The public record of these women as free mulatto women or free quadroons began to vanish in 1799 with the marriage of Dragon's and Monplaisir's daughter, Maria Anna, to Dimitry. The marriage certificate refers to Maria Anna as the "natural legitimate child" of Dragon and notes that Père Antoine read "a publication of the marriage bans at their ceremony." These factors betray a certain ambiguity surrounding the marriage. White fathers typically referred to their white children by marriage as legitimate and their duly acknowledged children of color as their natural children. Here, Maria Anna receives both appellations. In reading the "marriage bans," Père Antoine—a priest who was reputed as being open to performing interracial "marriages"—seemed to acknowledge the potential impropriety of the marriage.[66] Despite these caveats, the ceremony proceeded with "no cause or impediment preventing [it]." By 1801, when Maria Anna and Dimitry gave birth to a daughter, she could be baptized as legitimate and recorded on the white register of baptismal acts.

In 1819, during the first decade of Louisiana statehood, Michel Dragon must have felt that he had some loose ends to attend to with respect to the future generations of his family. In April of that year, at age seventy-four and "somewhat unwell in body," Dragon called the notary Christoval de Armas to his home on Chartres Street and performed two related acts. First, he acknowledged his forty-two year old daughter Maria Anna Dragon, now wife of "Mr. Andrew Dimitry," as his "natural" daughter so that she could be "entitled, in all plenitude, to the rights that she may claim, and which she may enjoy in her said quality." A week later, he drew up a last will that sought to reinforce Francesca's claims to the household property and immovables (including slaves). Taken together, these two acts—the acknowledgement of his natural child and his last will—followed the pattern of a man attempting, from what he believed to be his death bed, to protect his *placée* and their child. Dragon's recognition of Maria Anna as his natural daughter, so Wiltz summarized, "shows very clearly that Mr. Dragon did not consider he was legally married, for this acknowledgement of a *natural* child was not necessary, had he married a white woman: both wife and child would have been legitimated by his marriage with a white woman." Furthermore, Wiltz continued, the will "shows that Miguel Dragon calls Maria Anna Dragon his natural daughter and declares that he has lived with M. F. M. C. B. for fifty years. In no instance does he call Maria Francesca Monplaisir his *wife* or his *spouse* in this document."[67] It is possible that Dragon agonized over these notarial acts instituted in his later years. Potentially, they were at cross-purposes with the aspirations of his family. In 1819 Dragon had a host of legally white grandchildren from the union of Maria Anna and Andreas Dimitry. Any hint that Maria Anna was merely a natural child and any attention called to his "*mariage de conscience*" to Francesca could have been disastrous for the status of the Dimitry children. However, failing to acknowledge and protect his own "wife" and child may have placed them in danger of financial ruin. Ultimately, the Pandelly trial honed in on this gap between the family's claims to white privilege and the documentary trail that remained.

Political rivalry perhaps partially accounts for Wiltz's motives. His rhetoric indicates that he thought he was performing a public service for the southern cause, a movement that in the early 1850s became increasingly strident. In 1848 the United States concluded a war with Mexico, a war largely understood—by southerners and northerners alike—as a strategy to augment the interests of elite southern slaveholders. However, by the early 1850s, planters and aspiring planters with designs on the Mexican territorial cession competed with the increasingly vocal demand that these lands be reserved for free white labor. In the context of this national debate, abolitionists and other critics of the southern way of life found a receptive audience, provoking southern intellectuals to refine their defense of their practices and ideals and to invest them with cultural meaning and moral significance.[68] By no means an intellectual, Wiltz considered himself a "steward" of the South, a role outlined in the thought of pro-southern thinkers such as the U.S. senator from South Carolina James Henry Hammond and the Virginian George Fitzhugh, a critic of industrial capitalism.[69] Inspired by his more famous countrymen, Wiltz sought to realign New Orleans with the rest of the American South on the issue of racial etiquette. "Is not all this strange proceeding in a Southern city?" Wiltz asked of the board's wavering attempts to protect Pandelly. "I will ask a question to some of the Assistant Aldermen: How and why is it, that when you are out of the Council room, you say George Pandelly is a *Negro*, or *mulatto*, etc., or say that you are convinced he is so, and when in the Council you deal with him as your colleague and support him as such?"[70]

In setting the "facts of the case before the public," Wiltz articulated two principal tenets of an emerging southern ideology: a commitment to white supremacy and a pledge to eradicate political corruption.[71] When Wiltz worried about the etiquette of race and citizenship in the "Southern City" of New Orleans, its *urban* character constituted one of his primary concerns, especially in the aftermath of the yellow fever epidemic. The anonymity amidst diversity characterizing urban settings and transforming individual and collective identity in places like New York, Paris, and London posed a particular problem for the metropolis of the U.S. South. In 1854, the same year as Pandelly's trial, Charles Gayarré addressed this concern in "A School for Politics," a piece of fiction exploring how an enlightened politician might negotiate the minefield of New Orleans' urban and highly partisan political terrain. "Let men lay their snares," his main character proclaims. "I will profit by their weakness—their lies—their vices—their treachery—but I will keep free from contamination. I will not corrupt anyone—but I will use the corrupt for noble and patriotic purposes."[72] This is the role that Wiltz purported to perform.

The southern national identity that would continue to emerge over the course of the 1850s was predicated on a more rural, pastoral ethos emphasizing codes of patriarchal benevolence, social deference, racial hierarchy, and bucolic order—qualities difficult to maintain in an urban environment, as the plague of 1853 so effectively demonstrated.[73] For example, on the same day that Wiltz's charges against the council appeared in the paper, the public watched in horror as a massive pile of bodies lay abandoned and decomposing in Lafayette Cemetery. Despite the glut of human corpses, Wiltz could claim that the "really disgusting" development was the board's equivocation with respect to his charges against Pandelly. Wiltz prevailed upon white citizens to correct the actions of their elected officials. "The strange conduct of some of the Assistant Aldermen in this case; the *underground charge of slander* imputed to me, and the cowardly threats and menaces proffered against me," Wiltz argued, "compel me to give to my fellow citizens and to the public a plain and correct statement of all matters relative to this affair within my knowledge."[74] When a female relative of Pandelly's acting with "the feelings of a mother and a wife" pleaded with Wiltz to rescind his allegations, he insisted that he did not harbor any personal animosity towards Pandelly or the family and that he, in fact, "never saw [Pandelly] until he was pointed out in a company of Firemen." It was the family's public aspirations that inspired him to "busy" himself with them: "as long as they were in ordinary business he had no objection, but whenever they pretended to get into public employment, then he was determined to put them down."[75] In Wiltz's mind, his call to action constituted a "true and correct" record of both the board's dismissal of his allegations and the history of Pandelly's family. He hoped to fix and enshrine a collective understanding of the affair that would advance his conception of the southern cause.[76]

During the winter and spring of 1853–54, another series of investigations paralleling those into Pandelly's origins were underway. The mayor and the Board of Aldermen and Assistant Aldermen (a seat on which Pandelly had recently resigned) had assembled a sanitary commission charged with compiling a comprehensive report on the course of the previous summer's yellow fever epidemic. The doctors composing the commission interviewed medical practitioners, consulted international experts, reviewed the available data, visited the problem of sewage and drainage, and pondered the proposition of quarantine. Constructing a sanitary map of the city, the commission recommended that the "low, crowded, and filthy tenements"—veritable "fever nests"—

submit themselves to the "cauterizing appliances of the city government"; that livery stables, vacheries, and slaughterhouses in the city's vicinity be abated; that cemeteries within the city limits be "closed against future use"; and that "kitchen offal and back yard filth, including the bad system and neglect of the privies . . . require the most active agency and timely surveillance of the Health Department."[77] The city-appointed experts on the commission recommended no less than a revolution in the relationship of New Orleanians to their environment. "Hence then, away with the nonsense about the difficulty of acclimation, which only tends to blind the ignorant; if we are to have a healthy city, we must have a *really clean one.*"[78] In other words, New Orleanians could no longer afford merely to adapt to substandard sanitary conditions; they must transform their practices and reform their habits, taking a proactive role in eradicating even the possibility of contamination. If New Orleanians were willing to take the necessary steps, "it would be altogether impossible for the yellow fever to originate here, or to be disseminated as an epidemic, if brought from abroad."[79] The urgency and vigilance they demanded of the New Orleans body politic echoed that urged by Victor Wiltz, who wrote of the inquiry into Pandelly's racial identity: "This question is of the highest importance to the community."[80]

By the time February arrived, the Pandelly case had generated so much interest that crowds of spectators flocked each day to the Presbytere. The ponderous and poorly maintained building on the downriver side of St. Louis Cathedral housed all the city's courts. Its galleries rickety and its roof having been haphazardly patched following an 1851 fire, the courtroom could not have been comfortable. According to an earlier visitor to the city, the building "has everywhere an ancient, fatty smell, which speaks disparagingly of the odor in which justice is held."[81] Nevertheless, the "eager crowd" gathered "long before the hour appointed for the resumption of this case, . . . [indicating] that the trial was one, the interest of which was not confined to the parties litigant, but one which concerned the whole body politic."[82] The crowds continued to multiply until the judge proposed moving the proceedings to another, more spacious, and better ventilated courtroom in the same building. "The breathing of the carbonic acid emitted from so many lungs," the judge concluded, "was . . . deleterious to health."[83]

Those who could not make it to the courtroom every day from the first of February until the thirteenth could follow the trial in the newspapers, a number of which carried an almost word-for-word transcription of the proceedings and offered a running commentary on its significance. In the *New Orleans Bee/l'Abeille de la Nouvelle Orleans,* for example, the "Pandelly Case" always led the list of "Local Items" and sometimes filled as many as two columns of the front page, where it titillated the newspaper's bilingual readership. This format, reminiscent of serialized fiction, produced a similar effect on the reading public. Broken up into the discrete units of the court proceedings of a particular day, the installments heightened the element of suspense and offered bits of debatable evidence. Giving readers the sense of being involved in the courtroom drama, the newspaper coverage turned the readers into an extended community of jurors. Appearing against the rest of the news in sharp relief, the "Pandelly Case" did not look like the usual court coverage, where summaries took up no more than a couple of inches of column space. Nor did it resemble articles on useful news from around the city, nation, and world that concerned the city's business community. The hectic pace of the newspaper was slowed for the Pandelly affair, an event not merely summarized but instead reported in courtroom time, reproducing the excruciatingly slow tempo of interrogation and testimony. Forcing citizens to confront each word as evidence, this mass examination of racial and cultural identity in New Orleans required that readers and spectators be willing to interrogate the history of the region and its people.[84]

The *Louisiana Courier* proposed the trial's sensational nature as a possible explanation for its popularity: "One great attraction has been this—that the trial is one so unusual, as has been remarked that it happens but once in a century."[85] A man's ancestry was to be publicly scrutinized in the minutest detail in order to get at the "truth" of his racial identity. Spectators, according to the *Courier,* could not be faulted for wanting to witness this historic intrusion into a family's private memories. Perhaps the editors of the *Courier* had a point. However, if one were to go back a few years in the court records, one would find cases similar to *Pandelly v. Wiltz*, at least three of which—*Cauchoix v. Dupuy* (1831), *Bollumet v. Phillips* (1842), and *Dobard et al. v. Nuñez* (1851)—had been appealed to the Louisiana Supreme Court.[86] *Cauchoix v.*

Dupuy had all the trappings of romance, originating on the "eve of marriage" of a questionable man to a "respectable woman." Cauchoix, rumored to have been a "man of color," sued for $6,000 to recover his reputation as a white person. Initiated in the nearby parish of St. Bernard, *Dobard et al. v. Nuñez* detailed a much more complicated quest for the preferred racial identity. A veritable class action suit, the list of plaintiffs—consisting of the members of two very large families suspected of being "colored"—was three columns long. Testimony and accompanying documents such as genealogical tables, baptismal and marriage certificates, and epitaphs constituted a case record of more than four hundred pages. One of the witnesses for George Pandelly, Bernard Marigny, testified on behalf of the plaintiffs in *Dobard v. Nuñez* as well. Marigny—the living emblem of Creole culture who famously and stylishly gambled away his fortune and developed out of his losses the Faubourg Marigny (a substantial part of Pandelly's Third District)—seemed to be making a career out of testifying to the whiteness of his friends and neighbors.

Given the precedent of these cases during the previous twenty-five years, it is difficult to see why the *Courier* would refer to Pandelly's case as one that happened "once in a century." One possible reason that the Pandelly affair struck spectators as exceptional may lie in the comparative stakes involved in these trials. Most obviously, Pandelly's claim of having suffered the equivalent of $20,000 in damages may have escalated public interest in the trial because it fixed a dollar amount—almost half a million dollars in early twenty-first-century terms—to the injury caused to Pandelly's reputation by an allegation of blackness.[87] It can also be argued that the other cases had not been as public as the Pandelly case. Although involving the public scrutiny of ancestry, the earlier cases revolved around questions of a typically private nature. In these instances, charges of mixed ancestry came into being in order to contest a marriage rather than to oust a public official, possibly rendering these trials of lesser consequence to the general population. In contrast to Wiltz's audacious use of the newspaper as a forum for his grievances, in *Cauchoix v. Dupuy* a "Spaniard from Havana, unaccustomed to writing in French" sent his incriminating letter concerning a quadroon aunt directly to the family of Cauchoix's intended bride.[88]

In the wake of the local yellow fever epidemic and the apparent failure of the nation's political system to contain anxieties over race, slavery, immigration, and territorial expansion, the Pandelly affair helped shape and elaborate a crisis over the terms of racial, cultural, and national identity and over the boundary between intimate family life and matters of public concern. The Pandelly affair "concerned the whole *body politic*" not only because, as Wiltz indicated, it was the public's duty to set straight the errors of politicians but also because the white citizenry was witnessing one of their own confront the immanent threat of social death. Pandelly was understood to be a member of "one of the oldest families of the state"—in short, a Creole.[89] Pandelly's ancestral claim to the place predated even the territorial claim of the American government in New Orleans, and his sudden disenfranchisement would have a ripple effect throughout the city. The case threatened to overturn the precedent of tradition and to force a realignment of kinship and friendship networks. "A close, but legitimate investigation" of Pandelly's status would potentially reveal a disturbingly imperfect layering of history, an incongruity between the past and the future that had to be worked out in that particular present.[90] The public—packed so densely in the courtroom that a lawyer worried that the floor might give way—sensed what was at stake in this excruciatingly detailed examination of the "blood" of their peer. In the trial, they witnessed the violent distortions their memories and their histories would be forced to undergo in order to make their identities politically, socially, and racially acceptable. In short, they witnessed at close range the process of "Americanization."

In the "Archive of Our History"

Understood as historiographical project—or, as one reporter put it, an investigation into the "archive of our history"—the trial offered testimonial accounts from a number of the most elderly citizens of New Orleans, "so many relics of a past century, those who had lived under three different governments, existing on the identical spot."[91] It is ultimately this uneasy coexistence of three regimes in the recent history of the city that Pandelly and, by extension, the witnesses and spectators would have to account for. As a foray into the New Orleans archive, the trial offered spectators a chance to cull their memories for a better, more edifying story about themselves. In the spirit of historical revision, the newspapers primed their readers by transporting them to a distant past. The *Courier* called upon its readers to imagine "the time when this great city was in the womb of the future, and the place where she now rears her proud proportions a howling wilderness—a vast cane-brake where naught existed but the wild beast and the 'wilder still Indian,' where the alligators and other reptiles left their shiny marks."[92] From the vantage point of the "womb of the future," the reader could descend into the "howling wilderness" of the past assured of the promise of future American glory.

Similarly, another newspaper set the tone for this historiographical endeavor by pausing to meditate on the court building itself, "with its massive arches, and its ponderous Moorish architecture." The scene, according to the *New Orleans Bee*, "carries the mind of the spectator back to the time when royal helmets glittered in the Place d'Armes—when the Inquisition was in all its force—when New Orleans was thronged by savages and was the center of a vast Indian traffic—when miscalled Justice was administered under the same roof—when the nobles and the courtly dames of Spain and France perambulated its vestibules, and when the down-trodden and despised Colonists were held in subjection by foreign bayonets."[93] Underscoring the necessity of distancing the present from a corrupt past, the commentary portrays a colonial population suffering at the hands of "Moorish" and "foreign" influences—the "Inquisition," no less. "Bizarre" social customs characterized by courtly processions and the wearing of royal helmets accompanied a "miscalled Justice," including, of course, lax regulations regarding interracial relationships.[94] In order to win his case, George Pandelly had to present a compelling narrative of his ancestry, one that would convince the jury that his family had remained lily-white in spite of the challenges to purity posed by past regimes. Both settings of the past—the howling wilderness and glittering royal helmets—share a central image, a presence that would become crucial in Pandelly's narrative of his genealogy. He would call upon the "still wilder Indian" and the "throng of savages" to mediate for him the possible discrepancies in his bloodlines.

The Pandelly case was multidimensional in its methodology and its approach to the past. Acting as historians, participants in the trial consciously wove an account of the past from varied and contradictory primary and secondary written, oral, and visual materials. In this historiographical project, private recollections and public documents vied for priority and authority. The *Louisiana Courier* recognized as peculiar the extent to which dim recollections attained the status of fact: "In such a case as this, where genealogy is the question, hearsay testimony and tradition are allowed, which is not allowed in any other case."[95] Genealogy, then, was not merely a matter of establishing the factual details of family lineage; it also involved describing how the broader public had perceived those family relationships over time. Supplementing and transforming the official record, "hearsay testimony" and "tradition" augmented the status of memory and reputation over documentary sources. Witnesses on both sides engaged in this struggle over memory with accounts of their "racialized" encounters with members of the Dragon-Dimitry-Pandelly family. One witness for the defendant, despite having admittedly suffered a head injury and substantial memory loss, recalled an incident in "1820 or 1821" while attending a ball, "a decent one for white people where rich and poor were to go." He recounted watching as the commissary of the ball "took the misses Dimitry and removed them from the ballroom. [He] saw them brought to the doors. . . . This was done because it was said that they were colored people and that colored people were not to be admitted there."[96] Offering his supplementary narrative of the suspected African origin of the family, another witness related a similar decades-old episode in which whites took offense at the presence of the Dimitry children. "Mr. Dimitry was present at the examination in company with two children. [Witness] can't say whether they were male or female. Mr. Bernard Marigny came into the room and on seeing Dimitry and the children, he exclaimed *'Quoi! Il y a des nègres ici!'* (What! There are Negroes in here!) Mr. Dimitry . . . left the room right away."[97] Not only were these events located in the distant past, but they also forced witnesses to interpret complex social contexts involving multiple actors.

In one respect, the vague and ephemeral nature of these recollections often worked to enhance their credibility as evidence. One witness for the defendant could not locate the exact source of his knowledge about the racial identity of the family. To the question of how he knew of the public perception of one of Pandelly's ancestors as a "mulatress," he answered "he knows it because the public knows it." Being asked to point to a particular source of such knowledge, he responded that "it would be very difficult for him to do so. Nobody occupied himself about the origin of the woman. The witness never occupied himself about it. Doesn't recollect any conversation that he had with anybody about the origin of Françoise."[98] The witness admitted the uncertain nature of racial identification and the insecurity, yet pervasiveness, of public knowledge, but he could offer and the court could elicit this kind of testimony as authoritative. Neither the witness nor any of his peers had "occupied himself about the origin of the woman" and her family because their status as free people of color had been taken for granted. If the maternal ancestors of Pandelly had been free women of color, then the *lack* of conversation about them of them worked to confirm their social condition.

Meeting the testimonial evidence with oral accounts that stressed the cultural "whiteness" of the family, Pandelly's lawyers offered their own version of tradition, specifically the high visibility and respectability traditionally accorded to various family members. Chief among these was Pandelly's uncle, Alexander Dimitry, an educator who assumed responsibility for the public school system in the Third District and reinvigorated it on the model of Horace Mann, the influential American reformer who overhauled the New York school system into a powerful purveyor of U.S. civic identity.[99] In his opening testimony, according to the *Bee*, Pandelly's lawyer "eulogized [Alexander Dimitry] in a style only commensurate with his merits, and very ingeniously sought to make him a party to the suit."[100] Given that Dimitry, a one-time editor of the *Bee*, would not die until 1883, this assessment enacted a curious erasure. It attempted to remove Dimitry, a Creole of Creoles, beyond the pale of racial suspicion and also perhaps to rescue his livelihood. Dimitry "kept a school" in Raymond, Mississippi where the attendance had plummeted from fifty scholars to five after "the attack of Mr. Wiltz." During the trial, "Professor Dimitry" could be seen giving public lectures on "Greece and her morals" at the Lyceum Hall in New Orleans. After Dimitry's death, his intimate friend Charles Gayarré continued to insulate Dimitry and the entire Creole population from rumors of and evidence of black blood.[101]

The social prominence of the family combined with its members' "associations" to make a powerful case for its white racial identity. According to many witnesses, the Dimitrys-Pandellys always had white friends and associates and attended white schools and convents. Bringing the memory of the Catholic Church to bear on the question of Pandelly's racial identity, the Reverend Bishop Portier's testimony on behalf of the plaintiff invoked custom and tradition: "It was not the custom to marry white people to colored people from 1819–1826 . . . Marriages were sometimes not acknowledged by law, but were sometimes celebrated even in cases of mixed [race] marriages where one of the parties was dying. Those mixed marriages were celebrated in private before two witnesses and the clergyman who was only passive." Portier went on to distinguish the marriage of Pandelly's parents from this secret kind of marriage. "The marriage of Mr. Pandelly's father was celebrated openly and publicly by the officiating priest and in the parish church. It was not a private 'marriage of conscience.' The whole family was present and other white friends."[102] In other words, white attendance at the wedding of George Pandelly's parents constituted proof that his mother's whiteness had been traditionally accepted.

By incorporating a previous case from 1833–34 as a hybrid source that was both testimonial and documentary, Pandelly and his lawyers attempted to give legal weight to social tradition. This case within the Pandelly case tangentially concerned the racial identity of Pandelly's grandmother, Madame Andreas Dimitry née Maria Anna Dragon. Two free women of color, Pauline and Josephine Forstall, sued the Dimitrys in order to recover some property their parents had long ceded to Madame Dimitry. The women claimed that their property was given to a free woman of color with the same name as Madame Dimitry. Since Madame Dimitry claimed to be white, she could not be this person and thus must return their property. Ultimately, Madame Dimitry managed to keep her real property *and* the property of her white reputation, provoking the curiously worded judgment that the Dimitrys were "in possession [of the right] to be treated as persons not born of Negro extraction."[103] The plaintiff's lawyers gambled a bit in their use of the testimony from this previous case. On the one hand, it called attention to the fact that the racial identity of the family had been called into question before. If each generation of the family had to fight so hard to establish itself as part of the white population, could the jurors legitimately consider the family to be such? On the other hand, it allowed the plaintiff to refer to events even more remote than current octogenarians could remember. By introducing the records of the case into evidence, the plaintiff's side offered direct testimonials of people now dead who had been well acquainted with Pandelly's maternal ascendants, thereby substituting rumor and hearsay from the past for current public knowledge. Furthermore, the *Forstalls v. M. and Mme Dimitry* case could serve as a documentary proof of the Dimitrys' official enjoyment of white privilege.

Taken together, this extensive testimonial evidence was intended to make sense of the equally voluminous documentary evidence. The spectators and jurors were asked to consider baptismal and marriage certificates of many members of this large family, death certificates, last wills and testament, and the occasional letter. The court summoned a number of prominent notaries, each of whom came armed with his own records and those of past notaries that had been entrusted to him. The official archivist of St. Louis cathedral testified in the case as well, offering his interpretation of various church documents stretching as far back into the past as 1756. These documents were all primary sources of a sort, bits and pieces of history and traces of activity that the lawyers, jurors, and spectators had to place in a larger narrative. In this endeavor, both sides relied on a number of secondary sources that they considered "authoritative." Since 1848, Charles Gayarré, the future nativist spokesman and a friend of the Dimitrys, had been composing sweeping histories of Louisiana's colonial experience, published in French and English as *Histoire de la Louisiane* and *History of Louisiana.* At the time of the trial, the ink had hardly dried on his four-volume expanded version (1854). Pandelly's lawyers referred to it in order to establish the "true facts" of Louisiana custom, its landscape, and its population during the colonial period. Gayarré, for example, marks the arrival of Africans in the colony as 1721, long after the birth of Pandelly's questionable ancestor. "It was a physical impossibility," Pandelly argued in his petition, "that a single drop of negro blood could run in [his] veins."[104]

Pandelly's lawyer introduced other authoritative interpretive tools to suggest that the very terms used to express racial difference must be historically situated. Regarding the term *quarteroon*, understood in Pandelly's day as someone of three-fourths white ancestry and one-fourth African ancestry, the plaintiff cited a Spanish dictionary definition that applied the related term *quarteron* to those of mixed Indian and white ancestry, suggesting another interpretation of the Spanish colonials' use of the term to describe Pandelly's maternal grandmother. The possibility of Indian ancestry gave Pandelly a wider stage on which to secure his racial identity. In the city's transition to a more "American" understanding of race and culture, the Pandelly trial attempted to press the complex and multidimensional strands of evidence—historical narrative, aural testimony, written documentation, and physical appearance—into an identity that could be understood in binary terms.

Performing Race: The *Basanne* Woman Selling Ashes in the Street

At the same time participants and spectators of the trial were performing the function of historians, Pandelly, in an equally important respect, was performing a version of history: the historical narrative of his racial identity. Properly understood as a series of overlapping and competing performances, the trial was, in the words of Joseph Roach, "so rich in revealing contradictions" because it made "publicly visible through symbolic action both the tangible existence of social boundaries and . . . the contingency of those boundaries on fictions of identity."[105] Here, Roach speaks of the performances of burial rituals and the specific boundary of life and death. However, there is a symbolic similarity between dying and the predicament of George Pandelly during his trial. The dying person (or the unburied corpse) occupies a transitional space, as one who must be held apart from the community and then reincorporated as something else. If the designation "free man of color" constituted a type of "social death" for Pandelly, then the trial marked his prolonged encounter with the possibility of the "passing away" of his status in society. In Roach's terms, Pandelly was an "effigy" representing the racial anxieties of the community. In addition to the performative function of Pandelly's position, the trial itself can be seen as theater, the performance of the trial operating through auditory, visual, and documentary media. According to one legal theorist, performance is personal in that it "requires live participation of a human actor." It is social because "communicative success depends on the live performer actually appearing before a live audience." And it is dynamic, expressing meaning that "revolves around 'becomings' rather than 'beings.'"[106] Pandelly's trial was all these things. Pandelly, Wiltz, and their lawyers coordinated all kinds of evidence in order to perform Pandelly's identity primarily to the prescribed audience of the jurors, but ultimately to the entire community of New Orleans.[107]

In the search for Pandelly's origins, the spectators listened as witnesses related "long 'yarns' of what their grandfathers and grandmothers, uncles and aunts, and old Negroes and Negresses, old 'aunties' and 'uncles' and 'old Ethiopian octogenarians' told them."[108] These yarns unraveled through the maternal line in the direction of a central figure, Pandelly's great-great grandmother, Marianne Delha. The testimony of Bernard Marigny, the plaintiff's first witness, demonstrated the elusiveness of this figure and the difficulty Pandelly encountered in reconciling her existence with the narrative of his whiteness. Marigny, who had been acquainted with the family for a half century, attempted to confirm the "respectability" of the Dimitry family. According to Marigny, Madame Dimitry, Pandelly's grandmother, had always been "a good virtuous and moral lady." Her sons had been prominent school instructors and officials, the family living a subdued and "retired" life.

However, slightly beneath this litany of such code words as *respectable*, *virtuous*, and *moral*, which signified "white," ran testimony that worked to negate the family's *status.* Attempting to account for the ways in which the public's knowledge about the Dragon-Dimitry-Pandelly family had continually outstripped their status as white persons, Marigny's language often slipped and embarrassingly contradicted his overall confirmation of their white identity. "The daughter of Michel Dragon," Marigny stated, "married Andreas Dimitry—their children *intermarried with whites* (Here the clerk translated in so low a tone of voice that no one but those immediately around him could hear.)"[109] Furthermore, Marigny could not in his testimony suppress or deny the power of rumor. "Witness," the record states, "has heard and has 'grown old' that Mrs. Dimitry was of African origin." And then there was the undeniable childhood memory of that ambiguous spectral figure, the aged Marianne Delha, "an old woman of the family who sold ashes on Chartres Street whose color was *basanne* (bronze)."[110]

Ultimately, Pandelly's argument for his white ancestry rested on the identity of this elusive woman. Was Pandelly's great-great grandmother the "mulatresse slave of a M. Lallande" or "Marianne 'La Sauvagesse,' an 'Alabama Indian woman,' a 'mestizo,' actually the issue of an Indian woman and of a white person named Lallande D'Appremont . . . born in or about the year 1707 . . . on the Tombigbee river?"[111] She could possibly have been either or both. In the early eighteenth century, the French established outposts in the region of the Gulf Coast encompassing Mobile, Biloxi, and New Orleans, and their interactions with various tribes of the Creek Confederacy, including the Alabama, ranged from cooperation and alliance to forced enslavement.[112] In the absence of an entrenched plantation regime in Louisiana during the early colonial period, fluid social relations among European, Native American, and African inhabitants and overlapping jurisdictions of French, Spanish, and Native American control gave rise to a variety of interracial and inter-status intimacies.[113] Diverse racial practices and complex racial categories (as well as those of class and gender) emerged at the nexus of efforts emanating from the French and Spanish metropoles to codify these relationships and local challenges to this standardization.[114] A century later, the reputation of Louisiana as a site of extensive métissage frustrated Pandelly's claims of racial purity, but it also provided a loophole for establishing his whiteness. If Delha had been an Indian, Pandelly would be confirmed as white; if she had been of African descent, he would become a man of color. As Wiltz's laywer Cyprien Dufour claimed in his introductory remarks, "If plaintiff's family was African a hundred years ago, it is so still."[115]

Framing the question of Delha's identity in terms of "African" versus "Indian" allowed Pandelly and other "white" Creoles to explain their seemingly mixed origins and account for the tinge of color in their faces by incorporating the "Indian" into their genealogies. In the Creole imagination, "going native" was part of the circuitous path to "being white."[116] In a previous slander case, *Boullemet v. Phillips* (1842) the plaintiff Stephen Boullemet had argued that his descent from Indians or "Sauvages" rendered him white rather than colored and thus eligible for service in the Louisiana militia.[117] In his novel *The Grandissimes* (1880), George Washington Cable lampoons the narratives of Indian ancestry offered by the "most respectable" Creole families. The chapter "Family Trees" parodies the fascination among the Creole elite with public genealogy, particularly the way in which noble Indian blood combined itself in the prehistory of the state with noble European blood. While the Grandissimes family had managed throughout the libidinous history of the colony to keep itself "lily-white," the Fusilier clan claimed as its maternal ancestor the Indian princess Lufki-Humma: "the darkness of her cheek had no effect to make [Agricola Fusilier] less white, or qualify his right to smite the fairest and most distant descendant of an African on the face."[118]

Philip Deloria has suggested that white constructions of Indian otherness have proceeded along two axes: a "noble savage" axis that located Indians with respect to "positive and negative values" and a second axis focused upon the "relative distance" of Indian others from the white self. According to Deloria, Americans imagined Indians to be incorporated as "interior" or excluded as "exterior" to the nation or community depending upon the social, political, and aesthetic demands of a given context.[119] As "interior" as they could possibly be, Cable's Indians inhabit the bodies and bloodlines of Cable's Creoles. However, with succeeding generations, their "noble" qualities become increasingly "savage," leaving the Creoles with a virulent xenophobia and a fear of social change more broadly. "In a flock of Grandissimes might always be seen a Fusilier or two; fierce-eyed, strong-beaked, dark, heavy-taloned birds, who, if they could not sing, were of rich plumage, and could talk and bite, and strike, and keep up a ruffled crest and a self-exalting bad humor. They early learned one favorite cry with which they greeted all strangers, . . . 'Invaders! Invaders!' "[120] As a "feathered people" in a very literal sense, Cable's Creoles are squawking birds, hell-bent on protecting their territory.[121]

Adrien-Emmanuel Rouquette (1813–1887), son of a prominent Creole family and perhaps the most celebrated Creole to have "played Indian" during the antebellum period was decidedly more noble. He ranged during his formative years from his home on the outskirts of New Orleans near Bayou St. Jean to a nearby Choctaw settlement, where he fished and frolicked with young Indian boys. After a stint of schooling in Kentucky and New Jersey where he learned to speak English but forgot French, he was sent to college in Paris for re-immersion in his mother tongue. Under the influence of the Romantic writer Chateaubriand, whose *Atala* immortalized the American savage princess in the minds of educated Europeans, Rouquette eventually returned to Louisiana and took to the forests to find his own Atala. Before he could marry the Indian princess of his choice, she died of consumption. Sent again by his family to France, this time to recuperate from his heartbreak, he wrote *Les Savanes*, a volume of poetry with Native American themes that garnered some acclaim abroad. According to his most generous critics, Rouquette, "the American Lamartine," penned verse that "respired the perfumes of the forest."[122]

Rouquette's loss eventually propelled him into the priesthood and missionary work among the Choctaw residing across Lake Pontchartrain in Saint Tammany Parish, where he erected a number of rustic chapels. In various historical accounts of Rouquette's life, the Choctaw settlements provided an apt background for his displays of selflessness and courage, his own performance of a "noble savage" identity. However, hardly the "people of nature" imagined by Romantic writers, Rouquette's native hosts formed the remnant of a ravaged, displaced nation, barely eking out a living on the edges of the bustling metropolis. Having traveled to New Orleans in 1834, John Henry Latrobe recalled that the Choctaws he encountered in the city "had been to their new home [in the Oklahoma territory] and returned. They are generally displeased with it and are wandering off in various directions."[123] Despite the maligned status of Indians on the national scene, Rouquette often served his Indian constituency with sensitivity and courage. During the Civil War blockade, he risked his life by ferrying food, quinine (to treat malaria), and other supplies to the settlement. Actions such as these and his lifelong involvement in their communal life earned him the nickname "Chata-Ima," a Choctaw phrase meaning "one of us."[124]

During his trial, Pandelly and his lawyers developed an account of Indian "interiority" and a parallel account of African "exteriority" that absorbed possible "savage" elements, allowing for a more "noble" rendering of Pandelly's racial identity. Offering a study in comparative racial thought, the participants in the trial drew on multivalent discourses concerning the physical, mental, and moral aspects of racial difference. By the mid-nineteenth century, the scientific community had largely abandoned an environmentalist understanding of race in favor of theories ascribing racial distinctions to inherent biological differences. In this schema, the particular physical "defects" of blacks, Native Americans, and other nonwhites rendered them inferior—in body and mind—to "Caucasians." These scientific readings of race mingled in the popular imagination with literary and artistic portrayals of racial others that, although based on assumptions of nonwhite inferiority, often enshrined the seemingly inherent racial qualities of nonwhites with powerful moral and spiritual characteristics. Thus, as they read novels by James Fennimore Cooper or viewed such theatrical performances as *Metamora, Last of the Wampanoags*, Americans audiences could celebrate Indian culture as heroic and virtuous even in the face of racist policies of Native American removal and extermination.[125] Similarly, they might imbibe from writers such as Harriet Beecher Stowe or Lydia Maria Child "romantic racialist" portrayals of African Americans as ideal Christians or exhibit through participation in blackface minstrelsy that peculiar double emotion of desire and repulsion that Eric Lott has characterized as "love and theft."[126] Juxtaposing the "blood of Pocahontas" against the "blood of the African," the Pandelly affair offers a glimpse into how the academic theories and popular portrayals of blacks and Indians resonated practically when local white identities were at stake.[127]

On its most basic level, the Pandelly case is a protracted exploration of the question of interracialism: what qualities would Caucasian blood exhibit if it were to become mixed with the blood of other racial groups? Much of the testimony reflected a more general American fascination with racial "amalgamation." Expressed in positive or negative terms, alternatively reflective of fear or desire, ideas of racial mixture fueled important political discussions in the aftermath of the Mexican War about the social efficacy of American expansion further into Mexico and other parts of Latin America with large mestizo populations.[128] The specter of racial mixture also loomed over debates about the possible incorporation of free blacks and former slaves into the United States as citizens. During the late 1840s and early 1850s, American ethnologists understood mixed-race people to be perfect test cases for their theories of the origins and implications of racial difference. Accordingly, the U.S. Census added a mulatto category for its 1850 enumeration, instructing census takers that an accurate recording of this category would contribute to important scientific knowledge.[129] Subsequently, *Types of Mankind*, an 1854 compendium of American ethnological writings, shored up and popularized Josiah Nott's theory that the production of weaker and sterile "hybrids" led to the degeneracy of the parent races. Alternatively, apologists for Indian removal chalked up evidence of Native American civilization to the influence of mixed-blood elites, and abolitionist writers accessed the empathy of readers through mixed-race characters.[130] Embodying the convoluted logic of racial reasoning that would legitimate their dehumanization and simultaneously affirm their sexual desirability, near-white "fancy women" commanded some of the highest prices on the slave market.[131] The multiple and contradictory significations ascribed to mixed-race people by Americans of various political persuasions echoed the sentiment of one of the witnesses in the Pandelly case: "There is nothing more mysterious than the product or offspring of mixed races."[132]

To solve this mystery, the lawyers asked the jury to scrutinize the facial and other physical features of a succession of witnesses, always referring to some ideal type of Indian or African. Establishing the basis for judging phenotypic evidence, Christian Roselius, an attorney for the plaintiff, argued: "The distinguishing features of the aborigines of our country never run out; they themselves were fast wasting away by civilization or in other words by ruin; . . . there was something about them, distinguishing traits of character and features that never disappeared, no matter what the predominance of the Caucasian blood—the piercing eye, the lordly mean, the noble bearing will still be there. . . ."[133] Roselius distinguished between actual Indians, "they themselves" and their "traits of character and features," lifting their "piercing," "lordly," and "noble" aspects from their physical placement in Indian bodies and depositing them in white ones. Roselius's theory about the persistence of "Indian" qualities in the "Caucasian" population served as an operating assumption during the trial. One of the witnesses recapitulated Roselius's assertions: "Indian blood and features will reappear in the third or fourth generation."[134]

However, the quality and inheritance patterns of Indian blood was only half the question the trial attempted to answer, and this strategic use of the Indian proved to be a somewhat imperfect mask for a multiracial heritage. The injection of Indian blood into the Creole veins of the Dragon-Dimitry-Pandelly family did not completely quell the anxiety over what manifestations black blood would take. Many of the witnesses claimed to have heard of the family's Indian heritage, but a large percentage of them—including the plaintiff's own witnesses—reported having heard "vague rumors of African blood."[135] The task put forward by Wiltz's initial challenge and extended in the protracted civil trial was to identify the traces of this African blood in various documents and also in the physical appearance of various family members. To launch this investigation, the spectators needed a theory not only about discerning the presence of Indian blood, but also about detecting the presence of African blood. On this question, the various participants in the trial offered competing and contradictory ideas. In his argument, Roselius claimed that the presence of black blood would certainly be apparent. While Indians had a "bearing that could not be reduced to servitude, if so, but a short time," Africans, he implied, seemed to be natural slaves. Furthermore, any expert could "distinguish [Indian] features from the deformed and debased features of the African, who is but a step above the brute."[136] Other participants in the trial were not so sure that African blood was so easily detected. The same witness that endorsed Roselius's theory of the persistence of Indian traits doubted that African ancestry produced a similar effect. "African blood" the witness concluded "vanishes as it becomes intermarried with white."[137] Did black blood disappear without a trace, or did it produce physical "deformities?" The fundamental inconsistency framing this search for black blood fed an intense anxiety in the Creole population by raising the pressing questions of the day: How does one secure a white identity? How might one rewrite a heritage of mixture to resemble more closely a white genealogy? How are the physical and cultural markers of identity to be interpreted?

Indicated by a set of physical attributes (or more appropriately the lack of a certain set of attributes), Pandelly's "whiteness" required his lawyers to enlist the three-dimensional body as an integral part of the performance of the trial. In his study of circum-Atlantic performance, Joseph Roach defines the concept of surrogation as an essential component of coping with loss. "Into the cavities created by loss through death or other forms of departure," Roach writes, "survivors attempt to fit satisfactory alternatives."[138] In effect, the Pandelly case reveals a kind of reverse process of surrogation. The claims of Pandelly and his accusers depended upon an extrapolation from the kinds of identities available and desirable in the present through a line of ancestors stretching into the past. Both sides of the case constructed a narrative about the origin of Pandelly's maternal line, and both sides proceeded by calling forward various people to represent that elusive female progenitor, Marianne Delha. This operation entailed what Roach calls "the doomed search for originals by continually auditioning stand-ins." It also performed the opposite but supplementary function, legitimating the stand-in by imposing "narratives of authenticity and priority."[139] The arena for debate and dispute as well as the very raw materials of identity emerge from the "supplemental excess" created by the impossibility of an exact fit between the original figure (Delha) and its representation (Pandelly). As one critic puts it, "the excess meaning conveyed by the representation creates a supplement that makes multiple and resistant readings possible."[140] *Pandelly v. Wiltz* sought to standardize these competing readings of the racial performances of Pandelly and his family.

Pandelly was not even the main "effigy" in this case. He brought the suit, but no descriptions of him appear in the trial transcript or in any of the newspaper reports. Instead, his maternal ancestors became subject to the most intimate scrutiny. The witnesses and attorneys did not debate Pandelly's facial angles or the width of his nose; nor did they run their fingers through his hair to discern its texture. They reserved these invasive and, at times, humiliating forms of interrogation for the Dragon-Dimitry-Pandelly women. The only extended set of musings on the physical characteristics of Pandelly's male relatives concerned his uncle who attended college at Georgetown. A witness discussed the "Mediterranean" and "Indian" elements of the uncle's appearance and commented at length on the effect of this combination on the young women in the area. By far, the family's women suffered most of the close scrutiny. In a sense, these women formed a succession of effigies through which the participants in the trial understood and codified racial identity. Thus, they represented the most immediate embodiment of racial and cultural liminality.

During the first days of the trial, Roselius, Pandelly's lawyer, set the tone for the way the audience should regard these women. Pandelly's mother, Euphrosine, was present in the courtroom, and witnesses referred to her features from the witness stand. The newspaper account in the *Bee* noted that during the examination of one of the plaintiff's key witnesses "Mrs. Pandelly was in court. She is apparently of unmixed Indian blood and about fifty years of age. Her straight black hair, which she loosened and exhibited to the jury was slightly interspersed with white."[141] While Pandelly's mother was available for exhibition, his grandmother, Madame Dimitry, presented more of an obstacle to the lawyers. Eventually, Roselius secured a judgment that the jury should make a field trip to view the woman in her sickbed. According to Roselius, the jurors were to decide "from an inspection of [Madame

Dimitry] to what race she may have belonged." As can be expected, this notion was controversial. Wiltz's lawyers objected to the special excursion to the Dimitry residence, but the judge ruled in favor of Roselius "for the reason that it was a case that seldom happened; that juries were often taken from the court room to inspect levees, surveys, etc. and that in criminal cases it was common to take the jury to the spot where the crime was committed."[142]

This characterization is significant on two accounts. First, it enters the grandmother "into evidence" as an "object of scrutiny"—not much different to the jurors than a levee and, incidentally, performing a similar function. Just as a levee must protect the city by holding back the tremendous flow of the Mississippi, Madame Dimitry must perform her own protective duty by mediating and displacing the problem of interracialism. This description applied to Wiltz as well. His lawyer described Mr. Wiltz "as one willing to throw himself into the breach in order to restore the parity of the elective franchise and of our public bodies."[143] Second, the judge's sentiments constitute the apparent racial characteristics of the woman as a particular *place,* the "scene of the crime." Thus the trial transforms Pandelly's maternal relatives from mere women into three-dimensional embodiments of and potential sites for the illicit activity of racial mixture, and they become living archives, depositories of racial transgressions and aspirations.[144]

By far the most extensive and predominant evidence on both sides consisted of descriptions and evaluations of the physical characteristics of Pandelly's maternal relatives. Mrs. Pandelly and Madame Dimitry presented themselves to the court as official evidence. However, the attorneys Roselius and Dufour attempted to secure accurate descriptions of the ancestors extending back to Delha, who had died during the period of Spanish occupation. In fact, Roselius summoned the records of the 1833 case, *Forstalls v. Dimitrys,* for exactly this reason. Considering recent developments in the then "science" of ethnology and the proliferation of a discourse ranking the physical characteristics and mental capacities of the races, the Pandelly trial displayed a relatively unsophisticated approach to racial identification. The lawyers attempted to extract testimony that sounded authoritative. Drawing on ethnological theory, they asked witnesses about such things as forehead size, facial angles, and shape of nose. Invariably, witnesses seemed puzzled by this line of questioning and fell back on their own ways of detecting race—

namely, by reading hair texture and skin color. Despite Roselius's intention of charging this task to "experts," the people who testified to the race of Pandelly's family were ordinary people—his friends and neighbors and acquaintances of the family. Moreover, the earlier case, *Forstalls v. Dimitrys*, contains racial "evidence" that is even less codified. In an important sense, the trial indicated a respect for the ability of average citizens to forge a workable understanding of racial difference without the benefit of the newly developing science. This understanding took into account tradition and custom as well as current ideas about the physical appearance of a mulatto or mestizo.

Thus much of the testimony hinged on vague recollections of what the women looked like and how they presented themselves to the public. The lawyers asked witnesses to recall certain details about Françoise Monplaisir, Pandelly's great grandmother, and Marianne Delha, his great-great grandmother, and to make relative judgments about their racial identities. The series of questions presented to a witness from Baton Rouge typifies the thrust of the examination:

> Were you acquainted with Marianne Delha? . . . Did she look like the daughter of a white man and a Negro or the daughter of a white man and an Indian? Was her hair straight and coarse or not? What was her complexion? Could she speak the Indian dialect? . . . Were you acquainted with Françoise Monplaisir? Did she speak the Indian dialect? Was her hair straight or not? Who was darker Françoise or Mrs. Dimitry? Are Indians and Negroes more pale in old age? Are mulattos and quarteroons or other colored people darker in old age? . . . Was Françoise Monplaisir's hair always well combed? Was she in the habit of wearing a *tignon* when not dressed to go out?[145]

Taken as a whole, these curiously phrased and seemingly disjointed questions reveal the thought processes and preoccupations of a culture desperately trying to sort through its origins. So much depended on hair texture, the specific shade of skin, the clothing and grooming habits, the parentage, and the linguistic skills of these long-dead women. Furthermore, an "accurate" interpretation of this hodgepodge of characteristics hinged on the collective expertise of the contingent community of citizens. With the sanction of the court, witnesses offered "authoritative" opinions on such matters as the relative darkness of mulattos, Indians, and Negroes in old age and the transferability of cultural traits such as language and idiom.

As can be expected, this body of testimony produced competing descriptions culled from the deepest recesses of the memories of New Orleans' oldest residents and from similar recollections offered in a court case twenty years earlier. According to the descriptions, the women could have represented a number of different racial categories. The court, therefore, had the task of sorting through descriptions of various physical features and reassembling the women as Africans or Indians. According to testimony from the 1833 case, "Delha's long straight hair and her features left no doubt on this subject. She was evidenced entirely free from African blood."[146] The information provoked a different interpretation by Wiltz's witnesses. While Delha's hair may have been "flat and straight," her complexion raised considerable suspicion among those who had known her. One witness testified that "Marianne had the complexion of a *griffone* [a person who is three-quarters black]." According to another, more animated witness, "She was as black as the bottom of a kettle."[147] African ancestry seemed to have manifested itself more visibly in Delha's daughter, Françoise. While a number of people testified to Françoise's mestizo appearance, there were equally as many accounts of Françoise as a "mulattress." A neighbor who had seen Françoise's hair both "in *negligé*" and "well-combed" remarked that "the hair of Françoise was the hair of a woman of her caste, that of a mulatress," undulating *(ondée)* and "raised."[148]

Verdict and Repercussions

On February 12, 1854, ten days into the trial, the lawyers made their summations, and the jury members went into chambers and deliberated. The next day, they emerged with a verdict in favor of Pandelly's whiteness. While there was no indication that it was offered into evidence, an early-nineteenth-century portrait of Pandelly's grandmother depicted a youthful, recently married Marianne Dragon in full regalia, confirming her high-born social status (see illustration insert). This aspect of her reputation carried the day for her grandson. In spite of this affirmation, the court ignored Pandelly's appeal for damages. In the end, Wiltz had merely to pay the cost of the suit, a far cry from the

$20,000 that Pandelly sought. Like the official response to the yellow fever epidemic, this verdict sent a mixed message to the public. Just as the municipal bureaucracy identified yellow fever as its responsibility, the courts and spectators claimed racial identification, specifically the codification of blackness and whiteness, as a special public interest. As had the yellow fever epidemic, the Pandelly affair forced the residents of New Orleans to know "the proven truth concerning themselves and the city in which they dwelt." Or perhaps more to the point, they should be able, if challenged, to "prove some truths" and make an acceptable history from the racial memory of the city.

Officially, Pandelly was vindicated. The court had decided that Wiltz had unfairly and perhaps maliciously accused him of having African ancestry. Furthermore, it endorsed the American racial hierarchy in its valorization of whiteness (and Indianness) over Africanness or blackness. In a very important sense, however, the case failed to dispel the suspicion surrounding George Pandelly. Pandelly had considered the $20,000 to be evidence of the gravity of Wiltz's transgression and spoke of donating his award to charity. In failing to reward Pandelly monetarily, the court perhaps attempted to discourage others from bringing similar cases. However, the court seemed to be letting Wiltz (and anyone else who might have claimed to be concerned about the public good) off the hook. Furthermore, the court's opinion seemed to insinuate that, despite his efforts to prove his whiteness beyond doubt, Pandelly might indeed have descended from Africans.

Perhaps shaken by these periodically resurfacing insinuations, descendants of the Dimitry family continued to affirm their white identity publicly. In 1892–93, Charles Patton Dimitry, a historian and a son of Pandelly's uncle Alexander Dimitry, wrote a series of articles on genealogy for the *New Orleans Times Democrat* that in some ways reflected his commitment to the romantic historical tradition popularized in Louisiana by Charles Gayarré. Dimitry placed the colonial families of Louisiana in a long tradition of European royal grandeur and chivalry and lamented the processes by which "the gallant men and the graceful women disappear, and are seen no more."[149] Dimitry's journey takes him through successive doors as he glances back on scenes from medieval France, Florence, and Verona: "as the nearer doors open and more modern vistas appear, the vistas revealed are the vistas of Louisiana—the fairest scene of all—her forests, her prairies, her dark and odorous lagoons, Bienville, with light helmet decked with feathers and clad in half-armour, walks in the *Place d'Armes* with his officers, while the rolling of drums . . . beat a salute at morn to the flag of the *fleur-de-lys*." This scene of both the natural and royal origins of New Orleans forms an apt background to his genealogies.[150]

For late nineteenth-century cultural critics in New Orleans, the issues of purification and sanitation were paramount. Cable's account of the yellow fever epidemic of 1853 credits New Orleanians' ingenuity for developing a logical and scientific course of action for future epidemics.[151] Nevertheless, Cable became a major proponent of civil rights for blacks after the end of Reconstruction and his endorsement of longstanding racial mixture in the city would prompt white Creoles, Gayarré chief among them, to attempt to sanitize New Orleans' interracial past. In 1921, Gayarré's protégé Grace King published *Creole Families of New Orleans*, perhaps the most popular genealogical work in this vein. As King would do in coming decades, Charles Patton Dimitry rewrote the Dimitry family line, removing racially questionable figures. According to his interpretation, Françoise Monplaisir had been the issue of Louis Chauvin de Beaulieu and one "Charlotte Orbanne Duval d'Epresmenil," and Marianne Delha, the woman at the core of the Pandelly trial, fails to appear. This ongoing reworking of the family history by removing potentially African blood from the family veins testified to the anxiety and desperation felt by the Dragon-Dimitry family about their ancestors. As hard as they tried, however, the Dimitry-Pandelly descendants failed to remove their family from public suspicion. When directing me to the Pandelly case, an archivist at the New Orleans Public Library leaned in to tell me, "We all know the Dimitrys are black."[152]

As for George Pandelly, his reentry into Creole society was probably anticlimactic. His seat on the council being irretrievable, he returned to his previous job as clerk in the Fifth District Court of New Orleans. On April 29, 1854, almost three months after his big trial, he clerked for a small, seemingly insignificant case that should have inspired his sympathy. Echoing the 1833 case, *Forstalls v. Dimitrys*, a young man brought suit against one of his wife's tenants who refused to pay the woman rent because he claimed that he understood himself to be renting from a woman of color with her same name. In the course of the case, the woman had not only to prove that she deserved the rent money, but also that she was a white woman. As Pandelly copied and recorded the documents of this case, he surely recognized the woman's predicament. Little did he know at the time that this case would expand and erupt in a few years as *Desarzant v. LeBlanc.* In contrast to his intense but fleeting fame, the woman's predicament would give her a lasting notoriety, an ongoing and instructive existence in the folklore of New Orleans.

2

Failing to Become White

SHORTLY BEFORE THE CIVIL WAR, Anastasie Desarzant sued her neighbors for slander.[1] The neighbors had committed the insufferable offense of publicly calling Desarzant a woman of color. This offense not only wounded her pride, but it would also thwart her attempt to marry Maurice Antoine Abat, a leading white citizen. By instituting a slander case, Desarzant hoped, as had George Pandelly, to preempt damage to her reputation and become marked officially as white. If the court deemed her a woman of color, her liaison with Abat could aspire only to *plaçage*, and their children would never be considered legitimate under Louisiana state law. Actually, her position would have been exactly that of the neighbor who had accused her of being *nègre*. Unlike Pandelly's attempt, her case failed miserably; her supporting evidence unraveled bit by bit until there was no doubt in the court's mind that Desarzant was of African descent. After failing to obtain secure social status as a white person, after failing to "pass," Desarzant continued to live in the cultural imagination as an emblem of racial transgression. This woman who used all the resources at her disposal to prove her whiteness became notorious: ironically a century and a half later she was known only by her Afro-Creole nickname "Toucoutou."

Ostensibly, Desarzant had always known that she was the daughter of Justine Bacquié, a free woman of color, and Jean Laizer, a white man who made regular Sunday visits to see her and her siblings during their childhood. Desarzant and her siblings had grown up in the same household, and some of them, also with the last name Desarzant, were clearly identified in the public record as free people of color at the time of the trial. One brother, well known in the neighborhood, held membership in the Société d'Economie et d'Assistance Mutuelle Frères, a club "composed exclusively of colored persons."[2] In May 1853 in a transaction notarized by Abat, Desarzant loaned money to her brother Armand's wife. Although the initials *f.w.c.* (free woman of color) do not appear next to Desarzant's name, her brother and his wife were clearly marked by Abat as *f.p.c.* (free people of color).[3] A third brother, Maître Desarzant, a printer by profession, regularly published material for the Sisters of the Holy Family, an order of nuns of color founded by Henriette Delille.[4] An older sister, Louise Desarzant, married and recorded the baptism of her children on the official registry for people of color. Creoles of color in the mid-nineteenth century had two popular expressions for passing: "*passe-à blanc*" and "*blanc fo'cé.*"[5] While the first term seems to depend mainly on the perceptions of others, *blanc fo'cé* gives the impression of actively forcing or falsifying a perception of whiteness. That is the role that the court record suggests that Desarzant played in her act of passing.

Just as Pandelly had four years earlier, Desarzant enacted a double performance. In her attempt to perform the role of a white person, she too had to perform the function of the historian, deploying her documentary and testimonial evidence strategically to prove the long history of her whiteness. Desarzant's case rested primarily on three pieces of documentation, each of which placed the others under a certain amount of suspicion. The first document, Desarzant's baptismal record dated January 1824 and entered in the white registry of baptisms, named "Justine Martin" of Saint Domingue and "Jean Desarzant" as her parents. Desarzant's second document, a passenger list from a ship entering the port of New Orleans in 1809, "proved" that her parents "Françoise Martin" and "Jean Desarzant" hailed from Switzerland. From the first piece of evidence to the second, her mother's first name and birthplace had changed. Desarzant's third piece of documentary evidence consisted of records from a previous legal proceding. Just as Pandelly had attempted to use documents from a previous case in order to sustain a judgment of whiteness rendered years before, Desarzant enlisted a previous judgment on behalf of her white status in order to prove this status once again. In *Abat v. Mourier*, an 1854 case for which George Pandelly had coincidentally served as clerk, Justine Bacquié, acting not as Desarzant's mother but as the servant of color who had raised her, produced a sworn document attesting to the white parentage of Desarzant.[6] Unfortunately for Desarzant, this evidence trail had taken far too many detours.

Even before her trial concluded, the case began to spawn cultural commentaries. Joseph Beaumont, a Creole of color barber and musician, immediately penned the Creole folk song "Toucoutou," a devastating critique of racial passing.[7] Mocking Desarzant's aspirations toward whiteness, the catchy tune followed her around the city and secured her place in New Orleans' cultural memory. In 1911, when Creole of color activist and writer Rodolphe Desdunes wrote his community memoir *Nos Hommes et Notre Histoire*, he was so moved by Beaumont's rebuke of Toucoutou that he credited him with embodying the "spirit of the people."[8] One could still hear "Toucoutou" sung in the neighborhoods of New Orleans as late as the 1920s, and cultural historian Edward Larocque Tinker, a white native New Yorker, deemed it "probably the most cruel" of the Creole songs.[9] In his attempt to rescue Toucoutou from "the malice or hatred of [the song's] long dead author," Tinker dredged up the original court record and wrote the historical romance *Toucoutou* (1928), thus establishing himself as the protector of Desarzant's legacy. Because Tinker failed to cite the original case, the court records remained obscure, insuring that those interested in the case would have to accept his version of the circumstances as truth.

As these cultural commentaries demonstrate, the Toucoutou affair was not settled once and for all by the Louisiana Supreme Court in the late 1850s. Rather, it proved a powerful symbol, focusing the struggle of New Orleanians over racial, cultural, and legal legacies.[10] As satirical folk song, as historical event, as romantic melodrama, the Toucoutou affair morphed its way across generic boundaries, gathering cultural significance as it went.[11] In its own time, the case encapsulated antebellum anxieties over race, gender, and status. As a contest over marriage and family, it raised questions about the public contracts and private obligations forming the substance of these institutions. The case allowed the practice of *plaçage* to resonate across racial lines within New Orleans' families and forced New Orleanians to incorporate the legacy of these interracial arrangements into their sense of place and belonging. By the late 1850s, when this case wound its way through the Louisiana legal system, lawmakers had gone a long way toward remapping the status categories of free and slave over the racial categories of white and black. The Toucoutou affair exposed the perils of that process for free people of color. Even after the regimes and institutions of the Old South had nominally fallen away, Desarzant's existence at the crux of binary racial and status categories rendered her a powerful symbol. Toucoutou's predicament and the decades of commentary on it reveal the ongoing challenges to Americanization posed by New Orleans' history as a port city forced to manage multiple and competing regimens of racial and cultural performance.

Defending the Status of "His Wife"

Inasmuch as *Anastasie Desarzant v. P. LeBlanc and E. Desmaziliere, his wife* was a slander case, it is surprising that there is so little testimony about specific episodes of slander, leaving one to wonder what actually provoked the trial. The transcript offers a vague sense of the nature of the alleged infraction. In their recapitulations of the events, Beaumont, Desdunes, and Tinker all highlight the feud between Toucoutou and Eglantine. The record of the trial, however, suggests that the initial animosities involved Antoine Abat and Pierre LeBlanc. According to a conversation between one witness and LeBlanc, Abat had accused LeBlanc of being—despite his name—a man of color. This suggestion supposedly so infuriated LeBlanc that he set out to "prove that Abat's wife was a colored woman." LeBlanc and his romantic partner, Eglantine Desmaziliere, then advertised Desarzant's presumed status as a woman of color to the neighborhood. Upon meeting Maurice Eugène Abat, the young child of Desarzant and Abat, LeBlanc would frequently proclaim "A pretty boy for a mulatto." Both LeBlanc and Abat engaged in extensive pretrial lobbying in the neighborhood. LeBlanc allegedly bribed witnesses to testify in his favor. Abat attempted to defend the honor of Desarzant against her detractors, threatening one elderly woman with violence should she speak against Desarzant.[12] Alarmed by the prospect of his own exposure (whether or not he felt he had anything to conceal), LeBlanc seemed to have launched a preemptive strike against his accuser's wife, who proved to be a relatively easy target.

According to the 1850 census, Desarzant and Abat lived together in Faubourg Marigny with two young sons who had taken the last name Abat. Everyone in the household was listed as white, and in 1854 Desarzant and Abat registered a third son, Maurice Eugène Abat, on the record of white births. On May 16, 1857, Abat and Desarzant had appeared at the registry of marriages, a municipal office, and filed papers for a marriage license. While it was common for couples known to be interracial to contract "marriages of conscience" through their priests, it was increasingly difficult—not to mention illegal—for them to marry in the civil sphere. If Desarzant were indeed a woman of color, Abat and Desarzant's audacity would invite pubic ridicule. Accordingly, LeBlanc's and Desmaziliere's challenge as to the appropriate status of the Abat-Desarzant union set in motion a highly charged wordplay on the category of wife and the institution of marriage over the course of the trial. In the preparatory documents introducing the case to the court, the uses of the word *wife* wove a complex web of meanings bouncing back and forth among different levels of legitimacy. Throughout the initial exchange of plaintiff's petitions and defendant's responses, the figure of the wife and the concept of marriage underwent a process of intense scrutiny, nervous justification, and ironic dismissal.[13]

This contestation took its most bitingly sarcastic form in the filing of the case. Most likely on Abat's advice, Christian Roselius, the lawyer for Desarzant, crafted the lawsuit in such a way as to render Abat and Desarzant the true defenders of marriage as a contract binding those of the same race or status. While naming Desarzant as the sole plaintiff and using her birth name protected the socially prominent name of Abat, it also registered respect for public convention and state law by demonstrating Desarzant's willingness to forego access to the coveted title of wife until the legal challenges to her identity were settled. Furthermore, the naming of the case implied that LeBlanc and Desmaziliere were the truly irreverent people. In 1850 their living arrangement had resembled that of Desarzant and Abat except Desmaziliere and her children had all been listed on the census as mulatto.[14] *Desarzant v. LeBlanc* mocked their pretensions of a legitimate union by linking LeBlanc and Desmaziliere together in a very public formal setting. Moreover, Desarzant's original petition insisted that any judgment in the case should apply to the defendants *in solido* and that this shared responsibility for the defamation of Desarzant's character should be understood as an aspect of their shared union as man and wife.

In his careful preparation of Desarzant's petition, Roselius provoked a round of impassioned responses by LeBlanc and Desmaziliere. It is clear that they felt this case was a ridiculous imposition on their time and energy. Desarzant filed her claim in late June 1857; when the defendants finally responded with separate documents a little over four months later, they questioned the very basis of the case. Although the key passages in their respective responses were virtually identical, this lack of formal solidarity demonstrated their separate legal identities. Both responses took exception to the petition, arguing that there was no basis on which to sue them *in solido* because they were not in fact married to one another. Nor could they ever be—according to LeBlanc's petition, "Eglantine Desmaziliere is a colored woman and this defendant a white man." Shedding light on what they believed to be the true nature of the Desarzant-Abat union, both defendants doubted that Desarzant was as concerned over the institution of marriage as she claimed to be. "The plaintiff knows full well," they asserted, "that there is no other connexion between [LeBlanc and Desmaziliere] than that which exists between the plaintiff herself and a gentleman of whom she bears publicly the name." The language of their petition reinforced the moral and legal understanding of an interracial union as an "illicit connexion," a formulation offered by the court in an 1847 case.[15] Stalling further, the codefendants attempted to drive the case deeper into the bureaucratic mire by insisting that the official documents be served on them in French, their mother tongue.

Over the course of the next six weeks, in a flurry of legal paperwork, the two sides came to agreement over the wording of a petition. Desarzant agreed to "amend the . . . original petition by erasing therefrom the words 'his wife' wherever they occur in describing the defendants," basing her decision to sue the two together on her understanding that they "acted in concert and in pursuance of a preconceived scheme." Despite the vehemence of the defendant's protests and Desarzant's final concession, the court filed the case in its original form. By leaving to posterity this association of LeBlanc and Desmaziliere as man and wife, the case presents a picture of the institution of marriage on the brink. The official understanding of racial classification and the qualifications for legal marriage left no room for ambiguity, and the case depended on this clarity to demonstrate the drastic implications ($10,000 worth) of this kind of slander. However, as the name of the case suggests, the Toucoutou affair demonstrated that—legal proscription notwithstanding—decades of custom would be difficult to discipline.

As the initial skirmish over LeBlanc's racial identity and the subsequent attempt to position LeBlanc and Desmaziliere in a "correct" relationship to one another suggest, the Toucoutou affair signified the eruption of a more generalized anxiety over racial classification. The Pandelly affair and the Toucoutou affair have much in common; each required proof of racial lineage, a white ancestry that would stand up to the most intense public scrutiny. Pandelly's strategy of integrating the mediating figure Marianne Delha, the "Alabama Indian," helped him account for his apparent "black blood." Toucoutou, on the other hand, could claim no such intermediary figure. In fact, her lineage pointed in an altogether different and more racially ambiguous direction—away from New Orleans back through "La Ysla de Cuba" to Haiti, or as the witnesses in the trial preferred to call the island nation, "St. Domingo."

The Specter of Haiti, 1809

For the participants in the trial, the year 1809 was an important historical touchstone. That year a ship's log recorded the arrival of "Françoise Martin" and "Jean Desarzant" at the port of New Orleans, and a number of the witnesses in the trial also arrived in the city then. For New Orleanians in the late antebellum period, 1809 still signaled foremost the influx of refugees from Haiti by way of Cuba. Over a decade of slave insurrection and revolutionary violence in France's premier colony had sent waves of refugees to nearby islands and to cities along the eastern seaboard and Gulf Coast of the United States. By far the greatest number, over 25,000, settled in Cuba, waiting for the chance to return to their native soil. Out of consternation about Napoleon's European campaigns, the Spanish launched a general crackdown on "Frenchmen" in Cuba in 1809, and many former residents of Saint Domingue/Haiti uprooted themselves once again, finding their way to southern Louisiana. From May 1809 to January 1810, the port of New Orleans received 9,059 refugees from Cuba, who nearly doubled the urban population of Orleans parish.[16] The ship's log that Desarzant presented to the court listed her parents' nationality as "Suisse," Laizer's apparent country of origin. However, "Desarzant" and "Martin" more likely arrived in New Orleans as part of the mass exodus of "Frenchmen" from Cuba.

While George Pandelly could trace his family line directly to Europe, lingering only temporarily in the indeterminacy of colonial Louisiana, Desarzant had the more difficult task of maintaining a narrative of whiteness through the deepest recesses of the Caribbean.[17] In its dual legacy, the specter of Saint Domingue/Haiti frustrated Desarzant's hopes of becoming irrefutably white. On the one hand, mention of Haiti as "St. Domingo" provoked memories of life in France's most productive colony and the fluid nature of the racial and status categories once operative there. Sliding up and down the status hierarchy, enslaved Saint Dominguans, as one historian has noted, "could become *affranchis* [free people of color], who could later convert into *petits blancs*, and these become *grands blancs*."[18] Those with financial resources and social ingenuity could climb the racial ladder of the French colonial system, an intricate apparatus with, in the estimation of one former Saint Dominguan, as many as 512 rungs.[19] Those who "whitened" themselves this way learned to tread confidently on a creolized middle ground between two racial poles. On the other hand, as the world's only black republic, Haiti met the U.S. racial binary with a binary of its own, nominally privileging blackness over whiteness. Accordingly, Jacques Dessalines, its first president, famously ripped the white from the French tricolor and adopted the original Amerindian designation, Hayti, as the new nation's name. The first Haitian constitution deemed Haitians of any color as "black" and offered citizenship to anyone of African or Amerindian descent. To underscore the racial aspects of belonging, the Haitian government barred whites from owning land. The term *blanc* indicated one's status as a "foreigner" in Haitian creole.[20] The association of Desarzant with Saint Domingue/Haiti in the public imagination would recall either a Saint Dominguan racial ambiguity or a Haitian rhetoric of defiant blackness and illegitimate whiteness.

The refugees from Saint Domingue and the idea of Haiti had troubled American sensibilities ever since Saint Dominguans began to arrive in cities along the eastern seaboard and the Gulf Coast in the early

1790s. While some of the immigrants had been able to retain enough material wealth and slave property to establish themselves in their new locales, many others had only narrowly escaped with their lives and the clothes on their backs. Wherever they arrived in the United States, these traumatized victims of slave rebellion were met by local residents with a mixture of sympathy, curiosity, and trepidation. In their nascent republic, Americans read the meaning of their own revolution by triangulating it against the French and Haitian Revolutions. Much of the foreign and domestic policy of the Federalist era, culminating in the Alien and Sedition Acts of 1798, cast the French as the most threatening "aliens." Many Americans worried that their revolutionary experiment might careen out of control as the French Revolution had.[21] Many believed that the Saint Dominguan exodus could contaminate the American setting in a more immediate sense. The increased traffic between Saint Domingue and Philadelphia and the large number of Saint Dominguans seeking refugee in that city seemed to be an immediate cause of the devastating yellow fever epidemic that ravaged Philadelphia in the summer of 1793.[22]

In a nation that precariously balanced the ideals of freedom and equality with the practice of slavery, the events in Saint Domingue would continue to point to the inconsistencies in the national creed. Accordingly, antislavery reformers throughout the Atlantic world would draw on the Haitian example and particularly on Toussaint L'Ouverture's leadership as powerful symbols of the quest for liberty and the irrepressibility of the human spirit.[23] Seeing in the Haitian Revolution a harbinger of what might befall their own regimes, supporters of slavery and white supremacists would counter the image of Haiti as the ultimate symbol of freedom by mining events in Haiti for evidence of black misrule. These charged attitudes about Haiti/Saint Domingue held particular consequences for the reception of refugees of African descent. Whether free or enslaved, they were, in the eyes of many Americans, potential carriers of rebellion and discontent. A number of slave rebellions and plots could be directly or indirectly traced to a Haitian influence, including the 1795 Pointe Coupée rebellion in Spanish Louisiana, the 1812 Aponte Conspiracy in Spanish Cuba, the slave Gabriel's plot of 1800 in Virginia, and the alleged 1822 Denmark Vesey plot in Charleston, South Carolina.[24] For all these reasons, Americans equivocated over the proper response when boatloads of refugees from the French Caribbean arrived during the two decades encompassing the founding of Haiti.[25]

In Louisiana, where the bulk of refugees arriving in waves of migration from 1803 to 1810 doubled the urban population of New Orleans, the local response shifted according to the race and status of those seeking asylum. When news of approaching ships reached New Orleans in the late spring and early summer of 1809, residents began to mobilize charitable efforts. They collected monetary donations in excess of $5,000, an amount that rivaled the city's annual tax revenues of $7,650; they evacuated a fish market and transformed it into a temporary shelter; they amassed a store of blankets—all measures intended to aid white asylum seekers. Free refugees of African descent depended, to a large extent, on the charity and initiative of individual New Orleanians of color who coordinated relief efforts among their own population. Those fleeing as "slaves" suffered the brunt of the crisis: the 1808 general ban on the importation of foreign-born slaves and a suspicion over the character of this particular slave population combined to prevent this group from leaving the miserable ships.[26] Territorial governor William Claiborne, hand selected by Thomas Jefferson to tame the unruly cultural affiliations of Louisianans, juggled the conflicting interests of a francophone population that favored admitting the various classes of refugees and the "many good Americans" who balked at "so great an influx of foreigners."[27]

Officials also equivocated over the admission of free people of color and their general status in the territory. In 1806 the territorial legislature proclaimed: "Free people of color ought never to insult or strike white people but on the contrary, they ought to yield to them on every occasion and never speak or answer them but with respect, under penalty of imprisonment."[28] In 1808 city councilors debated the rights of a local free man of color to give fencing lessons, one official grumbling over reports that "mulattoes have the insolence to challenge whites to a duel."[29] In the midst of the 1809 migration, the exasperated Governor Claiborne attempted to enforce a ban on the admittance of free people of color—in particular those "males above the age of fifteen"—to the city. Nonetheless, by January 1810, the mayor of New Orleans reported to Claiborne that 428 free men of color had taken up residence in the city.[30] Later in the year, Governor Claiborne conceded that the conduct of free people of color "hitherto has been correct," but "in a country like this, where the Negro population is so considerable, they should be carefully watched."[31]

In 1811 Louisianans' fears of a possible Saint Domingue in their midst bore fruit when the largest slave rebellion in U.S. history broke out in the sugar parishes upriver from New Orleans. In sorting out the origins of the plot, authorities uncovered what they took to be a dense network of Creole and African enslaved people, fugitive maroons, free people of color, and privateers (who had congregated in the Gulf Coast colony of Barataria) acting in apparent consort. When New Orleanians mobilized to defend the city from the rebels, though, free volunteers of color, according to General Claiborne, "performed with great exactitude and propriety."[32] Imminent conflict with the British during the War of 1812 reawakened local anxieties over the loyalties of Saint Dominguan free people of color. They had already demonstrated that as soldiers they could be a formidable force. In 1813 free man of color Joseph Savary had raised a regiment of his fellow Saint Dominguans to support republican revolutions in Mexico and elsewhere in Latin America. However, the question of their ultimate loyalty and the virulent resistance of local whites to any hint of racial parity left U.S. officials in a bind. Claiborne worried that unless the United States demonstrated a complete confidence in free men of color, "the enemy would be encouraged to intrigue and corrupt them." For his part, commanding General Andrew Jackson counseled a middle course: promise men of color equal compensation and rights as "sons of freedom" and "fellow Citizens" but be ready to have them "moved in the rear to some point where they will be kept from doing us injury." Jackson's policy encouraged the brave service of Savary—whom Jackson promoted to the rank of second major—and other free men of color, but the failure of U.S. authorities to follow through on their broad promises of racial equality helped to cement the in-between status of free people of color.[33]

Fifty years later, concern over the legacies of Saint Domingue/Haiti for New Orleans as an Americanizing city permeated the case of *Desarzant v. LeBlanc.* Testimony in the case revealed the attempt on the part of many of the witnesses—of this extended community of refugees from Saint Domingue and their offspring—to revive and perpetuate the more fluid racial and status practices suggested by the memory of Saint Domingue. That is, their personal narratives and social etiquette corresponded to their hopes and aspirations rather than to their legal classification.[34] This practice manifested itself in Desarzant's trial in what Pierre Soulé called in his brief to the high court a "duplicity of names," a slippery series of personae ultimately referring to the same person. In her white incarnation, Desarzant was Madame Maurice Antoine Abat. To those who attested to her African ancestry, she was Toucoutou.[35] The woman on trial and thus in an in-between space called herself Anastasie Desarzant. Her brothers also had prominent nicknames. Acquaintances of Jean David Desarzant knew him as Maître Bacquié, his having taken one of the names of his mother. Likewise, the youngest brother Armand was known in the community as Bonblanc, a nickname that seemed to mock his phenotypic existence on the color line. A number of witnesses testified to Justine Bacquié's habit of using her different names in seemingly random combination. Françoise Martin, the woman from Switzerland whom Desarzant claimed as her mother, appeared as Justine Martin on the birth certificate of some of Desarzant's siblings and often called herself Justine Bacquié. One witness cleared up this confusion, testifying that Françoise Martin was Justine Bacquié's "real St. Domingo name." Considering this "duplicity of names," it is no surprise that the court denied Desarzant the existence of her white persona, Madame Maurice Abat. Instead, she came across as Anastasie Desarzant, the free woman of color nicknamed Toucoutou.

Official and unofficial names may have proliferated, but the "real St. Domingo" identity at the core remained a bedrock of sorts for New Orleans' free people of color throughout the antebellum period.[36] With commitments to liberty and equality that exceeded the scope of the United States, many of them retraced—both literally and figuratively—the path of their exile. After his "celebrated" service under Andrew Jackson, Joseph Savary continued to shuttle around the Caribbean and the Gulf of Mexico with other representatives of Republican France and Haiti, providing aid to revolutionary movements in Mexico and elsewhere.[37] Creole of color playwright Victor Séjour mined the cultural memory of the Haitian Revolution for his short story "Le Mûlatre": his title character abandons the Saint Dominguan plantation of his father to conspire in the forest with revolutionary maroons. Echoing a more general strategy of African Americans, New Orleans' Creoles of color contemplated a return migration to Haiti, particularly during the 1850s.[38]

Some New Orleanians of color, despite their expulsion from Cuba, continued to maintain ties of property and community on the Spanish island. As early as October 1814, Spain had invited free blacks to return to Cuba, an invitation that "large numbers" of free people accepted.[39] After losing her lawsuit, Anastasie Desarzant seems to have spent considerable time in Santiago de Cuba.

As much as Desarzant's extended network in Santiago might have embraced her after the court battle, during the period of the trial the specter of a Haitian legacy hovered portentously over Desarzant, undermining her search for a white racial identity. For many, her dogged pursuit of whiteness represented a betrayal of the possibilities that an attachment to Haiti and the experience of exile afforded. Before the trial, a male acquaintance told one witness, an old friend of Justine Bacquié's and a fellow migrant from Saint Domingue, "You had better testify in favor of Toucoutou who [because of her relationship to Bacquié] is creole of your country." "No!," the woman replied. "Eglantine has far more sense than Toucoutou, and moreover when I die, Eglantine I'm sure will come to my funeral but Toucoutou won't."[40] As someone who defended the middle ground of Creole identity, Eglantine Desmaziliere seemed to this witness more committed to a Saint Dominguan/Haitian way of life and more likely to perform the essential duties and rituals of friendship. In contrast, Desarzant's endorsement of Anglo-American whiteness placed her beyond the larger spiritual and cultural community. Another witness of color, described as a "creole of New Orleans," warned Desarzant of the consequences of her betrayals; when Desarzant remarked "how chagrined she was about this suit, witness consoled her and told her whenever any body wanted to get out of her class, such a thing couldn't but happen."[41]

In her truncated consolation, this witness demonstrated the parameters of the "tight places" in which New Orleans' Creoles of color found themselves in 1859.[42] On an individual basis, choosing to pass as white might finally secure the person a certain level of freedom, but this choice would also undercut the cultural resources of the group as a whole. When one of Desarzant's witnesses was asked by the defendant's lawyer Pierre Soulé whether she was herself white or colored, she upheld her racial indeterminacy, retorting defensively that she did not know. Although the witness eventually admitted to colored status, she maintained that she did not "see what that has to do with the case."

Despite this witness's insistence on the limited scope of the trial, however, the case had drastic repercussions for the sense of racial indeterminacy that the witness felt sustained her. In his brief to the high court, Soulé attempted to impose a more narrow racial logic than that being used by the witnesses, thus diminishing the authority of those who seemed to claim a more fluid racial identity. Toucoutou's mother, according to Soulé, "*is sought to be made* a white person by some two or three witnesses who presume to testify to her status while they can not say whether they *be* themselves white or colored."[43] This grammatical construction underscored Soulé's attempt to halt processes of becoming in favor of a consistent state of racial being.

Like that of Pandelly's nemesis Victor Wiltz, Soulé's urgent search for a coherent racial logic must be understood in light of the emergence of a southern nationalist identity. In particular, Soulé defended southern imperialist aspirations in the Caribbean and points south. Over the course of the late 1840s and 1850s, American mercenaries fueled the popular hunger for national heroes by launching a number of filibusters, extralegal expansionist expeditions, into the Caribbean and Latin America, often using New Orleans as a base of operation.[44] As Franklin Pierce's ambassador to Spain, Pierre Soulé himself had been the author of the infamous Ostend Manifesto (1854) that sought to extort Cuba from Spain. Even as he represented LeBlanc and Desmaziliere, Soulé served as legal counsel to the most famous American filibuster, William Walker, whose federal trial for overthrowing the government of Nicaragua and, thereby, violating the neutrality laws of the United States was underway in New Orleans at the same time as *Desarzant v. LeBlanc.*[45] Southerners such as Soulé with designs on an empire to the south had to be able to answer the kinds of objections raised by the late John C. Calhoun, who had opposed annexing "All Mexico" during the previous decade's Mexican-American War. "More than half of the Mexicans are Indians, and the other is composed chiefly of mixed tribes," Senator Calhoun had argued before Congress in 1848. "I protest against such a union as that! Ours, sir, is a Government of a white race! . . . Are they fit to be connected with us? Are they fit for self-government and for governing you?"[46] Those of Soulé's ilk would have a special stake in taming the racial identities proliferating throughout the former Spanish and French empires and bringing them within a stricter Anglo-American context.

When viewed as a battle waged over just this kind of project, the Toucoutou case reveals the instability of New Orleans' cultural and racial ground. The memory of Saint Domingue and the idea of Haiti figured as "friendly ghosts" for those *gens de couleur libre* seeking to secure their identities in spaces and legacies of racial ambiguity and black freedom. For Soulé, the search for the shelter of whiteness by Desarzant and others raised the large and ominous specter of Haiti, a disruptive presence that needed to be silenced.[47] Even so, a growing "American" influence in New Orleans and the intervention of the United States in hemispheric politics more generally nurtured another hazard for free people of color and impressed upon them a dire sense of their predicament in the racialized scheme of things. If the specter of Haiti were to expose Desarzant's African ancestry, another apparition even more threatening than her parents' native land lay in wait for her: the institution of slavery. In the decades leading up to the Civil War, the process of Americanization signified more than merely the encroachment of a binary system of racial classification; it also sought to standardize the categories of a slave regime, aligning a white identity with freedom and a black identity with enslavement.[48]

The Specter of Slavery

Under the imperatives of such an alignment, free people of color were especially vulnerable, their status rendered increasingly anomalous. The legal logic of this trend had been gaining force for more than two decades. An 1830 statute forced free people of color to leave the state if they had entered after 1825. In the early 1840s, those remaining in the state were compelled to register their names at the mayor's office. The prevalence of English surnames and the frequency with which other states such as Virginia and Maryland were listed as birthplaces suggests that New Orleans' indigenous *gens de couleur libre* held themselves exempt from this statute. However, in the mid 1850s, even those free people of color native to New Orleans increasingly suffered the burden of new laws requiring them to carry passes for such "privileges" as bearing arms and walking through the streets. The cause of the enslaved and the plight of the free people of color became inextricably linked in the legislative arena. In 1857, for the first time, lawmakers grouped together in the same section laws concerning slaves and those concerning free people of color, demonstrating the precedence of race over status. Tightening restrictions on manumission culminated in a general ban on that practice in 1857, when Louisiana finally conformed to the harshening slave codes of other southern states. In the spring of 1859, as Desarzant's wait for a hearing was coming to an end, the Louisiana legislature passed an act "to permit free persons of African descent to select a master and become slaves for life," a phrasing that underscored what lawmakers thought to be the underlying benevolence of their legislation. In a climate where fewer people gained their freedom and where free people were required by increasingly enforced laws to leave the state, free people of color in the city scrambled to defend their free status.

Throughout the antebellum period, enslaved people and free people of color found the court system to be a choice weapon, and they frequently escaped bondage and proscription through legal loopholes.[49] For Desarzant, establishing whiteness would work to secure her marriage plans, but it also would help secure her free status. This strategy pervaded *Miller v. Belmonti* (1845), for example, one of the most celebrated and serendipitous cases of the antebellum period.[50] Made famous by a "strange true story" of George Washington Cable, this case of "white slavery" purported to tell the story of Salome Müller, a German immigrant and "redemptioner." Presumably having been orphaned after entering into a contract of indenture in a far-flung Louisiana parish, Müller was said to have subsequently fallen into chattel slavery.[51] Two decades later, Madame Carl, a fellow immigrant, recognized Müller in the streets of New Orleans as the same white girl aboard her ship so many years earlier. Müller's long-lost godmother confirmed her identity after seeing moles on the inside of each of Müller's thighs, and with the support of the extended German immigrant community, the women pressed for Müller's emancipation from her owner of five years, Louis Belmonti. Before long, the high-profile case targeted her former owner, John Fitz Miller, as the ultimate villain in the story—the man accused of knowingly enslaving a white girl. Müller won her case in the lower court and prevailed again before the Louisiana Supreme Court and in several related cases. This version of the story is miraculous enough; however, sorting through the trial records demonstrates that the "Sally Miller" in the courtroom may not have been the German immigrant after all, but an enslaved woman of color known in some circles as Bridget Wilson. Stumbling on this avenue to freedom, Wilson endured and affected a series of name changes, eventually becoming, at the moment of her chance public encounter with Madame Carl, Salome Müller.[52] When mistaken for Müller, Wilson effectively passed for free and passed for white in one fell swoop.[53]

Whether she was known as Müller or as Wilson, the range of meanings ascribed to Sally Miller's appearance demonstrated the ambiguities suggested by near-white skin. Despite the whiteness of her skin, Miller had been held in bondage in Louisiana for twenty years, more or less. Her apparent whiteness had augmented the personal wealth of her masters, making her a potential commodity in the "fancy trade." In this specialized realm of the slave market, an enslaved girl or woman with a near-white appearance regularly fetched a higher price than the most able field hand. As luxury items, fancy girls provided an expensive canvas onto which slaveholders projected their sexual desires and social ambitions. Because of her white skin and delicate build, the ideal fancy girl was ill-equipped, according to the racial logic of the nineteenth century, for hard field labor. However, her status as a piece of property rendered her susceptible to the full range of her master's sexual fantasies and appetites in a way that a white woman's status would not allow. The fancy girl brought together whiteness and sexual availability in unsettling but titillating ways. Serving as a receptacle for white male anxiety about the potentially untamed sexuality of all women, white and black, the fancy girl was, in the eyes of her owner, simultaneously more sexual than the ideal white woman and more refined than the promiscuous black woman.[54] His ability to buy her in the first place and his subsequent discipline and mastery over her confirmed his place within the social hierarchy as well as his manhood.

However edifying for a white master's personal and social esteem, trafficking in what historian Walter Johnson has called "hybrid whiteness" held certain perils for slaveholders.[55] The closer a fancy girl's appearance to whiteness, the higher her value—to a point. The more convincing the performance of a white identity, the stronger her potential claims to freedom. Thus, Sally Miller forced her status beyond the tipping point from enslaved to free. The ultimate verdict in *Miller v. Belmonti* handed down by the Louisiana Supreme Court in 1845 turned to a large extent on the long-standing precedent that light or white skin carried with it the presumption of freedom. The presiding Supreme Court judge based his opinion on *Adele v. Beauregard*, a case from 1810 that conferred the presumption of freedom on mixed-race people. However, by the late 1850s, as Johnson has shown in his discussion of *Morrison v. White* (1857)—a similar case brought by fifteen-year-old Alexina Morrison—color on its own was not enough to guarantee freedom. Originally from East Texas and enslaved in Jefferson Parish near New Orleans, Morrison was originally granted freedom by a lower court. The case was bandied back and forth between the lower court and the Louisiana Supreme Court, where judges more conservative than those who rendered judgment on behalf of Müller asserted that the "presumption of freedom arising from her color must yield to proof of her servile origin."[56] When Salome Müller's identity as a pure German came convincingly under question, the Louisiana Supreme Court trod gingerly over her case, refusing to deny her the free status suggested by her white skin.[57] Suspended in legal limbo between slavery and freedom and blackness and whiteness, Alexina Morrison languished in prison and may have died there while her case remained on the Louisiana Supreme Court docket—where it still awaits a hearing.[58]

In the hardening racial logic of the late 1850s, just as a person could be, as one witness testified in Morrison's trial, "too white to keep," the person could also be the inverse—too black to remain free.[59] Providing a point of comparison for *Desarzant v. LeBlanc*, the case of Constance Bique Perrine demonstrated the drastic consequences of the presumption of blackness and thus enslaved status in the daily lives of free people of color. Only four days before Desarzant initiated her case in the Third District Court of New Orleans, another free woman of color, Constance Bique Perrine, brought a $2,000 lawsuit against the New Orleans police department for damages she suffered while in custody.[60] According to the testimony, Perrine had been arrested on the night of May 13, 1858, on St. Ann Street on charges of public drunkenness and disturbing the peace. Around the same time, police had also apprehended Anaïse, a runaway slave from a nearby plantation. At some point during the night, the identities of the two women became switched, and when Anaïse's master, a Mr. Rousseau, gave the police department permission to transport his slave woman to the calaboose and to punish her, the police took Perrine instead. "Tightly penioned and forcibly stretched upon a platform," Perrine was whipped ten times with a leather strap that measured at least three inches wide. During the beating, Perrine had continually protested that she was indeed a free woman, undeserving of such treatment. However, the officers continued, having been warned by Mr. Rousseau that Anaïse "was in the habit of giving herself out as free." When Rousseau finally came to retrieve his slave property, he was "confounded at the mistake." When Perrine's employer appeared at the precinct house to post bail for his cook and washerwoman, Perrine could barely walk, coming downstairs only "with great difficulty." Perrine miscarried a three-month-old fetus in subsequent days and lingered on her sickbed for close to four weeks. The $2,000, Perrine believed, would compensate her for pain and suffering, the loss of her child, doctor's fees, and lost wages. After an appeal process lasting almost a year and a half, she "won" her case, receiving a mere $150 for the medical bills and lost time.

Like Desarzant's case, *Perrine v. City of New Orleans* demonstrates the changeable status of status. Whereas Desarzant was in danger of slipping from the status of a white woman to that of a *femme de couleur libre*, Perrine, for a very frightening and eventful few hours, lost her rights as a free woman of color and became, effectively, a slave. Tellingly, Perrine sued the city and the chief of police not merely because she was whipped in their custody, but because she was "whipped as a *slave*."[61] If Perrine had indeed been the slave woman Anaïse, all seemed to agree that the customary ten lashes with a thick strap was appropriate punishment. Indeed, in the public imagination, the free woman and the slave were different sorts of people, and the free woman's body could not withstand the level of pain and abuse appropriate for the body of the enslaved woman. Accordingly, Perrine's doctor testified that "the infliction of ten lashes on a *free* woman at a particular time might occasion retentions, attended with serious consequences for a life time."[62]

Demonstrating the possibility of a downward shift in status, both Desarzant's and Perrine's cases pointed to the urgency of gaining a foothold where one was, of asserting social status in the face of its rejection. The notion that a white person could be taken as a free person of color or that a free person of color could be mistaken for a slave disturbed those who existed on the boundaries of those categories. The dollar amount affixed to these transgressions demonstrated the relative value of each social position. Whereas Perrine had decided that the amount of $2,000 would compensate her for both her extensive physical suffering and the embarrassment of having to endure, if even for a day, the position of a slave, Desarzant maintained that she had suffered five times that trauma, sustaining "damages and injury" to the amount of $10,000. During her trial, Desarzant must have felt the effects of gravity accumulating. If she were to slip far enough down the social ladder to be taken for a woman of color, the final rung into slavery may not have seemed far away.

Fears of slippage had undergirded the choices of Desarzant's mother, Justine Bacquié, all along, and her attention to etiquette sought to augment her own status and that of her children. Echoes of Bacquié's discomfort with social proscriptions resounded throughout the Desarzant slander case. For example, in the 1830s or 1840s, one of Bacquié's sons gained an apprenticeship with the nephew of one of the defendant's witnesses, a white woman. When this nephew barred Baquié's son from sitting at a common table with white workers, Bacquié—her honor and that of her family insulted—forced him to discontinue his employment.[63] The pressure to realign racial and status categories held especially dire implications for free women of color such as Bacquié who were engaged in liaisons with white men. In the atmosphere of the mid-nineteenth century, it was increasingly difficult to distinguish a free *placée* from an enslaved fancy girl.[64] In spite of laws that consciously worked to prevent a woman of color from achieving a reputation for virtue, Bacquié and other free women of color maintained their own codes of propriety. In part, this effort explains how Bacquié came to be Françoise Justine Martin's last name. According to a witness who had known Bacquié in Saint Domingue and Cuba, Justine had taken the name of her first "husband," a Mr. Bacquié. Somewhere between St. Marc and New Orleans and after the birth of two children who later died, "Mr. Bacquié left her and got married" to a white woman. "Being asked whether [Justine] married again, witness answers: 'she married again as she had done with Bacquié and others."[65] Bacquié's own arrangement with Jean Laizer, Desarzant's father, irritated her sense of dignity. Acknowledging the desire for a more formal commitment of Laizer to his family of color, Justine, according to one witness, "used to say that these [arrangements] were abominations."

Bacquié's daughters appeared to span the spectrum of respectful behavior. The testimony in the case merely hinted at the predicament of Desarzant's older sister Louise, who seemed to be generally condemned by the wider community of women of color. One witness self-righteously claimed that she "ceased visiting [Bacquié] as soon as her daughter Louise began leading a life that did not at all suit her."[66] By contrast, the evidence suggests that Bacquié's aspirations for Anastasie included as legitimate a marriage as possible and perhaps accounts for Anastasie's desire to pass as white and contract a legal marriage to Abat. One witness, an older white man who may have hoped to establish his own liaison with Anastasie, testified that he had run into Bacquié and Desarzant in the street. Upon remarking somewhat suggestively on how beautiful and "fine" the girl had become, Bacquié quickly and proudly replied: "That's my daughter and she is to be married."[67]

Holes in the Contract

In Saint Domingue, Cuba, and New Orleans, Justine Bacquié engaged in a lifelong struggle for a virtuous reputation and a more secure social status, and she bequeathed this struggle to her daughter. However, her intentions for her daughter's moral and social standing were at cross-purposes with those of Toucoutou's father, Jean Laizer, also known as Desarzant. His obligations to his white family shaped Laizer's social legacy to his children with Baquié. On one occasion, his fellow lodge member asked him, "Are you not ashamed being a married man to have such a family?" Laizer's response spoke volumes about the legal and racial boundaries operating in New Orleans: "These [children of color] are the holes eventually cut into the contract *(Des coups de canifs donnés au contrat)*."[68] His chosen metaphor—a contract with loopholes—raises questions about the nature and range of his social, familial, and personal relationships. Which contract did Laizer have in mind—his legitimate contract as a married man with his white wife, Hélène Ségoire? The informal arrangement with Bacquié, which had resulted in "such a family"? Or the social contract that would oblige a man in his situation to admit, if only for propriety's sake, to a sense of shame?

Whatever its nature, the contract functioned to some extent as a sieve. It would be difficult for the legal claims of his family of color to his paternity to hold water, rendering their social status exceedingly fragile. However, the family of color, despite formal restrictions on their inheritance, represented a potential drain on the financial resources of his white family. As a sieve, the contract worked to Anastasie Desarzant's advantage. By stepping forward to claim whiteness, Desarzant, as Laizer's child and one of the holes in the contract, attempted to capitalize on the inconsistency and illegibility of the various documents and testimony describing her relationship to Laizer. On the other hand, if this contract was meant to be a wall separating racial and status categories, the holes cut into it might also serve as windows. Through these, Laizer's public obligations might glimpse his private desires and vice versa, ultimately leaving unclear which were which, and thus problematizing both. When Laizer's contract was viewed this way, Desarzant's status as one of its loopholes worked to her disadvantage. Much of the trial's oral testimony and documentary evidence publicized her private filial connection to Laizer even though she would have preferred that it remain obscured.[69]

Jean Laizer died in 1850, but his legal and social maneuvers echoed through the courtroom, alternatively facilitating and confounding Desarzant's efforts to achieve a white identity.[70] In various official documents, he left traces of his obligations to both his white family and his family of color. His sense of duty to his white children was most apparent; his official will named only his legitimate white offspring, products of marriage to Hélène Ségoire in 1808, a union that lasted until her death in 1832. In the standard and expected manner, he bequeathed his whole estate, except a few slaves whom he emancipated, to his legitimate children, leaving them to partition the property fairly. However, other official records privileged his unsanctioned affiliation with Bacquié, charted through his own series of "duplicitous names." Jean Laizer, the upstanding white citizen, slaveholder, and member of the prestigious fraternal organization Polar Star Lodge No. 1 appears as a shadowy figure in the public records of his children of color. On their baptismal certificates, he retained the name Jean Desarzant from the ship record of his passage from Cuba to New Orleans. Further scrutiny into the identity of this mysterious man revealed Desarzant to have been the maiden name of Laizer's mother. Appropriately, his choice of this name for his children of color both confirms and obscures his connection to them, a connection that he records through his maternal line, not his "official" paternal line. In the baptismal records of some of his children, he appeared in two forms, first as the absent Jean Desarzant and secondly as himself, Jean Laizer, present at the ceremony and "*faisant pour le père.*"

In "making do" for their father, Laizer performed an ambiguous relationship to his "colored" children, a relationship mirrored in his concealed commitment to their material well-being. As was typical of men with two families, his will failed to tell the whole story of his legacy. Throughout the early years of the lives of Anastasie and her siblings, Laizer and Bacquié engaged in a number of transactions, sales of property designed to supply income for the children. For example, in 1830 Jean Laizer assisted in the sale of a house and lot in Marigny to his four children named Desarzant. Acting as their guardian, Laizer purchased this property for $1,200, having declared "that the said minors are orphans and that he has paid the price of their purchase with money entrusted to his keeping for account of and belonging to said orphans." The act indicated that Laizer had bought the property from a Zeline Bacquié, Justine's child from her liaison with her first "husband." This transaction may have worked to keep both the money and the property "in the family."[71]

Tracking Laizer's business and personal transactions and listening to the testimony of his friends and relatives undermines any distinction he hoped to maintain between public and private commitments. It is difficult to determine, therefore, which of these households—white or of color—constituted his genuine legacy. His white children's legitimate status, confirmed by his will, suggests that Jean Laizer's public face was his white family. After all, for propriety's sake he attempted to conceal his extramarital commitments from them, implying that they need not concern themselves with his clandestine attachments. However, he "made no secret" of his relationship to the Desarzant children in other contexts. According to one witness, his and Bacquié's parentage of these children was a matter of public notoriety among his friends as well as among the friends and acquaintance of Bacquié. One witness testified that Justine told her that "Laizer had served as godfather to their children so that he might go and see them. They called him '*Parrain*' [Godfather]."[72] As godfather, sanctioned by God and the church to step in where the birth father had failed, Laizer arguably augmented his status in the public imagination. Laizer participated in the lives of

Anastasie and her siblings as a kind of Sunday visitor, a benevolent and somewhat constant factor in their lives. The testimony of a few of the witnesses, close friends of the late Laizer, alludes to the existence of a community of "Sunday visitors." After meetings of the Polar Star Lodge No. 1, these men would make the rounds, dropping in on their mistresses and families of color in Marigny before returning home to their Esplanade mansions. One of Laizer's friends and neighbors, Manuel Prados, periodically accompanied him to Bacquié's house on Greatmen Street in Marigny—something of a meeting place.[73] According to Prados, he and others "visited another man by the name of Doublet and afterwards a builder by the name of Maurice Pidzetta, each of whom lived successively with a woman named Marie Jeanne Doublet who occupied the other half of the house in which Justine Bacquié lived."[74] It was during one of these visits, Prados maintained, that he saw Bacquié "suckling" a child believed to be Toucoutou. Indeed, much of the information on Bacquié trickled down to these prominent men through the women they "lived with." Another white male witness testified to the date of Anastasie Desarzant's birth, recalling that he lived with a "colored girl" who had been "confined" at the same time as Bacquié.[75]

Desarzant's lawsuit brought her white half-siblings into the courtroom, in the ultimate public gesture, to testify for the defense to their father's parentage of Anastasie and her siblings. Whereas Desarzant wished to conceal this relationship, the white Laizers revealed the family secrets, sacrificing the reputation of their deceased father in order to protect the ultimate prize of whiteness. Ironically, their full disclosure of Laizer's indiscretions helped topple the shaky barriers between the white Laizers and their relatives of color. As the testimony of Jean Laizer's legitimate white child Eugenie Laizer indicated, these two families—despite the efforts of Laizer to keep his affairs separate—had not been ignorant of one another. According to Eugenie Laizer, "Anastasie Desarzant always said she was the daughter of Jean David Laizer," and Eugenie's mother often told her of her "colored" relations. However, their appearance in court was not without its difficulties. Memories of the 1856 divorce trial of Virginie, another Laizer daughter, probably haunted them in the courtroom. Shortly after her marriage to Jean Lacaze in 1854, he had "abandoned their common dwelling" and taken up residence with Françoise, "a colored woman, his concubine."[76]

Just as Jean Laizer's marital and extramarital arrangements undermined the distinction between public and private, Lacaze's escapades threatened local social boundaries and the stability of his white wife's identity. According to the judgment of divorce rendered in her favor, the public nature of his abandonment of Virginie constituted his chief violation. Recognized by many acquaintances as the "real" wife of Jean Lacaze, Françoise—masquerading in the divorce trial as a mere "servant"—continually mocked Virginie Laizer's marital status. Speaking of his acquaintance with Mr. and Mrs. Lacaze, one witness clarified that "When I said I knew Mrs. Lacaze, I meant the mulatto woman. I do not know the plaintiff." Indeed, Virginie Laizer actually owned the home on Bayou Road that the pair occupied and in which they received visitors as man and wife. Remarking on the presence of only one bed in the succession of houses occupied by Lacaze and Françoise, witnesses had no doubt of the sexual nature of their relationship. The specific intimacy of their private relationship could not help but become public knowledge: one witness was certain that they shared this bed because "it was summer and all of the doors were opened," presumably allowing him to peer into the house or allowing aural evidence of their couplings to drift into the street. Moreover, Lacaze had bragged openly to friends about Françoise. One witness admitted that "Mr. Lacaze has spoken to me several times of this colored woman and that he had had carnal relations with her—and that he preferred this woman to any other." While it is impossible to know for certain Eugenie Laizer's true feelings about her half-sister Anastasie Desarzant, her testimony may have given voice to some of the resentment and social embarrassment suffered by her long-dead mother and her sister at the hands of their husbands.

For her part, Desarzant hoped to fill up the enormous breaches in her father's decorum with edifying stories about her identity, an attempt ultimately resulting in a struggle over the existence and nature of the holes in the official and unofficial contracts that constituted Desarzant's racial identity. Much of this struggle hinged on the question of "associations," as if whom one "frequented" was an indication of racial status. For every witness of Desarzant's who could claim that he or she "always sees white people" at Madame Abat's house, the defendants countered with a witness who had seen Desarzant at balls for people of color.[77] One witness testified that "Before the cholera,

Toucoutou used to frequent colored people exclusively," reprising the notion that epidemics could occasion severe reversals of power and identity. Other witnesses sent conflicting messages. One of Desarzant's witnesses, a Mrs. Ottman, believed Desarzant to be white. However, as Ottman testified, her sister once left a soirée at Ottman's house early, angered by the presence of a "colored woman" (Desarzant). Although she used to see Toucoutou regularly, another witness remarked that she had never been to Desarzant's house because "she doesn't frequent white people, and plaintiff *claims* to be white."[78]

If Desarzant's testimonial evidence grew more and more suspect over the course of the trial, her documentary evidence literally fell apart. Desarzant depended on the judgment she had won in her 1854 case and the subsequent order to obliterate all mention of her presumably "colored" status. This judgment hinged to a large extent on Bacquié's sworn statement of Desarzant's "true parentage." However, during *Desarzant v. LeBlanc*, the legitimacy of this statement dwindled under the testimony of those who claimed to have seen Bacquié afterwards in tears on Esplanade Street, regretting her oath. After Toucoutou called Bacquié an "old mulatress" and put her out of the house, Bacquié complained on more than one occasion, "Do you believe that a child, the issue of my womb, took me before the judge to take a false oath and declare that she was not my daughter?" Like this "false oath," other documents, seemingly sound at first glance, eroded under "expert testimony." For example, Aimé Willoz, the keeper of the baptismal registers in the St. Louis Cathedral, weakened his own document's authority in determining race, saying that it was "quite common to find colored persons registered on the registry of white persons. It is very seldom that white persons are inscribed on the registry of colored persons. . . . When such a case occurs, there is a marginal note made correcting the error." Indeed, the unreliability of church documents had provoked the adoption in 1847 of an ordinance requiring physicians and midwives to verify the parentage and race of each child delivered and to report these statistics monthly to the office of the recorder of births and deaths.[79] The judgments of medical professionals would supplant the dubious racial designations supplied by the church. Thus, even in the "official" record, racial identity was a potentially changeable quality, and one's identity could evolve over time.

Ultimately Anastasie Desarzant lost her case and her white privilege, demonstrating the power of marginalia, hearsay, and whispered asides. In fact, Desarzant's story took root in the murky but fertile ground of rumor and gossip and became an important cultural touchstone for years to come. The official book on the case closed to a large extent on December 7, 1859, when the Louisiana Supreme Court rendered its opinion without including the case in its reports. Perhaps it preferred to deemphasize this route to whiteness; perhaps it wished to protect the Abat family from further humiliation; or perhaps it rushed to close the docket in anticipation of the fast-approaching holiday season. In any event, the court's failure to report the case rendered it a needle in a haystack for future researchers and legal specialists. Nevertheless, the omission of the case from the court reports could not deter the trafficking of its memory along other avenues of public notoriety. Even before the verdict was given, the Creole of color barber-musician Joseph Beaumont composed a rapidly proliferating and mutating song about Desarzant that undoubtedly followed her through the streets and provided the basis for decades of cultural criticism.

Toucoutou as a "Site of Memory"

In the accounts of Beaumont, Rodolphe Desdunes, and Edward Larocque Tinker, the name Toucoutou continued to resonate within the ongoing and evolving predicament of racial identity. It became what Pierre Nora describes as a site of memory, a "double: a site of excess closed upon itself, concentrated in its own name, but also forever open to the full range of its possible significations."[80] As noted in the Prologue, the Toucoutou affair had until recently been "closed upon itself" to researchers in a very literal way. Tinker's novel *Toucoutou* had the effect of animating the documentary evidence but at the same time burying and obscuring it. Although the accounts of Beaumont, Desdunes, and Tinker appear to be separate and freestanding, they have been more like Russian dolls. Tinker's account has long enclosed the other two within it and aligned the features of their interpretations with his own.

Even so, Beaumont's version, a satirical Creole song, provided the engine propelling this memory into the future. His account has ensured the story's open-ended relevance across different but overlapping contexts. A barber by profession, Beaumont, called the "Béranger of the Creole people" after the popular French lyricist, composed infectious songs in the 1850s and 1860s.[81] Of Beaumont's Creole songs, Desdunes isolates "Toucoutou" as one of the most important.[82] Likewise, *Gumbo YaYa*, the W.P.A. collection of Louisiana cultural life, refers to "Toucoutou" as "one of the best known of all Creole songs," and it is reprinted there "because of the incongruity of omitting it from any representative Creole collection."[83] In *Nos Hommes*, Desdunes introduces the song "Toucoutou": "the couplets just as they have come down to us."[84]

Toucoutou	Toucoutou
Si vous té gagné vous procé Oh, nègue cé maléré. Mové dolo qui dans focé Cé pas pon méprisé.	If you win your lawsuit, Indeed, O Negress, this is bad; Bad for those who force it And the harm can not be disregarded.
Refrain: Ah! Toucoutou, ye conin vous, Vous cé tin Morico. Na pa savon qui tacé blanc Pou blanchi vous lapo.	Refrain: Ah, Toucoutou we know you! You are a little Mooress. Who does not know you? No soap will make you white.
Au Théâtre même quand va prend loge. Comme tout blanc comme y fot, Ye va fé vous prend Jacdeloge,[85] Na pas pacé tantôt.	At the theater, if you go there, Like all white people should, They will treat you like Jacdeloge, Who did not pass so well as white, did he?
Refrain	Refrain
Quand blanc loyés va donin bal Vous pli capab aller.	When these white lawyers give a dance Will you be able to go?

Comment va fé, vayante diabol, Vous qui laimez danser?	Will you, O beautiful devil, You who love to dance so!
Refrain	Refrain
Mo pré fini mo ti chanson Pasqui manvi dormi; Mé mo pensé que la leson Longtemps li va servi.	I have finished my little song Because I want to sleep; But I think the lesson will serve, For a long time to keep you meek.

Desdunes also records several stray verses and intimates the existence of many others. Imagined as a dialogue between Toucoutou and her concerned brother, the extra verses perform a filial relationship. While the brother emphasizes and tries to warn Toucoutou of her impending loss of social status, she denies their relationship and refutes his characterization of her predicament. "Why do you speak thus to me? / Like an evil vagabond? / A white person! Are you crazy? . . . / My name is not Toucoutou."[86]

Desdunes's account lacks precision about the song's path of transmittal—the way in which the verses may have "come down to us"; however, the song's colloquial language and its expanding repertoire of stanzas suggest the communal context of its composition and its passage across a contested space and time. As a barber and a member of at least two mutual aid societies, Joseph Beaumont had ample opportunity to act as a cultural maven, bringing people together, facilitating conversation, and stirring controversy. A resident of Marigny and thus a close neighbor of Desarzant and Abat, Beaumont was well-placed to gauge and shape local opinion. The germ of the song "Toucoutou" may have been hatched in the heated repartee of the barbershop, where grooming and language games often went hand in hand. Its popularity may have gathered steam during Beaumont's club meetings with other members gathered around the piano, the proliferating verses goaded on by the intake of alcohol and tobacco. In the weeks leading up to the December 7 verdict, New Orleans was entering the festive winter season that would culminate in late February with Mardi Gras. Beaumont's musical talents would have been in hot demand for countless parties, balls, and parades, and one can imagine "Toucoutou" echoing through the streets in an ever-evolving call and response.[87]

The performative context for the song invokes the cultural hybridity of the circum-Atlantic world where travelers in this creolized middle ground blended and transformed African and European traditions to meet their specific needs. Within the francophone black Atlantic, the meeting of Catholicism and African religious practices gave rise to voodoo, and its elastic ritual space and expansive pantheon encompassing both saints and *loas* disrupted distinctions between the sacred and secular realms.[88] Thus, it was not uncommon for spiritual practices to incorporate political and social critique and vice versa. In these ritual contexts, the composition and performance of "Toucoutou" during the season bounded by Christmas and Easter would have been wholly appropriate and expected. The use of Creole rather than French places the song in the context of these hybrid traditions and practices, and Beaumont exemplifies the spirit of Legba (Ellegua), the *loa* of the crossroads, which some critics might call a trickster, a catalyst for collective acts of creativity and dynamic interplay.[89] These satiric renditions thrived within a regimen of "play and display."[90] Highly improvisational, the composition of "Toucoutou" depended on Beaumont's individual talents, a spirit of exchange within a larger community, and a trove of historical memory accessible through performance, melody, rhythm, and gesture.

"Toucoutou" and other such songs were not transparent, and many analyses place the problem of translation in the foreground, extending George Washington Cable's observation that "There is an affluence of bitter meaning hidden under these apparently nonsensical lines."[91] Cable's formulation suggests the existence of an essential but concealed truth, but it is more appropriate to the genre of satire and the performative context of Beaumont's taunt song to consider the open-endedness of these songs.[92] Beaumont's composition merged the particular and the general, commemorating the Toucoutou case as a real historical event as well as offering it as an interpretive rubric through which people might continue to make meaning.[93] Drawing on both African and European satiric traditions, the song and its legacy holds unruly implications and presupposes an uneven interpretive context. One critic describes the "unstable ironies" of the satiric mode, pointing to the production of unintended meanings and exposing the contradictory impulses and forces underlying even those intended messages. As satire, then, "Toucoutou" thrives amid ambiguity in tone, motivation, and reception. Were Beaumont and his cohort making fun *of* Desarzant, or were they simply making fun? Were their performances meant to be thought-provoking or entertaining? Did their critique of the oppressive social context giving rise to the court case seek liberation from it, or did it facilitate the hardening of racial and status categories? Might the song have embraced all of these functions at once?[94]

The Creole strategies of racial passing provide an ideal subject for the genre of the satirical taunt song, both genre and subject giving rise to multidimensional social transactions. The humor of the song rests on what Henry Louis Gates, Jr., has called a "trinary structure," a framework dispelling "simple relations of identity" and the "binary political relationship . . . between black and white."[95] Beaumont and his cohort poked fun at Toucoutou, but they set their comparatively harmless taunts against a white society ultimately responsible for dictating the vicious terms of her exclusion. In mocking her efforts, the revelers provoked their own confrontation with Toucoutou at the same time that they redirected their outrage toward a third party: whites (or whiteness). The triple motion of Beaumont's humor back and forth among his community of revelers, Toucoutou, and white privilege mirrored the process of passing itself, one that Amy Robinson has described as similarly triangulated.[96] As one who was trying to pass, Desarzant suspended herself in a third space temporarily outside the confines of both free people of color and whites. For Desarzant, the act of passing entailed, first, a negotiation between herself and other *gens de couleur* because its members recognized her as one of their own ("*Ah! Toucoutou, ye conin vous!* / Ah, Toucoutou, we know you!") and threatened to impede her progress across racial boundaries. The group maintained its integrity by monitoring and potentially exposing those who might stray. As "passer," Desarzant also claimed a place among whites by adopting their habits and making a convincing case that, in terms of her appearance, seeing was indeed believing. By invoking a realm outside the two groups where strict distinctions did not yet apply, Desarzant's trial threatened to subvert white privilege: here, it was the *gens de couleur* that had privileged knowledge about Toucoutou and white society that was potentially duped by her.

Additionally, the context of racial passing allowed Beaumont and others to accentuate ironies, playing on the gap between what appeared to be objective reality and the admittedly subjective readings of that reality. In their view, serious rules and practices that claimed the authority of principle seemed arbitrary and absurd. In passing for white, Toucoutou had hoped that her white appearance would be the ultimate arbiter of her social station. In response, Beaumont stressed the inadequacy of appearances, indicating that things were not ultimately as they seemed. For Beaumont, the fair-skinned, blue-eyed Desarzant was a "Negress," a "little Mooress" *("négue, cé tin Morico")*, and he reminded her that *"Na pa savon qui tacé blanc / Pou blanchi vous lapo* (No soap will make you white)." Furthermore, he emphasized the disparity between the law in fact and the law in practice, asking *"Quand blanc loyés va donin bal / Vous pli capab aller?* (When these white lawyers give a dance, will you be able to go?)." If "no" were the answer to this open-ended question, the lawyers would have fulfilled their duty in helping to police hardening social boundaries. Yet, the history of quadroon balls and *plaçage* suggests that the answer to this rhetorical question was more likely to be "yes." Indeed, Abat's "marriage" to Desarzant was one of several high-profile relationships between white men in the legal profession and free women of color.[97]

Like much satire, Beaumont's "Toucoutou" was politically ambivalent, amenable to a wide range of social critique. Beaumont recognized that passing was most subversive when it was exposed and treated as an occasion to force public conversation about race and belonging. Thus Beaumont critiqued the social practices that constituted the status hierarchies of color and race. He chastised Toucoutou for bringing the matter into the legal arena, one that had sufficient power to bestow upon "whiteness" a property value exceeding that of "blackness" or "of color."[98] Furthermore, Beaumont mocked as absurd the liberties that whites enjoyed and that Toucoutou sought to attain. According to Beaumont, the main advantages of whiteness included such frivolous privileges as being able to go to the theater, and the consequences of blackness included being forced to sit in a segregated section of the audience, hardly a life-altering injustice. However trenchant Beaumont's social critique, though, it nevertheless held conservative implications. In trivializing the privileges of whiteness, Beaumont denied its real benefits and, in turn, masked with laughter and derision the terrifying plight of people of color, free and enslaved, in late antebellum New Orleans. Clarifying a status quo, the major lesson of Beaumont's song and his impetus for writing it in the first place was to "keep [Toucoutou] meek" and to ensure that she knew her place within the social hierarchy. The "triangle" between Beaumont (as Toucoutou's brother), Toucoutou (Desarzant), and the "white man at the ball" (Abat) mirrored the triangulated structure governing the act of passing. The sexual undertones of Beaumont's characterization of Toucoutou as an avid dancer ("you who love to dance so!") also shaped these associations into a "love triangle." In evoking the racial landscape of the "quadroon balls" and "*plaçage*," Beaumont encouraged a certain sexual propriety among free women of color.

When Rodolphe Desdunes published his community memoir *Nos Hommes et Notre Histoire* (1911), the racial terrain had shifted quite a bit. In the last decade of the nineteenth century, Desdunes and other prominent Creoles of color had challenged racial segregation with *Plessy v. Ferguson*, ultimately losing the case in the U.S. Supreme Court.[99] In that trial, Homer Plessy, a Creole of color who appeared to be white, had offered himself as evidence of the absurdity of racial classification. Plessy had enacted what Joseph Roach calls "whiteface minstrelsy," performing first the role indicated by his appearance, that of a legitimate traveler in the white section of a railroad car, and then the role indicated by his legal "blood" classification, that of someone who should be ejected from the car.[100] The Creole of color architects of *Plessy v. Ferguson* not only challenged the practice of racial discrimination but also sought to undermine the racial binary that served as its basis. The U.S. justice system echoed Beaumont, responding in no uncertain terms that "no soap will make you white!"

Desdunes's memoir walked a fine line between the desire to enshrine a coherent Creole of color identity and the need to acknowledge a common social and political agenda with non-francophone black Americans. Steeped in a transnational sensibility, Desdunes, whose Haitian father had served as an agent for emigration to Haiti during the period of Desarzant's trial, respected the cultural distinctiveness of New Orleans' Creoles of color and their placement within a French-speaking Atlantic world. In a 1907 pamphlet addressed to African American leader W. E. B. Du Bois, Desdunes offered New Orleans' Creoles of color as a likely "talented tenth" with important cultural qualifications, cautioning Du Bois to honor the differences between "Anglo-Saxon" Negroes and "Latin" Negroes.[101] For Desdunes, who was interested in a pragmatic alliance with the Anglo-Saxon black leadership, Beaumont did not represent the spirit of Legba, provoking and facilitating creativity in a three-dimensional communal context. Rather he was the individual genius lending Desdunes's "people" the cultural authority needed for the task of racial uplift. Beaumont, as literate *auteur*, gave Desdunes's memoir the status of a canon from which African American leaders such as Du Bois could draw.[102]

In particular, recounting the Toucoutou affair helped Desdunes dispel widely held ideas about the prejudices of Creoles of color—specifically those people who, following Toucoutou, either passed for white or took undue pride in their white features. "We have unfortunately too many colors and too many fads in the black race," Desdunes wrote. "[The amalgamated Negro] is a fool in his own house and esteems nothing so much as the fairness of his skin and the supple strains [sic] of his hair."[103] Less interested in the performative aspects of Beaumont's song, Desdunes accentuated the ethical dimension of satire, noting that Beaumont's songs always revealed "a depth of thought" and taught "a moral based on life as it is."[104] Read in this light, "Toucoutou" was a warning about the rules and codes of living, literally, on Du Bois's "color line." Using Beaumont's song "to show how our people reacted to the foolish controversy over the color of the skin," Desdunes concluded, "These circumstances created division among our people. Some approved, others disapproved the idea of wishing to pass into white society. The dissidents were in the majority."[105]

Even so, Desdunes remained sympathetic to Desarzant's claim that "she was of the Caucasian race, that she was *white*, as the expression was then used."[106] Here, he historicized whiteness and lauded Toucoutou's attempt to infiltrate and expose it. In his post-*Plessy* setting, he fought to reconcile the tension between the phenotypic absurdity of racial classification, played out so famously by his "people" in the *Plessy* case, and the very real consequences of being "black" in the Jim Crow South. Desdunes portrays Beaumont as a "race man," bringing the historical memory of passing into line with his current political cause for black racial unity. For Desdunes, Beaumont's song spoke to the ramifications of the Supreme Court decision in the *Plessy* case. Toucoutou became a cultural predecessor of Homer Plessy, embodying the legacy that he set straight. Whereas Toucoutou passed for selfish gain, Plessy passed in the interest of racial equality. Desdunes's description of Toucoutou's transgression of racial boundaries implicitly endorsed and canonized Plessy's heroic efforts to end segregation.

Like Desdunes's account, Edward Larocque Tinker's retelling of the Toucoutou affair sprang from the context of Jim Crow. However, whereas Desdunes attempted to anchor the memory within a black framework, Tinker attended to its implications for white New Orleanians. A white New Yorker, Tinker moved to New Orleans in 1916 upon marrying a Louisiana native. Fascinated with the unique cultural landscape of the Crescent City, Tinker conducted obsessive research on his adopted hometown.[107] He uncovered a number of what George Washington Cable would have called "strange true stories . . . natural crystals," possessing "harmony" and "unity" enough to "warn off all tampering of the fictionist."[108] The Toucoutou affair was one such story. Tinker gleaned most of his information on writers of African descent, including Beaumont, from Desdunes's *Nos Hommes*, and Tinker almost certainly recognized Beaumont's song as one of the Creole songs he heard sung regularly in the streets.

In telling a story about interracial sex and marriage, Tinker realized he was treading on volatile ground. When George Washington Cable broached these themes in his late nineteenth-century fiction, the vehement backlash against him had forced him into exile in New England.[109] In the 1920s white elites still fretted over the possibility—indeed, the probability—of their mixed-race ancestry.[110] Tinker used Cable as a guide for how (and how not) to shape his narrative and his characterizations. Despite his own professed commitment to the strangeness of the truth, Cable had consistently altered his "natural crystals" for maximum aesthetic and political effect. For example, when Cable dramatized the case of Salome Müller, the German slave girl, he failed to mention the possibility that Müller could have been Bridget Wilson. Instead, he played to an audience that would rather empathize with the plight of a mistreated white girl than with the heroism of an enslaved woman accessing an unlikely loophole to freedom.[111] Similarly, Tinker filtered the raw material of *Desarzant v. LeBlanc* through the interpretive lens of a 1920s context still dominated by the terms set by the city's polite society and a whites-only definition of Creole (see prologue).

With this in mind, Tinker offered a number of introductory remarks to his novel. First, he clarified the definition of the word *Creole*, emphatically denying that it implied a mixture of "white and negro blood." While the adjective *creole* could apply to anything "produced in Louisiana," including mules, eggs, and negroes, the noun "Creole . . . can mean only one thing and that is a pure white person born of European parents in Spanish or French colonies." Furthermore, he counseled his readers not to take some of the uncouth characters in his novel as representatives of the Creole population: "Indeed the Creoles themselves have coined a word to describe such people, and call them '*creolasse.*'"[112]

Unlike Beaumont the satirist and Desdunes the memoirist, Tinker bent the story to fit the codes and expectations of the genre of melodrama, placing Desarzant in the role of Anastasie Taquin, *née* Jasmin, the sympathetic heroine.[113] In stories meant to appeal to a white audience, as Tinker surmised, characters of color could dupe whites to a certain extent for dramatic effect, but ultimately the racial order and white authority must be restored. Under the terms of the racial etiquette of Jim Crow-era New Orleans, it would have been unthinkable for Tinker's heroine to deceive her white husband consciously, infiltrate the ranks of the white Creole society, and continue to draw sympathy from the reader. His Toucoutou is virtually blameless, exercising far less control over her life than did the Anastasie Desarzant of the actual court record. She is younger, born in 1830 (not 1824 as Desarzant was), and the trial occurs around 1849 instead of 1859. Taquin continues to have "nascent breasts" and "narrow hips" even after the birth of her son, her "little Zozo." She has no intractable siblings of color like those who appear in the court record and Beaumont's song to disrupt her tale of whiteness. Her sole brother disappears early in Tinker's account. Not until late in the action does Anastasie begin to realize her "status" and have the obligatory scene in front of the mirror, standing "so close her little nose almost touched its reflected image, she decided she looked white,—but was she? She must know."[114] Tinker places the blame for the egregious transgression of racial passing solely on the mother figure, Claircine, who has orchestrated the charade and left Anastasie ignorant of her racial ancestry. In stark contrast to Jean Laizer, who seems to have been an active if problematic presence in the lives of both his white and "of color" families, "Bazile

Bujac" dies of yellow fever when Toucoutou is a young child, thus breaking free of this cultural conundrum.

According to the conventions of melodrama, Tinker's formulaic plot resolves intermediary cliffhangers according to static moral frameworks and trades on racial and cultural stereotypes. Rather than offering the Toucoutou affair as an occasion to explore a variety of ethical frequencies, Tinker shaped the story according to a binary moral code where characters and their actions could be judged as unequivocally good or bad. Far from Desdunes's paragons of generosity and decency, Tinker's Creole of color characters are consumed with hatred and animosity and have few redeeming qualities. Instead of Desdunes's virtuous "spirit of the people," Tinker gave his character based on Beaumont the name Sans Façon—a term literally meaning without style or without the proper carriage or deportment. With the song "Toucoutou"—according to Tinker "probably the most cruel" of the Creole songs—Sans Façon gives the free people of color "a scapegoat upon which they could vent all the bitterness of their position."[115] Similarly, the loud and garish Eglantine Ferchaud ("hot iron"), Anastasie's rival and defendant in the case, harbors a "mean envy" of Anastasie's apparent whiteness. For Tinker, the performances and language games constituting individual and collective identity did not generate creative potential as they did for Beaumont. Rather, they revealed racial and cultural essences that, inhering in the blood, were understood to have always been there. Accordingly, Tinker's characters, chiseled from the rigid demands of melodrama, are best understood as types. A swashbuckling swordsman and duelist, Anastasie's husband Placide Taquin is a white Creole and thus not at all as placid as his name implies: "The deeply passionate blood of Spain mingled in his veins with the more volatile but equally ardent blood of his French ancestors."[116] Anastasie Taquin, formerly Anastasie Jasmin, is the typical *sang-melé*. Her richly wrought set of features conjure a floral metaphor, and a certain "softness" betrays her white skin, pointing to the enduring presence of otherwise hidden African characteristics.

Although Tinker's moral framework simplifies the hermeneutic challenges faced by his characters and the historical figures they are based on, it helps his readers organize the unruly Creole legacies of New Orleans according to the principles of Americanization. Memories of the Haitian Revolution and intimations of an irrepressible

Haitian influence in New Orleans haunted an American imperial project that gained steam in the first decades of the twentieth century. At the close of World War I, the United States had articulated a blueprint for democracy to be exported around the globe and had honed the segregationist practices that would safeguard this democracy from undue contention. Since the final decade of the nineteenth century, the United States had staked its claim as a white nation among darker people in Asia, the Caribbean, and Latin America. Tinker's *Toucoutou* was published in the midst of a U.S. military occupation of Haiti that lasted from 1915 to 1934 and that fed on popular perceptions of Haitians as cannibalistic, incompetent, and wholly savage.[117] In representing the Creole language, the Creole spaces of New Orleans, and Creole practices such as voodoo, Tinker staged his drama on the remnants of the Haitian legacy that had been so crucial to racial and cultural identity of nineteenth-century New Orleans.

Even though his ultimate goal was to deny a mixed-race Creole identity, Tinker mined this identity for dramatic tension. He drew, for example, on his long-standing interest in the Creole language, what he called "Gombo, the Creole dialect."[118] Whereas Beaumont's use of the Creole language opened up interpretive possibilities, Tinker's use of Creole and his theories of language reinforced white supremacy and racial essentialism. Tinker believed that language could be one of the most reliable keys to a culture: "*Cé langue crapaud qui trahi crapaud* (It is the language [or speech] of the frog that gives him away)."[119] However, Tinker also suspected that language offered disturbingly irrefutable evidence for cultural and racial mutability and change. Reconciling his commitment to white purity with his understanding of the malleability and infectious aspects of language, Tinker followed Charles Gayarré's conditions for appropriate language use. In his denunciation of Cable's *Grandissimes*, Gayarré had insisted that "an educated gentleman of the depicted epoch never addressed his wife or daughter in the jargon of the negro."[120] Alternatively, though, the "jargon of the negro" could be used by even the most devout cultural conservatives to lampoon people of African descent and those such as Cable who argued publicly for black civil rights.[121]

As many cultural critics have demonstrated, dialect writing, even if circumscribed to some extent by racist assumptions about speech and language, accommodated a number of perspectives across a broad political spectrum.[122] Cable's rendering of Creole and other Louisiana dialects formed an essential part of his appeal to social liberals. However, opponents of black equality, including the "friend of the Indian," Abbé Adrian Rouquette, could also access the satiric power of the Creole language to lampoon African American culture and racial liberals like Cable. For example, Rouquette's "Critical Dialogue between Aboo and Caboo"—a discussion between a white Creole patriarch of yore and his besieged progeny over Cable's allegations of their mixed-race ancestry—ends with sage advice from a younger kinsman to his elder. After Caboo dismisses Cable as a "High-Priest of Negro Voudouism" and suggests that Aboo simply disregard "every word not written by [Cable] in the beautiful *patois* of Lamartine and Chateaubriand," the swamp around them comes alive with "strange voices—voices of Bull-Frogs, sounding like human voices." A derision of Cable's views and talent, this chorus culminates in a "Weird Solo by a Zombi Frog," whose "strange, ventriloquous voice" testifies: "*Savan Missié Kabri, / Ki konin tou gri-gri. / Koté Bayou Koshon, / Où ganyin plin dijon, / Li té dansé Kongo / Avek Mari Lavo* (I know Mr. Cable, who knows how to work gris-gris. On the shores of Bayou St. John, in plain sight, he dances the Kongo with Marie Laveau)."[123]

In this dialogue, Rouquette charts the central fear of white Creoles that they might slip along a continuum from a magisterial French past, through the present New Orleans landscape faintly reminiscent of the French colonial legacy, straight into the pulsating heart of darkness. Tinker also privileged French as "a most subtle, intricate form—the height of sophistication" but clearly worried that the Creole language—a "simplified 'pidgin' "—might harbor something closer to the truth.[124] Indeed, these linguistic shifts might signal deeper shifts in the racial fabric of New Orleans society. In her guise as a white woman speaking French, the character Toucoutou presents a troubling reminder of the instability of Creole identity. "Due to the liquid quality of her voice and accent, she spoke a French that was far more melodious than that spoken by the French themselves."[125] Had she passed so well for white because her accent was indistinguishable from that of other white New Orleanians who were acceptably exotic because of their historical and geographical distance from France and cultural distance from Anglo-America? Or did the melody and liquidity of her voice represent, as Tinker would have it, the "efforts . . . of an inferior race to learn the language of a superior?"[126]

Early in the novel, Tinker moves the action to Congo Square, a patch of cleared ground just across the ramparts from the city proper. From the earliest French colonial days until the late antebellum period, enslaved people had been allowed to congregate there during prescribed hours on Sundays to sell their surplus wares.[127] What began as a necessary market in lean times quickly took on a social and religious function as well. Enslaved people seized on the relative autonomy to flirt with one another, worship their gods, and enjoy themselves. The exiles from Saint Domingue found special refuge in Congo Square's music, dancing, and ceremonial practice. Holding a longstanding significance in the cultural and racial geography of New Orleans, Congo Square—a middle ground and meeting ground between sacred and secular, business and pleasure, local and foreign, and black and white—exemplified the processes of creolization.[128] A characterization of Congo Square became obligatory for any traveler's report or fictional account of the oddities and otherness of Creole New Orleans.

However, under the gaze of white onlookers, the varieties of mixture occurring in this space also helped to stabilize whiteness. Never having "seen anything more brutally savage and at the same time dull and stupid," the Anglo-American architect Benjamin Henry Latrobe contemptuously held himself apart from the crowd of "*blacks*" at Congo Square when he visited the city in the late 1810s.[129] In witnessing the spectacle at Congo Square, white onlookers who merely watched confirmed their racial (and moral) distance from black and mixed-race participants who intoned the "ejaculatory burdens" of "unutterable songs," who "[threw] their bodies into the most startling attitudes and the wildest contortions," and who coaxed unusual sounds from exotic instruments made of such unlikely material as a mule's jawbone.[130] Tinker's description of atypical bodies engaged in unfamiliar motion echoes the voyeurism and disgust of these previous accounts. "Fat Arada mothers, notorious for their elephantine hips and fleshy bustles, danced with the best of them, every part of their ungainly bodies quivering like huge blobs of jelly."[131] Of course, his Toucoutou is present in the scene, first as merely an onlooker. However the "maddening rhythm" ultimately riles the African spirit that lives deep within her, and she unconsciously begins to dance. "Her whole soul went into the synchronized sway of her muscles as her body moved to the music."[132] If Toucoutou were authentically white, she would have been as repulsed by the scene of Congo Square as Latrobe had been. At the very least, she would have been able to hold herself aloof, suspended in a pose of objective observation. Instead, Tinker's depiction of the powerful draw the African rhythms have on her soul and body serves as a less-than-subtle foreshadowing of her future predicament in the courtroom.

As we have seen, the specter of Haiti/Saint Domingue hovered over the court case, threatening to expose Desarzant's African ancestry. In the spirit of the U.S. occupation of Haiti, Tinker attempts to domesticate this troubling presence and to assert the values of white supremacy. Tinker's Toucoutou stands in a long line of Haitian voodoo queens. Her grandmother was Comba Nea, voodoo priestess and chief instigator of the Haitian Revolution. Her mother, Clarcine, would draw strength from this legacy long after relocating to New Orleans. When appeals to the Virgin Mary do not cure her lover and Anastasie's father, Bazile Bujac, of yellow fever, Claircine enacts a secret ritual that frightens the young Anastasie as she watches through a keyhole. "Crouching beside the cross, [Claircine] began to intone quietly strange muttering words. . . . 'Heru mande, heru mande, heru mande, Tigi li papa.' "[133] For Tinker, this ritual, replete with the "monotonous maddening beat of the ancestral tam-tam" and the "rhythmic reflection of the thudding big drum" is unacceptable and somehow even incomprehensible in a New Orleans setting.[134] The young Toucoutou recoils in horror: "Certainly that wild figure [Toucoutou] had seen could not be the same person who fed and dressed her every day and whom she adored." Overcome with grief and bewilderment, Toucoutou "crept miserably" back to her bed which seemed "a little white island on which she had been set adrift—alone—in a limitless black universe."[135] Tinker turns the memory of Saint-Domingue/Haiti—the sole black republic in the hemisphere—on its head. He imagines the population of New Orleans as Toucoutou on her white island of a bed, threatened on all sides by the possibility of racial impurity.

For Tinker and his reader, the stakes are clear. By the 1920s, the figures of the mother and daughter voodoo queens both named Marie Laveau had a wide currency in the folk life of New Orleans as a symbol of the incongruous power supposedly wielded by mixed-race women in the nineteenth century.[136] New Orleanians had long expressed an anxiety over voodoo ceremonies as sites of potential interracial sexuality.

One late-nineteenth century memoirist recalled an antebellum raid on one such ceremony: "Blacks and whites were circling round promiscuously, writing in muscular contractions, panting, raving and frothing at the mouth. But the most degrading and infamous feature of this scene was the presence of a very large number of ladies (?) [sic], moving in the highest walks of society . . . that were caught in the drag net."[137] Would a Haitian cultural legacy symbolized by Toucoutou's grandmother, Comba Nea, voodoo priestess and the fomenter of a slave rebellion, continue to live in her granddaughter and be allowed to infiltrate white New Orleans through Toucoutou's legitimate marriage to one of its "leading citizens"? Tinker hoped to assure his readers that it would not.

For Beaumont, to be a person of color was to exist in dynamic and creative tension with "polite" white society. For Desdunes, being a Creole of color was to take pride in one's culture and training, a potential gift to the larger black political community. However, for Tinker "blackness" was a dangerously chaotic prospect for Toucoutou and those who lived on the color line. Thus, when readers finally join Anastasie in the courtroom in the latter part of the novel, they recall the spectacle of the voodoo ritual and the dance at Congo Square and sympathize fully with Anastasie's plight. In this liminal space of insecure racial identity, Anastasie teeters on the brink of both social and existential ruin.

(Open) Endings

In Tinker's rendition of the story, Toucoutou, her family, and New Orleans' white society all get something of a fairy-tale ending. Facing the impending dissolution of their marriage, Toucoutou and Placide Taquin, her husband, escape an encroaching social judgment. When a charivari arrives at their doorstep to ridicule the Taquin family and to extort a donation to Charity Hospital, the young family has already fled a safe distance from white New Orleans, to Cuba, where they would ostensibly live as they pleased. In reality, the trial conveyed a more ambiguous legacy for the Desarzant/Abat family and for racial identity of New Orleanians more generally. Evidence of an actual marriage does not follow the record of Desarzant's and Abat's 1857 application for a marriage license. In fact, their license application contains the additional notation "null and void." However, when the census taker came to their door in August 1860, they were, with a few alterations in their relationship's presentation, still living together as man and wife. Although Anastasie and her children were duly recorded as "mulatto," she now unabashedly gave her name as Anastasie Abat. Moreover, her former nemeses, foregoing their righteous defense of marriage, also lived together under a common name as Pierre and Eglantine LeBlanc.[138] Apparently, Desarzant went to Santiago de Cuba for periods of time, perhaps to visit friends or relatives or perhaps to get away from the version of her case popularized by Beaumont, by then ringing through the streets. In June 1871, while on one of these Cuban excursions, Desarzant fell ill and died at the age of forty-seven. Papers from Desarzant's succession state emphatically that "the said Anastasie Desarzant never was married." However, she trusted Abat to accept responsibility for their minor son, Maurice Eugène Abat.[139] After Desarzant's death, in accordance with an 1868 law passed by the Reconstruction legislature permitting fathers to legitimate their "natural" children, the elder Abat drew up the necessary papers, recognizing Maurice as his legitimate child in 1872. Confirming Tinker's readers' worst fears about the possible infiltration of the white race by people of color, Maurice E. Abat had by 1930 moved to Fairfield, Connecticut, where he ostensibly lived as a white man.[140]

Between the end of Desarzant's trial in 1859 and Abat's conferring of legitimacy upon his son Maurice in 1872, much had happened in New Orleans. After Abraham Lincoln won the 1860 presidential election, the state of Louisiana—albeit with considerable opposition from New Orleans' Unionists—joined other southern states in seceding from the United States and helped provoke Civil War. A humbling Union occupation that began in May 1862 and continued until the war's end gave way to a Reconstruction politics in the city that, often violent, proved to be a font of radicalism. Republican activists, with *gens de couleur* in the vanguard, campaigned tirelessly for universal male suffrage, fair labor regimes, and what the 1868 Louisiana Constitution described as "social, civil and public rights."[141] Republicans moved to desegregate schools and public conveyances. Moreover, activists of color helped to legalize interracial marriage and legitimate the existing children of interracial unions, thus making official and public the formerly private and quasi-legal ties that bound them to their white relatives across racial lines. Most dramatically, of course, enslaved people once held as private property congregated in New Orleans and elsewhere demanding their rights as citizens. Not only did Reconstruction politics publicize what was formerly private; it also provoked uneasy relationships among individuals and groups, creating stranger bedfellows and more dramatic social reversals than New Orleanians could have imagined before the war.

The plight of Pierre Soulé, the lawyer for LeBlanc and Desmaziliere's collective defense against Desarzant's charges, captures the social implications of these developments. In the wake of Union occupation, Soulé, the outspoken pro-southern expansionist, had exiled himself—as had many of his compatriots—to Mexico City, where he earned "a precarious livelihood by the practice of law in a foreign language." When the northern correspondent Whitelaw Reid happened upon Soulé's New Orleans residence, the "Catholic negroes—mostly of the old Louisiana free negro stock" had taken charge of it. Holding a fair to benefit schools for the formerly enslaved, the Creoles of color enacted "one of the curious revenges of these avenging times." Tongue in cheek, Reid painted what he felt to be an absurd picture: "negroes raffling fans and picture frames and sets of jewelry in the Soulé parlors; negroes selling ice-cream in the Soulé dining room; negroes at his piano; negroes in his library; negroes swarming amid his shrubbery; and yet as handsome, as elegantly dressed, and in many respects almost as brilliant a party as he himself ever gathered beneath his hospitable roof."[142] In this scene and in New Orleans more generally, cultural insiders faced an overwhelming wave of gawking outsiders eager to secure their own power and authority in the city, state, and nation. In conjunction with the establishment of federal authority over the city, native *gens de couleur* attempted, despite their previous status as slave owners and potential slave owners, to forge common bonds with freed people, both groups assuming public roles previously denied them.

Illustrations

Bird's-eye view of New Orleans. Lithograph by J. Bachman [Bachmann], circa 1851. Courtesy of Library of Congress.

Family scene, yellow fever in New Orleans, 1853. The Historic New Orleans Collection.

Marianne Celeste Dragon, grandmother of George Pandelly. Attributed to the School of Salazar, circa 1796. Oil on canvas. Collection of the Louisiana State Museum.

Birth home of Anastasie Desarzant in 2002, Greatmen (Royal) Street between Frenchmen and Elysian Fields, Faubourg Marigny. Photograph courtesy of the author.

Congo Square scene. From George Washington Cable, “The Dance in Congo Square,” *Century Magazine*, February 1886, 525.

Self portrait, Julien Hudson, 1839. This elegantly styled free man of color exemplifies the ethos of "dandyism" made possible by tailors such as François Lacroix. Oil on canvas. Collection of the Louisiana State Museum.

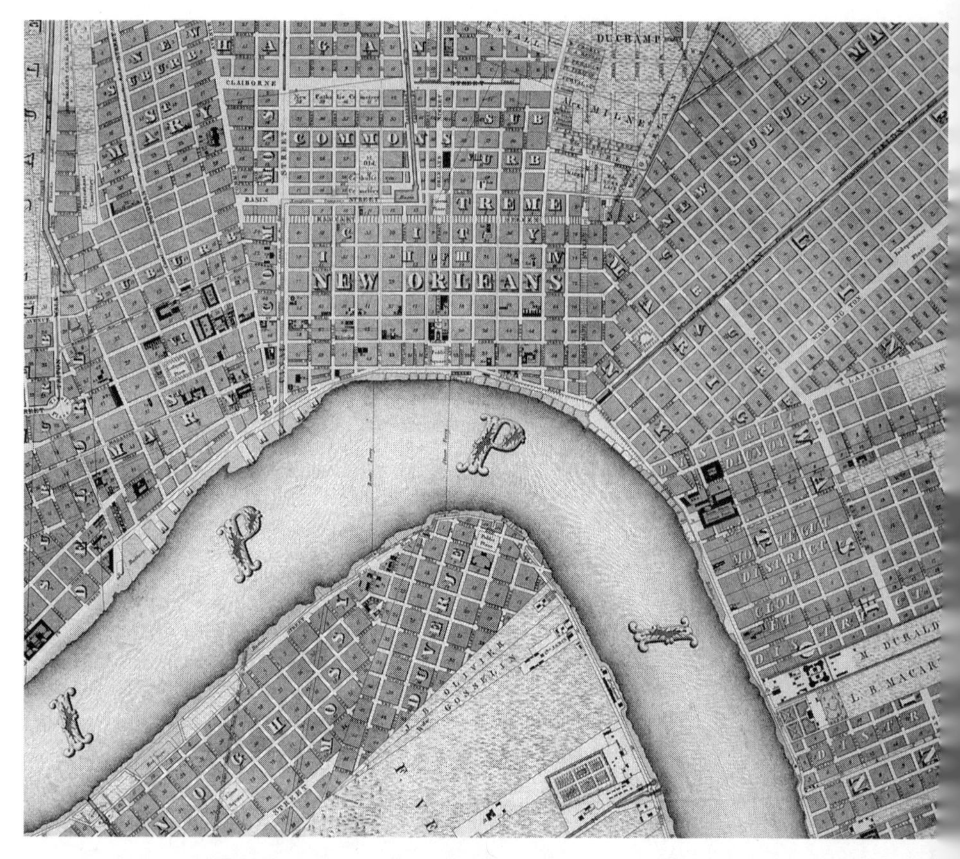

Detail from topographical map of New Orleans and its vicinity, Charles F. Zimpel, 1834. The detail shows the French Quarter, parts of Tremé directly above it, and Marigny to the right. New Marigny extends upward from Marigny. The land to the extreme right would become the Bywater neighborhood. Note the juxtaposition of the dense city grid and the relatively open space demarcating family-owned plantation land. The Historic New Orleans Collection.

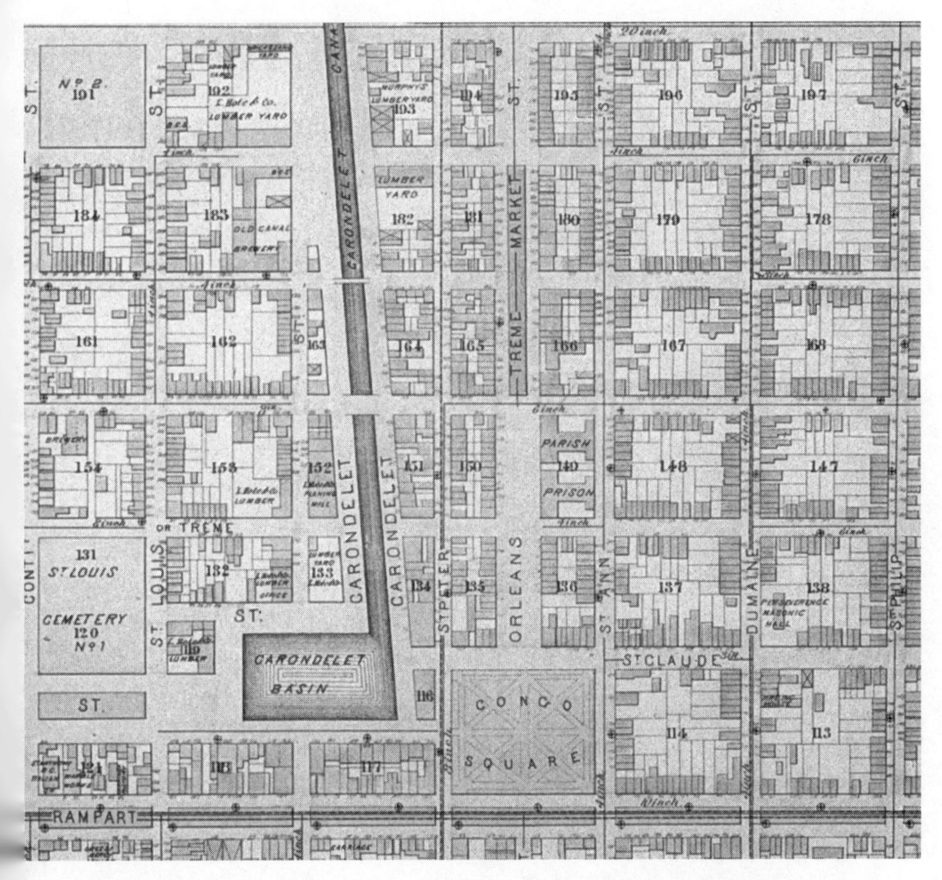

Map of Tremé, from Esplanade to Canal and Burgundy to Roman, Robinson Atlas, 1883, plate 7, showing Congo Square, St. Louis Cemeteries Nos. 1 and 2, Tremé Market, Bayou Road, Claiborne Street, Canal Carondelet, and Carondelet Walk. François Lacroix and other free people of color invested heavily in this area. The Historic New Orleans Collection.

La Cathedrale/the Cathedral, New Orleans, 1842. Lithograph of St. Louis Cathedral by free man of color Jules Lion. The Historic New Orleans Collection.

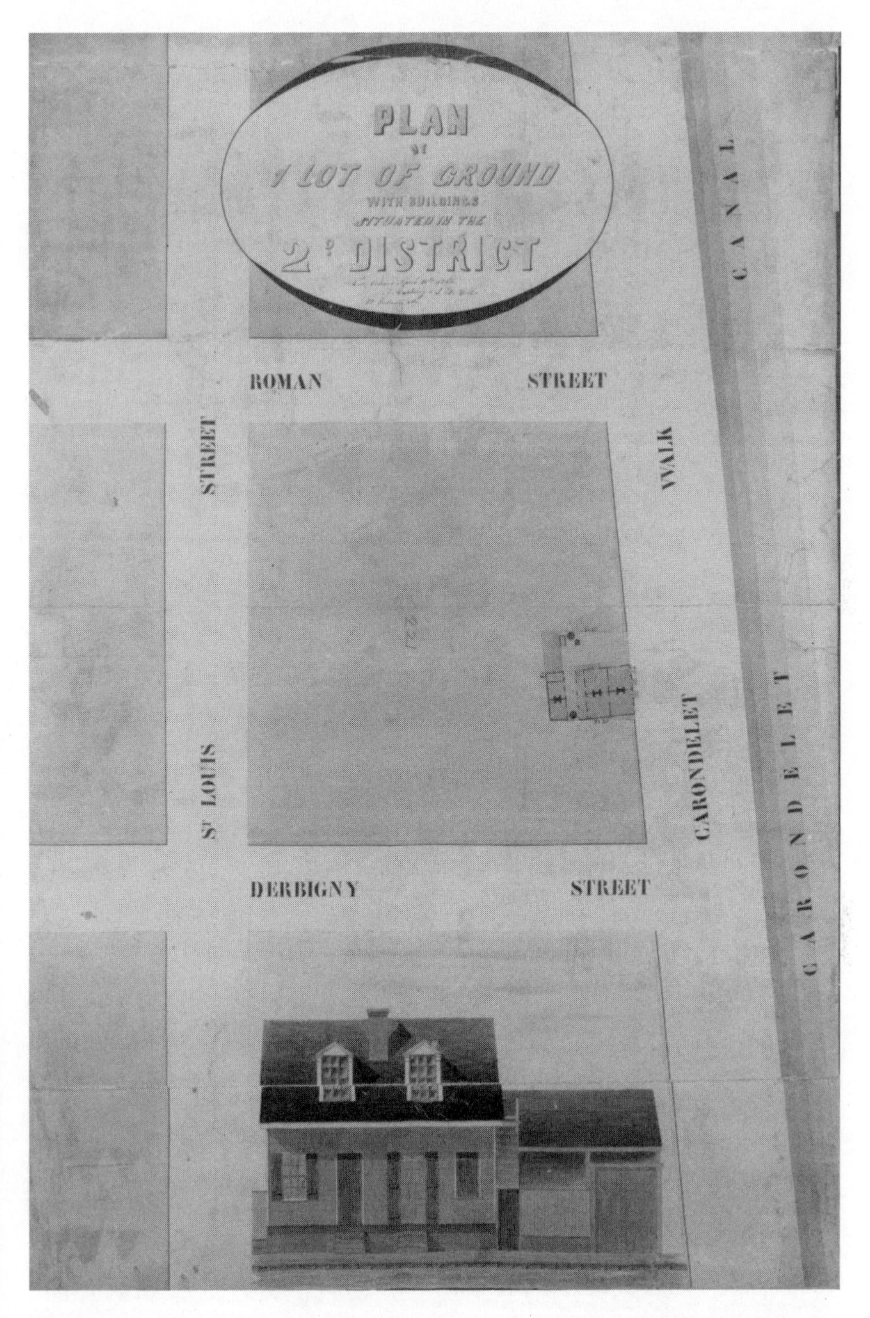

Elevation and floor plan of a typical Creole cottage on Carondelet Walk. Note the lack of a center hallway. Courtesy of the New Orleans Notarial Archives Research Center.

Rodolphe Desdunes, from *Nos Hommes et Notre Histoire* (Montreal, 1911), frontispiece. Courtesy of Harry Ransom Humanities Research Center, University of Texas at Austin.

Henriette Delille, circa 1850. Courtesy of the Sisters of the Holy Family of New Orleans Archives.

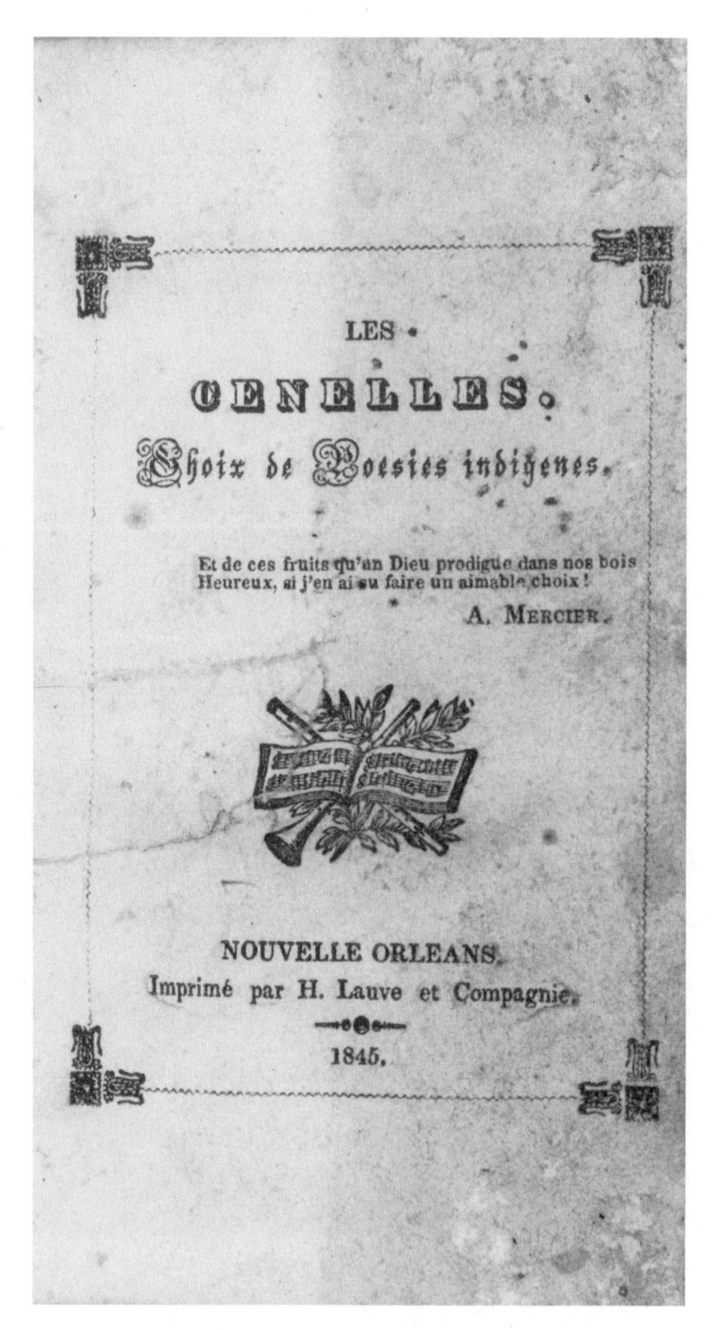

LES

CENELLES.

Choix de Poesies indigenes.

Et de ces fruits qu'un Dieu prodigue dans nos bois
Heureux, si j'en ai su faire un aimable choix!

A. MERCIER.

NOUVELLE ORLEANS.
Imprimé par H. Lauve et Compagnie.

1845.

Title page of *Les Cenelles* (New Orleans, 1845). Courtesy of Harry Ransom Humanities Research Center, University of Texas at Austin.

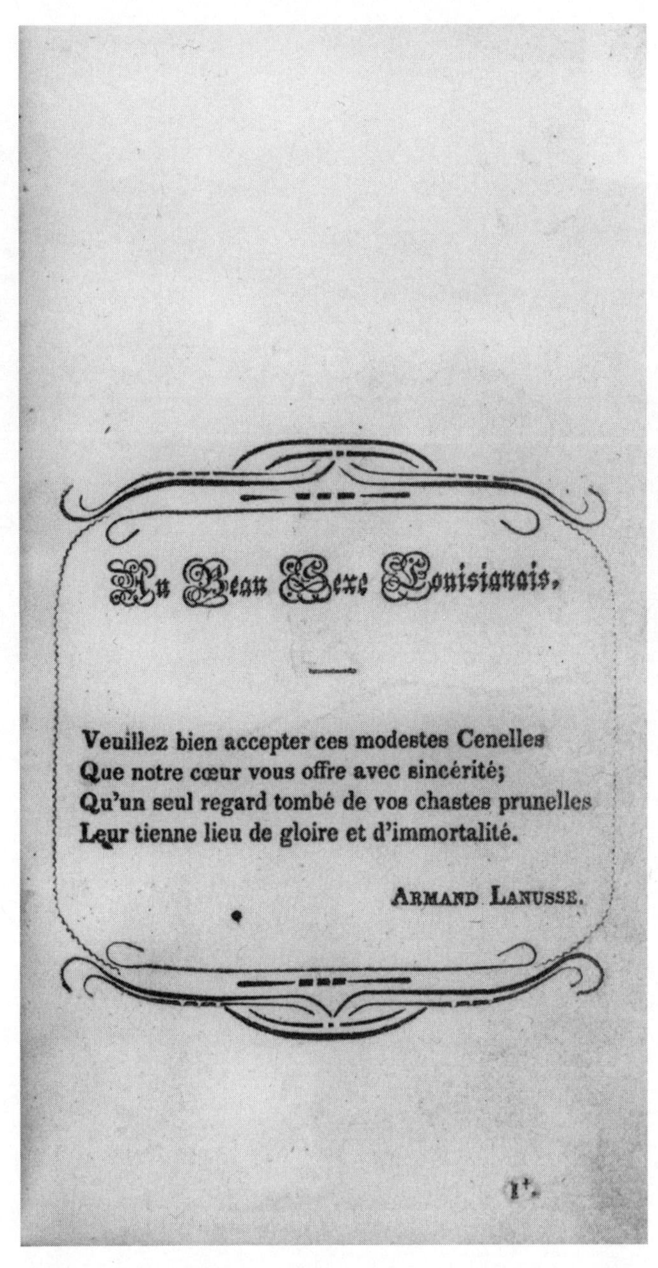
Au Beau Sexe Louisianais.

Veuillez bien accepter ces modestes Cenelles
Que notre cœur vous offre avec sincérité;
Qu'un seul regard tombé de vos chastes prunelles
Leur tienne lieu de gloire et d'immortalité.

Armand Lanusse.

1*.

Dedication page of *Les Cenelles* (New Orleans, 1845). Courtesy of Harry Ransom Humanities Research Center, University of Texas at Austin.

Funeral procession of Captain André Cailloux. *Harper's Weekly*, August 29, 1863.

Dr. Louis Charles Roudanez, proprietor of the *New Orleans Tribune*. From Rodolphe Desdunes, *Nos Hommes et Notre Histoire* (Montreal, 1911). Courtesy of Harry Ransom Humanities Research Center, University of Texas at Austin.

Jean-Charles Houzeau, coeditor of the *New Orleans Tribune*. From *Ciel et Terre*, IX (1887–1888).

The New Orleans riot, 1866. *Harper's Weekly*, August 25, 1866.

The New Orleans riot, 1866. *Harper's Weekly*, August 25, 1866.

3

Claiming Birthright in the Creole City

IT IS POSSIBLE FOR US to imagine the world of François Lacroix, a Creole of color and one of the most successful real estate moguls of his time. On a typical morning in antebellum New Orleans, Lacroix would awaken in his bedroom, which was tastefully furnished with mahogany pieces perhaps expertly carved by one of the many Creole of color cabinetmakers in town. The armoire offered Lacroix a full view of his wardrobe: shirts, trousers, and overcoats of the finest Parisian fabrics. A high-end tailor by profession, Lacroix "presided over the bazaar of New Orleans fashion," outfitting some of the most prominent men in the city. He and his tailoring partner, Etienne Cordeviolle—remembered later as a "very flashy elegant looking fellow"—literally created the identity of the well-dressed Creole gentleman. An 1853 advertisement for Lacroix's tailoring business boasted "the best and most extensive assortment of clothing of every description, made in Paris." An 1874 newspaper reminisced about Lacroix's artistry: his coats "passed muster before the severest tribunals of Europe"; his trousers "made the dandies of Rotten Row or the Champs-Elysées groan with envy."[1]

His translation of Parisian style to the semitropical climate of New Orleans acculturated francophone identity to this context of Americanization, keeping it alive at least on the level of personal style. In New Orleans, as in other urban and urbanizing settings, the correct clothes could mean the difference between social success and public ostracism. Remarking on the appearance of the "Creole gentleman,"—a "very fair specimen of the *juste milieu*"—one 1842 visitor to the city offered an extended excursus on the "science of clothing" and the virtues of a good tailor. "There is a very silly saying, that it takes nine tailors to make a man, whereas the truth is, that one first-rate tailor not only makes *many* men, but what is more essential, many fashionable men! Were it not for creators of this class, what a set of nincompoops would the present race of dandies be! Strip them of their clothes and they are mere nothings . . ."[2] Lacroix and other important Creole of color tailors participated in a transnational expression of what it meant to be French and urban. Their artistry coincided with and facilitated the emergence of what Parisian poet Charles Baudelaire would articulate in 1863 as an ethic of "dandyism." Committed to founding a "new species of aristocracy" that might stem "the rising tide of democracy, which invades and levels everything," the haughty, blasé men engaged in the "vague institution" of dandyism would have "no other profession save elegance" and "no other occupation than that of cultivating the idea of beauty in their person."[3] Dandyism would not have been practicable without the artistry of tailors such as Lacroix. Chronicled by Martin Delany as a prime exemplar of the "practical utility of the colored race," he and Cordeviolle earned reputations as international trendsetters: "The reported fashions of Cordovell [sic], are said to have frequently become the leading fashions of Paris; and . . . many of the eastern American reports were nothing more than a copy, in some cases modified, of those of Cordovell."[4]

Lacroix put his unique imprint on New Orleans by setting the styles and also by buying and selling property. Speculating on the growing economy of New Orleans and its environs, Lacroix and Cordeviolle bought, sold, and collected large sums in rents on large parcels of property throughout the 1830s and 1840s. After they dissolved their partnership in 1848, Lacroix often conducted business with his brother Julien, a grocer by profession and himself the owner of a large cache of real estate. In the middle decades of the nineteenth century, it would have seemed virtually impossible to trace a route through New Orleans without traversing at least one Lacroix property.

If he had a tailoring job to complete, Lacroix might, upon leaving his house, make his way from Rue D'Amour (Love Street) in Marigny to his establishment on Chartres Street near Bienville Street in the heart of the French Quarter. Later in the antebellum period, he would have to cross Canal Street to reach his shop on the corner of St. Charles and Common Streets. Otherwise, he might begin making the rounds of his various properties. In spite of his "perfect army of lawyers and agents," he preferred, according to one witness at his probate hearing, to collect his own rents.[5] One can imagine Lacroix on one of these expeditions, his finery distinguishing him from most passers-by and his meticulous appearance and "staid demeanor" contrasting with his surroundings. New Orleans continually fell short of emerging expectations about urban hygiene. Sidewalks, streets, and gutters collected all manner of filth. Sluices along the Mississippi allowed river water to stream periodically into the city to help manage the river's flow and to refresh the city streets; in particularly low-lying areas, much of this water lay stagnant and putrid where it mingled with the droppings of horses and mules and the contents of chamber pots. Throughout the late 1840s and early 1850s, the city mounted a campaign to poison the stray dogs plaguing the city but failed to provide adequately for the removal of their carcasses, which were often left to decompose where they fell.[6] One shudders to think of the condition of the cuffs on Lacroix's silk pants or that of his fine leather slippers.

In his amblings, Lacroix very literally marked his territory, staking claim to his various properties in person, reminding those who were mere inhabitants of his houses—structures ranging from elaborate townhouses to Creole cottages to condemnable shanties—of his ownership status.[7] So palpable was Lacroix's entitlement that when he paused for refreshment at a neighborhood café, one might detect undercurrents of deference and resentment flowing through the establishment. Whether he passed his time reading the latest installment of *L'Abeille* or *Le Propagateur Catholique*, two of the newspapers to which he subscribed, or chatting with white and *gens de couleur* business acquaintances, Lacroix presented himself as an architect of his social world rather than as simply an actor within it. In the café and other public social spaces, Lacroix the mere owner of property became Lacroix the proprietor, an exemplar of the social status attributed to ownership and the cultural values conveyed by it.

Lacroix was one of a small but prominent group of highly visible and active Creole of color real estate magnates in New Orleans. Joining him were another pair of high-end tailors, the partners Joseph Dumas and Julien Colvis; poet Camille Thierry; dry-goods businesswoman Eulalie Mandeville; and a host of others who took advantage of the availability of property in the expanding faubourgs. To own and deal in property in New Orleans in the middle decades of the nineteenth century was risky business for anyone, and particularly for people of African descent. Throughout the late antebellum period, their free status was increasingly challenged and their liberties circumscribed, leaving them susceptible to laws and statutes that could possibly render them slave property.[8] While some took the route of the Lacroix brothers and stuck it out in New Orleans, others such as Joseph Dumas and Camille Thierry chose exile in France.

After the Civil War, Creole of color businesspeople occupied a social, political, and economic space fraught with inconsistency. As native proprietors, they shared the concerns of dispossessed white residents of New Orleans. As people of African descent, they sought rights within the framework and jurisdiction of a Reconstruction government composed largely of "outsiders." Competing interests and threats to their status produced a tangle of loyalties for Creoles of color, with potentially disastrous consequences for their property holdings. For example, in 1876, after the rupture of the Civil War, "old Lacroix" died, leaving a tremendously embattled and devalued estate of 134 individual lots and 92 whole squares of land, most with buildings and other improvements. Upon the death of his wife Cecile in 1856, Lacroix's properties had been worth over $250,000 (close to $6 million in early-twenty-first century currency). By 1876, amidst a sharp economic downturn in the city and after the 1874 seizure of much of his estate for unpaid taxes, that sum had shrunk to just under $67,000 (a paltry $1.2 million today).[9] The contest over this more modest sum revealed the high stakes involved in determining the relationships among racial status, national imperatives, and civic belonging.

Often, discussions of Creole of color property ownership in New Orleans take as a starting point the remarkable wealth of Creole of color women and the less than legitimate status of Creoles of color in the codes of kinship that prohibited extensive inheritance across color lines from white fathers to children of color.[10] Certainly the increasing *inability* to inherit and thus accumulate real wealth describes the fundamental predicament for these people situated in between racial and status categories. The illegitimacy of interracial liaisons held drastic implications for the economic, the social, and particularly the moral legacies of Creoles of color. The Lacroix case demonstrates the difficulty New Orleans' *gens de couleur* had in defending *legitimate* accumulations of property and status, asserting authority, and securing posterity in a world that seemed to be closing in around them.

Resonating in overlapping temporal frames, questions of posterity force historical actors to reflect on the past and to express anxiety over the future from the vantage point of a particular moment of present crisis. In the case of probate proceedings such as that of Lacroix, the most immediate crisis is death, and the struggle over inheritance resonates as a conversation between the dead and the living over the meaning of accumulated property and experience. Family histories and legacies become public in probate court, and legal proceedings reformulate these legacies, particularly in cases such as that of Lacroix in which the line of descent and status of heirs was called into question. Two concepts coexist and compete in this process: contract and birthright.[11] Probate courts redraw contracts regarding land and other forms of property, and these documents redirect title and signify new ownership at the point of the previous owner's death. Contracts of this sort erase and supersede past arrangements and attempt to proceed anew from a space of "cleared ground."

In practice, this space is more like a palimpsest than a tabula rasa. Understanding inheritance as a birthright in addition to a mere contact disrupts a smooth legal transaction from one claimant to another and from present to future by introducing the problem of history and of overlapping and contradictory claims. Heirs, especially those who struggle with one another over legitimacy, must demonstrate their birthright with convincing stories and commit themselves to the maintenance and consequences of these stories.[12] Enlisting legal and literary methods framed in technical and moral terms, entitlements constitute legal fictions that often belie usurpation or theft when seen from the perspective of competitors. "Contract" recasts the theft in rational terms of consent and reciprocity, and "birthright" creates an aura around that contract, promising the ultimate bearers that the property in question always has been rightfully theirs. To claim birthright is to offer an interpretation of the past that culminates in one's own right to ownership and, thus, authenticates one's custodial status. Birthright admonishes its bearer to reconcile symbolic meaning and actual title and to transform the anxiety and regret the dying feel regarding future generations into a suitably continuous narrative of entitlement and belonging.

The legal and contractual struggles constituting the probate records of the Lacroix family and others dramatize this process, especially when considered alongside the literary and cultural debates about who the legitimate heirs to New Orleans might be. The suspended identities of those under the microscope of probate proceedings find release in literature and other forms of expression that take apparitions seriously. The lines of inheritance articulated and denied by legacies of property give physical and material weight to the routes traced by fictional characters and the authors who created them. A consideration of the various perspectives of differently located New Orleanians—white Creoles and "Americans"; white Creoles and Creoles of color; Creoles of color who stayed and Creoles of color who chose exile—situates the issue of Creole of color belonging in the context of numerous competitions for ownership status in the city. These legal and literary contestations highlight the asymmetries of power governing the shifting cultural and political landscape. Demonstrating the paradoxical nature of entitlement, they mark mid-nineteenth-century New Orleans as a complicated "point of entanglement" where overlapping national, diasporic, and intensely local understandings of belonging alternately challenged, displaced, and reinforced one another.[13]

A foray into this rich nineteenth-century legal and narrative space raises a number of questions: Who were the rightful proprietors of New Orleans? How did this proprietorship resonate in regional, national, and transnational contexts? How did these proprietors achieve their dubious position of ownership? What constituted a birthright to New Orleans, and what was its value? Ultimately, within the mid-nineteenth-century context of social upheaval and reversal, how might a potential heir have distinguished between a birthright and a "mess of pottage"?[14]

Race and a Logical Harmonics of Place

Traditionally, birthright has included most prominently the claim to territory and has bestowed upon its bearer the responsibility of defining and refining that territory and defending it against encroachment. Demonstrating historical grounds for ownership and developing a cultural aesthetic of place are strategies that reinforce title and, when skillfully interwoven, ascribe meaning to particular places.[15] This process proceeds on a legal basis in probate court and other official settings. On a more general level, historians, artists, writers, and ordinary people claim and contest birthright in various media. The cityscape of New Orleans has functioned in various genres as a storyboard, its physical aspects enhancing fictional and symbolic narratives by providing the context in which New Orleanians performed the various components of their identities.[16] Responding to the imperatives set forth by Americanization, the shift from French and Spanish colonial practices to Anglo-American racial and status categories, New Orleanians who sought whiteness constructed palatable stories about their racial purity, stories that nonetheless underscored their cultural uniqueness.

Alongside these narratives, Creole of color poets and writers detailed their own spatial practices in New Orleans. In 1845 they published *Les Cenelles*, often cited as the first African American poetry anthology. Although many critics have chided the *Cenelles* poets for failing to launch a direct attack on racism and slavery, this elegant and delicate volume expressed a concern for the limited mobility of their caste and charted a variety of alternative paths.[17] Led by the teacher Armand Lanusse, these free people of color inscribed an alternate sense of belonging on their poems and mapped out their shifting social worlds. The name of the anthology, *Les Cenelles*, derives from an abundant berry found in and around New Orleans; Creole of color suitors traditionally presented the preserves of the fruit to their prospective sweethearts.[18] By offering their poems under the name of this native berry, the poets emphasized two of the major themes of their work: amorous love and a contested sense of belonging. In so doing, they established the ground upon which social relationships moved and within which cultural values took root.

Translating the narrative and physical remnants of their experience into a form that would meet present political and cultural needs, nineteenth-century critics—white and of color—labored over decades to construct for New Orleans a mythology of place that could sustain favorable historical narratives and buttress individual and social identities.

Narrative accounts of belonging often hinged upon the presence of free people of color as in-between people. Thus, the formulations of Creoles of color responded to, even as they were shaped by, the status of their group in the contemporary imagination as symbols of racial impurity and compromised birthright. *Les Cenelles* was but a small voice in a loud debate that would get more strident over the course of the nineteenth century, culminating in the furious clash between the senator, historian, and judge Charles Gayarré (1805–1895) and his nemesis, the popular writer George Washington Cable (1844–1925).

A resident of Faubourg Marigny and one-time neighbor of François Lacroix, Gayarré had fashioned himself as chief architect of New Orleans' cultural and geographical mythology. Grandson of Etienne Boré, one of the most prominent sugar planters in the state, Gayarré embodied the white Creole identity: "in [his] veins there ran the mingled stream of French and Spanish blood" and, it went without saying, no hint of the African.[19] He was ubiquitous on the lecture circuit in New Orleans, and his historical corpus expanded from the humble *Essai Historique sur la Louisiane* in 1830 to a four-volume history and meditation on the French, Spanish, and American legacies in Louisiana completed in 1866 and reissued in both French and English several times over the next few decades.[20] After the Civil War, he composed a history of the reign of Philip II of Spain (1866), the historical romances *Fernando de Lemos* (1872) and *Aubert-Dubayet* (1882), and several articles in local and national magazines. In her literary eulogy to Gayarré, his protégé Grace King, herself a prominent writer, genealogist, and protector of New Orleans' cultural identity, proclaimed, "He held [Louisiana's] archives not only in his memory, but in his heart, and while he lived, none dared make public ought about her history except with his vigilant form in the line of vision."[21]

Writing in a romantic nationalist tradition, Gayarré attempted to express what Charles Baudelaire called "the divine palimpsest," a rendering of his territory that generated a harmony in which "all the echoes of memory . . . form a concert—pleasant or painful, but logical and without dissonance."[22] In creating and maintaining this logical harmonics of place, Gayarré addressed the burning political question of whether French-speaking Creoles and English-speaking Americans could be co-proprietors in New Orleans.[23] This rivalry was not merely symbolic. The Louisiana Purchase and subsequent transfer of authority to the United States had set in motion various rivalries and contests over land ownership and land use. Because titles that carried weight under the Spanish or the French might not be honored by the Americans, Creole families and individuals fought with each other and with the Americans over the terms of their proprietorship. Waged in court and other legal arenas, the battles provoked by this initial confusion over status and belonging echoed well into the nineteenth century.[24]

Gayarré's first "poetical" rendering of the history of Louisiana, the 1848 speech "Poetry and Romance of Louisiana" given at the People's Lyceum in 1848, can be read as a response to the municipal schism of 1836–52, a particularly dramatic incarnation of the cultural and political power struggle between "native" Creoles and "invading" Americans.[25] Gayarré imagines an end to cultural divisions between Creoles and Americans, dramatized most significantly by the municipal schism. Securing Creole rights to the territory required taming racial ambiguities in Creole identity that stemmed from French and Spanish colonial legacies of racial mixture. Augmenting a general distinction between Creoles and Americans in order to reconcile it, Gayarré gave Creoles a unique identity that was also squarely American. In the process, he sought to demonstrate to readers that all Creoles were white and that all whites were superior to blacks. In other words, his geography of cultural proprietorship easily morphed into a geography of whiteness.

Making identity manifest in the land itself, Gayarré enshrined his native Louisiana "both physically and historically," that is, in terms of its landscape as well as the actions of its great men.[26] In characteristically overwrought language, Gayarré placed his hypothetical ideal proprietor, "his whole soul glowing with poetical emotions . . . under yonder gigantic oak, the growth of a thousand years." From the vantage point of a "hill of shells," the reader and observer overlook a "placid lake where all would be repose if it were not for that solitary canoe, a moving speck hardly visible in the distance . . . on that very line where the lake meets the horizon, blazing up with the last glories of the departing sun."[27] Under the influence of Gayarré's pen, the landscape becomes suitably poetic for his poetic white Creoles. His depiction of the transformation of Indian land into the colony of Louisiana performs many of the functions of landscape painting, a technique increasingly popular in the middle of the nineteenth century.[28] As Gayarré was writing his histories in the mid-1850s, Richard Clague, the "father of

Louisiana landscape painting," was finishing his schooling in France. He returned to Louisiana in 1858 to chronicle Louisiana's unique low-lying landscape of bayous, moss-hung oaks, and cypress trees.[29] Erasing the bloodiness of conquest, his landscapes clear the land for new title. Likewise, Gayarré's scene establishes the author and his reader (as landscape painting establishes the painter and viewer) as owners of the territory. Souls aglow, Gayarré and his prototypical Creole are heirs to a place dominated for a thousand years by a gigantic and steady oak tree. All history—human and natural—culminates in the gaze of Gayarré and his model proprietor, seated as they are atop a hill of shells, a remnant of Native American proprietorship. Gayarré's (Indian) canoe is "hardly visible" as it makes its way over the horizon. It lingers there to be summoned by those, such as George Pandelly, who called on Indian ancestors to attest to the "purity" of their blood.

Thus Gayarré prepared Louisiana for its admittance into the wider U.S. national imaginary during the Jacksonian age, a democracy of white men predicated on recasting the horrors of conquest as the precondition for national regeneration.[30] Accordingly, his history achieves a reconciliation of (white) Creoles and (white) Americans by demonstrating their mutual respect, racial purity, and common contributions to Louisiana culture. His symbolic and strategic use of Andrew Jackson's legacy as a mechanism of reconciliation demonstrates the terms of this process. The capstone of his four-volume *History* is the 1815 triumph of Andrew Jackson, using local troops, over the British at the Battle of New Orleans. Although militarily insignificant because it occurred after the War of 1812 had technically ended, this battle was an important early test for Louisiana, which had achieved statehood only in 1812. The military success demonstrated a potential unity between French colonials and Americans, and Jackson, fondly remembered by Gayarré as a frequent visitor to his grandfather's plantation, provided a powerful symbol for how the new social order could be made palatable. Indeed, Gayarré's invocation of General Jackson as a bridge between Creoles and Americans mirrors the more explicit enshrinement of Jackson as part of New Orleans' public culture in 1854. In that year, the reunified city government—spurred by a Gayarré-led committee—renamed the Place d'Armes, the most prominent public space in the *vieux carré*, Jackson Square. For the center of it, the committee commissioned a statue of Jackson astride his horse, poised battle-ready on hind legs.[31]

Through the strategic deployment of symbols such as Andrew Jackson, Gayarré demonstrated the terms of the Creole-American détente. Future cooperation in business and marriage depended on their mutual expression of national belonging and racial brotherhood. To this end, Gayarré aggressively defended a native Creole and American proprietorship against waves of mid-century immigration and the specter of racial equality looming after the Civil War. Gayarré served as a chief spokesman for the nativist Know-Nothing party in Louisiana in the aftermath of the yellow fever epidemic of 1853 and the breakdown of the two-party system. In the closing decades of the nineteenth century, he emerged as a defender of white supremacy and a vehement proponent of racial segregation. In this respect, he helped police the lines between native white New Orleanians—both Creole and American—and offensive Yankee, black, and immigrant outsiders. In the post-bellum years, Gayarré framed his writings on race chiefly in response to fellow New Orleanian George Washington Cable, the son of Protestant American migrants to the city. After Reconstruction, Cable, a former Confederate soldier, became a champion of civil rights for blacks, thus troubling Gayarré's precious cultural calculus.[32]

In making the "freedman's case in equity" in the mid-1880s, Cable appealed to the honor of the southern gentleman, bidding the bronze statue of General Robert E. Lee, standing alone and without horse atop its pedestal in New Orleans' Tivoli Circle (now Lee Circle), to abandon its silence and speak the wisdom of "our whole South's better self."[33] Taking up his own challenge in a series of magazine articles and national lecture tours, Cable argued the merits of desegregated railroads and schools, affirming the rights of black Americans to full civil equality.[34] To make "crude, invidious, humiliating and tyrannous" distinctions on the basis of race, according to Cable, would be morally untenable, but it would also inhibit a "just assortment of persons . . . on merits of exterior decency."[35] Revealing "class-mixing" to be of paramount concern, Cable would far rather find himself seated next to a "quiet, well-behaved colored man or woman" such as Lacroix than a "profane, boisterous or unclean white person."[36] Whereas his political writings downplayed the prospect of racial amalgamation, Cable's fiction, most notably *The Grandissimes* (1880), emphasized the tangled bloodlines and hybrid idiom of Louisiana Creoles, suggesting that the line between black and white was arbitrary not merely because it masked more important class distinctions, but more importantly because it had been too often crossed. These traversals manifested themselves in the presence of mixed-race people, but also in the emergence of an amalgamated Creole language—"strange talk" spoken by rich and poor, white and black, slave and free.[37] Cable introduces these characterizations of a hybrid Creole identity from the perspective of Joseph Frowenfeld, a recent American immigrant of German descent. Witnessing the confusion of the 1803 cession of Louisiana to the United States, Frowenfeld remains above the fray, the picture of cool righteousness.

National in scope, the impact of Cable's formulations of the "Negro Question" and his solution to it drew the most substantial and visible criticism from Atlanta's Henry Grady, editor of the *Atlanta Constitution* and chief architect of the New South ideology.[38] In New Orleans, Gayarré's response was unrelenting and particularly venomous, coming in the form of articles in the New Orleans' newspapers and lectures throughout the city.[39] In his "The Creoles of History and the Creoles of Romance," a widely disseminated address first given at Tulane University in 1885, Gayarré answered the assessments of Frowenfeld—understood by Gayarré as the "moral and intellectual personification" of Cable himself—with a stunning defense of the history and racial identity of his people. He incongruously projected the practice of segregation into Louisiana's past. From 1724, the moment of its promulgation, the Black Code, "raised Alpine heights, nay it threw the Andes as a wall between the blacks or colored and the natives of France as well as the natives of Louisiana or creoles," mandating from the "very beginning to the late war of secession, the strongest line of demarcation—I may say an impassable one."[40] In the eyes of Gayarré, Louisiana—as colony, territory, and state—had been ruled by level-headed men with "views very different from those of a modern sentimentalist" such as Cable, who "wants to make the world believe that black is white and white is black."[41] Moreover, those at the upper echelons of (white) Creole society—even those Germans, Swedes, and Greeks who had come into the colony—spoke "no other language than French—real French—not a hybrid jargon."[42]

The success of Cable's dialect writing and his well-attended national speaking tours with Mark Twain would insure that his national renown would trump that of Gayarré. However, locally it was clear that

Gayarré's interpretation of New Orleans history would prevail into the twentieth century and shore up Jim Crow practices.[43] Gayarré's efforts awarded him a public immortalization similar to that of Jackson: a monument depicting the "Goddess of History" was dedicated to Gayarré in 1886 on Esplanade, the old Creole thoroughfare.[44] Cable's optimism about Creole (and southern) honor and his willingness to confront tangled bloodlines and modes of speech ultimately forced him, to Gayarré's delight, into exile in New England. "Now I wash my hands of him," announced Gayarré, "and making my last bow to that amiable gentleman, I turn him over to the tender mercies of the 'American savagery.' "[45] If Cable were foolish enough to think like a damned Yankee, he might as well be one as far as Gayarré was concerned.

Within this struggle over birthright in New Orleans, Creoles of color as an in-between people played an important role, best exemplified in Cable's *Grandissimes* and Gayarré's response. Set during the fraught 1803 transition from French to American rule, the novel depicts, among other contestations, the struggles of interracial half-brothers to come to terms with their coexistence and to resolve the right to belong in New Orleans. Cable demonstrates this internecine conflict in the naming of his two principal characters, Honoré Grandissime and Honoré Grandissime f.m.c. (free man of color), half-brothers of the same father, one "white" and the other "of color." Although his characters are not technically twins, in naming them Cable employs a twin-brother motif in order to examine the socially constructed nature of their differences in social position, opportunity, entitlement, and fate.[46] Honoré Grandissime the younger is Apollonian, blindingly handsome, unsullied by menial labor, and immune to the physical defects brought on in literature by moral failings. Even though he is a merchant, a profession that should raise suspicions in a market of sugar and slaves, his skin and his conscience are clear. His bloodlines seemed clear as well: "His whole appearance was a dazzling contradiction of the notion that a Creole is a person of mixed blood."[47] His dusky doppelganger, Honoré f.m.c., cuts an equally remarkable figure with "a strong clear olive complexion; features that were faultless . . . a tall well-knit form attired in cloth, linen and leather of the utmost fineness."[48] While the younger Honoré's beauty is that of innocence (he "was able at any time to make himself as young as need be"), Honoré f.m.c.'s beauty derives from his maturity and its attendant anxieties ("hair en queue, the handsomer for its premature streakings of gray").[49] Honoré f.m.c. becomes more feminine as the novel progresses. At the pinnacle of the action, when the white Honoré is most vibrant, the emasculated Honoré f.m.c. languishes stylishly on a divan, his weakening constitution typical of female heroines of Victorian literature.

For much of the novel, the reader is not certain to whom Cable refers and must infer the racial identity of the Honoré under question from situational and physical cues. For these two characters, who exist together in a kind of shadow relationship, Cable suggests that Gayarré's hope for a reconciliation between white Creoles and Americans did not go far enough, leaving as it did Creoles of color out of the equation. In spite of the earlier birth of Honoré f.m.c., the reader encounters him as the "impersonator" of his younger white brother, who is not required by law to carry initials after his name. Honoré f.m.c. is "almost the same, but not quite," trapped in a narrative where his actions can only be read as mimetic.[50] His social stigma dictates that he bear the burden of this "difference," even if at times he turns it to his advantage. The half-brothers Grandissime—one the swashbuckling public face of a proud but diminished colonial family, the other, darker brother a well-dressed but shadowy figure—hold the fate of the city in their relationship. The white Grandissime has status and authority but little money; the Grandissime f.m.c. holds as much real estate and other assets as François Lacroix but lacks a public social foothold. In their 1803 Louisiana Purchase setting, merging their identities more fully and legitimately would strengthen local culture against the onslaught of the United States and encroaching "Americans."

In this novel of sibling rivalry and fading French cultural and familial legacies, Cable's concerns mirrored the themes of the Biblical story of Jacob and Esau. Where there are two brothers, is there a fair way for a father to pass on a birthright? Could the heirs in question reestablish equilibrium under the inevitably unequal terms of inheritance? What personal, social, and cultural consequences might ensue from these negotiations? Would the Honorés Grandissime, in the spirit of Jacob and Esau, overcome initial strife and contention to pave the way for new levels of reconciliation? Cable seems to answer these questions by affirming the familial bond across racial lines, thus promoting peace in a troubled New Orleans. In his newly "redeemed" post-Reconstruction setting of 1880, Cable offers the Honorés Grandissime as an example to the South and ultimately to the nation of how to reckon with historical wrongs and achieve interracial cooperation. Just as he would five years later in *The Freedman's Case*, Cable affirmed class distinctions over those of race, much to the dismay of Gayarré.[51] When the Honorés forge a blueprint for the public remedy of the legacies of caste and slavery by creating "The Grandissime Brothers," a jointly owned business that publicly announces their kinship, the younger Honoré states the nature of his true relationship to Honoré f.m.c. more succinctly: "God knows . . . my very right to exist comes after yours. You are the elder." For Gayarré, this economic union and the filial recognition it rests on constitutes "the milk of the coconut" of Cable's betrayal of local culture, and he dismisses this "novel partnership, the partnership of bastardy and legitimacy, and the partnership of black and white" as sheer idiocy.[52]

Cable's depiction of a renewed birthright based on interracial harmony seemed to resonate with a sense of sober charity toward blacks within a national debate on the "Negro problem." However, a closer look at the fate of Cable's f.m.c. reveals Cable's deeper affinities with his nemesis Gayarré. Polarizing the debate within New Orleans' literary history around Cable and Gayarré obscures their common ground and the ways in which each reinforces racist practices and white supremacist ideologies. Again, the story of Jacob and Esau provides an interesting foil. The reconciliation reached between the Biblical twins Jacob and Esau was possible in part because Esau came into his own as a patriarch. Only after marrying, begetting a large progeny, and acquiring territory and an army is Esau able to extend his forgiveness to Jacob. In literature based in an Americanizing New Orleans, free people of color did not have the same recourse as Esau, even in Cable's vision. Cable's solution to the interracial family struggle was to have Honoré Grandissime f.m.c. wither from unrequited love and die a questionably suicidal death by drowning in the Mississippi River.[53]

Because his short stories and novels have often served tourists as guides through the city and because he made a vocal formulation of the "freedmen's case," George Washington Cable has carried the literary historical burden of challenging Gayarré's racist reformulation of the narrative of social space.[54] However, the fate of his most famous Creole of color characters aligns his vision with Gayarré's formulation of race and proprietorship.[55] Cable contrives abrupt demises or, as in the short story " 'Tite Poulette" (1879), a sudden revelation of "pure whiteness" for his problematic Creole of color characters, disrupting narrative pace and logic. Likewise, Gayarré's insistence on white supremacy and racial purity strikes an incongruous chord with his often public admiration of the industry of free people of color as well as his suspicion that "hybrids" would "continue, as they do daily, to creep into the Caucasian ranks, where their traces will soon be lost sight of, and forever obliterated."[56] It was quite possible for Gayarré in an 1877 essay on "The Southern Question" to maintain with Cable and others that "So far as I am personally concerned, I have no hesitation in saying, so intense is my love for intellect, honesty, and high-mindedness, that I would rather breakfast, dine, sup, and even sleep, with a noble-hearted, refined and classically educated hybrid than with a dishonest, ignorant, and brutish white man."[57] Even though Gayarré ultimately ascribes "our parents' sins, whites and blacks" to the "law," he acknowledges that "hybrids" are "entitled to address well merited reproaches to their Caucasian parents."[58] In his own fiction, Gayarré goes to the brink of signifying that some of his characters have African ancestry, only to give them a "Spanish" identity instead. For example, in *Fernando de Lemos* (1872), Gayarré's character Trévigne, the College d'Orleans "charity case" later revealed to be of Spanish nobility, has the requisite features of an "octoroon": dubious parentage, "slightly olivaceous" skin, and eyes "like two orbs of jet, half concealed under the long silky eyelashes."[59] That a prominent Reconstruction-era Creole of color, editor of *l'Union* and *la Tribune de Nouvelle Orleans*, was named Paul Trévigne further marks Gayarré's character as a man of color.

Given these unsightly but not uncommon incongruities in narrative logic and racial reasoning, perhaps we must look to Creoles of color themselves for more formidable resistance to the Gayarré-Cable paradigm. *Les Cenelles* and other writings by Creoles of color staged a meeting between their own formulations of belonging and the proprietary language of those who would come to be known as white Creoles, or simply Creoles. Both white Creoles and Creoles of color sought to animate and legitimate their growing marginality, transforming it from a position of declining influence to a marker of cultural authority in the city. The position of the *Cenelles* poet-narrator was similar to that of Gayarré: both sensed and feared a social slippage of their previously privileged group, but their respective poses reflected different racial and cultural realities. Exercising an authority newly grounded by his political affiliations and by his consolidating whiteness, Gayarré canonized the history of his group and fashioned it into the official heritage of the city. His Creoles were "*gentils hommes* . . . as their names show, being generally preceded, among the French, by the aristocratic prefix: *de.*" Duly "titled"—even if in most cases these titles were of their own creation—his Creole men became suitable mates for pure white women, whether "Creole" or "American."[60]

While Gayarré both preserved his Creole identity and actively acculturated it to a context of Americanization, the *Cenelles* poets lingered in cultural limbo, tracking their tentative movements around their native New Orleans and through the francophone diaspora and perhaps providing a more thorough guide to their racial and cultural landscape. Just as Gayarré attempted with his *History of Louisiana*, the Creole of color *Cenelles* poets prepared a space for themselves on the land, naming and populating local settings. These poets drew on a Creole of color tradition of claiming ownership, making narrative return to New Orleans spaces not because they wished merely to fulfill their nostalgic desires, but in the hope of bringing their experiences of marginality and diversion to bear on the question of belonging.[61]

Much like Gayarré, Creoles of color also understood the battle of 1815 and their service under Andrew Jackson as an example of their birthright to New Orleans, but they drew upon different memories of the importance of the Anglo-Creole alliance. Highlighting Jackson's proclamation that his free troops of color should be given equal rights, they participated in parades commemorating the war, reminding the wider population that they had not yet received their due.[62] Their performances might have accompanied readings of "The Campaign of 1814–1815," a popular poem by Hippolyte Castra not included in *Les Cenelles* but prominent enough among Creoles of color to survive in their families' "copybooks."[63] Military service was not the only path taken by Creoles of color to demonstrate entitlement to the land. In his contribution to *Les Cenelles*, "Le Retour au Village aux Perles (The Return to the Village of Pearls)," a poem originally written in 1828, Nelson Desbrosses creates a frivolous yet free landscape of amorous love. The title of the poem is a nickname for Bayou Road, given by Desbrosses because of the "large number of beautiful young women in the neighborhood." He naturalizes the love he feels for the female subject of the poem and the features of the land: "Oh flowering tree, testimony to our desire / I see you again and there is no denying it / Dear little stream, it is to you that my soul / Today wishes to entrust its fortune."[64] His account of his romantic relationship constructs for him a poetics of possession that is no less powerfully felt than Gayarré's proprietorship. This poetics further authorizes his presence as a "return" *(retour)* to a space he already knows and by extension a place where he may forge a right of trespass. Moreover, claiming access to Bayou Road places the poet on an in-between path, the old high ground connecting Bayou St. John and the city, a Native American trading route historically populated by *gens de couleur libre.*[65]

Making their claims on landscape, the *Cenelles* poets and their narrators often linger between life and death and outside the spatial and temporal constraints of legitimate activity. They describe a crumbling relationship to their social world and place their commentary in the mouth of ghostlike figures. The solitary phantoms of *Les Cenelles* trace hesitant lines that often intersect in cemeteries and other desolate landscapes. "Banished from the entire world, . . . / I am alone, always alone in this field of tombs, / Where the willow's weeping branches sway." Whereas Gayarré's symbolic proprietor sits under a "gigantic oak," aglow with the satisfaction of ownership, the dejected apparition of *Les Cenelles,* this "orphan among the tombs," "rests in the shadow of an ancient cypress," having searched in vain for the shelter a family tree would provide.[66]

The anguish of the poet is palpable even to a modern reader skeptical of Romantic poetic conventions. However, a trip to the New Orleans notarial archives reveals documentation of extensive Creole of color property ownership during the same period of the poet's lament. There we find François Lacroix and others—including a number of the *Cenelles* poets themselves—buying and selling property en masse. Lacroix and the poets constructed and maintained a sense of place that manipulated genre and moved swiftly among different levels of understanding. Just as the concept of inheritance juggled the tangible qualities of contract with the figurative aspects of birthright, a sense of place was simultaneously concrete and abstract, set in stone and up for interpretation. It revealed itself in various discourses and allowed legal claims, custom, and myth to compete for attention and recognition.[67]

The patterns of ownership and the stylish amblings of Creoles of color such as François Lacroix constituted genuine acts of artistic creation not fully captured by characterizations such as that of Cable's Honoré Grandissime f.m.c., who skulked down back alleys at dusk. Metaphorical and figurative though it is, the poetry of *Les Cenelles* attempts as well to lay claim to actual territory. How are we to reconcile the anxieties expressed by the poetry and the evidence of seemingly secure Creole of color proprietorship? The remainder of this chapter attempts this reconciliation and witnesses the ways in which sentimental expression and legal fact welcome and refuse alignment.

Fashioning a City

Purchasing, selling, and managing properties all over the city, Creole of color landowners built notions of community and shaped their immediate environments. Yet their activities diverged both from historians' expectations about opportunities available to free people of color and from the social restraints they encountered increasingly frequently throughout the middle of the nineteenth century. When discussing the shaping of New Orleans' neighborhoods, chroniclers of New Orleans' culture have cast a tragic eye over what seems to have been a diminishing Creole presence in the city. They invoke the name of Bernard Marigny as a prototype of the white Creole. This scion of Louisiana emerged victorious from the contests over official title during the late colonial and territorial period of the early nineteenth century, only to lose his holdings just downriver from the *vieux carré* through mismanagement and an apparent gambling addiction. During the first decade of the nineteenth century, Marigny appeared countless times in notarial offices, subdividing and selling off his plantation lot by lot, in many cases to *gens de couleur*, many of them Saint Dominguans in flight from their island homeland.[68] Emphasizing the role of Marigny on the land places the land under Gayarré's narrative sway, illuminating the poetic but fading glory of the original French and Spanish colonial families. However, the fact that *gens de couleur libre* frequently purchased and inherited properties in Marigny should caution us against premature lament over a "lost" Creole era. Locating Creole of color real estate moguls on the land situates these neighborhoods within the pragmatic ethos of a bustling metropolis and provides an occasion to witness how people of color made sense of the fact that slipping social status and restricted mobility often coincided with considerable wealth and economic flexibility. Most importantly, it exposes the "mental and physical labor" of establishing a legacy, the work required in transforming contract into birthright.[69]

For Creoles of color, fashioning the city constituted one of the key means of fighting for legacy within New Orleans. As architects of the city grid, François Lacroix and his brother Julien facilitated the development of important hubs of commercial activity and community interaction in the Creole faubourg of Marigny, as the former Marigny homestead would come to be called, and that of Tremé, a neighborhood carved out of the extensive plantation of Claude Tremé and other "habitations" and common areas just behind the *vieux carré* toward the lake.[70] Faubourg Tremé responded to the Mississippi River levee with the Carondelet Canal, the man-made bayou connecting the back of the city to Lake Pontchartrain, an alternative port accessed from the Gulf through Lake Borgne. Pumping money and resources directly into the francophone sectors of the city, the canal conveyed goods for local use in the cultural interior of New Orleans. Although the canal teetered on the brink of decay and technological backwardness, reflecting the waning position of Creole neighborhoods and the seemingly inevitable ascendancy of English speakers, the neighborhood constituted an important site of white Creole and Creole of color identity formation.[71] Locals had the upper hand in this neighborhood. According to the narrator of an 1854 novel, during the summer months the water of the canal was "so thickly covered with water plants that, if lake-killers [ships entering by way of Lake Pontchartrain] weren't located here and there, one could easily mistake it for a long, narrow greensward. Many a stranger has lost his life here by trying to cross this betraying meadow . . . No year passes without twenty to fifty corpses being fished out."[72] In "Adieu," his contribution to *Les Cenelles,* Camille Thierry mourned his impending journey to France along the banks of the canal. He emphasized the powdery path and the abundance of green crickets, allowing the intimacy of nature to offset the bustle of the marketplace and the hum of constant real estate development.

While this atmosphere of commerce and conversion may have assaulted the ear of the poet, the businessman Lacroix thrived in the vicinity of the canal. The industry it promoted spurred the development of land long held as part of the city commons. In 1839 the two-block-long Tremé Market opened a block away from Carondelet Canal, offering extensive shelter for vending meats, vegetables, and other goods and easily accessible by the streetcar, which passed through the middle of it.[73] Over the course of the late 1840s and early 1850s, Lacroix acquired a great deal of the property lining the banks of the canal as well as lots and structures in the immediate neighborhood that served residential and commercial purposes. Lacroix consolidated his properties in what would become the social and commercial center of Tremé and the neighborhood developing rapidly (due to the efforts of Lacroix and others) toward Lake Pontchartrain. A significant portion of Lacroix's holdings clustered near the intersection of the Carondelet Canal and North Claiborne Street, an important line of demarcation in the nineteenth century, the last major artery between the grid of the city and the swamp.[74]

Residentially speaking, nineteenth-century New Orleans snaked along the banks of the river, the back of town—remnants of old family plantations—being too swampy for urban habitation. However, the poor quality of the land extending back toward the lake from the *vieux carré* did not deter Creole of color landowners and others from gambling on the future market for it. Their speculation on surrounding swampland literally shaped New Orleans by identifying new potential for urban development and impacting the growth of the city well into the twentieth century. One by one, families with estates dating back to the earliest colonial periods surrendered to their own debt or to attractive offers by real estate speculators. Rural land previously considered undesirable to city-dwellers because of its swampy condition presented an increasingly attractive investment opportunity, particularly for free people of color. François Lacroix's real estate portfolio included vast stretches of former plantation property that had recently been incorporated into the city proper. For example, within the span of one week in 1837, Lacroix and his partner Etienne Cordeviolle acquired seventy-three new lots that had just been carved out of the Ancienne Habitation Blanc in the area between Tremé and the lake. The still-unimproved lots were valued at over $15,600 (over $400,000 today) when Lacroix sold them to his brother Julien in 1852. Lacroix also speculated heavily on quasi-rural land closer to Lake Pontchartrain that would not be developed until the 1940s, land downriver from Marigny in a section of town that would come to be known as the Bywater, and a neighborhood toward the lake from Marigny designated New Marigny—where the boundaries of Lacroix's acquisitions in 1873 were demarcated with reference to "projected streets." Both he and his brother Julien occasionally bought property across the river in McDonoghville and other farther-flung areas.[75]

Occupying geographically marginal space of questionable hygiene, much of Lacroix's real estate holdings teetered on the brink of social acceptability. The health department continued to cite one particular property in New Marigny on the corner of Music Street and St. Claude, a lot sunken "two feet below the banquette (sidewalk)" in which cesspools never failed to form.[76] Because these areas had been far removed from the *vieux carré*, they had long been considered receptacles for those whose existence troubled the city's sense of morality and healthiness. From 1743 until 1808 a series of charity hospitals occupied the swampy, virtually unusable lands of the city commons. People who failed to recover from their ailments did not have far to go: the city's first cemetery, Saint Louis 1, was established in the rear of the hospital, bounded by Rampart, Conti, St. Louis, and Tremé Streets.[77] In 1831 the city authorized the construction in the area of a new parish prison, a landmark of prison design featuring an interior courtyard, galleries, and accommodations segregated by race, gender, and type of crime. Prisoners with means paid for special accommodations in the Orleans room on the third floor.[78] Some of these borderline neighborhoods also gained notoriety as unofficial red light districts, and in the final decades of the nineteenth century the bordellos of Storyville occupied prime real estate on and around Basin Street in Tremé.[79]

Perhaps the most famous marginal site was Congo Square, a cleared patch of ground just across the ramparts from the *vieux carré* that functioned as both a market and a ritual performance space for New Orleanians of African descent. Because the surplus goods they traded there filled an important need in the early New Orleans economy, masters had long permitted and even encouraged this space of relative freedom for their slaves. An 1819 city ordinance reserved Sundays for "the assemblies of slaves for the purpose of dancing or other merriment," and Congo Square proved the most convenient setting. By 1822 a city directory reported the area to be "very noted on account of its being the place where Congo and other Negroes dance, carouse, and debauch on the Sabbath, to the great injury of the morals of the rising generation."[80] To the dismay of authorities and to the delight of exotica-seeking tourists, as the city grew up around Congo Square, it continued to foster a limited economic and cultural resistance to increasingly restrictive laws governing slavery and interracial and interstatus mingling.[81]

Places of exclusion, confinement, and literal as well as figurative marginality, the edges of the city also constituted sites of potential for those such as Lacroix who had the means and power to access and transform them.[82] In their efforts to establish their birthright to their property, Lacroix and other prominent Creole of color proprietors demonstrated that the faubourgs and the extended "back-of-town" area could foster the institutions and social activities that would sustain and augment the group identity of Creoles of color. Whether people responded to the private development schemes of Bernard Marigny and other large proprietors or took advantage of the city's efforts to develop the old commons, up to 80 percent of the lots in Tremé and 75 percent of the lots in Marigny passed through the hands of *hommes* or *femmes de couleur* at least one time during the antebellum period.

Among the many real estate developers in Tremé were tailors Joseph Dumas and partner Julien Colvis, who lived on St. Philip Street near St. Claude; the brothers Bernard and Albin Soulié, active Tremé realtors who lived on Tremé Street and had offices on North Rampart; and financier Drausin B. Macarty, who held property on St. Philip and North Robertson Streets. Macarty married a member of the Courcelle family, which was also heavily invested in real estate in the area.[83] Along Bayou Road, the old colonial thoroughfare, families of *gens de couleur* also formed economic bonds and marriage ties with one another that served to keep title and ownership status relatively consolidated. For example, François Boisdoré and neighbor Louis Doliolle each owned considerable property lining Esplanade Avenue. In 1832, when the city wanted to widen the important street though their plantations, the Doliolle-Boisdoré alliance held out for five years until the men received what they considered to be a fair price. Boisdoré surveyed and auctioned off a large parcel of his valuable land in 1844. Once a captain in Andrew Jackson's battalion of free men of color, Bazile Demazilière bought substantial property on Bayou Road, and his family married into the neighboring Decoudreaux family, a member of which would become the mother of Paul Trévigne, a prominent Civil War-era journalist.[84] Although he resided on Love Street in nearby Marigny throughout the antebellum period, by the early Reconstruction period Lacroix had relocated to Orleans Street between Congo Square and the Tremé market.

Cultural networks and religious institutions reinforced neighborhood affiliations expressed through kinship patterns and business practices. One of the most resonant battles over Americanization in antebellum New Orleans took place within the Catholic Church and had profound consequences for cultural identity in the Creole faubourgs. Increasingly influenced by the Anglo-American church establishment, the religious hierarchy sought to minimize the role of the city's lay leaders or *marguilliers*, who were overwhelmingly drawn from the francophone population. Heavily invested in Scottish Rite freemasonry, the *marguilliers* struggled against a Catholic leadership that opposed the freemasons on both theological and political grounds.[85] When the official Catholic hierarchy wrested control of the St. Louis Cathedral in the *vieux carré* from the francophone lay leaders, the faubourgs offered physical shelter for their ceremonial lives, practices that often challenged the racial separation endorsed by the municipal government or the emergent Catholic establishment. Located on the corner of St. Claude and Dumaine, Perseverance Lodge No. 4, housed a white masonic organization with roots in Saint Domingue, but the building also served as a meeting place for Creole of color freemasons.[86] In 1867, under directives from affiliates in France, this lodge and others throughout the city officially integrated their membership.[87] Among *gens de couleur*, associations formed in Masonic lodges spawned a host of mutual aid and benevolence organizations, burial societies, and social clubs. These institutions thrived on a spirit of rivalry and contention with one another even as their performance cultures signaled their common ground. At the 1863 funeral of Marigny resident and Union captain André Cailloux, for example, various social organizations turned out in full regalia in a show of mutual respect and appreciation for the fallen war hero. After his body lay in state at the Society of Odd Fellows, his own lodge in Marigny, the entourage paraded with his hearse to St. Louis Cemetery on the other side of Tremé.[88]

In the faubourgs, residents continued to infuse the Catholicism issuing from the city center with their local interpretations and spiritual practices. Until the early twentieth century, Catholic parishes based their membership on residence rather than racial identity, allowing the Creole neighborhoods of the city to adapt the conservative directives of the official church fathers to local needs. The establishment in 1842 of St. Augustine Church at the corner of Hospital and St. Claude Streets in Tremé simultaneously affected a compromise with and registered concern over a growing conservatism among Catholic officials. It also allowed the Creoles of color to leverage their financial means to secure pews for themselves and for enslaved people. Working through the St. Augustine parish, church officials cooperated with Creole of color leaders to establish support among a disgruntled francophone population and to promote a sense of piety and education among *gens de couleur.* Part of a complex that had once served as the main building of the plantation of Claude Tremé and later as the site of Charles Gayarré's alma mater, the Collège d'Orléans, St. Augustine Church stood on ground that exemplified the layering of economic, educational, and religious activities that would continue to thrive within the parish.

The process of transforming this ground into sacred space forced the Church hierarchy to incorporate the informal collaborations among pious women—white and of color—already taking place on the property. In 1834 the Frenchwoman Jeanne d'Aliquot purchased part of the defunct Collège d'Orléans in order to expand her school for free people of color and slaves, a school that had been operated by the white Ursulines and Sisters of Mount Carmel. Two years later Aliquot and a number of her pupils, including the free woman of color Henriette Delille, formed the Sisters of the Presentation. Over the next sixteen years this informal association of laywomen transformed into a pious community and, finally, a religious order affiliated with the Sodality of the Blessed Virgin Mary in Rome. In conjunction with the establishment of St. Augustine in 1842, Bishop Blanc of New Orleans took a crucial first step in this transformation when he sanctioned the order as the Sisters of the Holy Family.[89] The protection of the Church, in particular of Père Etienne Rousselon of St. Augustine Church, provided Delille and the nuns of color with a base for their often-subversive activity, establishing what some have called the "feminine face of Afro-Catholicism."[90] Against the terms of the Code Noir, Delille not only offered moral instruction to enslaved people but taught them how to read and write as well. Defying the spirit of the Louisiana Civil Code, she acted as a witness to a number of "marriages of conscience" between whites and free people of color. Against the wishes of her church superiors, she purchased property and continued, though informally, her cross-racial association with Jeanne d'Aliquot.[91] In spite of laws preventing educational and cultural initiatives among *gens de couleur libre*, François Lacroix and other wealthy Catholics of color, such as fellow tailor Joseph Dumas and broker Thomy Lafon, provided funding and support for the Sisters. In the year before his death, Lacroix was listed in the city directory as a caretaker of a hospital operated by the Holy Family order.[92]

Just as Tremé was establishing itself as a cultural haven for free people of color, François Lacroix and his brother Julien exerted a similar influence over the growth of the Marigny neighborhood. In addition to accumulating property cut from the grounds of the old colonial-era Marigny plantation, the Lacroix brothers played a major role in the development of the contiguous neighborhoods of New Marigny and the Bywater. Many of the defining institutions of Creole of color identity established in the area owe their genesis to the Lacroix brothers and landowners like them. For example, the Couvent Institute Catholique, a school for indigent orphans provided for by the will of Marie Couvent, may never have been established had it not been for François Lacroix. He and his wife donated property in New Marigny for the school, and he served on its first board of trustees.[93] This institution would play a major role in consolidating the political and cultural opportunities of free people of color before and after the Civil War. Armand Lanusse, editor of and contributor to *Les Cenelles*, served as headmaster of the school, and Paul Trévigne, who would become a civil rights activist in the post-bellum years, taught mathematics there. By attending to the status of orphans, the school seemed to answer one of the chief concerns of the *Cenelles* poets, who worried that the liminal space of the graveyard might be the only place for those who could not secure their lineage and claim an inheritance legitimately.

As Frenchmen Street descends through the heart of Marigny toward the river, passing Washington Square Park, it comes to a vibrant point with Victory Street (now Decatur) and Esplanade. The Frenchman Street area exemplified the urban ethos that New Orleans rapidly achieved in the middle decades of the 1800s, anchored in a set of properties passed back and forth between François and Julien Lacroix in a series of somewhat secretive transactions. By the time of Julien Lacroix's death in 1868, both sides of Frenchman Street as well as the downriver block of Esplanade between St. Peters and Chartres were owned by a Lacroix. A complex of buildings designed for mixed residential and commercial use housed warehouses and apartment buildings, adding to the layers of urban density and urban anonymity that had already fully eclipsed the old Marigny homestead. The centerpiece of this important part of the neighborhood was Julien Lacroix's grocery store, where people of refinement could buy staples as well as delicacies imported from Europe. Bernard Marigny, the namesake of the neighborhood, had a credit account with Julien Lacroix.

Whereas François the tailor outfitted the well-dressed Creole gentleman and lady, Julien the importer and grocer literally defined Creole "taste," conditioning the palate of the upper echelon of New Orleans society. Providing people the means to entertain well, his store was well stocked with beverages such as Bordeaux and Madeira, white wine, claret, champagne, vermouth, and schnapps and non- and semi-perishable foodstuffs such as sardines, mackerels, herring, smoked beef, and capers. If his household effects are any indication, he seemed to live more extravagantly than his wealthier brother, owning even more mahogany furniture, his embellished with marble accents. In addition to his formal dining room, which could accommodate twelve diners, Julien's residence had two parlors, one of which was outfitted with another dining room table and twelve more chairs.[94] Fully equipped to host large parties in his apartments above the store, Julien Lacroix may have created much of the social scene of the neighborhood himself. In 1850 he counted three enslaved people, a man and two women, as part of his household, and they may have provided elegant service at such gatherings.[95] After his death, his widow operated a dance hall on the upper floors of a contiguous Lacroix building.[96] During the mid-nineteenth century and for many decades to come, Julien Lacroix's lively intersection at the foot of Frenchman Street provided the backdrop for a tasteful and eclectic social scene.

Creole of color landlords such as the Lacroix brothers were literally invested in New Orleans, and their assets thrived in an Americanizing city where racial codes were becoming stricter. Somewhat counterintuitively, their success in building and speculating depended on the stability of the New Orleans economy and the racial hierarchies supporting a slave system that consistently devalued black lives and thus their own "blackness." Managing racial and status hierarchies was in large part a spatial problem requiring each person to assume his or her "proper place." Recent studies of the emergence of Jim Crow detail the uneven and often contested development of the practices separating the races and their reliance on a rigid either-or racial designation.[97] Nineteenth-century New Orleans must be looked at through another lens, one attuned to the contradictions of spatial integration in spite of racist legislation and of racist legislation in spite of racial ambiguity.[98] Making sense of the fact and the fate of Creole of color estates such as that of Lacroix demands that we maintain a delicate critical balance that mirrors the in-between status of Creole of color proprietors. Understanding how people of African descent managed their title and entitlement to the social and physical space of New Orleans can help explain a central conundrum of race in the city—that racial identity mattered deeply and yet there was ample opportunity to defy racial codes and rules. As an in-between people, Creoles of color lived their lives at the crux of this paradox.

Intimacy, Insularity, and Creole of Color Identity

Historians often remark on the "insularity" of the Creole of color community, charging *gens de couleur* with cutting themselves off from "blacks" or "Negroes" even though they could not gain the status of "whites." Some further note a pervasive contradiction to official rules of racial realignment, pointing to the "intimacy" that this Creole of color community shared with white Creoles and immigrants.[99] For instance, the city's francophone Masonic lodges were widely reputed to have accepted members across lines of race well before the official integration of the lodges in 1867.[100] Moreover, French-speaking white freemasons often took an interest in each other's mixed-race families. The lawyer-politician Pierre Soulé, a prominent Douglas Democrat and lawyer for the defense in *Desarzant v. Le Blanc*, fostered the artistic career of Creole of color sculptor Eugène Warbourg, the mixed-race son of his Masonic confrere Daniel Warbourg.[101] Indeed, the uniqueness or insular nature of this social group depended to a large extent on interracial intimacy. That is, what separated them from other blacks—in addition to their francophone culture—was a legacy of semi-legitimate sexual relationships across the color line and an ensuing degree of autonomy and control over their own financial and spatial mobility. As a result, Creoles of color held themselves immune to an 1840 law requiring free blacks to register at the mayor's office. Those rosters generally excluded native free people of color, listing instead "out-of-state" free blacks with English names from states along the eastern seaboard.[102] Because free people of color historically maintained privileged relationships with influential whites, they were able, for a while, to avoid legal indignities such as this, eking out both social space and actual space within New Orleans. In city directories and in some legal documents, François Lacroix and other prominent men and women did not always carry the dreaded initials *f.m.c.* or *f.w.c.* after their surnames.

When juxtaposed against the "city," with its official municipal codes, the realm of the faubourgs constituted an alternative public where the neighborhood inhabitants arrived at their own consensus about what kinds of identity were preferable (or at least permissible).[103] The customs and practices of insularity and intimacy between whites and free people of color reconstituted Americanizing laws emanating from city hall. Nothing prevented whites and free people of color from purchasing property from one another or patronizing one another's businesses. Someone like François Lacroix, for example, could expect service in any café he chose to enter. Creoles of color such as Lacroix, Nelson Fouché, and Louis Charles Roudanez gained reputations across racial lines as exceptional tailors, cigar makers, or doctors and had mixed-race clienteles. Creoles of color active in real estate often rented to white tenants and vice versa.[104] In addition to these professional relationships, free people of color and whites experienced close intimacy in their residential patterns, living side by side, and census data throughout the nineteenth century reveals a number of interracial households.

Facilitating this insularity and intimacy, the "Creole cottage," the dominant mode of architecture in the Creole faubourgs, mediated the ongoing transaction among official laws, public custom, and private desires, freedoms, and transgressions. Perfected by Creole of color builders such as the Doliolles and the Courcelles, it differed from the typical American-style house, which came into fashion in antebellum New Orleans with an emphasis on the front entrance and an elaborately flowered and manicured front lawn. In contrast, the emphasis of the Creole cottage was more on the rear of the house. Usually lacking a front gallery and set right on the sidewalk, the Creole cottage expanded towards the back, opening up onto an interior courtyard and focused toward the kitchen and rear quarters. Even the "gable sided" roof typically sloped from front to back.[105] Whereas American-style houses actively greeted the public, these rear-oriented buildings prioritized privacy, giving the Creole faubourgs a feeling of intimacy and insularity, suggesting there was more to them than met the eye. The floor plan of the typical Creole cottage, however, suggested a lack of privacy *inside* homes, featuring multiuse "walkthrough" rooms, two to the front and two to the rear with no center hallway such as that characterizing an American townhouse.[106] When American architect Benjamin Latrobe visited the city in 1819, he commented on the cultural nature of this difference: "We derive from the English the habit of desiring that every one of our rooms should be separately accessible, and we consider rooms that are thoroughfares as useless. The French and continental Europeans generally live, I believe, as much to their own satisfaction in their houses as we do in ours, and employ the room they have to more advantage, because they do not require so much space for passages." Latrobe predicted that the American style would predominate as more carpenters and architects migrated to the city from the "Eastern border of the Union."[107]

The experiences of *gens de couleur libre* who lived in and built cottages of their own contrasted sharply with the domestic realities of enslaved people. In one important sense, New Orleans and other urban areas held out the possibility of freedom in anonymity to enslaved people and offered many the opportunity to make a literal escape aboard any number of steamboats docked at the levee. Meeting these challenges, lawmakers attempted to narrow the loopholes to freedom and shelter the marketplace of slavery from this kind of resistance.[108] Legislation passed in 1857 stipulated twenty-five lashes for slaves who disturbed the "public peace" by gambling or singing "obscene songs," insulting free persons, or carrying a cane or stick in public. Ship captains caught with fugitive slave property aboard their vessels and convicted of this offense would "suffer imprisonment at hard labor for a term . . . not less than three years" as well as fines and reimbursements.[109] The guidelines of "display" and police "surveillance" governed the spatial and domestic options available to slaves in New Orleans as elsewhere. Slave owners corralled their slaves as products for sale, and the cultural map of New Orleans was pockmarked by physical slave markets where buyers could peruse slaves on display. Slave pens were clustered at the corner of Chartres and Esplanade, just around the corner from Julian Lacroix's grocery store. Solomon Northup, whose narrative depicts his capture as a free man in New York and subsequent sale to the deep South, recalls his experience on the market in New Orleans: the trader "would make us hold up our heads, walk briskly back and forth, while customers would feel our hands and arms and bodies, turn us about, ask us what we could do, make us open our mouths and show our teeth, precisely as a jockey examines a horse which he is about to barter for or purchase."[110] Confined to visible quarters within private homes, slaves could not stray too far from the gazes of their masters. The Civil Code further encapsulated the constraints on the mobility of enslaved people: "Slaves, though *moveables* by their nature, are considered as *immoveables*, by the operation of law."[111]

When walking in the streets, enslaved people were obliged to carry and show passes demonstrating their status and immediate purpose. Written passes of this sort, working in tandem with slave law and the threat of punishment, sought to align a slave's "purpose" and that of his or her master. Imagining this conflation of purpose to be natural, masters often overlooked the violence that facilitated the subjugation of enslaved people, preferring instead to ascribe the forced compliance of their enslaved property to bonds of affection and sentiment.[112] For example, when questioned during the probate hearings of François Lacroix about the whereabouts some of Lacroix's former slaves—a mother and three children—a friend of the family expressed bewilderment and consternation that they had fled the Lacroix residence upon the arrival of Union troops in New Orleans. Before the war, these slaves had tended dutifully to the sickly Mrs. Lacroix who died in 1856, but they seized their opportunity for freedom as soon as it presented itself.[113] In their cottages, then, elite Creoles of color fashioned a domestic life designed to inoculate them against the many confinements suffered by enslaved people and to convince themselves that their own slaves were indeed "part of the family."

The most storied interracial households in New Orleans were the results of a *plaçage*, a relationship in which a white man would literally place a woman of color paramour and their children in a small cottage. Throughout the antebellum period, city boosters concerned with intermingling blood as well as the public image of the city sought to curtail these arrangements and such accessory institutions as quadroon balls. Nevertheless, interracialism made its mark on the physical space of the city. In one frequently acknowledged legend, Bernard Marigny recorded the history of *plaçage* in the layout and naming of the streets in his faubourg. Although they've since been changed to correspond with Burgundy and Rampart Streets in the French Quarter, Rue d'Amour and Rue des Bons Enfants (Love and Goodchildren streets) designated thoroughfares associated in public knowledge with the practice of *plaçage* and the partial inheritance of a white father's estate by his natural children of color.[114] Within the very public space of the streets, white Creoles and Creoles of color acknowledged private transgressions of official rules concerning race and status.

Local Diversions: "Sacrificing" an Estate

Disclosing his family's tangled relationships and detailing the disintegration of his vast estate, the probate proceedings of François Lacroix provided the occasion for competing performances of racial, cultural, and familial identity. When considered in the context of the swath of history they encompass—from the 1830s and 1840s until the 1880s and beyond—these documents attest to the changing terms of interracial intimacy and cultural insularity for Creoles of color in the mid-nineteenth century. They reveal multiple shifts in racial etiquette and the changeable grounds for entitlement and social and political belonging. In the years leading up to and after his death, François Lacroix's estate forced to the surface his concerns over his own posterity, his family's financial and social security, the sense of community he helped construct within the Creole faubourgs, and the persistence of that sense of community relative to other claims on the destiny of New Orleans.

The most provocative and most extended testimony taken during the Lacroix proceedings concerned the claims of his white "daughter-in-law" Sarah Brown Lacroix and his granddaughter Maria Cecilia to a portion of his estate. His relationships with them in life suggested his concerted effort to manage interracial intimacies in his own family and insular social world. I use quotation marks in describing their kinship because the "marriage" of Sarah Brown and Victor Lacroix, François's son, existed in social and political limbo. Falling outside the bounds of legality, Victor's and Sarah's nuptials were celebrated in 1862 in a purely religious ceremony at St. Alphonse Church, a newly consecrated church in the American sector of the city, the interior of which had not even been completed. A "marriage of conscience," this interracial union could not have existed in the civil sphere.[115] Although couples would be able to legitimate interracial unions such as this under the Reconstruction government beginning in 1868, by that time Victor Lacroix had already been brutally murdered by opponents to radical Reconstruction in the infamous riot at Mechanics' Institute on July 30, 1866, an event that dramatized the perils of a black identity in New Orleans.[116] A martyr to the cause of civil and political equality for African Americans, Victor Lacroix would never be able to legitimate his union with his white wife, thereby securing his nuclear family's financial and social heritage. Instead, the timing of his death injured his "wife's" sense of propriety and jeopardized the racial and social identity of their children.

At some point in 1866 after Victor's death, Sarah Brown Lacroix traveled from her house on Gasquet Street across Faubourg Tremé to the home of François Lacroix, who lived at the time on Orleans Street near St. Claude. She brought with her witnesses who could testify to her character; "certify" to the Lacroix family that her "conduct was that of a respectable lady."[117] She hoped this testimony would provide a counterbalance to her residence in a neighborhood known for prostitution and other morally suspect living arrangements.[118] This intimate visit was an interesting twist on the racial etiquette of the city, which in its institution of *plaçage* provided the context for Creole of color women to seek financial security and protection from white men. Here, Sarah Brown Lacroix, a white woman, pled her case for respectability before the prominent patriarch of her late "husband's" Creole of color family, begging him to lend financial support to her and her children. Old Lacroix appeared to resist a public acknowledgement of his son's interracial alliance with this persistent woman. Seemingly reluctantly, Lacroix provided her with clothing and a house at first, benefits that he supplemented gradually with food and finally money. By December 1866, François Lacroix had assumed responsibility for Cecile and Victoria Lacroix, two of Sarah Brown and Victor's children, as their "undertutor."[119] Considered alongside his consistent and active efforts to shore up Creole of color institutions and build community networks, François Lacroix's attempts to set Sarah Brown Lacroix up in housekeeping seemed particularly reluctant. An older Creole of color gentleman supporting a young white woman, he performed in the volatile and confusing context of early Reconstruction the inverse function of the white suitor of the Creole of color *placée.*[120] The role reversal may have held a particular irony for François Lacroix, whose own mother, Elizabeth Norwood, had been *placée,* the longtime "wife" of French immigrant Paul Lacroix.[121]

At François Lacroix's succession hearing, Sarah Brown Lacroix attempted to create legitimacy for her position. At the time the marriage ceremony was performed, she claimed, she had failed to realize that her new husband Victor was a man of color. Having met him only a month and a half before the wedding, Sarah assented to marry a man whose "complexion" she testified later, "was as fair as mine."[122] In 1865 the couple even had the baptism of their first child, a son, listed on the white registry of baptisms. Soon after her son's birth, Sarah Brown Lacroix met her father-in-law, the well-known Creole of color real estate tycoon, presumably only then realizing the racial identity of her new family. Whether she was telling the truth or not, her identity must have undergone an extensive and sudden transformation. What passed as her white nuclear family, unconnected to many relatives beyond the borders of her house, was suddenly part of a vast and prominent family of color with a network of properties across the city. If her claims to a Lacroix identity were successful and she publicly wed herself to a historically and legally degraded group, she would have suddenly accessed a web of property ownership that could potentially offer much more geographic and economic mobility than an association with that group would normally dictate.

However, Sarah Brown Lacroix would have to fight hard for this recognition, and judging from various documents, she found it difficult to embrace the colored status that being a Lacroix would have designated. In the 1870 census she was listed as the widow of Victor Lacroix, but she and her six-year-old daughter "Cecilia" were also listed as white. By 1875, a year before François Lacroix's death, she was listed as Sarah Brown in a city directory.[123] Exhibiting a commitment to the growth and maintenance of an insular Creole of color community, François Lacroix arranged his affairs in a way that suggests that one main concern was to protect his investments from white ownership. Although Lacroix contracted business with white people, his personal records indicate that he was not particularly interested in fostering relationships that would threaten to carry his wealth across racial lines. Over the course of his life, the circle of people he seemed to trust shrank drastically. In the early part of his career, he was a generous patron of a number of Creole of color institutions. In the 1850s he began to limit his primary business relationships to family, particularly his brother Julien. By the end of his life, he refused to will his property to Victor's family or to his other son, Edgar, reputed to be something of a gambler. It seemed as though Lacroix, burdened by generational anxieties, could not trust even his own family members with the legacy of his wealth and property.

The financial and relational predicament of the Lacroix family in the aftermath of the Civil War and Reconstruction indicated the constraints of a social world that was becoming perhaps too intimate and insular. What was once a large and thriving estate dwindled and dispersed among warring family members and creditors until there was practically nothing left. Lacroix's estate suffered in large part because he refused to meet official regulations and expectations regarding its management and dispersal. Specifically, he declined to pay his taxes, and he died without a will, leaving his civic and familial obligations unmet. These failures constituted a public spectacle in the 1870s, beginning with the civil sheriff's seizure of much of his property in 1874 and culminating in his succession, which remained open and contested for nearly forty years. Merely cataloguing his property claimed the full-time attention of notary Christopher Morel for two weeks in 1876; at his succession hearing one tax official claimed that in ten years' experience, he "never had so big an undertaking" as the Lacroix estate, which "took up the greater part of our time for two or three years." Even the judge in the Lacroix succession had an interest in it, his father being one of Lacroix's creditors.[124] The auction of the estate continued unabated until the 1880s, occupying multiple columns in the local newspapers. The city's leading newspapers had also carried the story of the sheriff's sale, allowing readers a glimpse at close range of Lacroix's financial decline, which many portrayed as physical and mental as well.

If his social demise was a spectacle, it was one that Lacroix himself engineered. The fate of the Lacroix estate can be understood as his commentary on the increasingly limited terrain for New Orleans' native proprietors during a period of humiliating occupation by the Union army and the subsequent Republican administration.[125] The deterioration of his legacy also provided the raw material for others to come to terms with their own slipping financial and social status. In one sense Lacroix's inaction can be seen as a protest, a defiant display of belonging aimed at the new authorities who seemed to have taken over. For example, François Lacroix clashed with Union officials when he complained that they occupied his properties without compensating him—a complaint he shared with other New Orleans landowners, white and of color.[126] His allowing himself to be listed, for the first time, as white on the 1870 census further indicates his intransigence before public officials in the wake of shifting regimes. The refusal of Lacroix to pay his taxes prompted editors of the *Daily Picayune* to argue convincingly that his actions were a direct response to rising tax assessments by the Reconstruction government, thus echoing a common concern of proprietors not only in New Orleans but also across the South.[127] "He did not wish" to pay his taxes, the *Picayune* argued. "Spurning all proffers of assistance, laughing at every warning, deriding every prayer of his friends, old Lacroix permits—nay he practically commands—the sacrifice of one of the most magnificent estates in the South."[128] This "sacrifice" allowed him to register his generational concerns about the future of his family and his city in the years before his death and from beyond the grave. It also allowed him to articulate one of the major themes of the history of New Orleans in the mid-nineteenth century: the fight of Creoles, natives of the city, white and of color, to avoid being erased from its legacy.

The portrayal of Lacroix's predicament in the mainstream press, "curious and interesting" enough to occupy two-and-a-half columns on the front page of the *Daily Picayune*, registers an uneasiness on behalf of white native proprietors with the idea that his was a conscious and forceful protest. In reporting on the auction of the estate, "a drama such as seldom if ever seen enacted in this city," the *Daily Picayune* memorialized him (even before his death) as a walking apparition. "Apathetic and apparently unconscious," his smile was "vacant" and his daily walks home wordless. He sat daily "on the steps of the rostrum smoking a cigar while the auctioneer knocks down his houses and lands for a mere song." His stoic pose and his positioning on the bare wooden steps suggested the ways in which, for the editors, his predicament shadowed that of a slave at auction. The former tailor Lacroix reportedly attended the daily auction "dressed in the shabbiest of linen, with his shirt open at the throat, with his bushy, gray hair unkempt," testifying to the extent of his destitution.

Giving Lacroix voice would have been admitting that his concerns had social (as opposed to eccentrically individual) meaning. As a particularly visible "native proprietor," Lacroix functioned to other owners as a reminder of their own dispossession and, further, an emblem of the extensive nature of that dispossession—topics that provoked significant anxiety and discomfort. Interestingly, the public discussion of his downfall includes a description of Lacroix's "dwelling," now located at 70 Dumaine Street in Tremé, complete with an imagined account of its interior. In veritable ruins and having "much the look of a stranger," the Creole cottage, as described, occupied the space of the past, its physical condition set in sharp relief against the tall, stately, modern brick buildings to its left and right. Moreover, the *Picayune* writers ascribed the ruined condition of the house, and by extension of Lacroix himself, to the crowded and chaotic state of its interior.[129] Living amid a "confusion and congregation of curiosities," Lacroix faltered because his domestic space failed to establish adequate division and partition within, relying on walls of "paste board planks . . . divisions merely for the eye, not for the nose or ear."

Furthermore, his home harbored only two relics of any importance, and those were inadequately maintained. Evidence of his own failures to fulfill his duties to the previous generation, his 103-year-old mother whittled away her remaining time in the front room "in an immense and venerable rocking chair." Her refusal to pass away at such advanced age suggested that all was not well with her son. In the back room, the greatest and most important piece of furniture was a "venerable iron safe, somewhat rusty but still preserved from all outside attacks." A reflection of his own intransigence, Lacroix's safe demonstrates his unwillingness to invest in the future of his family and his city in their current state. Trapped at the crux of these anxieties of inheritance, Lacroix may have sacrificed his estate, but in their accounts of him, the newspaper editors effectively sacrificed Lacroix's social legacy.

Seen in this manner, he was the "monstrous double" of the native white proprietor, the victim "neither divisive nor trivial, neither fully part of the community nor fully outside it," that allowed his white counterparts to "deflect" their ownership anxieties away from themselves.[130] Even so, the judge responsible for Lacroix's succession two years later felt a distinct sense of unease regarding his descendants' bickering over their fair share of the estate: "If [Lacroix] has done wrong [in not clarifying the terms of his legacy] it comes with very bad grace from his son [Edgar Lacroix] to cast stains over the ashes of his father."[131]

It is constructive to consider François Lacroix and Charles Gayarré to be a twinned pair, much like Cable's fictional pair Honoré Grandissime and Honoré Grandissime f.m.c. Native proprietors and custodians of Creole—white Creole and Creole of color—identity, Gayarré and Lacroix registered grave concerns over their inability to fulfill their own proprietary obligations and over the next generation's ability to carry and extend their legacies. Writing about the population of color in an 1877 essay, Charles Gayarré wondered "what will become, in the end, of that unfortunate class, neither white nor black, hanging like Mohammed's coffin between heaven and earth, and rejected by the two races from which he proceeds."[132] Toward the end of the century, Gayarré and his own beloved white Creoles were left in a similar lurch. Defending his birthright had proven to be as costly to Gayarré as it was to Lacroix. Gayarré had sunk a fortune of roughly $500,000—twice the assets of Lacroix—in Confederate bonds and currency. Having considered exile to rich archives in Spain, Gayarré instead fled, as many of his compatriots had, to rural plantation land when New Orleans fell easily to Union troops in 1862. After the war's end, when the federal government required former Confederates to swear oaths of allegiance or have their property confiscated, Gayarré objected. According to legend, when Secretary of State Seward suggested that he and other Louisianans "bend your stiff necks, eat dirt, [and] creep on your bellies to your seats [in the U.S. Congress]," Gayarré forcefully declined, affirming what he believed to be the strong character of Louisiana's "true sons."[133]

During the last decades of the nineteenth century, Gayarré looked on as "Creole culture," as he had come to know it, effectively disappeared and became mere tourism lore.[134] Most of his 1872 novel *Fernando de Lemos* finds the title character (based on Gayarré himself) lurking—much like the *Cenelles* narrators—in a graveyard, where he spends countless hours mulling over lost lives and various moral, spiritual, and philosophical issues with the old gravedigger Tintin Calandro.[135] Gayarré's physical decline seemed even swifter than that of Lacroix. Although Gayarré suffered from poor eyesight, he attempted to earn his living solely on his writing. He spent his later years writing historical fiction, complaining that his painstakingly researched histories had not earned more money, and waging war on Cable's popularity in newspapers and magazines. In his fiction, he could contrive an outcome of financial solvency: Tintin bequeaths de Lemos a small fortune, which de Lemos uses to secure comfortable lodgings overlooking St. Louis cemetery. In real life, Gayarré's pride was at least as stubborn as Lacroix's. After refusing for years to accept so much as a donated slice of bread, Gayarré finally availed himself of a monthly stipend provided by an organization of "charitable ladies" headed by the mother of his protégé Grace King.[136]

In literature, such as Cable's *Grandissimes*, New Orleans' free people of color functioned as tragic failures, anachronistic apparitions whose fate was to be excised from the social fabric. In the literary and actual terrain of New Orleans, Creoles of color were "squeezed out," their ghostly remains functioning as surrogates for the class and racial anxieties of the literary and social establishment. Against these representations, it is possible to read Lacroix's sacrifice as a tactic of diversion instead. Veering from expected paths and procedures of ownership allowed Lacroix to speak from beyond the grave and echo the ghostly voices of the *Cenelles* poets. Even if Lacroix's dramatic sacrifice of his estate did not yield the sense of entitlement he might have wished for his family and his social group, it did help to characterize New Orleans as a complicated and provocative terrain where standardizing techniques of national consolidation would meet considerable local resistance.

Insularity and a commitment to a geographically local identity were not the only proprietorship options pursued by Creoles of color in the nineteenth century. Many sought breathing room from this predicament through exile, a more obvious detour from the threat of Americanization. Because focusing on Creoles of color in physical or imaginative exile allows us to see at close range the layered manifestations of competing obligations, loyalties, and sources of inspiration, it sheds light on their sense of birthright, especially on its implications for ownership and entitlement.[137] Many exiles fail to burn every bridge leading back to their native land, keeping alive the possibility of some form of return. Inasmuch as they charted an alternate proprietary path, Creole of color exiles bequeathed a parallel legacy to that of the New Orleans-bound Lacroix family.

Vagabond Proprietors: Maintaining Birthright in Exile

Charles Gayarré's is not the only possible twin of François Lacroix's legacy. We might also consider Lacroix's story alongside the activities of "vagabond proprietors" who chose to leave an Americanizing New Orleans. Lacroix's own partner Etienne Cordeviolle retired from business in New Orleans sometime before 1852 and migrated to Paris, where he drew a healthy income from his clothing designs.[138] Rival New Orleans tailor Joseph Dumas also sought exile in Paris. During the 1830s and into the 1840s, Dumas and his partner Julien Colvis operated a clothing business across Chartres Street from Lacroix and Cordeviolle and amassed a similarly large fortune in real estate.[139] Their properties consisted of lots and buildings in the *vieux carré* and Faubourgs Tremé and Marigny as well as extensive holdings across Canal Street in the so-called American sector of the city. In addition to these real estate investments worth $177,100 in 1846, the partners also held promissory notes from customers worth almost $30,000 and joint property in their store and its merchandise amounting to just over $10,000.[140] When Dumas moved his family permanently to Paris in 1845, he and Colvis dissolved their business partnership, but their personal relationship continued to flourish.[141] Dumas served as the undertutor to Colvis's children, one of whom, Dr. Joseph Colvis, married Dumas's own daughter and joined the Dumas family in France.

Because the French government had abolished slavery and extended political rights to people of African descent in 1848, New Orleans' Creoles of color considered France and its colonies to be attractive refuges.[142] The Parisian metropole in particular provided shelter for those such as pianist and composer Eugène Macarty, sculptor Daniel Warbourg, and physician Louis Charles Roudanez, all of whom demanded a more hospitable climate for their artistic and professional ambitions.[143] In the 1850s urban free people of color in New Orleans drew upon their circum-Caribbean connections to assist refugees and relatives from the rural Attakapas region (encompassing Lafayette and Opelousas), where violence against free blacks had reached a terrifying pitch. In this effort, they responded to periodic requests from the Haitian government that free African Americans bring their industry and education to the hemisphere's premiere black republic. For Louisiana's free people of color, this represented a homecoming of sorts. "Haitian by his education and his manners," Emile Desdunes—the father of late-nineteenth-century New Orleans activist and historian Rodolphe Desdunes—served as the emigration officer of Haitian president Soulouque in the 1850s. Creole of color exiles also sought refuge in Spanish-speaking locales—particularly those with pronounced francophone populations of African descent such as Santiago de Cuba, where many of their ancestors had relocated during the uprisings in San Domingue. Extending a legacy of cooperation between the Mexican Republic and New Orleans' free people of color—many of whom had fought in the Mexican War of Independence (1810-1821)—the builder, investor, and cigar maker Nelson Fouché launched a particularly inventive scheme to relocate one hundred Creole of color families—all of whom would assume the rights of Mexican citizens—to Eureka, a colony he organized near Veracruz.[144]

Within their exiles, *gens de couleur libre* developed a network of transatlantic legal and literary practices to sustain their property rights and secure their identities, and a number of Creole of color real estate brokers and managers emerged to fill the needs of these long-distance proprietors. Drausin B. Macarty, described by a local business report as a "quadroon—gentlemanly and correct," had by 1854 established himself as an agent for several "absent parties" and from 1849 to 1854 increased his own holdings from $15,000 to $40,000.[145] Macarty's brothers-in-law Bernard and Albin Soulié followed suit, and after the Civil War Albin also retired to France.[146] Entrusting his New Orleans' fortune to broker Sidney Thezan, poet Camille Thierry used his claims on New Orleans to prepare for and maintain his exile in Bordeaux, France. Thierry's property, worth $43,195 at its height, included stock in the New Orleans Gas Light Company, shares in the Citizen's Bank of New Orleans, a U.S. bond, and six pieces of real estate, including lots and houses from which he drew income from rents. Thierry's poem "Adieu," published in *Les Cenelles* in 1845 expresses his own mourning for Tremé's Carondelet Canal: "The north wind today chases me / from your shores." The poem's sense of urgency, inevitably, and nostalgia offered a fitting tone for a host of other exiles who in the 1840s and 1850s chose to leave New Orleans rather than suffer the indignities of life there. "Farewell! I have no fear that these long days of absence/ Will make me forget you: / I love to remember, and memories of you / I will have near the hearth."[147]

Far from constituting an absolute break with New Orleans, the real estate activities of Creole of color landlords as well as the poetry of the *Cenelles* poets married an exilic status to a politics and poetics of belonging, their practice of exile reinforcing their proprietorship in New Orleans. The emotional logic of exile prefigures a return, especially in the realm of poesy. Enriched with a variety of perspectives, poetic return brings a sense of renewed and focused vengeance. Whereas Gayarré's construction of Louisiana reinforced the racialist project of Americanization, the *Cenelles* poets refused to consolidate their claims in the nation, exploring other possibilities for identification. If Gayarré created a narrative that knit together culture and race by aligning the French and Spanish colonial legacy in Louisiana with quickening notions of whiteness, the authors of *Les Cenelles* and other exiles exposed the rough seams of that narrative fabric by identifying with both the politically radical aspects of French history and the criticisms leveled by French-speaking *gens de couleur* against the racism and status hierarchies of French colonialism. In contrast to Gayarré, they appealed to the Africanist presence at the center of European experiments in the New World and, armed with this rhetorical ammunition, reasserted their rightful proprietorship of Louisiana.

While their poetry did not make a formal break with French Romanticism, the *Cenelles* poets traced "the itineraries of the Negro race," the alternate routes taken by those denied full claim to either a French or American national identity.[148] In the United States and across the Caribbean, restrictive laws severely curtailed the political expression of people of African descent. Published despite a Louisiana law restricting the publication of writings or speeches "having a tendency to produce discontent among the free colored population of this state," *Les Cenelles* resonated within a transnational atmosphere of francophone black Atlantic protest.[149] The poets' pelagic critical sensibilities echoed those of Martiniquan *homme de couleur* Cyril Bissette, for example. In 1822 slave owner Bissette and three associates had been seized and imprisoned in Martinique for agitating for political rights for *gens de couleur.* Convicted and branded with the mark of the galley slave, the men were ultimately deported to Paris, where Bissette launched his influential journal *Revue des Colonies* (1834–1842) and adopted a radical abolitionist position.[150]

Keeping a "coup d'oeil" on the colonial regime, Bissette—a relative of Josephine, the wife of Napoleon I—compiled news not only from France's various New World colonies, but also from those of England, Spain, and other European nations.[151] Keeping its eye on the Old World as well, *Revue des Colonies* charted developments in Algeria, which France had invaded in 1830, provoking a violent clash with local resistance that would last for decades. The journal paid special attention to the United States, highlighting both the internal predicament of Americans of African descent, enslaved and free, and U.S. imperial designs in the Western Hemisphere, particularly with respect to the black island nation of Haiti. The most radical outlet for abolitionism in France, Bisette's journal attracted an eclectic group of contributors, including the Martiniquan poet Pierre Marie Pory-Papy, who later joined Bissette as a member of the 1848 French National Assembly; the French Catholic priest and political activist of the late eighteenth and early nineteenth century, literary historian Henri Grégoire; New Orleans *homme de couleur* playwright and poet Victor Séjour, also in exile in Paris; and the Haitian brothers Ignace and Emile Nau, founders of the controversial Haitian *cenacle*, a group of writers critical of the regime of Haitian president Jean-Pierre Boyer. Articulating the political and cultural potential of the emerging francophone critical sphere, Emile Nau emphasized the importance of Africa on Haitian character: "there is in the fusion of the European and African cultures which constitutes our national character, something that makes us less French than the American is English. This advantage is a real one."[152] In a sense, these francophone writers anticipated the more radical break with French formal traditions and linguistic practices made in the twentieth century by the négritude poets, who also delved within diasporic contexts for their African roots.[153]

The pendulum of exile and return swings throughout *Les Cenelles.* Refusing to commit to one location, the poets tie together various points of reference and create a new geography steeped in their own patriotic pride and personal sacrifice. For example, in the Père Lachaise cemetery in Paris, the inscription on the tombstone of Victor Séjour, the Creole of color dramatist and the most celebrated contributor to *Les Cenelles*, charts a rich legacy and destabilizes the relationship between metropole and colony: "Victor Séjour, Son of Haiti and Louisiana, Free Man of Color of New Orleans, Successful Playwright of Paris, Greatest French Language Dramatist of France's former colony on the Mississippi."[154] This description of Séjour (whose very name means sojourn or stopover) skirts around New Orleans, Louisiana, and the Mississippi—sites within the geographical boundaries of the United States—enclosing them instead within a French colonial legacy. Séjour's geographical affiliations are Haiti and Louisiana, France's former colonies, and the cosmopolitan cities of New Orleans and Paris. His racial affiliation is "man of color," and his cultural expression is that of a "French language dramatist." However, Séjour is ever mindful of France's shortcomings. In an age of emergent nationalism, Séjour's memory occupies fissures in both French and U.S. national identity, searching among multiple metropoles and hinterlands for territory where it might move critically and productively.[155]

In his only contribution to *Les Cenelles*, Séjour aligns his Gallic pride with that of Napoleon Bonaparte, superimposing his own exile over the grandest French exile of all. The reader of "Le Retour de Napoléon"—written on the occasion of the return of Napoleon's remains to France—recognizes the predicament of the Creole of color in the thinly veiled account of Napoleon's confinement: "Ah! When, solitary and pensive, on St. Helena he stood, / He turned his gaze toward a distant France / As he would toward a golden star; / His face burned bright with the fires of memory; / He cried out: 'My God, I would relinquish my soul, / To see her once again.' "[156] Illuminating the critical context of the Creole of color poet's perspective, Séjour mediates his outsider status with the figure of Napoleon, himself an outsider of sorts: the Corsican emperor of France. Imagining Napoleon from St. Helena rather than Elba, he promises that his own exile from New Orleans will not be forever. To exemplify a useful and productive *"retour,"* however, Séjour's homage to Napoleon must be selective. Séjour does not refer, for example, to Napoleon's failed campaign to reinstate slavery in the colony of San Domingue or his betrayal of the "black

Napoleon" Toussaint L'Ouverture, but instead argues for his embodiment of the "popular will" of France against the "illegitimate" claims of the few. Even so, Séjour subtly fuses the iconography of Napoleon and Toussaint. A meditation on this stanza reveals the image of Toussaint's final and permanent exile set inside the temporary exile of Napoleon. Toussaint wasted away in a French prison, never to return to his island home; Napoleon languished in his island exile preparing his return to glory. On a more practical level, Séjour's poem may have later parlayed the vanity of the French emperor Napoleon III into tangible benefits for a struggling Haiti. "It is an open secret," Rodolphe Desdunes revealed in a 1907 essay, that "through the influence of Séjour" and his intimation that the reign of Napoleon III (1852-1870) could be considered a "*retour*" of Napoleon I, "the sympathetic Emperor became very partial towards the colored race," particularly those citizens of the black island nation of Haiti.[157]

Articulating a multidimensional past within the French diaspora, Séjour envisions himself as heir to both the French republican spirit and the Haitian Revolution. By including Séjour in *Les Cenelles*, Lanusse sought to make him an emblem for his Creole of color readers, reminding them that, although anchored in New Orleans, their social group should by no means consider itself confined by the city's increasingly insulting laws. Earlier, in 1837, Victor Séjour published "*Le Mulâtre*" in Cyril Bissette's *Revue des Colonies.*[158] Touted as the first known short story by an "African American," Séjour's *Le Mulâtre* is set in Saint Marc, San Domingue, the birthplace of his father, and the surrounding countryside. Having left New Orleans a year or two before, Séjour imagines from his new home in Paris a world of "picturesque vegetation" and "bizarre forms of natural life," including newly enslaved Africans, white planters, mulatto children, and rebellious maroons. Emphasizing the itinerancy of New World lives, Séjour briefly frames his narrative with the meeting of a traveler of indiscriminate race and Antoine, an old but imposing "negro." After remarking about the increasingly tense master-slave relationship and prefiguring the violence of the Haitian Revolution, the "old negro" relates an Oedipal family romance of the brutalities of slavery and the tangled familial relationships and abbreviated lineages it creates. While the internal story clearly takes place in the context of slaveholding Saint Domingue, the narrative's frame—the stage where Antoine and the narrator meet—remains unfixed and destabilizes the reader's sense of history and time.

The action of Antoine's story culminates in a struggle between Alfred, a white slave master, and Georges, his slave and the mulatto of the title, for the honor and dignity of Laïsa, Georges's enslaved wife. Laïsa finds herself in the same predicament as Georges's deceased mother, the Senegalese beauty violated by Alfred so many years before. Threatened with rape, Laïsa strikes Alfred and, under the terms of the Code Noir, is condemned to death. Vowing revenge, Georges escapes to the forest to join a maroon community whose slogan "*Afrique et liberté*" contests France's investment in the triangular trade by confronting hollow pronouncements of a French *liberté* with memories of capture from Africa.[159] Years later, after Alfred has married a white wife and produced a male heir, Georges returns to obliterate Alfred's entire bloodline. Georges kills Alfred by decapitation, but not before his severed head speaks the secret that Georges has clamored his entire life to know. In honor of his mother's dying wish that he not seek the identity of his father until he reached the certain age, Georges has worn an unopened pouch around his neck containing his father's portrait. Now the mortally wounded Alfred admits that Georges is not only his slave but his son as well. Revealing the extent of his grief but also staying true to his original vow, Georges commits suicide. Whereas Gayarré or Cable would compel the death of the man of color in order to allow the white Creole to begin anew with a clean slate, Séjour's tale of birthright forces the demise of all involved. However, recalling the maroons, their appeal to *Afrique* still circulating in the forest, Séjour's mid-nineteenth-century reader would undoubtedly look past the intimate carnage of the family drama toward the ultimate collective revenge of the Haitian Revolution.[160]

From the perspective of liberal politics in the Parisian metropole, Séjour's identification with the progressive legacies of the French Revolution, his attempts to cast the Napoleonic period in the most republican light possible, and his interest in Haiti as the cradle of black freedom placed him in the company of such acquaintances of his as Cyrille Bissette and the Romantic writer-politician Alphonse de Lamartine, Victor Hugo, and Alexandre Dumas, each of whom New Orleans Creoles of color claimed as inspiration.[161] Influenced by his participation in various salons frequented by these revolutionaries and by the trans-American network facilitated by Bissette, Séjour's artistic and social sensibility countered the isolation of his exile with the community of those who respected the moral status of the exilic condition.[162]

From the perspective of the *Cenelles* poets located in the alternative metropole of New Orleans, Séjour's fame and influence placed him in the vanguard of a network of French and francophone radicals, many of whom made their way to the faubourgs of the Creole city after the backlash against the radical upsurge of the Revolution of 1848. In the Creole faubourgs of New Orleans, they often collaborated with Creoles of color in spite of state and local laws prohibiting the transgression of lines separating racial and status groups.[163] Indeed, *Les Cenelles* owes its publication in part to an interracial collaboration of this sort. The radical republican newspaper *la Tribune de la Nouvelle Orleans* was the fruit of one of these collaborations in the Reconstruction period. Thus, the public culture of the Creole faubourgs, experienced as intimate and insular in the context of an Americanizing city, maintained its resistant quality in large part due to the infusion of people and ideas from Europe and the Caribbean. Somewhat paradoxically, these insular and intimate spaces thrived because of their more cosmopolitan aspects. Thus, *gens de couleur* did not necessarily have to leave home to reap the benefits of exile. The Creole faubourgs constituted rich sites of cultural exchange and continual renewal from without.

Bringing circum-Atlantic traditions and formulations to bear on the local needs of New Orleans' residents, a dissident religious culture—encompassing such practices as spiritualism and voodoo—paralleled and often clashed with official Catholicism, even that of the city's considerably more progressive francophone parishes.[164] Operating through mediums—persons with demonstrated expertise in channeling the thoughts and voices of the dead—spiritualist religious practices resonated within the predicament of exile and facilitated communication across boundaries of all kinds. A religion often attributed in the United States to the awakenings of the Fox sisters, two white farm girls living in upstate New York, spiritualism—with Anglo-American adherents ranging from William Lloyd Garrison to Abraham Lincoln—had dual origins in European utopian thought and African syncretic religions practiced among the enslaved population of the

French Caribbean.[165] Its emergence during the 1840s among European émigrés and *gens de couleur libre* in New Orleans brought it, in a sense, back to these roots, and Creoles of color served as some of the most sought-after mediums in the city. Meeting in interracial circles in private homes, spiritualists channeled Biblical figures, various saints, and French and Haitian revolutionary leaders and conveyed values of equality and universal brotherhood. In his small apartment and blacksmith shop on Toulouse Street on the edges of Tremé, the Creole of color healing medium Valmour administered to those suffering from a range of diseases and ailments throughout the sickly decade of the 1850s. He gained such a reputation that the French émigré and mesmerist Joseph Barthet appealed to Valmour for advice in his own practice and subsequently likened him to Jesus Christ.[166] Widespread interracial support bolstered his reputation for years, until in 1858 authorities forced Valmour underground, accusing him of "monkeyshines" and practicing the voodoo arts of "gris-gris."[167]

As this assessment demonstrates, the resemblance of the popular Valmour's techniques to more explicitly African practices distressed public officials. The nineteenth-century careers of a number of enormously influential voodoo practitioners—most famously the mother and daughter both named Marie Laveau—demonstrated how this Haitian syncretism of western African religious practices and Catholicism permeated the cultural, social, and political life of New Orleans. In times of private and public crisis, many New Orleanians sought the expertise of Laveau and others when their more traditional resources failed them. During the 1853 yellow fever epidemic, Laveau the elder gained a reputation as an effective healer. She also made the rounds of parish prisons, administering especially to those men condemned to execution. In an especially dramatic display of her influence, Laveau reputedly intervened during the public execution of two prisoners. At the solemn ceremony fittingly conducted at the rear of Congo Square, a lightening bolt interrupted the process and prematurely snapped the ropes from which the men dangled.[168]

Awed by the supernatural dimension of voodoo, white New Orleanians also worried about the implications of voodoo for their claims to racial purity. At home in the *vieux carré* and beyond Tremé along the banks of Bayou St. John, both the mother and daughter Laveau officiated over interracial voodoo ceremonies where people of all descriptions mingled indiscriminately. Characterizing a typical voodoo ceremony as a veritable "interracial orgy," a *New Orleans Times* reporter fretted in 1872 about "The sudden entrance of a hoydenish flaxen-haired white girl, who whirled around the room in the arms of a negro blacker than the ace of spades. . . . There could be no mistake about it. Set adrift on the rapids of depravity in real earnest, she had reached the center of the vortex."[169] Furthermore, voodoo practitioners, many of whom worked as cooks, domestics, or—like both Marie Laveaus—hairdressers in white homes, might potentially publicize the secrets of white society to the broader community of color. As a twentieth-century folklorist mused, "All the family skeletons must have come out to dance for Marie [Laveau]," thus placing her, in many respects, above the law.[170] Unlike Valmour, who apparently refused donations for his spiritual assistance, the younger Laveau successfully marketed voodoo to locals and tourists clamoring for a taste of the exotic, and in the process she amassed economic wealth to complement her cultural and political capital. Both women confounded the press of their day; in 1874, the younger Laveau led a curious press corps on a futile search for her famed St. John's Eve ceremony on Bayou St. John. They also continue to elude historians and folklorists who must confess the difficulty of distinguishing between the mother and daughter.[171]

In their religious and cultural practice, Valmour, Laveau, and others used their experiences as displaced New World Africans to shape the spiritual terrain and leverage power within the neighborhoods of New Orleans, thereby transforming their local setting with knowledge from elsewhere.[172] When Rodolphe Desdunes remembered the effects of the chastening political and social atmosphere on the New Orleans population of color, he remarked, "There are moments in the life of a people who suffer when it is good for them to change their climate."[173] Reflecting particularly on the expatriation of Creoles of color en masse in the 1840s and 1850s and his own father's role as an immigration agent for Haitian emperor Faustin I, Desdunes had in mind the promise that physical migrations held for an oppressed people. However, as the literary culture of the *Cenelles* poets, the religious culture of spiritualism and voodoo, and the proprietary culture of the Creole of color landlords demonstrated, one need not leave in order to "change [one's] climate." The spirit of exile could be nurtured from within as well as from without. That is, those who left could maintain imaginary and real ties to New Orleans, and those who stayed could draw on connections to other places to fight for their own conceptions of freedom and equality.

Composed and published in Bordeaux, Camille Thierry's final volume of poetry, *Les Vagabondes* (1874), demonstrates the paradox of exile and belonging. *Les Vagabondes* seems to be a symbolic preparation for death in a foreign land, an extended apology for having strayed so far from home, and a lament over this displacement. Thierry's literary pose as an abandoned and disinherited heir to birthright in New Orleans paralleled anxieties about the decline of his New Orleans estate, the value of which helped him maintain a level of comfort in exile. In the early 1870s, just as Thierry was composing the volume and readying it for publication, the value of his New Orleans property diminished significantly. In a final visit to New Orleans to strip his friend and broker Sidney Thezan of authority, Thierry attempted to forestall the postwar financial decline experienced by so many New Orleanians.[174] Yoking together the poems he had written thirty years earlier for Lanusse's anthology and new poems apparently written during these last years in Bordeaux, Thierry claimed with his poetry what was increasingly difficult to demonstrate with his property: that he was indeed a Creole of New Orleans.

Particularly provocative in creating the space of New Orleans and other locales, the new poems continued to demonstrate the viability of seemingly lost lives and stories for the exilic political sensibility.[175] Thierry humanized marginal figures who would appear as grotesques in the work of Gayarré, for example. In "Mariquita la Calentura," Thierry revises our appraisal of a character who also appears in Gayarré's *Fernando de Lemos.* For Gayarré, Mariquita is wholly "other," a withered character who curses the fate of the privileged boys of antebellum New Orleans, a madwoman remembered by readers of the novel not as a Castilian woman but as a "half-crazed negress."[176] Alternatively, Thierry's character Mariquita haunts the cityscape, inspiring sympathy from the narrator: "Poor, poor Mariquita! . . . / What have you done to me, old woman? / Have you thrust in my soul / All the sadness of the future?"[177] Thierry the vagabond and Mariquita the ghost occupy space in socially transgressive ways. Extending past injustice well into the future, the timeless sense of haunting practiced by both allows them to retain potency in their mobility. The ghost of the old woman and Thierry's memories of New Orleans cross seemingly secure boundaries—between life and death, between France and the United States, and between past and future. These thoughts, "thrust into my soul," even violate the boundary of Thierry's body, collapsing temporal distance and internalizing geographical space. Temporality, public and private property, and bodily integrity all lose their sanctity when apparitions are on the loose.

Infusing his collection with such spatial irreverence, Thierry forges an expanded global sensibility, thus strengthening the claims of New Orleans' particular "forgotten people." The poems in his collection visit a range of sites throughout the francophone diaspora, drawing together a disparate cast of suffering characters and peoples in common cause. In its pages, the "regrets of an old mulatresse," reduced to the status of a beggar after being forced by circumstances and age to leave San Domingue and her white paramour, find a historical parallel in the story of Diane de Poitiers, the powerful mistress of King Henri II, relegated after his death to a life of isolation by Catherine de Medici, his legitimate wife. In the politically trenchant poem "Abd-el-Kader," Thierry recounts the resistance of the Berber leader El-Kader to the 1830 French invasion of Algeria, thus adding to an eclectic if contradictory pantheon of heroes that included Napoleon I and Toussaint l'Ouverture. Thierry imagines the resolve of El-Kader, this "*brun capitane*," in his forced exile to Morocco. "And there, exhausted yet sublime / to search his intimate thoughts / for some new, superhuman plan / for tomorrow's battle."[178]

Thierry's attempts to mobilize his vagabondage and to rescue his own legacy of property in New Orleans were ultimately in vain. Thezan's firm went bankrupt before Thierry could safeguard himself, and in 1874 Thierry died in Bordeaux, nearly destitute. However, the problem of exile and return that he addresses in his poetry underscores the creative detours taken by the Dumas family. In "La Chanson de l'Exilé (Song of the Exiled)," Thierry writes "Exile, my friend, I fear it, / But must I stay here? . . . No!" Initially conceived as a flight from a particular place, Thierry's ideal exile continues as a flight from general stagnation in the speaker's renunciation of fear—"Courage! There is another river."[179] Thus, the exile establishes from somewhere the legitimate authority to stake a former claim.[180]

Evident in their continued ownership of Louisiana property and their maintenance of friendships on both sides of the Atlantic, the particular flexibility of the Dumas family's exile became most apparent during and after the Civil War, when the family attempted to parley its financial wealth into moral capital and political power in Republican Louisiana. To secure this property, Joseph Dumas made a rare trip to New Orleans in 1863–64 to take an oath of U.S. citizenship, a step that denied Confederate claims to national status and that may have prevented the seizure of his real estate by federal forces.[181] Francis E. Dumas, the son of Joseph Dumas, operated in the context of the Civil War and Reconstruction as a "*brun capitaine,*" an Abd-el-Kader of New Orleans' Creoles of color. Commissioned by Union general Benjamin F. Butler as a captain in the Second Regiment of the Louisiana Native Guards, Francis Dumas ultimately freed his slaves and organized them into a company under this regiment. His prowess as a soldier eventually led to his promotion to the rank of major. Playing a prominent role in a battle at Ship Island, Mississippi, Dumas and three other officers earned special commendation as officers who were "constantly in the thickest of the fight, and by their unflinching bravery and admirable handling of their commands . . . reflected great honor upon the flag under and for which they so nobly struggled."[182] Dumas's prominence continued into the Reconstruction era, when he ran for governor of Louisiana in 1868, losing by two votes on the second ballot to moderate Republican Henry C. Warmoth.

We might better understand the Reconstruction-era political significance of Creoles of color by pairing the active presence of Francis Dumas during Reconstruction with the fate of François Lacroix's martyred son, Victor Lacroix. Shortly after his death in the riot of 1866, Victor Lacroix was summoned from the grave during a spiritualist séance. Through the Creole of color medium Henry Rey, Victor encouraged the religious radicals to press forward in their commitment to the goal of universal manhood suffrage.[183] Both Francis Dumas and Victor Lacroix used radical politics during the Civil War and Reconstruction as points of entry from which to claim their rights to New Orleans and their status as citizens of the United States. Thus, they seemed to answer their fathers' anxieties over the status of Creole of color birthright. By sacrificing an estate and relocating to Paris, the elders Lacroix and Dumas paved the way for their sons' attempts to bring their francophone legacies to bear on the shaping of a newly reconciled U.S. identity.

I PAUSE HERE WITH A consideration of the predicament of Maria Cecilia Lacroix, François Lacroix's granddaughter via the "marriage" of Victor Lacroix and Sarah Brown. Over the years following Lacroix's death, Sarah Brown Lacroix relentlessly petitioned his succession to recognize the claims of Maria Cecilia to the estate of her grandfather. Because her white mother embraced the Lacroix legacy, Maria Cecilia eventually became arbiter of her grandfather's estate. Even so, she seems to have lived as a white woman throughout her life.[184] As executor, she inherited frequent legal proceedings that were finally—albeit incompletely—settled in 1912. She stood by almost helplessly as Lacroix's determination to will legitimacy and respectability to race and property relationships devolved in the legacy of his own real estate. In an ironic turn of affairs, the city bought a vast portion of Lacroix's estate cheaply, making it a prime location for the development of New Orleans' most infamous red light district, Storyville.[185] In the late nineteenth and early twentieth centuries, the brothels of Storyville institutionalized extralegal interracial liaisons by providing tourists and local white men a convenient way to indulge in interracial sex. The creation of Storyville also quarantined the moral consequences of this practice to a well-delineated section of town.[186] The city continued and contained the tradition of *plaçage* by accessing a portion of the former property of François Lacroix. The creation of Storyville represents the late-nineteenth-century culmination of efforts to manage the almost two-hundred-year-old legacy of interracial liaisons and the moral and proprietary anxieties associated with their existence and propagation.

4

Establishing Propriety in the City of Sin

MADAME DELPHINE, a *femme de couleur libre* well past her prime, had come to visit Père Jerome, the priest of the church she had recently begun to attend. Having sensed the priest's sympathy for the women of her class and their white paramours, she sought advice about her daughter, who "was just passing seventeen" and was suspended in a very temporary limbo between maidenhood and womanhood. Madame Delphine wanted desperately to find a suitable "guardian" for her daughter, thus insuring the girl's respectability. She was aware that her daughter was ripe for *plaçage*, the extralegal but institutionalized sexual liaison of a white man and a free woman of color. To temper the moral, financial, and emotional uncertainties of such a prospect, Madame Delphine enlisted the priest in her campaign for the moral and spiritual status of her daughter, the child of her own *plaçage*.

While delivering his morning sermon, Père Jerome had already noticed the two women. Madame Delphine, a woman of "dark and faded" features sat beside another "in better dress, seemingly a girl in her teens, though her face and neck were scrupulously concealed by a heavy veil, and her hands, which were small, by gloves."[1] To Père Jerome, the odd pair elicited a range of anxieties. The image of a young veiled woman in a church called to mind a marriage ceremony, but the veil was as heavy and impenetrable as a funeral or death shroud. The girl presented a "beautiful figure" but withheld the full impact of her beauty from strangers: "the slight effort of Père Jerome's kind eyes to see through the veil was in vain."[2] Her face and hands covered, the girl refused access to those wishing to inspect her features for racial markers. In declining to submit herself to the gaze of potential suitors and the machinery of racial classification, she confounded the efforts of New Orleanians who would insist on a central mandate of Americanization linking racial purity and social propriety. Enlisting a spatial metaphor to describe the terms of her exclusion and to suggest further the conspicuous marginality of those engaged in *plaçage*, Père Jerome summed up the "dilemma" of the girl with potentially white skin and "black blood": "She has no more *place* than if she had dropped upon a strange planet."[3] At their conference, the priest and the mother admitted their conundrum: now they "don't know what to do with her."

The three figures—Madame Delphine, her pubescent daughter, and the priest—form a conspiratorial trinity at the heart of George Washington Cable's 1879 short story "Madame Delphine," a tale of the quest for racial purity and cultural legacy. Cable attached these pressing concerns over the terms of legitimacy and proprietorship to the actions and strategies of Creole of color women. By adding the dimension of priestly advice, he asked his reader to ponder the implications of *plaçage* for the sexual and moral purity of Creole of color women and by extension for social propriety more broadly understood. The plight of women of color threatened to spill over the boundaries of their own race and gender and compromise the moral standards and social institutions of the citizenry at large. Indeed, the unseen face of the girl forms a kind of narrative center for Cable's story. Maintaining anonymity in masquerade, she could potentially be anyone.[4] Aptly named Olive, she teetered on a dangerous precipice of racial and moral indeterminacy, a cipher for anxieties over cultural and racial propagation and legitimate proprietorship.

On an individual level, her mere existence as a mixed-race, near-white woman raised the possibility of her passing as white. The ambiguity of her racial status further exposed the failures of paternal obligation. Thus, in Cable's story, the mother and the priest must conspire for Olive's protection in the absence of a father figure. As a potential *placée*, Olive threatened to reproduce her social proscription and compromised moral position in the lives of her future children, especially troubling the prospects of any daughter she might have. Addressing the plight of the near-white woman in the context of Americanization threatened as well to reveal as chimerical the racial and proprietary claims of white families—or, more accurately, families that hoped to demonstrate and maintain a white status. If a white "husband" were under the contractual "obligations" of *plaçage* as well as those of marriage to a legitimate white wife, which bonds would he honor with his love and affection and with the legacy of his property and his name? Even if the question of legitimacy were settled in the legal sense, might the "placed" woman and her family of color exact a moral and emotional claim on the property and sentiments of the "husband"?

Destabilizing the racial and financial status of whiteness, the shadow of *plaçage* also troubled Creole of color aspirations to an uncomplicated proprietorship and secure moral legacy. As sexual partners and daughters, *femmes de couleur* often received donations of real estate and other property from white paramours and fathers despite increasing restrictions against such conveyances. These gifts often functioned as seed capital for more extensive participation in the real estate market and other business ventures, and Creole of color women acquired and managed property on a scale approximating that of Creole of color men such as François Lacroix and Camille Thierry.[5] However, the moral unease and social insecurity associated with *plaçage* threatened to compromise their ownership claims and those of Creoles of color more generally. The practice of *plaçage* and the property issuing from it dramatized the extent to which legacies of sexual propriety competed with the more tangible but perhaps less enduring legacies of real estate. In other words, when Creoles of color reached for immortality by exercising their aspirations to ownership and securing their right to belong, they encountered the limitations that reputations of immorality and illegitimacy would exact on these claims.

Difficult to address in the most stable legal circumstances, these concerns over race, gender, and property took an especially complex form in antebellum Louisiana. Then, as now, Louisiana was a "mixed jurisdiction," combining aspects of civil law deriving from the Napoleonic Code and Anglo-American common law.[6] During the first decades of the nineteenth century, legislators, judges, and other legal advocates labored to develop a civil code that might reconcile the lingering vestiges of French and Spanish colonial practice with the territory's new U.S. affiliation. Especially pertinent to our consideration of the property of free women of color, the Louisiana Civil Code evolved so that the terms of inheritance overwhelmingly favored white families. Particularly instrumental in shaping family law, the Civil Code of 1825 explicitly denied interracial couples the means by which they might legitimize their unions and refused a child of color the right to claim a white father. Suspended between "legitimate" and "illegitimate," the status of "natural" son or daughter was the most secure position that children of these unions could hope to occupy, a father's formal legal recognition by notarized act being the only means to that end. New stipulations of the code prevented white fathers, even those who had acknowledged their paternity, from bequeathing their property to their "wives" and children of color either while living or after death and, moreover, required them to will the bulk of their property to their legitimate heirs, both consanguineous and collateral.[7]

The changing legal landscape placed the property of women of color—especially those who had been *placées*—under considerable suspicion. Cable's "Madame Delphine" does more, ultimately, than raise the question of the place of the mixed-race woman in New Orleans' social life, the problem of not knowing "what to do with her." It addresses the problem of the property of women of color as well. At the end of Cable's story, Olive has seemingly avoided the stigma and legal challenges of *plaçage*. Sacrificing her maternal role and privileges, Madame Delphine has suddenly produced extensive (and fraudulent) documentation "proving" Olive's white status, thus rendering her eligible for legitimate marriage to the white husband of her choice. However, Cable's story is not a fairy tale that ends happily ever after, and his narrative choices speak to his difficulty in envisioning a morally and culturally edifying New Orleans. Like other of Cable's Creole of color characters who can not bear the weight of their social predicament, Madame Delphine is so stricken with grief after her daughter's wedding that she dies in Père Jerome's arms in the midst of confessing her charade.

Cable began the story by directing an ambling visitor toward a certain piece of architecture, "a small, low, brick house of a story and a half, set out upon the sidewalk, as weather-beaten and mute as an aged beggar fallen asleep."[8] Taking place long after the main events of the story, the initial scene calls attention to the fact that the dilapidated house "is in'abit; 'tis live in" by generations of quadroon women, perhaps even by Olive and her descendants.[9] The sad condition of the dwelling described by Cable suggests the moral compromises made by those practicing *plaçage*, but it also points to the dogged permanence of these social relationships despite decades of codification and legislation meant to undermine them.

Literary and historiographical battles over the reputations of Creole of color women echoed characterizations of their moral, legal, and proprietary status offered by the civil courts. In the decades leading up to the Civil War, the significant real estate holdings of Creole of color women acted as a focal point for fears and concerns over legitimacy and legacy, and a number of high-profile cases, legal assaults on the ownership claims of *femmes de couleur libre*, served to crystallize these anxieties. In spite of efforts to disinherit them, women of color managed to secure property and shape tangible and moral legacies. Their struggles provoked unsettling confrontations over the nature of their belonging and raised questions about the gendered dimensions of birthright. For example, what was the status of women's legacies, especially if they called to mind the context of *plaçage?* Under what circumstances could a woman claim an heir's status to legacies of property and morality, and how in turn might she bequeath these to her own heirs? How did the moral status of *plaçage* function to maintain the property of whites and malign the property of nonwhites? Debated in literary, historiographical, and legal terms, these questions and the responses they elicited revealed the complexity of passing on reputations of propriety and legacies of property to and for Creole of color women.

Our Men and Our History, Our People and Our Story

A review of Creole of color histories shows that the mixed-race Creole woman (often perceived and portrayed as "beautiful") presents a problem similar to the dilemma of Olive. Like Cable and his characters Madame Delphine and Père Jerome, historians do not seem to "know what to do with her." For most cultural and racial groups in the United States, claims to national legacy have required a rigidly gendered historical script of male public action and prominence on the one hand and female domestic propriety and moral duty to children and the less fortunate on the other.[10] Historians have evaluated the actions and cultural production of Creoles of color with these models in mind. The

English-language version of Rodolphe Desdunes's community memoir *Nos Hommes et Notre Histoire* (1911) is renowned among researchers by its more inclusive translation as *Our People and Our History.* However, the more literal and masculine translation as *Our Men and Our History* more aptly captures the tenor of the historical representation of Creoles of color.

Continually resurfacing in subsequent histories, the men who represented for Desdunes the pinnacle of Creole of color achievement spanned the disciplinary and professional categories. Desdunes introduced Armand Lanusse, poet and schoolmaster; Norbert Rillieux, scientific genius and Eli Whitney of the sugar industry; Paul Trévigne, teacher and editor; Eugène Warbourg, internationally known sculptor; Joseph Abeilard, skilled but unappreciated architect; Oscar Guimbillote, conscientious physician; Basile Crokère, real estate developer and fencing master; Edmond Dédé, distinguished pianist; and François Lacroix, Thomy Lafon, and Aristide Mary, property owners and generous philanthropists. In the decades since, historians have echoed and expanded on Desdunes's list of illustrious Creole of color men, whether or not they have chosen to accentuate the francophone aspect of Creole culture.[11] What usually passes as Creole of color history is nothing less than a litany of male excellence and thus makes the case that the group deserves a place in a national or revolutionary narrative.[12]

When women make an appearance in histories of the antebellum *gens de couleur libre* and their descendents, two women figure most predictably and most prominently—Henriette Delille, the "foundress" of the Catholic order the Sisters of the Holy Family, and Madame Bernard Couvent, the philanthropist whose will bequeathed the money and buildings for the Société Catholique pour l'Instruction des Orpheleins dans l'Indigence. Segregating their stories, Desdunes reserves one of his twelve chapters for a discussion of the "Creole woman of color," and Delille and Couvent are especially prominent. Taking the defensive, Desdunes opens with a caveat designed to rescue the "fairer sex" from rumor and hearsay. "Most of the Creole women," he explains, "were exemplars of piety and charity." For him, the genre of history takes on the role of a civil court, separating fact from fiction and forever clearing the names of slandered parties. "If there are minds today so vile as to try to blemish the memory of these noble women, seeking to lower them to the level of the brute, we will appeal the matter to the tribunal of history, which at all times and in all countries has vindicated the innocent." Entering his testimony on behalf of their piety and charity, he claims "The Creole woman was as chaste and as pure in her hovel as was her more fortunate sister living in the midst of luxury."[13]

Foregrounding Delille and Couvent as exemplary Creole of color women allows Desdunes to reject *plaçage* and to emphasize instead the contribution of Creole of color women to education and service to the poor, public roles deemed particularly acceptable for women in the nineteenth century.[14] Desdunes's two values of piety and charity merged in the activities of these two women, especially in Delille, who explicitly circumvented her family's and her community's expectations that she become *placée*. Born to a relatively wealthy Creole of color family in 1813, Delille imbibed French literature and culture early on, demonstrating her ability to entertain a future suitor with elegant music and sophisticated conversation. However, instead of following her sister Cecilia into a liaison with a wealthy white man, Delille began to take "instructions in faith and morals" with the French nun Jeanne D'Aliquot. Moreover, Delille actively campaigned against the institution of *plaçage*, condemning it as demoralizing and degrading. Within the shelter of the school and convent on Tremé's St. Claude Street, Delille served as godmother to a number of free women of color, officiating at their baptisms jointly with the French priest Father Etienne Rousselon. The collaboration of the white priest and the devout woman of color performed, in a sense, the inverse of *plaçage*. These efforts complemented Delille's public work among the poor people of color and the enslaved, especially notable efforts in light of the fact that other members of her family had passed for white. Delille's resistance against *plaçage* and the prejudice of her caste has earned her a place for posterity among Creole of color "revolutionaries," prompting late-twentieth-century efforts to canonize her as a saint.[15] Despite Delille's pious acts, religious authorities in the nineteenth century continued to find it difficult to perceive of women of color as "real" nuns and barred them from wearing the officially recognized habit and veil. When a young novice, Sister Marie, presented herself thusly veiled before Archbishop Napoléon Perché in 1872, he drove her from the room, demanding "Go take that off! Who do you think you are? You are too proud, too proud! That dress is not for you! Go take it off *at once!*"[16]

While Delille serves as Desdunes's ultimate model of piety, Madame Bernard Couvent exemplified charity. Specifically, Couvent provided a foundation for the development and enrichment of the Creole of color community. In providing the resources and inspiration for the Institute des Orpheleins, Couvent sought to relieve the plight of underprivileged and orphaned children.[17] In the process, she also provided an academic refuge for wealthier Creoles of color in the Marigny neighborhood and throughout the Creole faubourgs, creating a structure for generations of Creole of color teachers, writers, and intellectuals. The first accounts of Madame Couvent's charitable gift had more to say about her legacy than about Couvent herself, lending Desdunes's attempt to write her into a Creole of color history a retroactive cast.[18] "It is believed she was born in Africa," Desdunes writes of Madame Couvent, explaining why she lacked a presence in the cultural memory of "his people" during his day, especially since others left tangible traces of their lives in a good family's "copybooks" or a network of descendants and relatives. "We have very little information about Madame Couvent. People often spoke of this aged lady. They extolled her piety and her charity, but nothing is known of her birth."[19] He also hints at the prevalence of class elitism among wealthy free people of color who might have considered her priority of educating poor orphans to be a "genuine reproach."[20] Because of increasing constraints against free colored education in the years preceding the Civil War, Couvent's school, a haven for distinguished Creoles of color, had an enormously important function. The list of teachers, benefactors, and directors of the school includes Armand Lanusse, compiler of *Les Cenelles;* Paul Trévigne, coeditor of *l'Union* and the *Tribune;* François Lacroix, real estate broker and tailor; Thomy Lafon and Aristide Mary, wealthy philanthropists; and ultimately Rodolphe Desdunes himself.[21] Thus, Couvent created the entire context for a Creole of color educated elite.

By the time of Desdunes's writing, decades of travelers had commented on the physical beauty, sexual desirability, and perceived availability of New Orleans' mixed-race women. With New Orleans' official red-light district of Storyville in its heyday in the early twentieth century, many famous bawdy houses organized prostitution around racial variations, promising locals and conventioneers alike the fantasy of an interracial liaison. In a 1906 edition of *The Sunday Sun*, a periodical devoted to Storyville news—what one chronicler has called a "cynical blackmail sheet of the lowest kind"—Lulu White, the "Queen of Diamonds" and proprietress of the famous Mahogany Hall, boasted of being "surrounded by the finest and prettiest lot of octoroon beauties to be found in the country."[22] Desdunes countered this association of mixed-race women with sex and sin with a litany of their industry, religious service, and selfless dedication to social welfare, thus setting in motion a historical narrative that confronted prevailing assessments of the moral status of Creole of color women.

In spite of Desdunes's efforts, though, the reputations of Creole of color women continued to suffer at the hands of historians of Louisiana well into the twentieth century. Joseph G. Tregle, Jr., excluded women such as Delille and Couvent from his important 1952 article reappraising the myths of "early New Orleans society" and emphasized the practice of prostitution among "free Negro women": "Those of the women favored by nature set themselves up in bordellos all over the city, even in the most respectable neighborhoods, or roamed the streets in open pursuit of trade."[23] In Tregle's view, *plaçage* carried an undeserved aura in the historical mythology of the city: "tradition notwithstanding, there is little evidence to suggest that these most handsome of the Negro population were anything far removed from their less striking prostitute sisters." Concurring with the testimony of "an irate New Orleans housewife" in an 1825 issue of *Niles Weekly Register*, Tregle portrays the "quadroon" as "heaven's last worst gift to white men."[24]

Concerned chiefly with piety and charity or a lack thereof, these historical accounts of Creole of color women have tended to bestow on them the hefty burden of upholding the "good names" of all New Orleanians, white and of color alike. However, the histories do not provide a sense of the various dimensions of this burden, thus compelling us to turn to elsewhere if we are to begin to understand the contradictory impulses and the high stakes involved in representing (and being) Creole of color women.[25] Images of Creole of color feminine piety are quickly chased down by legacies of their sexual impropriety. As Monique Guillory has shown, these competing ascriptions continually surface in the palimpsest of the city's built environment. For example, after their incorporation, Delille's Sisters of the Holy Family relocated to Orleans Street in the *vieux carré*, occupying a building made infamous as the former site of a number of quadroon balls. In the Orleans ballroom, Creole of color women had entertained white men of high social standing and curious visitors such as Bernhard, Duke of Saxe-Weimar-Eisenach, who in 1826 registered an ambivalent response to the quadroon balls. Finding that "the colored ladies . . . conducted themselves with much propriety and modesty," he nevertheless "did not remain long there that I might not utterly destroy my standing in New Orleans."[26] In this space, the nuns labored to create an atmosphere of sanctity in the face of the inheritance of sin and notoriety attached to their location and the women of their caste who formerly frequented it.[27]

The conflicted picture of Creole of color femininity parallels and draws on the multivalent image of the "tragic mulatta" figure in literature. Like this more general incarnation of hybrid racial identity, Creole of color women characters have often served to delimit hard and fast racial and moral categories, and they seem tragic because they are trapped between them. Some authors have situated the tragic mulatta at the regrettable but inevitable culmination of overwhelming historical, biological, and natural forces. Alternatively, others have placed her at the vanguard of destabilizing emancipative processes. In either case, she is a powerful stereotype; the emotions attached to and elicited by her presence are never neutral.[28] In a wide array of fictional representations, the mixed-race woman finds herself in a delicate situation, caught in an odd balance between public censure of and public attraction to her existence. In effect, she comes to embody the contradictions of social codes that dually shun and facilitate interracial sexual relationships, and she must find ways to manage and manipulate anxieties of race, gender, and property before she and her whole lineage succumb to them.

Whatever we may think of the melodramatic fate of Cable's Madame Delphine, who breathes her last breath in the platonic embrace of a kind priest, the urgency driving her conspiracy for Olive's whiteness attests to how difficult it has been for Creole of color women to preserve their moral and proprietary status. Her sense of desperation also attests to the limited resources at their disposal. In writing "Madame Delphine," Cable revised an earlier attempt to depict the ethical dimensions of the *femme de couleur*'s plight. In his story "'Tite Poulette," Madame John, the character analogous to Madame Delphine, allows the wedding of her "daughter" to a white man to proceed by producing "real" (instead of manufactured) evidence of the girl's whiteness. "Take her! She is thine!" Madame John interjects as the two lovers bemoan the forbidden nature of their love. "I have robbed God long enough. Here are the sworn papers—here! Take her; she is as white as snow—so! . . . I never had a child—she is the Spaniard's daughter!" This abrupt ending elicited criticism from an anonymous Creole of color woman who read the tale in its serialized form and chided Cable, "The ending is not the truest truth . . . If you have a whole heart for the cruel case of us poor quadroons, change the story, even yet, tell the inmost truth of it. Madame John lied. The girl was her own daughter; but like many and many a real quadroon mother, as you surely know, Madame John perjured her own soul to win for their child a legal and honorable alliance with the love-mate and life-mate of her choice."[29] Thus, in "Madame Delphine" Cable grounds Delphine's private and internal suffering in unjust laws and social conventions and, in an effort to get at the "truest truth," depicts the grief of the mother as the price exacted by caste restrictions.

In fictional accounts, *femme de couleur* characters display a predictable set of physical characteristics: "alabaster" skin, dark eyes, a slight wave in the hair, or a "bluish tinge in the half moon" of the fingernails.[30] Like those of the mixed-race tragic mulatta, the features of Creole of color woman often register as "beautiful." Following Sterling Brown, we might understand an accentuation of the "beauty" of near-white characters of color as a form of "race flattery," descriptions affirming the self-perceptions of white writers and readers.[31] We might also consider the appearance of these female characters in light of the long-standing challenges "beauty" has posed in Western thought. Thinkers as diverse as Plato and Dante have described the apprehension of the beautiful as an experience that overwhelms the visual sense, arresting other sensory processes. Transfixed by a beautiful object or person, one might be more easily led to an apprehension of the divine. On the other hand, under the spell of beauty, one might veer too far from the path of morality. Among enlightenment thinkers such as Edmund Burke and Immanuel Kant, a pervasive response to beauty's perceived power to undercut rationality has been to distinguish between the sublime and the merely beautiful, whereby beautiful things would pale in comparison to those eliciting the more profound, metaphysical, and ultimately moral experience of the sublime.[32] Considered in this light, the beauty of Creole of color women characters threatens to disarm the judgment of readers and beholders, pushing them outside their social and cultural comfort zones and leaving them ashamed, grasping for satisfactory justifications for their distracting desires. Troubled by the prevalence of concubinage of *femmes de couleur* by white men, Spanish colonial governor Esteban Miró articulated one response to the perceived problem of mixed-race feminine beauty, attacking the problem at what he thought to be its root: Miró issued a declaration ordering free women of color to cover their reputedly alluring and overabundant heads of hair with turbans or, in local parlance, *tignons.*[33]

It is no surprise, then, that contemporaries and historians have been circumspect about attributions of beauty to Creole of color women and reluctant to frame their discussion of *femmes de couleur* with such a charged concept.[34] John Latrobe allowed the word *pretty* to suffice in his description of the waltzing techniques of the quadroons he observed while quadroon-ball hopping during his 1834 visit to New Orleans: "The dance to me is a detestable one . . . nothing would ever induce me to let a wife or daughter or sister of mine join in its mazes. It is pretty, in the same way that an indecent picture may be a pretty one to every sense but the moral one."[35] In the judgment of one mid-twentieth-century historian, the beauty of New Orleans' *femmes de couleur* had not attained the level of the sublime, which would have allowed their names to have been "engraved in bronze, inscribed on marble or immortalized in verse. In fact their fame ended in the grave. They were exhibited on a flimsy pedestal which crumbled with their fading youth."[36] Faced with such widespread criticism, Desdunes countered by relegating the physical beauty of the women below the level of their spiritual beauty: "The Creole woman knew how to study, to think, to pray. She was generous, helpful, and pious. Her virtue, her charity, and her devotedness could never be doubted. These virtues will always be her most beautiful ornaments."[37]

Nevertheless, literary portrayals of Creole of color women abound with descriptions of their beauty, in particular that of the fleeting, overripe, and doomed variety associated with tropical flora. Alexis de Tocqueville's traveling partner, Gustave de Beaumont, captured this quality when, upon seeing what he took to be a white woman seated in a colored balcony, he exclaimed "What? Colored? She is whiter than a lily."[38] In Lydia Maria Child's Reconstruction-era novel *Romance of the Republic* (1867), the garden district home of the two interracial sisters, Rosabella and Floracita, is so bedecked with bouquets and floral arrangements that a young visitor from Boston declares, " 'Flowers everywhere! Natural flowers, artificial flowers, painted flowers, embroidered flowers, and human flowers excelling them all,'—glancing at the young ladies as he spoke."[39] The floral metaphors continue in William Faulkner's *Absalom, Absalom!* (1936), whose Creole of color woman has "a face like a tragic magnolia."[40]

For a number of writers, the beauty of Creole of color women and her representation as near-white lead to progressive politics and precipitate a critique of socially prescribed hierarchies. For the abolitionist writer Lydia Maria Child, the plight of New Orleans' *femmes de couleur* radiates outward from the city across the country more generally to bolster a campaign against racial prejudice. In *An Appeal in Favor of That Class of Americans Called Africans* (1833), Child uses the specific case of the quadroon women of New Orleans—"much distinguished for personal beauty and gracefulness of motion"—to illustrate the injustice of a Massachusetts law prohibiting interracial marriage.[41] Linking the problem of race prejudice to that of slavery, she explores this theme more fully in her short story "The Quadroons," published in the Boston abolitionist journal *Liberty Bell* in 1842. Rosalie, the mixed-race daughter of a wealthy New Orleans merchant, "highly cultivated in mind and manners, graceful as an antelope, and beautiful as the evening star," falls in love with Edward, a young Georgian.[42] After contracting a "marriage sanctioned by Heaven, though unrecognized on earth," they move to Georgia, and Rosalie gives birth to their daughter, Xarifa.[43] In the sheltered atmosphere in which they raise her, "the rare loveliness of the child increased daily and was eventually ripening into the most marvelous beauty."[44]

Predictably, this Edenic domestic setting falls apart when Edward tires of Rosalie and legally marries a woman of his race and class, someone who complements his growing social and economic aspirations. Thus abandoned, Rosalie eventually dies broken-hearted. Despite her father's and a potential suitor's attempts to protect her, Xarifa falls victim to the "carelessness" of her maternal grandfather. Because he had failed to emancipate his daughter Rosalie, she and Xarifa had not been "free women of color" after all, but slaves. After the grandfather's death, Xarifa is auctioned off in the Savannah market, her exorbitant value of $5,000 attesting to her near-white beauty and her carefully cultivated tastes, talents, and sensibility. After tiring of "courting her" in a more traditional manner, her new master finally takes her by force. Driven insane, Xarifa dies, her "beautiful head fractured against the wall in a frenzy of despair." The extent of the carnage, Child assures us in typical Romantic fashion, is not hyperbole: "Reader, do you complain that I have written fiction? Believe me, scenes like these are of no infrequent occurrence at the South. The world does not afford such materials for tragic romance as the history of the Quadroons."[45]

New Orleanian Alice Dunbar-Nelson—wife of poet Paul Laurence Dunbar, a contemporary of Rodolphe Desdunes, and an accomplished historian and fictionist in her own right—foregoes the melodramatic death scene in her portrayals of the Creole of color woman's predicament. She only subtly hints at the African blood of her characters. For Dunbar-Nelson, the intensive sheltering required to safeguard the morality of New Orleans' *femmes de couleur* placed as stifling a limit on their identities and human urges as the institutions of *plaçage* or slavery did in Child's representations. In Dunbar-Nelson's short story "Sister Joespha," the character Camille—afflicted with such beauty that "even Father Ray lingered longer in his blessing when his hands pressed her silky black hair"—"took the white veil" at sixteen. In spite of her growing sense of confinement, she ultimately chooses to continue her life as Sister Josepha behind the "heavy door" of the convent. If she were to abscond down Chartres in the direction of Canal Street as she dreamed of doing, she would have "no name but Camille . . . no nationality, for she could never tell from whom or whence she came; no friends, and a beauty that not even an ungainly bonnet and shaven head could hide. In a flash, she realized the deception of the life she would lead, and the cruel self-torture of wonder at her own identity."[46] Likewise cloistered "in a great French house with a grim sleepy *tante* and no companions of [her] own age," Odalie, the title character of another of Dunbar-Nelson's short stories, loves the young *gallant* Pierre from afar, with no hope of making her love known and no understanding of the codes of flirtation that would allow him to flit among young "butterflies" as his whim dictated. Broken-hearted, Odalie requests of her prim protectors, an aunt and a judge, that they return her to the convent of her childhood education.[47] In her turn of the nineteenth-century context, the social and moral predicament of Creole of color women allowed Dunbar-Nelson to ponder the terms of women's sexual propriety more broadly and to portray legitimate, though socially vexing, feminine desires.[48]

Across decades, literary genres, and the political predilections of their creators, then, mixed-race woman characters have prompted anxiety over the shaky premises of racial categorization and the various moralities governing interracial desire.[49] They have also given rein to the specters of social and biological determinism within a national context seemingly predicated on individual determination and social mobility. In these stories, mixed-race women characters have been "raised" as carefully as livestock and "cultivated" as diligently as hothouse flowers to perform roles not of their own choosing. In *Marie* (1835), Gustave de Beaumont prefigures the title character's doom in his first description of her: "Her glance was melancholy and moving as a dream of love; yet one could see shining in her great dark eyes a flash of that ardent light of the Antilles; her brow would bend, weighted by an indefinable sadness. . . ."[50] Likewise, in "Un Mariage de Conscience" (1843), a short story by free man of color Armand Lanusse, a young and nameless mixed-race girl seems from the moment of her birth to have been racing headlong toward her death under the wheels of her former "husband's" carriage. Despite the strict moral upbringing provided by her aunt, the young girl, obliged by her mother, attends the quadroon balls, where she is seduced by Gustave, the "*empressé cavalier.*"[51] He soon tires of her and legitimately marries a white woman, bringing on the tragic death of the young girl of color. In "By the Bayou St. John," Dunbar-Nelson describes the languorous attenuation of the hopes and dreams of the mixed-race Creole woman, attributing it to the "eternal feminine." This manifestation of fate echoes the haunting beauty of the bayou itself: "The blossoms of orange and magnolia mingle their perfume with the earthy smell of a summer rain just blown over. Perfect in its stillness, absolute in its beauty."[52]

As readers, we think we know who this mixed-race character is and what she is fated to do. In literary accounts, the perfect stillness and absolute beauty of Creole of color women have anchored in their constancy the swirling passions and compromised actions of others. However, because she is what Karen Halttunen might call the ultimate "painted woman," there are limits to our knowledge of her and myriad ways in which she might defy cultural roles and rules.[53] Other prominent characterizations of *femmes de couleur* as independent, politically savvy, and proud press against and trouble these widespread portrayals of their pervasive and debilitating melancholia. In Cable's *Grandissimes*, the character Palmyre, "a woman of the quadroon caste, of superb stature and poise, severely handsome features, clear tawny skin and large, passionate black eyes," evokes the stereotype in her appearance.[54] Recalling the independence and power of the real-life voodoo queens Marie Laveau, Palmyre, once a slave cultivated to provide genteel service to plantation mistresses, became known as the "Philosophe" after receiving her freedom and was "noted for her taste and skill as a hairdresser, for the efficiency of her spells and the sagacity of her divinations."[55] Palmyre's characterization is more typical of mulatto male characters whose white blood tends to make them more intelligent and less submissive than their pure black half-brothers, and she elicits the fear and respect of white characters. She languishes from time to time on sickbeds, to be sure, but unlike Child's Rosalie, for example, she displays "mental acuteness, conversational adroitness, concealed cunning and noiseless but visible strength of will."[56] Palmyre pines for the white Honoré Grandissime, but her yearning does not incapacitate her. After working *gris-gris* against a prominent member of the Grandissime family late in the novel, she escapes his punishment and vanishes beyond the boundaries of polite society, resurfacing as the elusive Madame Inconnue, resident of Bordeaux, France.

In the *Mysteries of New Orleans* (1854–55), Baron Ludwig von Reizenstein's "urban mystery" serialized in a radical German-language newspaper of the city, the major mixed-race character, Lucy Wilson, is similarly resourceful and independent. The reader first encounters Lucy—the proprietress of the "Mulattoes Settlement," an outfit regularly holding quadroon balls—as a woman with a face of "dazzling whiteness." In her late teens, she is "of striking beauty and surprising height," her "raven black hair cover[ing] her shoulders with luxuriant fullness."[57] Something of a female *flâneur*, she donned the "complete man's outfit" of Emil, her equally striking German immigrant lover, and "left the house and passed down Orleans Street, a polished dandy."[58] As in other portrayals of *plaçage*, the passionate and stormy relationship between Emil and Lucy offsets the dutiful and temperate union of Emil and his legitimate white wife. However, in Reizenstein's account, the illicit interracial union is the more legitimate one. Indeed, Hiram, a mysterious and wandering freemason, prophesizes an imminent judgment on the city for its thorough investment in slavery: Lucy and Emil will bear a son, a "yellow savior," who will usher in from New Orleans "the rise of a new dawn that will break over the South of the United States."[59] In the wake of the yellow fever epidemic of 1853, Lucy gives birth to this savior; leaving him in the hands of a protector, she and Emil board the bark *Toussaint L'Ouverture* bound for Haiti. Similarly to Palmyre, Lucy slips away from New Orleans proper and beyond the margins of the text. As voodoo priestesses and as Madonnas of color, Palmyre, Lucy, and other uncontained and uncontainable mixed-race characters signal white anxiety over the instabilities of their own identities and the illicitness of their own desires. Thus, they point to the ongoing challenges women of color pose to social, racial, and moral order in the city and, by extension, the nation.

As these varied literary representations demonstrate, the practice of *plaçage* and the presence of mixed-race characters—or any such hint of interracial sex—thrust us into a complicated moral, legal, and cultural universe that demands a consideration of the multiple ways historical actors have made meaning of their lives. In *Nos Hommes et Notre Histoire*, Desdunes is interested, in one sense, in *histoire* as "history." However, the other translation of *histoire* is "story." Reading Desdunes's title as "Our People and Our Story" instead of "Our People and Our History" or "Our Men and Our History" allows us to limn the mutually reinforcing dialogue between reality and representation and between fact and fiction.[60]

Les Cenelles and Feminine Propriety

Let's turn once more to *Les Cenelles*, Armand Lanusse's 1845 compilation of Creole of color poetry. In chapter 3 we considered how the *Cenelles* poets imagined and reconfigured their sense of cultural belonging. They also used their art to manage the complexities of gender relationships among French-speaking *gens de couleur libre*. In particular, *Les Cenelles* provides a lens into the problems posed by *plaçage* and women's property to the moral and familial legacies of Creoles of color. Chided by literary critics both for the perceived aesthetic limitations of their work and for their reluctance to connect their artistic expression to the explicit political mission of antislavery, the *Cenelles* poets have nevertheless focused attention on "some of those areas most closely touching upon their lives."[61] In particular, they preoccupied themselves with the gender and racial anxieties provoked by *plaçage*. As *hommes de couleur* with a stake in the integrity and destiny of their cultural group, the poets engaged in a very public courtship with *femmes de couleur*, inserting themselves in a sexual and moral economy that would seem otherwise to deny them a voice.

Despite evidence of the frequency of legitimate marriage between free men and women of color, most accounts of *plaçage* describe a siphoning off of the "most desirable" women of color from the market of potential mates for free men of color, implicitly or explicitly portraying these men as frustrated losers in a high-stakes sexual competition with white men. Creole folklore caricatures the free man of color as a "fiddler crab," presumably denied access to the sexually charged interracial arena of the quadroon ball except in the role of a musician providing entertainment: "*Milatraise courri dans bal, / Cocodrie poté fanal, Trouloulou! / C'est pas zaffaire à tou, C'est pas zaffaire à tou, Trouloulou!* (Yellow girl goes to the ball; Nigger lights her to the hall. Fiddler man! Now, what is that to you? Say, what is that to you, Fiddler man?)."[62] In *The Grandissimes*, Honoré f.m.c. longs to marry the proud *femme de couleur* Palmyre. When he finally proposes, he does so by letter written in English, a language in which he is less than proficient. In his absence his confidant, the American "immigrant" Joseph Frowenfeld, reads the sad missive to Palmyre. "Star of my soul, I approach to die. It is not possible for me to live without Palmyre . . . Halas! I pine! Not another ten years of despair can I commence. Accept this love. If so I will live for you, but if to the contraire I must die for you. Is there anything at all what I will not give or even do if Palmyre will be my wife? Ah, no, far otherwise, there is nothing!" The garbled syntax sits ineffectually on the page, voiced by Frowenfeld who bristles "with annoyance at being made a proposing medium." Honoré f.m.c.'s absence in this scene attests to his impotence, particularly when compared with the high profile of Palmyre's former fiancé—the maroon leader and fomenter of slave rebellion, the late Bras Coupé—and that of her current (unrequited) love interest—the *homme de couleur*'s half-brother, the white Honoré Grandissime. Among such strong racial types, Honoré f.m.c. comes across as particularly emasculated, a sexual and political nonentity—a portrait that resurfaces in the historiography. In his account of the sexual landscape of *plaçage*, for example, historian Joseph Tregle portrays free men of color as a psychologically troubled population, "frequently a bitter and contentious part of the community," largely as a result of their social and sexual exclusion.[63]

Drawing on the formal qualities and general themes of French Romanticism, the *Cenelles* poets add dimension to the figure of the surly "fiddler crab" and attempt to work through the terms of their courtship of women of color and, thus, the terms under which their group might propagate itself.[64] Even as it lashes out at social injustice and the slipping status of Creoles of color, *Les Cenelles* presents a double-edged sword. It seeks to restore a publicly maligned Creole of color manhood, and at the same time it admonishes Creole of color women to shape up and to keep their chastity, a specific kind of sexual morality, intact. The poems seem to reject *plaçage* outright; yet the poets certainly realize that the social and economic standing of their community relies to some extent on the relationships and legacies formed under the institution. At least two of the poets, Pierre Dalcour and Camille Thierry, were children of *plaçage*.[65] Thus, the volume has revolutionary as well as conservative implications.[66] Like their French counterparts, the *Cenelles* poets used poetry as a platform for addressing and ultimately transforming what they perceived to be social ills. However, emulating Alphonse de Lamartine, the French poet-politician and one of the most often excerpted poets in *Les Cenelles*, Lanusse and his colleagues enlist notions of feminine virtue to help them express what is ultimately a conservative faith in continuity.[67] In "Vision," Joanni Questy's narrator, a humble orphan, implores the divine vision of a woman to "*Speak* to me, Alas!" When she does, she confirms her supernatural powers of preservation: "'I will, granting your prayer, / Keep watch over your path. / You will tread this land / Under the shadow of my hand.'"[68] Clearly, the poet's sense of continuity, his sense of stability, relies on the constancy of this vision of what a woman should be and say.

An understanding of the Romantic style is of paramount importance to a reading of *Les Cenelles*.[69] In particular, the poems exhibit a paradox of voice by which, in the words of one critic of the French Romantics, "They declaim their spiritual solitude in the accents of one standing before a large audience."[70] Lanusse and his fellow poets forge a space that forces the public and private to overlap, allowing them to articulate private grief, pleasure, and intimate transgressions and to gesture toward their public relevance. The apostrophic mode, the extensive use of "*Hélas!*" and the overabundance of exclamations mark these poems as written speeches and thus help them perform a prescriptive rather than a merely descriptive function. On the one hand, *Les Cenelles* assumes that its primary audience is something like the "general public" and that the dominant group will take notice of the poets' defiance of the institution of *plaçage*. We see this public aspect of the poetry in both its apostrophic form and its publication as a physical object. In the words of one mid-twentieth-century critic, the triumph of "this pathetic little book" is "that it came into being at all" in the climate of increasing social and legal restriction for *gens de couleur libre*.[71]

However, we must also take the volume's dedication at face value and read the poems as if they really were meant for a private audience of Louisiana's *beau sexe*.[72] "Please accept these modest Cenelles / Our heart offers you with sincerity; / A single glance fallen from your virtuous eyes / Will take the place of glory and immortality."[73] In this dedication and the poems that follow, Lanusse and his fellow contributors provide both a public record of the chastity of Creole of color women and a private model of chastity for Creole of color women. Concerned also with their posterity, they offer this record, this "simple monument" to future writers and historians.[74] Moreover, they insist that, for these writers of the future, the general character and appearance of these women will not have changed. "These [future] poets will see [in *Les Cenelles*] how those who preceded them thought and how they praised the charming ladies of Louisiana whose beauty, grace, and loveliness will doubtless be preserved in all their marvelous purity by those who succeed them."[75] In preserving these graces, the *Cenelles* poets bequeath some conservative gender formulations to future generations of women and writers.

Ultimately, however, *Les Cenelles* is about more than proffering a vision of an ideal woman for her own sake; it is about a relationship between Creole of color men and women under siege by *plaçage*, and it registers further a concern for cultural legacy, the propagation of their cherished social group into the future in a recognizable form. In evaluating the potentially chaotic—because not legally sanctioned—relationships issuing from *plaçage*, the *Cenelles* poets traverse controversial interpretive ground marked by the related themes of incest, orphanhood, sexual piety, and racial purity. The poets often took the position of protective brothers or scorned lovers.[76] In some poems the poet seems to be both the protective brother and the scorned lover at the same time. The most powerful example of this dualism occurs in Joanni Questy's poem "Causerie (Chat)." On the surface of things, the voice of this poem is the voice of a brother, warning his sister against involvement with a questionable (one would guess white) man. In flashes, the voice of the poem also seems to be that of a jealous lover reprimanding his love. Questy's address appeals to this sister-lover as someone who shares a (possibly illicit) secret. "Mircé, if you love me, if you are my sister, / Listen to the counsel of a brother who loves you; / I am a poor devil, and also a big talker, / And then again something else. This you know for yourself!"[77] The speaker's provocative "and then again something else" echoes throughout the poem in the plaintive and spiteful tone with which he implores his "sister," whom he desperately characterizes alternatively as "pauvre enfant" (poor child) and "Démon, mutin!" (demon, sneaky one!), to remain chaste. "Think for a moment of the love which binds us," writes Questy. And, later, "Ah! Do you know, Mircé, my dear child, / What that man really is? And do you know, cruel one, / What takes place inside me, in my heart, in my blood, / When I happen to catch one of them in my sight!"[78] Linking the desires of "that man" with the turmoil inside the narrator's own body, the combined phrase "in my heart, in my blood" alludes to both a romantic and a filial connection.

The undertones of incest in this context are not surprising, given the prevalence of literary and legal pairings of themes of incest and the quest for or anxiety over racial purity.[79] This concern manifested itself in the Louisiana Civil Code, where the article banning incestuous marriage immediately follows the article banning interracial marriage.[80] However, by attending only to the prohibition of the incest taboo in the context of legitimate unions of marriage, the code leaves the status of "natural" or "illegitimate" children up in the air. Because they could never be legitimated, interracial unions were not shielded by law from incest. In other words, these less-than-legitimate arrangements carry with them incestuous connotations and blur the distinctions between sister and wife and between brother and husband. The theme of incest presents two fundamental problems. First, it highlights the conundrum at the center of the white Creole quest for racial purity. Incest represents only an extreme form of the kind of endogamy white supremacists would champion, since the only way to be certain of the "racial purity" of one's family in a world of racially ambiguous people is for siblings to intermarry. The anxious theme of incest also speaks to the moral limits of a hybrid Creole identity: certainly to champion a vibrant atmosphere of indiscriminate mixing is not meant to condone marriage and sex among siblings. But how might these incestuous relationships be effectively policed? In response to these concerns, the *Cenelles* poets adopt a somewhat paradoxical position. They fear that the "arrangements" between "their" women and white males might precipitate the demise of their delicate social group even though these relationships had a strong hand in shaping this community. Thus, the poems present the ironic quest of a mixed-race Creole people for racial and cultural purity. Following the purifying logic of Americanization, the poets reject its binarism, hoping to delimit and fix the in-between position of Creoles of color within the delicate racial hierarchy of New Orleans and to secure a viable identity for their fragile cultural group.

In the symbolism of *Les Cenelles*, the incest theme surfaces in the likely context of French Romantic poetry and attaches itself to another important theme, that of orphanhood.[81] The concern of Creoles of color with orphans had a basis in reality. Planning for Madame Couvent's Institute Catholique des Orpheleins was just underway in 1845. Couvent had been concerned about the education and social protection of free children of color without the security of paternal acknowledgement. As she was well aware, the child of *plaçage* would be at the mercy of the whim of the father, whose failure to acknowledge his natural children would render them orphans in a figurative if not a literal sense. Moreover, even those natural children acknowledged as such by their white fathers would legally be able to inherit only a limited amount of property under Louisiana law, leaving a father's moral and financial obligations (in the nonlegal sense) unmet. Thus, natural is a status category that approaches and mimics legitimacy without ever actually reaching it, leaving unsecured the natural child's inheritance and other claims to belonging and underscoring a Creole of color anxiety over status and cultural permanence.

Although many of the poems include characters with no parents or no family, the major excursion into the realm of orphanhood is Bo . . . rs's lengthy poem "L'Orphelein des Tombeaux (the Orphan of the Tombs)." The complicated narrative structure of this poem includes an observer walking through a graveyard, an orphan in mourning beside the tombs of his sister and adopted father, and a spectral vision of "an angel of fifteen, crowned with jasmins!" who apparently died before she could be defiled.[82] In that limbo between life and death and maidenhood and womanhood, the angel of fifteen recalls *plaçage* and conjures up her double, the orphan's mother, whose existence is only vaguely hinted at by the poet as "the sad memory of a touching voice." The identity of the angel is ambiguous: she may be a vision of the mother as Virgin Mary, a potential lover taken too soon, or an image of the dead "sister," a girl who had presumably been his adopted father's daughter and, thus, of dubious kinship to him.[83] Suggesting a troubled co-orphanhood and a sibling rivalry complicated by gender, the poet triangulates the relationship of the sister, the "father," and the orphan. A visit to the sister's tomb occasions the death of the father, cutting short the father's vow to "shield [the orphan's] days from the ravages of time." A visit to the father's tomb inspires the vision of the virginal sister-lover, bringing on the orphan's own demise. The orphan's dying wish is "To hold within my arms that timid virgin! / To be carried away in the pools of her moist eyes!"[84] The spectator and the reader are left to contemplate the carnage wrought by the unintended consequences and unfulfilled promises of *plaçage*.

Les Cenelles mines the interlacing themes of incest, group identity, and orphanhood in order to reveal alternate paths to gender propriety for both men and women. The formulations of the poets suggest a hope that rigidly enforced notions of gender and sexuality would reinstate a sexual compatibility between Creole of color men and women and, therefore, shore up the racial and cultural durability of their group.[85] The poets have a clear and explicit sense of what a woman should not be. In "A Mon Ami, P. (To My Friend, P.)," August Populus counsels his friend to avoid women with excessive pride, vanity, and "frightful jealousy."[86] Lanusse also chastises the pride, vanity, and artifice of a woman who has "insisted" that he write a poem about her. Although charmed to some extent by her beauty and compelled to honor her request, Lanusse pens a "bitter satire" against her:

> Everyone admired this grace so pure
> Which appeared yesterday in fresh attire
> Which you had chosen with exquisite taste;
> But I feared then to form my own opinion,
> For old Olinda, the self-declared connoisseur,
> Was whispering to me that you looked dreadful.
> It is true that one could perceive in her eyes
> The reason that made her speak so.
> *(Tout le monde admirait cette grace si pure*
> *Qui paraissait hier dans la fraiche parure*
> *Que vous aviez choisie avec un gout charmant;*
> *Mais j'y craignais d'assesoir mon propre jugement,*
> *car la vielle Olinda, qui se dit connaisseuse,*
> *Me confiait tout bas que vous étiez affreuse.*
> *Il est vrai qu'on pouvait dans ses yeux déceler*
> *Quel était le motif qui la faisait parler.)*[87]

Concerned with more than merely pride, Lanusse, in "A Elora (To Elora)" directs his attention to the "self-interest" that would inspire a young girl to "[flee] marriage [*l'hymen*] and its severe code / To adopt one less sure but more accommodating."[88] According to this logic, the placed woman has forsaken community and her own morality for wealth and property. His use of *l'hymen* instead of the more neutral *mariage* focuses attention on the bodily compromises such young girls made for the sake of material possessions. Indeed Lanusse catalogues some of the gifts that one might expect when contracting such an arrangement: "Some new furniture, a dazzling jewel case . . . [a] silk dress." According to the *Cenelles* poet, *placées* may live royally; however, they try in vain to "hide a horrible ugliness," for "those who live in the lap of luxury / Have written on their foreheads: indignity, dishonor!"[89]

Counterpoising these "faults" and "weaknesses" against representations of the women as "pure" and "chaste," the poets focus on individual and figurative women, convey a thorough image of feminine "virtue," and link it to masculine prowess. In "A Ida (To Ida)," M. F. Liotau addresses a dark-eyed, ebony-haired, lithe-bodied sixteen year old. He stresses that it is not her physical attributes that draw him to her, but "it is this virtue which opposes without fear / The will of a obscene and venal heart, / This sweet naïveté, this innocent stamp / On your virginal brow."[90] In "defending His law" rather than succumbing to the advances that lure adolescent girls of her type, Ida assumes iconic proportion in the structure of morality supported by *Les Cenelles.* The virtuous young Creole woman acts as a kind of muse for these poets: their status as legitimate artists seems to depend on the propriety of the women. "Virgin, it is you who forever lives in my heart, / Who makes my heart beat; / Who revives the hope in my soul,/ A soul that bears the burden of misfortune."[91] The propriety of the women allows the poets to engage in courtship on their own terms, to be the kind of men they want to be. Their witty word games and their playful acrostics must fall on "innocent" ears.[92] Furthermore, the youth and innocence of the ideal Creole beauty provide a rich canvas on which the men might enact a kind of "harmless" Romantic libertinism. Valcour B.'s "happy wanderer" sings "Confident now and then of my vows, / To be constant and true, / I see a weakness in an innocent young girl; / I laugh—faithful only to pleasure, / My flame burns as long as my desire; / I take flight to a new love." Likewise, P. Dalcour writes of a character that must ceaselessly float from Amélie to Coralie from "blond" to "brunette."[93]

Ultimately, however, the poets pose as sympathetic protectors of their vulnerable sister-lovers. In "La Jeune Fille au Bal (The Young Lady at the Ball)," Lanusse situates the action in the midst of what appears to be a quadroon ball, thus anticipating the social and moral dangers of *plaçage*: "Our young dancers demand your hand, / Go flutter about, Emma, I'll follow you with my eyes. / The fiddle has sounded!!"[94] Far from the mute and displaced "fiddler crab" of popular myth, the Creole of color man has a voice and assumes a central position as watchman over the communal conscience. Under the sway of the festive atmosphere of the ball and the promise of an attenuated claim to prosperity, the young Emma's body continues to perform in spite of its limitations: "You suffer from exhaustion, yet you waltz still! / Oh! What is it with this child? She is mad, my God."[95] Thus, the "fiddler crab" steps forth to offer her the comfort of familiarity and empathy and some sage advice that she fails to heed: "Come, come close to me, and rest yourself a bit." Likening Emma to a moth entranced by a flame, he predicts her downfall: "Near that candle where captivated by his own pain, / he perishes, consumed by carelessness."[96]

Les Cenelles puts forward a sense of women's sexual morality that resonates with the moral prescriptions of the Catholic Church, their religious milieu.[97] Taken as a whole, the poems set up a triangle of complicity among the young women, their mothers, and the priest figure. In one poem in particular, the very structure of the St. Louis Cathedral has been emptied of its significance. "Church of Saint-Louis, old temple, shrine / Here you are today, empty and deserted! / Those who were entrusted here below to your care, / Scorning the needs of the sacred tabernacle, / Have led the Christian army astray."[98] This portrait of an empty church and a despondent Catholicism resonates with the opening scene of Lanusse's "Un Mariage de Conscience," when the narrator stumbles upon a mixed-race girl who is praying in vain to the unresponsive Virgin Mary in the empty sanctuary of the St. Louis Cathedral.[99] In "Epigramme (Epigram)," Lanusse levels partial blame for *plaçage* against the clergy. Like Cable's Père Jerome, Lanusse's priest is a witness to the corruption of young women, even if he is not, as is Père Jerome, an active agent in arranging an interracial liaison. Lanusse depicts an uncompleted conversation between a mother and a priest: "Might I not, father—how does one say?—*place* my daughter . . ."[100] Lanusse leaves the priest's answer to the mother's suggestion of a possible *plaçage* unspoken, allowing for the possibility of the priest's complicity.

Perhaps as a corollary of the logic of universal siblinghood/orphanhood, the *Cenelles* poets reserve their harshest criticism for the mother figure. In Romantic nationalist literature, women, when not figured as the national mother or the Virgin Mary, convey a necessary sexuality and remind citizen-readers of the chimera of universal siblinghood. In "Epigramme," Lanusse condemns the mother as a hypocritical, opportunistic "*bigote.*" He provides a scathing epigraph by the French poet Verjux to "A Elora": "This child without her mother, would maybe have been wise. / As wife, to her husband she would have given care; / Mother, she'd have seen to the needs of all her young."[101] In the text of the poem itself, he repeats the sentiment: "To those who would abuse her simplicity / Her mother offered her complicity."[102] In accessing the orphan's identity, the *Cenelles* poets announce a preference for paternal descent, distancing themselves from this mother figure and her legacy of (im)morality. In a slave society where the condition of the child follows that of the mother, maternal inheritance carries a dangerous and devalued legacy, especially for those who stand to inherit the status of the woman of color. The poets seem to suggest that with mothers such as these, to be an orphan would be preferable.[103]

In a strong sense, *Les Cenelles* serves as a form of prescriptive literature for pubescent girls, emphasizing propriety and chastity over maternally sanctioned *plaçage* and the promise of property and wealth. However, the property of Creole of color women often constituted one of the most critical sources of conflict in antebellum New Orleans, particularly if it involved the contested estates of prominent white men and their *placées* of color and children. In this sense, *plaçage* threatened to undermine the legacies of all Creoles, white and of color. We can witness the complex issues of property, moral and racial purity, and cultural propagation in the estates of two kinsmen, Eugène and Augustin Macarty, and the women with whom they spent their lives, Eulalie Mandeville and Céleste Perrault. Like the cases of François Lacroix, Joseph Dumas, and others, the contested property claims of Mandeville and Perrault emphasize the divergent themes of interracial "intimacy" and Creole of color "insularity." Even more than the men's cases, they illustrate how moral judgments and notions of cultural legitimacy attached themselves to the in-between position of Creoles of color. The trials of Mandeville and Perrault also allow glimpses into the circum-Atlantic connections among Creoles of both colors, detailing familial and social lineages that extended through the Caribbean to France.

The Macarty Women and Feminine Property

Despite the hotly contested property of each, neither Mandeville nor Perrault was the most well-known of the Macarty women. That distinction belongs to the white Creole Madame Delphine Lalaurie née Macarty. On April 10, 1834, an angry mob chased Madame Lalaurie from her home, provoking a flight that is said to have ended in France. Earlier that day, her slave cook, literally chained to the oven, had set fire to the house. When the neighbors came to rescue the Lalauries and their burning property, they were astonished to find Lalaurie's slaves in varying degrees of neglect and suffering. "We saw," wrote the editor of *L'Abeille*, "where the collars and manacles had cut their way into the quivering flesh. For several months, [the slaves] had been confined in those dismal dungeons with no other nutriment than a handful of gruel and an insufficient quantity of water." The editor of another paper was more detailed: "We saw one of these miserable beings. The sight was so humble, we could scarce look upon it . . . he had a large hole in his head; his body from head to foot was covered with scars and filled with worms." The spectacle of the contorted and abused bodies of slaves roused the scorn of the New Orleans citizenry. However, as many raconteurs of the tale have noted, they may have also experienced the guilt of not having addressed the matter sooner. Some months before the fire, a young girl—to become in subsequent versions of the tale the "most prominent ghost" of the "haunted house"—fell or jumped from the roof of the house, fleeing Delphine's whip. Having missed the opportunity to take revenge on Delphine's person, her neighbors instead ravaged her property, killing her horses and smashing her abandoned getaway carriage at the lake. They emptied the contents of her house into the street, burning piano, tables, and chairs and ripping up fine mattresses and textiles. When acclaimed traveler and observer Harriet Martineau encountered the house a year later, she noted its symbolic function: "The house stands and is meant to stand, in its ruined state." The story of Madame Lalaurie and the "haunted house" has provoked an extended argument over the morality of slavery and the humanity of slave owners and has provided a major point of interest in the New Orleans tourist industry.[104] It has functioned as an important monument to the moral objection of New Orleanians to the potential excesses of slavery.

The story of Madame Lalaurie—née Delphine Macarty—has also constituted one of the most prominent entries of the Macarty family into the cultural memory of New Orleans. However, when Charles Gayarré's protégé Grace King sought to immortalize white Creole families in *Creole Families of New Orleans* (1921), a beautiful hardback with a lace-edged oval depicting a street scene of the *vieux carré*, she understandably failed to include this sordid tale. Instead, Madame Lalaurie surfaces in her account as Delphine Macarty, one of the "ladies who . . . irradiate the pages of the chronicles of New Orleans," giving substance and permanence to the Macarty name.[105] King presents what seems to be a remarkably detailed account of this white Creole family superimposed upon a chronicle of the key historical events of Louisiana's colonial period. In her imaginative genealogy, the history of the Macartys is inexorably intertwined with the history of Louisiana, earning them the honorific title of Creole.[106] For King, the patriotism of the Macarty women reconciled competing aspects of Louisiana's cultural life during periods of transition, combining a defiant protest against Spanish and American pretensions to power with a feminine grace. It echoed Gayarré's defense of the honor, purity, and, thus, marriageability of white Creole women: they "have entered the mansions of the highest nobility with the dignified footstep of perfect equality, and I could fill up a long list with the historical names of barons, viscounts, counts, marquises, dukes and princes who were happy to place their coronets on the fair brows of Louisiana's creole daughters."[107] Thus, the Delphine Macarty of King's legend is not the emblem of horrific abuses against her slaves but the young and beautiful bride of a Spanish nobleman and matriarch of a prominent family.[108]

The opening passage of King's Macarty chapter betrays, in addition to the story of the "haunted house," a second and related lapse. The Macarty men, perhaps more than the memory of Madame Lalaurie, have presented an unfortunate obstacle to King's exposition on Creoleness: "The good old Creole name of Macarty has become only a memory in New Orleans. The male members of the family are extinct . . ." The female Macartys continue to redeem King's narrative, having "carried the Macarty traits and qualities into the other families until there is hardly one that does not bear a representative in their genealogical record."[109] In the context of King's historical genealogy, the Macarty men have regrettably reneged on their social responsibility to pass on their genes and to perpetuate a white Creole aristocracy, essentially leading to cultural death in Americanization. While there is a sense in which fond memories of greatness in fact serve King's purpose by creating an aura around the ever-illusive past, the fading of "the good old Creole name of Macarty" into "mere" memory perplexes and frustrates her. The vitality and virility of the Macarty men should have protected them from both active extermination and passive "passing away." At the very least, these traits should have inoculated them against the charms of *femmes de couleur* who, "in regard to family purity, domestic peace, and household dignity," were in King's opinion "the most insidious and the deadliest foes a community ever possessed."[110]

Despite King's assertion of the name's extinction, however, a quick perusal of the 1920 *Soard's New Orleans Directory* reveals at least two Macartys living in New Orleans during her time and other descendants of the family living under the names McCarty and McCarthy. In one of my own early-twenty-first-century trips to the Louisiana Division of the New Orleans Public Library, I met a woman of color, a self-described Creole by the name of McCarthy, doing genealogical research on her nineteenth-century Macarty relatives. Rather than negating King's claims, however, this revelation challenges us to search for alternate meanings of "extinction" and alternative modes of propagation in this illustrious bloodline. The search for the Macarty legacy leads directly to the heart of cultural and racial viability—to two highly contentious court cases challenging the property of free women of color. As far as white New Orleans was concerned, the Macarty men did not die a quiet and peaceful death; their passing threatened the very fiber of white Creole society and exposed the shaky foundation of racial and gender rules and roles.

In *Old Families of Louisiana* (1931), Stanley Clisby Arthur collected his own assortment of previously published genealogies, including an article by Charles Patton Dimitry, a relative of George Pandelly who had taken to documenting the whiteness of white Creoles. In his entry on the Macartys, Dimitry claims emphatically that Eugène Macarty did not marry.[111] Grace King echoes Dimitry as to Augustin Macarty's marital status, and she neglects to make mention of his cousin Eugène, one of the wealthiest and most visible men in the antebellum *vieux carré*. Both genealogical accounts consciously discount the lifetime romantic commitments of the two men to Creole women of color, each relationship spanning almost fifty years. Furthermore, the two men had a number of children of color whom they recognized and provided for in one form or another. Since they provide the conditions for the "contamination" and "extinction" of the Macarty name, Creole of color women are central to these genealogies even in their absence. Both men died in the mid-1840s, within a year of one another, and the successions of each provoked white members of the Macarty family to challenge the rights of their kinsmen to pass on property to women of color and to provide protection for their families after their deaths.

"Illicit Connexions"

In the late 1840s and into the 1850s, Eulalie Mandeville and representatives for Céleste Perrault found themselves in the Louisiana Supreme Court defending their "marital" property—no trivial issue in New Orleans. In exposing the "absurdity" of Cable's *Grandissimes*, for example, Charles Gayarré would protest the portrayal of Honoré f.m.c. as the colored heir to the Grandissime estate, intimating that New Orleanians had traditionally taken it as their duty to challenge these cross-racial inheritance claims in court. Maligning the proprietorship of Creole of color women who often rented furnished rooms, Grace King associated the economic decline of New Orleans with the property of a Creole of color former *placée:* "The appearance of the first such placards [for a *chamber garnis*] is the appearance of a first taint spot in the value of property in a locality—a symptom of corruption."[112] Thus, the Macarty cases presented a number of interrelated questions about the relationship between "property" and "propriety," contested terms that suffered under the weight of *plaçage*, as we have already seen in surveying the literature and historiography of Creole New Orleans.

Although Mandeville and Perrault were involved in long-term commitments with their "husbands," these seemingly stable relationships represent only one possible outcome of *plaçage*, a practice with many faces. Sometimes the relationships took on the qualities of legitimate marriages. Often they were quite temporary, a rite of passage for a young white Creole man in his late bachelorhood. The relationships gestured toward contractual accountability but ultimately operated according to the whims of those involved.[113] While the experiences of Mandeville and Perrault do not represent the typical *plaçage*, they provide a unique insight into the legacies of propriety and property that the practice conveyed. In reviewing these experiences, I resist the urge to overindulge the sentiment of love. The longevity of the relationships seems to suggest that these cases of *plaçage* were grounded in something like "true love." However, I am more interested in the ways in which the potential for interracial affective bonds threatened the sense of propriety of white Creoles as well as Creoles of color. I am also interested in how and why these practitioners of *plaçage* deployed and withheld expressions of romantic, filial, and parental love and affection.

At some point in 1792 or 1793, late in the Spanish colonial period,

Eugène Macarty and Eulalie Mandeville began to live together, forming what the Louisiana Supreme Court in 1847 called an "illicit connexion." The "connexion" was certainly lopsided in a number of ways. Eugène Macarty was known as a white man, a member of one of the more visible and active military families, and Eulalie Mandeville, widely known as Madame CeCe Macarty, was understood to be a woman of color, occupying a liminal and changeable legal and social status. However, in other ways, Mandeville had as much or more claim to social status as Eugène Macarty. Eulalie Mandeville was the daughter of Philip Mandeville de Marigny, the wealthiest man in Louisiana, and half sister to Bernard Marigny—the "Creole of [white] Creoles," the namesake of Faubourg Marigny.[114] In the 1840s, a member of the Marigny family remembered that Eulalie Mandeville had "resided in the house of my grandmother as one of the family."[115] The potential and actual siblinghood of white men and women of color—here presented in the public record of Mandeville as Marigny's "natural sister"—provides an interesting twist on the theme of incest running through *Les Cenelles.* Fulfilling the role of "protective brother" delineated two years earlier by the *Cenelles* poets, Bernard Marigny claimed during the trial that Mandeville "passes in [his] family as being his natural sister" and that he "has known her since he can recollect."[116] Marigny's language is casual, depending on "recollection" rather than law and contractual record to determine kinship. He thus contributes to and participates in a legacy of an informal but powerfully felt recognition of racial mixing, a legacy that Grace King and others attempted to erase during the late nineteenth and early twentieth centuries.

The relationship of Eulalie Mandeville to her "natural family" was financial as well as emotional. Philip Marigny made frequent gifts to Eulalie Mandeville, including land at Terre aux Beoufs and various sums of money, including a one-time donation of $3,000 (around $65,000 today) delivered, as Bernard Marigny testified, "*de main au main*" (from hand to hand).[117] Bernard Marigny followed his father's example and donated to his half-sister lots of land in what would become Faubourg Marigny. These bequests suggest a colonial history of recognition of codes of obligation accompanying interracial kinship.[118] In contrast to Mandeville's financial liquidity, Eugène Macarty, at the time of the "illicit connexion," had no apparent means of support. A number of witnesses remembered that Macarty had been dependent on his brother, Jean-Baptiste de Macarty, when he met Mandeville and that he had procured a modest loan (by Marigny standards) of $2,000 from his own sister in 1793. These funds had evaporated by the next decade, forcing Macarty to start a business from scratch, selling wood harvested on land owned by Eulalie Mandeville.

Despite Macarty's modest beginnings, he quickly became successful in New Orleans as a moneylender, building a reputation described in numerous accounts as "usurious." As a household, the Macarty-Mandeville alliance was extremely fruitful and industrious. Mandeville steadily built a dry-goods business and acquired a solid reputation. Early in the century, Mandeville identified a gap in the economy of territorial Louisiana and used slaves and other resources provided by her family to fill the basic need for dry goods. As one witness remarked, "that line of business was then considered very lucrative as there were few competitors."[119] She quickly grew into a "*grosse marchande*" with excellent credit and "five or six negresses selling for her and besides these, eight or ten other persons [selling] for her on commission."[120] With an enslaved sales force of thirty-two in 1830, Mandeville—by then the largest slaveholder of color in New Orleans—expanded her business into nearby parishes. Reinvesting her profits in real estate, she became a landlord as well.[121] When witnesses testified to her character in this challenge to her property, the words *shrewd*, *frugal*, *laborious*, and *active* carried considerable weight with the court. Throughout their decades together, Macarty and Mandeville took care to separate their accounts and investments legally and in the public imagination. Witnesses described a division of fiscal responsibility in the Macarty-Mandeville household. Both parties vocalized this division repeatedly so that eventually people knew to apply to Mandeville to buy or lease property and to Macarty to borrow money.[122] Although Macarty frequently "invested" Mandeville's money for her, Mandeville always signed her own checks and had her son, Eugène, Jr., deposit her money into her separate account.

The Macarty-Mandeville household economy also involved raising the Macarty children and tending to their affairs. By the time of the trial, the household included three adult children, all sons, in New Orleans and one adult son in Santiago de Cuba on the eastern part of the island of Cuba, a city with strong historical ties to the francophone world of San Domingue/Haiti and New Orleans. Another son living in

Cuba had already died, leaving two children of his own. During the 1820s and 1830s, the Macarty-Mandeville household acquired a transnational character, and the children in Cuba participated heavily in building, leveraging, and helping protect the family legacy. In several trips to Cuba, Eugène Macarty, Sr., made a series of loans to his son Barthelemy for the maintenance of Dolorida and St. Etienne, two sugar plantations outside Santiago, and for the management of the enslaved people who labored on them. Even though these plantations never made much money and eventually brought Barthelemy to the brink of financial ruin, Macarty continued to invest in them and to lay the groundwork for the education of his grandson. When Eugène, Sr., finally liquidated his Cuban property, he received $3,000, and by the time he made out his will in 1845, his total assets amounted to a little more than twice that sum. Declaring himself as "never having been married," Macarty bequeathed $2,000 each to his brother Theodule Macarty and a nephew and $500 to a favorite niece. He also freed two slaves, the "mulâtre François" and the "negresse Rosette." Leaving $300 each to his natural children with Eulalie Mandeville, his will directed his relatives to give him the most modest funeral possible. Apparently, he had not been the millionaire that the public believed him to be. Thus, his collateral heirs turned to the property of Eulalie Mandeville, the wealthiest free woman of color in the antebellum United States, whose assets totaled over $155,000 (close to $4 million in today's currency). In the end, however, they could not penetrate Mandeville's careful decades-long preparation of her claim to her property.

A year before Eugène Macarty's death, his cousin Augustin Macarty died, leaving his *placée*, Céleste Perrault, in a situation similar to that of Mandeville. In the lawsuit *Badillo et al. v. Francisco Tio* (1851), the Macarty family sought possession of Augustin's estate, valued at over $55,000.[123] While the immediate concerns of the two cases—to wrest control of a man's estate from his mistress of color—resemble one another, *Badillo v. Tio* displays some interesting differences from *Macarty v. Mandeville.* Like that of his cousin, Augustin Macarty's "illicit connexion" commenced in the latter part of the Spanish colonial period. A "nobleman and an officer in the Spanish army," he dwelt with one of his uncles, "also a Spanish officer who lived with a woman of color." Under the influence of this "licentious" uncle, Macarty took up with several women "of that class" in succession, "until in 1799, he took Céleste Perrault with whom he lived nearly fifty years." In spite of this union, the testimony in the case reveals that Augustin Macarty and his universal legatee presented a weaker argument than had Mandeville about who constituted the "natural" family and who did not. In fact, Augustin Macarty left not only a small "natural" family consisting of Céleste and their son Patrice, owner of a dry goods business in Pensacola, Florida, but also a trail of former mistresses and children of color half-related to one another. The story of his sexual and familial involvements paints a much more complicated picture than his cousin's.

Also, Augustin Macarty had followed the somewhat popular but less successful strategy of appointing an intermediate agent as a conduit through which he could provide for his "widow" and their children, a practice that was not unheard of among those with legal savvy.[124] To the Macarty relatives, it seemed further as if Francisco Tio, the universal legatee of the will, had been interposed on behalf of not only Céleste and Patrice but also on behalf of Josephine Macarty, Augustin's daughter by "his first concubine" of color, Victoria Wiltz, and her children.[125] Tio himself was "married" to Josephine Macarty, and the case mentions a number of children including Phelonise and Brigitte, the latter of whom offered her own testimony in the trial. Thus, Céleste Perrault's public defense of her property represents an attempt to weave a plausible tale of genuine intimacy from the web of "illegitimate," "natural," and "legitimate" familial relations that Augustin Macarty left in his wake.

It also demonstrates how the court could be an arena of struggle over the legal and moral inconsistencies governing *plaçage* and the status of interracial families. Much of the testimony presented to the court referenced Civil Code article 227 regarding how an illegitimate child might go about proving paternity, in spite of the fact that the code explicitly restricted children of color from claiming a white father. "Proof of paternal descent" could be made in three ways, according to the code: in a private correspondence in which the "father acknowledges the bastard as his child," when the "mother of the child was known as living in a state of concubinage with the father and resided as such in his house at the time the child was conceived," or "when the father in public or private has acknowledged him as his child or has called him so in conversation or has caused him to be educated as such."[126] The court's admission of these terms in spite of the interracial restrictions on them, allowed some of Macarty's "heirs" to present themselves as such even within a set of seemingly ironclad legal proscriptions. References to this article dramatized Augustin Macarty's moral failings, the extent to which he wavered back and forth between implying his paternal status and outright denying it. They also demonstrated the proximity of Patrice, the son of Perrault, to the status of Macarty's "natural child." The court judged Patrice to be the child of Macarty, citing not the actions of Augustin Macarty himself, who had failed to sign his certificate of baptism, but instead pointing to Céleste's residence in Macarty's house as his "concubine" when her son was born. For his own part, Macarty employed terms of endearment that suggested friendly if not paternal obligation. He frequently wrote to Patrice as "*mon ami* (my friend)," stopping just short of calling him "*mon fils* (my son)," and he spent the last years of his life supporting Patrice Macarty's business.

Instrumental in shoring up Patrice Macarty's status, article 227 was less helpful in the case of the other children and served to characterize these relationships as incomprehensible under Louisiana law. Josephine Macarty, for example, had been born after Macarty left the house of her mother Victoria Wiltz, thus blocking her access to legal recognition by the court. Brigitte, whose mother went unnamed in the court record, had the lowest status of all the witnesses. She could not legally demonstrate her claim to be Macarty's child and, furthermore, could not convincingly testify to his relationship to her alleged half-sister Josephine. Although she told the court that Macarty mentioned *dans ses discours* with her that he had fathered Josephine, the court chose to believe instead white witnesses' accounts that Macarty habitually denied having any children. The legitimacy of the *discours* depended not on their public or private nature, but on the race and status of the listener.[127]

Within this space created by the extralegal status of Augustin Macarty's liaison with Céleste Perrault and his equivocation over the status of some of his children, a sizable estate had accumulated, property that Macarty hastily attempted in the months before his death to disseminate among the members of his family of color. In late 1844 Macarty made Francisco Tio the executor of his will and thus placed him in control of property totaling over $58,000. As the plaintiffs pointed out, Tio, although living with the woman who claimed to be Macarty's child, had never been especially close to Macarty. Instead, he was a known confidante of Perrault and the "husband" of Josephine Wiltz. After Macarty's death and with Tio's assistance, Perrault controlled his estate, including the fates of a number of slaves and the fruits of their labor, a house on Camp Street in the "American sector" of New Orleans, some lots of land throughout the city, and various items of furniture and clothing. The families of Perrault and Josephine Macarty also claimed other slaves, bank stock, insurance, cattle, rents and revenues from immovables, and cash. Significantly, Perrault sold a number of slaves immediately after Augustin Macarty's death, displaying a "sudden increase of wealth" and enabling her to take an eighteen-month trip to Paris. In the end, the Louisiana Supreme Court ruled in favor of the plaintiffs, charging Tio's interposition as a kind of fraud and ordering him to remit the assets of the estate to Macarty's collateral heirs.

"Contrary to Our Fixed Policy"

Taken together, the Macarty cases exposed the broad latitude of familial relationships protected by Louisiana law at various historical moments. The challenge before the court was to bring the story of these liaisons up to date, transcending time by changing their possible legitimacy in the past into a definite transgression of social norms. The trials thus attempted to account for the movement of these relationships within the public imagination through the first half of the nineteenth century. In a sense, Louisiana's unique Civil Code developed alongside the waxing and waning of public acceptability of interracial liaisons. One could read it as a tool that would protect legitimate families and ensure that parents and children would adequately perform their financial responsibilities to one another. The concept of the "forced heir" prevented a father or mother from disinheriting their legitimate children. Joint property laws gave women more power over their wealth than women in other states had.[128] Yet, this shoring up of family stability and financial security was inexorably linked with the movement toward problematizing interracial liaisons and disinheriting the children resulting from them. There is an inverse relationship between the development of family law and joint property legislation for married people—what one scholar has counted among the Civil Code's humanistic qualities—and the tightening strictures against *placées* and natural and illegitimate children. According to article 1468 of the 1825 Civil Code, those living in "open and notorious concubinage" could inherit only one-tenth the value of all movables, and "natural children"—those who had been acknowledged by their white fathers—could inherit up to one-fourth of the value of the father's movables, provided that there were no legitimate heirs to the property.[129]

Although both Macarty cases originated in the late 1840s, the judges looked to historical precedent and attempted to explain the actions of the Macartys in light of widespread interracial intimacies during the colonial period and an evolving Civil Code. The laws of the Spanish colonial period had permitted interracial marriage with the consent of both families. In spite of the legality of such marriages, however, many people—free people of color and white—declined to marry at all, primarily due to the expense and elaborate procedure, producing thickly intertwined relationships that cut across class, status, and color and that provoked open conflict between law and custom.[130] Complementing the relative permissiveness of the Spanish colonial laws regarding free people of color, the representative of the Catholic Church, Father Antonio Sedella, shielded free people of color from legal indignities and conducted many church-sanctioned "marriages of conscience" across racial and status lines. His generosity and openness reserved him a prominent place in the historical memory of Creoles of color as the kindly "Père Antoine."[131]

For those such as Gayarré and King who sought to supplant these memories, the colonial period also raised concern. The ability to trace one's heritage to one of the respectable French women—a "casket girl" rather than a prostitute—became a veritable genealogical imperative among white Creoles. In his widely printed speech "The Creoles of History and the Creoles of Romance," Gayarré addressed these controversial legacies of the Spanish period by pointing to the official measures taken by Spanish governor Miró to keep the races and social castes distinct. After taking a census of the free colored population, Miró, Gayarré reminded his listeners, "declared that the idleness of the free negro, mulatto and quadroon women, resulting from their living on incontinence and libertinism, must no longer be tolerated; that they must renounce their mode of living and betake themselves to honest labor." In any case, Gayarré seemed to believe that Miró had effectively undermined the particular appeal of women of color to white men when he forbade these women from "wear[ing] plumes and jewels and direct[ing] them to have their hair bound in a kerchief."[132]

Although the important nodes to be considered were the Spanish period and the Civil Code of 1825, the judges and witnesses grounded their understanding of *plaçage* by looking back to the laws and customs of antiquity. In their decision in *Badillo v. Tio*, the judges traced the path of the "Roman" practice of "unequal marriages"—in which a woman of "inferior condition" gave herself or was "given by relatives to a single man to live with him in a state of concubinage"—through the ages to Spain and then eventually to Louisiana under the Spanish dominion.[133] The court likewise chose to explain the excesses of the young Augustin Macarty with reference to his service in the Spanish military. In terms of her finances, Mandeville successfully navigated the fissures in the law, bringing her arrangement with Macarty literally "up to code." Before 1825, she consolidated her accounts, opening her own bank account and having her son deposit her money for her. She kept her business separate in fact and in the public imagination from that of Eugène. Her diligence in financial matters provoked the court to admit that she had managed her accounts independently since 1825 and that all joint financial decisions made prior to that were most likely legal and outside the bounds of the current law.

On the intimate level of the "family" and the emotional bonds associated with it, aligning the current interpretation of these relationships with their practice over time proved more difficult. Arguments for and against the inheritance rights of women of color and their families used the 1825 Civil Code to reinforce the parameters of legitimate marriage and inheritance. By far the most vocal opinions of the court upheld the values of "proper" (white) marriages, and the judges took every opportunity to scorn interracial arrangements and their offspring. Even while permitting her right to her property, the judicial opinion described the relationship of Mandeville and Macarty as "a sad instance of the grossest violation of every social law, of every lawful tie."[134] Likewise, for Augustin Macarty and Céleste Perrault, the opinion asserted they "openly flouted the institution of marriage—one of the chief foundations of society."[135]

A minority of the judges in *Badillo v. Tio* wrote their own opinion contesting the right of Josephine and Patrice, the children of Augustin, to prove their parentage under the terms of article 227. Unlike the judges who recognized the longevity of Perrault's relationship with Macarty (admitting that Patrice, although illegitimate, was in all probability Macarty's child), this adamant minority wished to restore the terms of Civil Code article 226, which stated that "free illegitimate children of color may . . . be allowed to prove their descent from a father of color only."[136] The court, they argued, should aggressively exclude all discussion of paternity—all "shameful investigation"—in trials of this kind. This refusal, they hoped, would protect the bloodlines, reputation, and property of whites from any association with free people of color and also narrow the opportunities for people of color to lay claim to these various kinds of legitimacy. "Here marriage between the two races is forbidden by law," their opinion states. "The honor of marriage shall not be debased by the connection. The law permits it only when the parent has taken so lost to shame, as to make an authentic act of his degradation, and without this absolute certainty, will not allow the shameful investigation in court for the purpose of enabling the colored child contrary to our fixed policy to diminish the father's estate to the prejudice of his white and lawful heirs."[137] The language of "honor" and "shame" demonstrated the stakes involved in segregating kinship claims according to race.[138] Enlisting rhetorical force to counter the ambiguity and variety of social practice, the judges wrote in terms of what the "law permits," requiring "authentic acts" and "absolute certainty." In the face of the historical memory and historical evidence of changeability, they reiterated the immutability of a "fixed policy"—one mandating airtight documentation and extensive elaboration on the affective bonds of families of color.

However, the Macarty cases tell a much more complex story of the transmission of "properties of blood" and affection (not to mention personal property) than the judges were willing to publicly admit. Ironically, the expression of these bonds forced the court to acknowledge their value at least on some level. In the final judgment for *Macarty v. Mandeville*, the court admitted that the "deceased and Eulalie had children as aforesaid, and no doubt parental love, the strongest tie on earth." The court remarked, in both cases, on the discord within the white branch of the Macarty family, their language reflecting the extent to which the emotional family did not match the legal family.[139] Augustin Macarty's letters to his relatives showed "that he was completely estranged from them and disclose a strong desire on his part to convince them that he was poor and that they had nothing to expect from him."[140] The court considered the children of Mandeville and Eugène Macarty "perhaps better entitled to inherit the proceeds of their labor than collateral heirs for whom they felt little or no regard."[141]

Despite the evidence of strain on these collateral relationships, the form of the plaintiff's appeal met the requirements of the law's evolving strictures on kinship. The list of relatives suing Mandeville was extensive, a veritable class-action suit extending for almost two legal-sized pages. Each relative claimed a carefully calculated share of the "marital property," with fractions ranging from 1/7 to 1/420 of the total estate. Even the infamous Madame Lalaurie of the Haunted House, acting as Delphine Macarty, claimed that 1/14 of the estate was due to her.[142] In the end, Mandeville won the case not because she represented a better claim to kinship—the meticulous genealogical preparations of the plaintiffs being more impressive to the court—but because she proved to the court's satisfaction that she had been independently wealthy. Augustin Macarty's relatives—many of whom had brought the earlier suit against Mandeville—demonstrated the legality of their relationships through a reputable intermediary who, when compared with Francisco Tio, seemed to the court to be objective and fair. Although the court was willing to acknowledge the potential strength of the familial bonds between white men and their families of color, this acknowledgement ultimately reinforced the authority of the increasingly stringent laws. "In spite of their strong emotional content," the court effectively said, "we are not legally bound to protect these relationships."[143]

When explicated in the courtroom and placed alongside the formal legal relationships constituting legitimate families, the kinship ties between free people of color and whites took desperate and chaotic shapes. "Natural kinship," the only distinction that carried weight where the question of inheritance was concerned, could be achieved only through the father's explicit notarial act. According to the dissenting judges, however, a father documented his "degradation" only when "taken so lost to shame." Furthermore, the groups of defendants assembled in court under the name of Francisco Tio, Augustin Macarty's universal legatee, were a motley crew. Brigitte, Josephine, Patrice, and Phelonise were alleged half-siblings, children of Macarty's by different mothers. Tio himself "lived in concubinage" with Josephine Macarty, Augustin's alleged child, whom Tio's father had "raised as his own" making the two lovers siblings in the emotional if not the genetic sense. When confronted with this tangle of relationships, the court expressed bafflement and disapproval. In a very explicit manner, the legal system constructed and responded to the kinship patterns of the *gens de couleur libre* as semi-incestuous and illegitimate. This public perception made the *Cenelles* poets' expression and exploration of these themes even more salient. If a brother could not protect the image of his sister's (lack of) purity in the public imagination and in the law, he could at least attempt to subvert these portrayals through his poetic depiction of her chastity. Nonetheless, as the cases of the Macarty women show, the venue of the court and the realm of civil law worked in contradictory ways. Even as the legal system sought to reinforce prevailing American notions of purity and proprietorship for whites, it also, to some extent, gave Creole of color women the opportunity to defend their ownership status.

Legacies

The contested legacies of the Macarty men invite concern over the legacies of Mandeville and Perrault. Following Cable, we might expect a legacy of a dilapidated cottage housing several generations of Creole of color women and with them the mystery of the city's atmosphere of ruin. Following Lanusse and the *Cenelles* poets, we might expect to find these women and their offspring in a moral conundrum powerful enough to compel poetic rescue. The probate records of Eulalie Mandeville and Celeste Perrault prove to be more banal than either Cable or Lanusse and his anthologists would have hoped. However, they do attest to the modes of detour accessed by Creole women of color and the terms under which they might have expected to keep their property intact.

After her trial ended in March 1848, Mandeville lived only a few months longer, dying on October 20, 1848, at the age of seventy-four.

Moreover, her succession documents describe her family relationships in terms evoking the spare sense of economy and organization guiding her business affairs after 1825. In making the distinction between "legitimate" and "natural" relations, the Louisiana law created parallel genealogical narratives for the Mandeville-Macarty family. In one sense, Mandeville died a solitary figure, in full possession of her estate, unencumbered with the financial obligations a "legitimate family" would compel. "The deceased never was married and left neither lawful descendants not lawful ascendant, nor collateral relations." However, in terms of the affective bonds shared by her "natural family," Mandeville served as the matriarch of a thriving lineage of free people of color that included, in 1848, four sons and two grandchildren. The presence of these heirs—Barthelemy Macarty of Cuba; Villareaux Macarty, Eugène Macarty, and Theodule Macarty of New Orleans; and two grandchildren, Isabel Rigaud and Eugène Rigaud, legitimate children of Mandeville's deceased daughter Emeriste Arthemise Macarty and her husband Etienne Cheri Rigaud—helps explain why the Macarty name was not as extinct in 1921 as Grace King might have hoped. Curiously, the documents comprising Mandeville's succession severed Mandeville from the Marignys, her original "natural family." Professing that she had no living natural brothers or sisters, they effectively erased the kinship ties evoked during *Macarty v. Mandeville* by Bernard Marigny, who would continue to live until 1868 and who could have used some of her money. Although she did not live long enough to enjoy her court-supported claim to her property, her six-figure legacy to her natural children and grandchildren went through the proper procedures swiftly. The papers documenting her succession are brief and to the point.[144]

Perrault's legacy, on the other hand, was as complicated as Augustin Macarty's, enlisting dozens of witnesses in Europe and America. Shortly after the conclusion of *Badillo v. Tio*, Perrault settled in Paris for good. According to François Lacroix, the wealthy New Orleans tailor who was "well acquainted" with Perrault, she lived in the Paris home of her "godson," André Martin Lamotte, an arrangement that seems to have caused some speculation of impropriety by the court, an insinuation that Perrault and this much younger man had been romantically involved. Answering these concerns, Lacroix and another witness, Dr. Louis Charles Roudanez—a physician and the future proprietor of the Reconstruction newspapers *l'Union* and *la Tribune de la Nouvelle Orleans*—testified to the status of Lamotte as a widower and reiterated that "Madame Celeste Perrault was very old," in her seventies during this period. Perrault confided to one witness before her death in late 1859, "My income is not enough for me to live in Paris, but Lamotte, who is a true son comes to my assistance." In addition to room and board, Lamotte's filial responsibilities included paying personal bills—Perrault's Parisian dressmaker and launderer admitted their acquaintance with Lamotte in written testimony—and arranging for her funeral. When her succession was opened in a New Orleans court, Lamotte presented years of accounts detailing her expenses and claimed $2,000 from her estate of over $9,000. Extending over a period of years, her case proved to be far too complicated for her real son and testamentary executor, Patrice Macarty, who died before it was settled. However embattled her estate was to become, Perrault claimed at least one aspect of her legacy without impunity: the good old Creole name of Macarty. According to one witness, "here [in New Orleans] she was called Céleste Perrault; Madame Macarty when in Paris."[145]

Perrault's flight to Paris represented her grasp at freedom and an attempt to wrest control of her property *and* her propriety from the moral climate of New Orleans. However, the freedom she claimed there was contingent on her denial of freedom to others. Lamotte's generosity was not the only means of support Perrault enjoyed as Madame Macarty in Paris. She drew as well on income provided by the hire of her slaves—Pauline and her two children, Angela and Emeline or "Mimi," and Zoe and Felicité—whom she entrusted to the care of a friend, the free woman of color Eugenie Frésinette, back in New Orleans. If she had taken them to Paris with her in the late 1840s and early 1850s, they might have accessed a window of opportunity for achieving freedom. The case of the enslaved Missouri couple Dred and Harriet Scott against their presumed owner had not yet reached the Supreme Court, where, in *Scott v. Sanford* (1857), Justice Roger Taney would deny enslaved people the right to sue "as citizens" and affirm the rights of U.S. citizens to their slave property wherever they might travel. Although an 1846 Louisiana law anticipated the restrictions of the *Dred Scott* decision, the Louisiana courts sometimes overrode this law, granting ultimate freedom to enslaved people who had traveled to free soil states and countries.[146] Of particular importance for French-speaking New Orleanians, France, following the institution of a 1791 law, immediately freed any enslaved person who set foot in France (the mother country, not the colonies), and in 1848 revolutionary France outlawed slavery throughout its empire. In the late 1840s, the Louisiana Supreme Court freed two enslaved women who had previously sojourned in France. By the early 1850s, however, the court—apparently reluctantly—began to apply the terms of the 1846 law in a stricter fashion.[147] If Perrault's slaves had traveled to Paris, they might have claimed immediate freedom under French law or, at the very least, may have capitalized on a favorable recognition by the Louisiana court.

Instead they were left to the harshening proscriptions against enslaved people and free people of color dominating the legal climate of New Orleans during the 1850s. In 1857 the Louisiana legislature prohibited manumissions, a law Perrault may not have been able to circumvent even if she had wanted to. As a slaveholder, Celeste Perrault Macarty was considerably more charitable than her "husband's" kinswoman Delphine Macarty Lalaurie: the will that Perrault McCarty prepared in 1850 intended to bestow freedom on her slaves at her death. Her sojourn in Paris required that they remain in her possession, bringing in $6 to $12 each a month ($150 to $300 in twenty-first-century terms), hardly a negligible sum for a widow in Paris. Tending to her slave property was also a substantial financial burden. During the 1850s Perrault's slaves suffered from a number of ailments including various "fevers," pain in the sides, rheumatism, and weakness, compelling frequent and expensive visits from one Dr. Androus, who saw Perrault's "servants" an estimated twenty-five times per year during the late 1850s. At Perrault's death, Androus also claimed reimbursement from her estate. Afflicted with typhoid in 1857 and incapacitated for well over a year, Mimi sometimes failed to bring in a monthly income; and Zoe and Felicité died sometime before 1857. The contingencies of Perrault's estate thwarted the hopes for freedom of those of her slaves who managed to survive the decade. At the outset of their arrangement, Perrault had specified to Frésinette that an amount of the money from each hire of the slaves should be put aside so that they might eventually purchase themselves outright. However, as Frésinette testified, she used the money saved for this purpose to purchase the mourning attire to be worn by the slave women in memory of Perrault. Thus, her three remaining slaves dutifully performed Celeste Perrault's status after her death by wearing black and by constituting over one-third of the value of her wealth.

5

Choosing to Become Black

ON MAY 1, 1862, Major-General Benjamin F. Butler of the U.S. Army took possession of the city of New Orleans and, within the first few days of the federal occupation, received some unlikely visitors. The captains of Louisiana's Native Guard, the militia regiments of *gens de couleur libre* that had organized in the defense of Louisiana and thus in support of the Confederacy, called upon him to inquire about their group's future and to "learn what disposition they [should] . . . make of their arms."[1] Just over a year earlier, they had joined other New Orleanians in a frenzied response to a call to arms issued on April 21, 1861, by a local committee dubbed the Defenders of the Native Land.[2] The next day, according to a pleased and partisan *New Orleans Daily Picayune*, "nearly two thousand persons, representing the flower of the free colored population of New Orleans," met at the Couvent Institute in Marigny, where Armand Lanusse served as headmaster, to form their own military companies. At this meeting, fifteen hundred men pledged to fight " 'shoulder to shoulder' with the citizens as their fathers did in 1814" under Andrew Jackson against the British.[3] Later in the week, Jordan Noble, the free man of color who had served as a drummer in the 1815 Battle of New Orleans, announced his own attempt to form a regiment of color.[4] One wealthy *homme de couleur*, Bernard Soulié, donated $10,000 (almost $230,000 today) to the Confederate cause.[5] The units composed of free men of color joined other local volunteer companies, including such organizations as the Jefferson Davis Light Guards, the Sumter Guards, the British Guards, and a company of middle-aged lawyers and judges that Pierre Soulé had helped organize.[6] Over the course of the next year, as anxieties about the course of the nascent Civil War mounted, these units periodically came together in motley assembly for public display of loyalty to Louisiana.

Notwithstanding the unified tone of these festive occasions, authorities had mixed feelings about the military service of the *gens de couleur libre* in this particular cause. The spectacle of volunteers of color made excellent publicity, but officials continually passed over the Native Guard for active duty and failed to supply it with the basic rudiments of militia service. The Native Guard was even disbanded for a period in early 1862 when the state legislature announced its intention to conscript only able-bodied white males.[7] Despite their characterization by the *Picayune* and other newspapers, free men of color were likewise ambivalent. Like the citizens of France, Britain, and other foreign nations living in New Orleans, they exhibited enthusiasm for the Confederate cause primarily to defend their stakes in the city and would have balked at conscription into the regular Confederate army. Nevertheless, in the days preceding the federal occupation, the militia, including the Native Guard, was poised to stand against the U.S. military in defense of its native Louisiana.

When the gunboats of the U.S. Navy finally approached New Orleans on April 24, the militia stationed in the city beat a hasty retreat, leaving one young woman to wonder about the leaders' level of intoxication.[8] When Butler disembarked from his steamer a week later, he "marched without opposition" up Canal Street, depositing the bulk of his troops at the Customhouse on the corner of Chartres and Canal and continuing to the St. Charles Hotel, where he intended to have his headquarters. The city seemed so safe and secure to Butler that he returned to his ship on the same evening and brought Mrs. Butler ashore, taking her to the hotel by carriage with only a single guard.[9] As a group, New Orleans' *gens de couleur* responded in various and conflicting ways to the federal invasion. The Native Guard, which had not retreated with the rest of the militia into the countryside, offered its assistance to Butler; others defied federal authority in the city. Armand Lanusse, for example, refused to fly the Stars and Stripes on the grounds of the Couvent Institute.

Although he initially declined the Native Guard's offer of support, Butler, deep within rebel territory and starved for additional troops, reconsidered the idea of resurrecting the group toward the end of the summer. After conferring with Charles Sauvinet, one of its former captains and a translator of French, Spanish, and German for the Provost Court, Butler carried out his proposal to "call upon Africa," finding the former captains "all very glad to take service with us."[10] On August 22, 1862, Butler issued an order allowing the Native Guard and other free colored citizens to enlist in the Union Army, eventually adding 3,000 troops to the force under his command.[11] For free men of color, who had traditionally seen military service as a potential pathway to expanded citizenship rights, their participation in the Union Army offered them the best chance yet for social and political inclusion.[12] As members of the Native Guard under Butler and later as members of the Corps d'Afrique organized by Butler's successor, General Nathaniel P. Banks, *hommes de couleur* served with distinction, producing such heroes as Major Francis Dumas, the highest ranking black officer in the Union Army when he was promoted in the fall of 1862 and, along with Martin Delany, one of only two blacks to attain the rank of major during the Civil War.[13] At the Battle of Port Hudson, Louisiana, in May and June 1863—the first battle in which troops of color were used in combat—Captain André Cailloux became a martyr for the cause of black freedom and social equality, leading a storied attack on Confederate forces and demonstrating to a national audience the valor of black troops.[14] Because General Banks declined at first to acknowledge many of the troops who had fallen, the bodies of Cailloux and others lay decomposing on the battlefield for forty-one days before they could be retrieved. After the recovery of his corpse, Cailloux received a hero's funeral. The grand procession combined military officials, members of an assortment of Creole of color fraternal organizations, and thousands of onlookers, free and enslaved, who had come to pay their respects to the man Rodolphe Desdunes would deem the American Spartacus.[15]

In tandem with their military service, soldiers of color agitated for civil rights. Soon after joining the Union Army, many troops of color asserted themselves in New Orleans' public spaces. In September and October 1862, soldiers protested the operation of "star cars," New Orleans' segregated streetcar system, procuring a tenuous compromise whereby black officers would be allowed to ride in cars designated for whites. When General Banks sought to purge the Corps d'Afrique of officers of color, many of them, including Major Francis Dumas, resigned from the Army in protest.[16] In a postwar rally, the Friends of Universal Suffrage political organization pushed the veterans of the Native Guard to "continue in proving their manhood by pursuing a course honorable to themselves and their race."[17] They did. During the Civil War and Reconstruction, Louisiana and New Orleans in particular served as a theater for an early "experiment" in presidential Reconstruction and as a "crucible" for the development of wartime, presidential, and congressional Reconstruction policy. Radicals in Louisiana hammered out practicable strategies to achieve universal manhood suffrage and desegregation.[18] Abraham Lincoln's hopes that an occupied Louisiana could be quickly restored to the Union under a conservative 1864 constitution that effectively did little for blacks except put an end to slavery proved shortsighted. By 1865 former Confederates had gained control of the state legislature and the city government, and the unrepentant Rebel mayor John Monroe had been reelected. In response to these developments, an interracial progressive movement clustered in New Orleans moved to reconvene the Constitutional Convention and considered instituting black suffrage. In 1866 its attempts provoked one of the bloodiest riots of the era, and the ex-Native Guard, who led a large procession in support of the convention, suffered numerous casualties at the hands of a police force made up of former Rebel soldiers. Known as the New Orleans Massacre, this event directly precipitated congressional passage of the Reconstruction Acts and paved the way for black political participation as voters and officeholders.[19] For blacks and people of color, military service would serve as a springboard into radical Republican political leadership in New Orleans as elsewhere.[20]

Given the very real albeit limited privileges enjoyed by *gens de couleur libre* before the war, it should come as no surprise that the path of the Native Guard from its inception as an arm of the Confederate militia to its service in the Union Army to its production of Reconstruction-era spokesmen for black rights was fraught with contradiction. As potential black leaders, ex-Native Guard members and other people of color who had been free before the war felt continually compelled to explain their early choices, to make sense of their fluctuating wartime allegiances.

General Butler recalled his concerns having been allayed by Sauvinet's reasoning: "If we had not volunteered, they would have forced us into the ranks, and we should have been suspected. We have property and rights here, and there is every reason why we should take care of ourselves."[21] At an 1864 dinner in Boston hosted by Massachusetts Republicans, Arnold Bertonneau, a former Native Guard captain, reminded the audience of the "extremely perilous" position of New Orleans' *gens de couleur* in the early days of the Civil War. "Without arms and ammunition or any means of self-defense . . . ," he reasoned "Could we do otherwise than heed the warning and volunteer in the defense of New Orleans? Could we have adopted a better policy?"[22] When testifying before a U.S. congressional commission investigating the 1866 riot, a former Native Guard captain, Charles Gibbons, suggested that people of color would have been "robbed of their property if not killed" if they had failed to support the Confederate government.[23] Despite the plausibility of these explanations, their dubious display of loyalty has clouded the posterity of New Orleans' Creoles of color ever since.[24]

For me, exploring the various dimensions of the political project of Creole of color Republican activists and its implications for expressions of racial and national identity is ultimately more interesting than the question of their ultimate loyalty. Despite their cultural affiliations with Louisiana as an outpost of French civilization and their own racial, color, and status prejudice, the lives and deaths of Creole of color radicals demonstrated the extent of their commitment to the possibilities posed by citizenship in the United States and to the idea of black equality. However, their conflicting and conflicted actions, attitudes, and histories required a good deal of translation on their part, and they strove to make their identities as French-speaking *gens de couleur libre* more palatable and their motives more comprehensible in their new political, social, and racial context. This chapter examines one of the major vehicles for these acts of translation: the two radical Republican newspapers funded and produced by a segment of the Creole of color elite, *l'Union* (1862–1864) and *la Tribune de la Nouvelle Orleans/the New Orleans Tribune* (1864–1868, 1869–1870). In a sense performing the feats of heroism and sacrifice that the Native Guard enacted on the battlefield with their journalistic and literary efforts, these newspapers constituted the most sustained attempt by Creoles of color in wartime and Reconstruction New Orleans to bridge the gap between their pasts as *gens de couleur libre*—a caste apart—and their future roles as potential leaders of a black political community.

In their establishment and editorship of these bilingual journals, Creole of color journalists bridged more than simply their pasts and futures. In the political, cultural, and racial maelstrom of Reconstruction New Orleans, the newspapermen facilitated discussion among a variety of opposed groups: New Orleans natives and the succession of new regimes, French-speaking *gens de couleur* and English-speaking blacks, and freed people and those who claimed to be their benefactors, to name a few. Thus, the newspapers elaborated on the traditional in-between position of Creoles of color by accentuating their function as cultural mediators. In keeping with the best of the Creole tradition of fluidity and adaptability to local contexts, Creoles of color "passed" as African Americans. In the examples of George Pandelly and Anastasie Desarzant, we have seen how racial passing as white could be an instrument of liberation at the level of the individual and the family. The efforts of the Creole of color newspapermen demonstrate that choosing to become black might be a means of communal liberation. Some historians have suggested that they embarked on this strategy of rhetorical blackness to promote their own interests; in the process, however, they invested their choice to pass as black with an ethical dimension and discovered an extant tradition in which English-speaking African Americans grounded the quest for freedom in the experience and expression of a consciously racially defined group.[25] Many historical accounts of the *Tribune*'s efforts implicitly or explicitly privilege the newspaper's universalist rhetoric over its use of racial reasoning or vice versa. Many see in the *Tribune*'s use of French and Haitian revolutionary traditions its profound difference from the voices of English-speaking African American politicians.[26] Alternatively, I understand their efforts as an induction of sorts into a predicament that Eddie Glaude has called "the tragedy of African-American politics." Continuing a tradition that had certainly not run its course by the mid-nineteenth century, African Americans, now joined by Creoles of color, forged a pragmatic and prophetic political response to the limitations imposed on American democratic ideals by white supremacy.[27]

Attending to the complex nature of their alliances, *l'Union* and *la Tribune* reveal the consequences and implications of the bridge-building exercises of the Creole of color journalists. The newspapers underscore the tensions and the possibilities raised by putting francophone and anglophone traditions of black leadership in conversation with one another in a city that, although anomalous in so many respects, clarified and exemplified both the probable pitfalls and potential promise of Reconstruction. Tirelessly, the Creole of color journalists pressed their identity and culture into the twofold service of participating in a black American community with its own intellectual protest tradition and of envisioning a national culture of social and political equality. In doing so, they drew upon the experience of their group in between black and white racial categories, in between French and American national traditions, and in between Louisiana's Confederate experiment and the Union triumph, thus pointing to the constructed nature of both race and nation. What were the barriers to the effectiveness of this project? In what terms might we speak of its success?

Introducing *l'Union* and *la Tribune*

In September 1862, shortly after the first battalion of the Native Guard was mustered into the U.S. Army, Louis Charles Roudanez, a Creole of color physician, founded the biweekly *l'Union*, the self-proclaimed "organ of the free colored population," and chose Paul Trévigne, a multilingual teacher at the Couvent Institute, as its editor.[28] Vocalizing the anxieties and concerns of the Creole elite, *l'Union* sought to make the precarious cultural group visible to Union occupiers who may not have understood the structure of New Orleans society.[29] Over the course of the war, the newspaper's radicalism deepened, its political advocacy became more extensive, and death threats to Trévigne forced the journal to reorganize. A week after it was disbanded, Roudanez and Trévigne launched a new newspaper, the *New Orleans Tribune/la Tribune de la Nouvelle-Orleans*, a more politically coherent effort drawing more consciously on the French Romantic protest tradition. While attending medical school in Paris from 1848 to 1853, Roudanez had taken to the barricades in defense of working people during the democratic socialist revolution of 1848, learning a great deal about public protest from his fellow radical doctors.[30] Drawing on this socialist pedigree and attacking any measure that restricted or limited the rights and opportunities of the freedmen, the *Tribune* built a positive social agenda inclusive of universal male suffrage, desegregation, civil rights, and economic and labor reform. During the fall of 1864 and the spring of 1865, a particularly intense period in New Orleans around these issues, the *Tribune* served as the "official organ" of a number of "Negro rights" groups.[31] From 1865 to early 1868, the *Tribune* also served as the official newspaper of the Republican Party in Louisiana.[32] A split among the staff members over the gubernatorial election of 1868 and the withdrawal of party patronage caused the paper to fold in April of that year, even though it reappeared sporadically without party affiliation until 1870.

Despite the founding and funding of these newspapers by Roudanez, the editorship of Trévigne, and the richness and eloquence of the French-language sections, the characterization of *l'Union* and the *New Orleans Tribune* as Creole of color newspapers does not adequately capture their complex programmatic stance. The newspapers also exemplify the porous nature of the racial boundaries of the Creole of color category, continuing the tradition of francophone collaboration across racial lines discussed earlier. While living in Philadelphia and trying to complete a book manuscript on the comparative faculties of men and animals, Jean-Charles Houzeau, a Belgian astronomer and natural scientist of aristocratic birth, contributed articles under the pseudonym Cham as *l'Union*'s northern correspondent. He arrived in New Orleans in the fall of 1864 to coedit the *Tribune*.[33] Houzeau spoke of his role first as an advocate for blacks: "People noticed that I used the pronoun 'we' when speaking of the oppressed race. Did I not have the right like a lawyer at the bar to identify myself with those whose rights I was defending?"[34] However, the act of his writing for the *Tribune* coupled with his generally dark complexion made feasible the rumor that Houzeau was, in fact, a person of color. His act of racial passing rendered him socially dead but ultimately more useful than ever to the cause of justice: "because I alone, all alone at first, among the white population took up the pen in behalf of the blacks, I forfeited my 'Caucasian character' . . . I was dead, more than dead even, vilified in the eyes of my race. The defiant stance that I took was so exorbitant, that the only way to explain it was to imagine that I might be of African blood myself."[35]

In addition to seeking allies across racial lines, the newspapers—as Houzeau's forfeiture reiterates—attempted to cross cultural barriers and represent the interests of those "of African blood" no matter what their cultural identity. To achieve this goal, the staff expanded to include English-speaking blacks, and the *Tribune* coordinated its activities with a wider local and national group of black American leaders. In 1865 the paper moved from Conti Street in the French quarter to 122–124 Exchange Alley, a pedestrian arcade linking Canal Street and the St. Louis Hotel. Before the war, the hotel contained one of the most notable slave exchanges in the country, and the headquarters of lesser slave brokers lined the alley.[36] Setting itself up in the same space that once offered the most blatant public display of racism and injustice, the *Tribune* attempted not only to address the effects of slavery, but also to subvert its legacy in New Orleans' built environment. Its posterity reflecting these efforts, the *Tribune* has gone down in history as "the first black daily in the United States."[37] The articulation of a political project that could both include Houzeau and present itself as a "black daily" relied on the unique position of Creoles of color in between cultural identities and racial categories.

From the different and somewhat antagonistic groups of Creole of color and black American, and from the vantage point of southeastern Louisiana, a Union outpost in Confederate territory, the polyglot, multiracial editors of *l'Union* and the *Tribune* tried to construct various viable political, economic, and social alliances. In effect, they imagined communities with both national and diasporic dimensions.[38] They utilized the resources and techniques of print media first to help create a national political entity, the voting black community, and then to vocalize the dimensions and concerns of that emerging political entity, giving themselves a central role. Both papers combined the news of French and English speakers under one masthead, determined to demonstrate the essential compatibility of the two populations. Expanding on *l'Union's* English section, which often seemed to be an afterthought, the *Tribune*, bilingual from the start, made a more concerted effort to communicate with the black and white English-speaking world. Houzeau remembered the importance of this decision: "For a long time, the English section was only a cut and paste collection from English newspapers. On the contrary, it needed to become a veritable '*Tribune*,' from which one spoke to the government and to the country." Working to "maintain the unity of ideas and policy in the center of the directing group," the French-language section would ideally act as a funnel, consolidating opinion and channeling it into the English-language section, which "would deal with the outside world."[39] Thus, the *Tribune* provided a forum in which the voices of blacks (and its editors' own voices as "leaders" of the black community) could communicate across and within linguistic barriers and comment on the ever-evolving political context.

Fueled by a sense of social importance and political urgency, the production of *l'Union* and the *Tribune* required tremendous commitment from those involved. Over the course of the decade, Roudanez spent $35,000 in support of the newspapers (close to $450,000 in early-twenty-first-century money), borrowing $1,200 in a last ditch effort to save the *Tribune.*[40] Houzeau typically worked eighteen-hour days for the newspaper, juggling various duties such as writing editorials in both French and English, holding "office hours" to meet with "special pleaders," handing out assignments, reading proofs, covering political and philanthropic meetings, and corresponding with other newspapers around the country.[41] While editing the newspapers, Trévigne continued to teach full time at the Couvent Institute, even when faced with death threats from Confederate sympathizers.[42] The personal risks and sacrifices and tireless work attending this day-to-day project of nation-building were, of course, no guarantee of its ultimate success.

Setting the terms of their emergence on the public stage as legitimate players, the editors of *l'Union* and the *Tribune* believed themselves to be facilitating a culture of free debate and the rational exchange of ideas: "The principle which governs our journal, which is essentially progressive is that every system, every social, religious, commercial, or political theory which fears the light of discussion—discussion entirely free, animated but always parliamentary—every thesis which fears controversy must confess to itself its own weakness."[43] The first volume of the *Tribune* reiterated the sentiment found in the pages of *l'Union* and announced its public accountability: "Convinced that a newspaper under the present circumstances representing the principles and interests which we propose to defend and advocate was much needed in New Orleans, we shall spare no means at our command to render the *Tribune* worthy of public confidence and respect."[44] In contrast to other newspapers in the city, which the Creole of color editors regarded as partisan to the Confederate cause, *l'Union,* in a two-part column entitled "Le Journalisme" and "Les Journaux," upheld ideals of impartiality and objectivity, rhetorically forsaking a status quo in which corruption and bribery in return for good press were the central motifs: "this one, a poet, offered me a gold pen; that one, a moralist, dispensed to my caretaker ladles of money which I was obliged to send back; this woman author brought me a magnificent desk." Rebuffing these advances, the journalist, as disinterested and objective architect of the common good, "blush[es] for them as I would for myself. They do not blush at all."[45] In the pages of *l'Union*, the virtuous journalist served as a bridge to safety and enlightenment across the morally pitted terrain of occupied and Reconstruction Louisiana.

Much of the rhetoric of the Creole of color newspapers indicates a deep belief that the ideal of an enlightened rational public sphere might be achieved by the "courteous combat" of reasoned, progressive discussion. However, the staff harbored no illusions about the limitations that American racism and the racial rigidity of Americanization imposed on this progressive vision of an expanded public that could include people of African descent.[46] Well aware that they addressed multiple and fractured publics, the Creole of color journalists drew on a vast arsenal of persuasive techniques and discursive traditions. Paul Trévigne in particular was known for his "easy-going style" and the "playful manner with which he communicated his ideas." Rodolphe Desdunes, who collaborated with Trévigne in the closing decades of the nineteenth century, remembered how Trévigne's fluid, yet razor-sharp critical voice would slip beneath the scope of white supremacist repression to strike its target: "[Trévigne] laughed as he chastised with his satire."[47] In their ability to navigate the chaotic and changeable expressions of national and racial allegiance, the journalists anticipated W. E. B. Du Bois's description, in *The Souls of Black Folk* (1903), of how an African American "double consciousness" might help negotiate the "problem of the color line."[48] The newspapermen drew on the fluidity of their position in between black and white and in between French and American to imagine both a racial community and a national community. Tapping into their extensive experience as a people constantly in transition, they took up the challenge of facilitating successful alliances. At every turn, the attitudes of their own group and others' perceptions of them complicated their program, requiring that the Creole editors address a central tension in their role as political figures and analysts: Did their in-between status place Creoles of color in a vanguard position with respect to the black population, or did it render them a buffer population, easily inserted between blacks and whites to absorb the tensions of an increasingly racialized political and social context? What were the essential differences between a vanguard identity and a buffer identity? Were these positions two sides of the same coin?

"Negroes" as "Fire and Brimstone"

By July 1862 General Butler's initial ebullience had soured considerably. He had hanged a "traitor" on a flagpole; he had insinuated the sexual impropriety of New Orleans' "fearless" Confederate women by decreeing that their public taunts of Union soldiers warranted their treatment as prostitutes; and he had recently been trying to sanitize New Orleans in preparation for the "sickly season." New Orleanians had taken to calling him "Beast." Writing in exasperation to his wife, who had retreated to New England in fear of an outbreak of yellow fever, the frustrated Butler confessed, "I am changing my opinions. There is nothing of the people worth saving. I am inclined to give it all up to the blacks. Such lying, meanness, wrong, and wickedness, that I am inclined to think that the story of Sodom and Gomorrah a myth, else why not rain fire and brimstone upon this city. I am afraid the Lord will do so in the shape of Negroes."[49]

The numbers seem to bear out Butler's prediction of a black apocalypse in New Orleans. Between 1860 and 1870 the number of blacks in the city more than doubled from 24,074 to 50,495, while the number of whites declined from 144,601 to 140,923.[50] James Parton, a northern reporter and chronicler of Butler's administration, recalled that upon the Union capture of the city, "great numbers [of blacks] soon flooded into the Custom-House, pervading the numberless apartments and passages of that extensive edifice, all testifying the most fervent good will towards the Union troops."[51] Portrayed in various accounts and histories as a swarm or deluge, the rapidly expanding black presence was seen as a punishment for past sins or a portent of future disaster, notions that underscored many observations about the character of public space in wartime and Reconstruction-era New Orleans. For Creoles of color who had been free before the war, the influx of freed people presented a distinct form of annihilation. The prewar *gens de couleur libre* had relied on the term *libre* for their privileged social and legal distinction from the rest of the nonwhite population. Distinguished after the war by such awkward monikers as the "old free" or "formerly free" population, this group witnessed its cherished legal and social identity melt with its numbers into the masses of freedmen. In 1860 New Orleans' free population of color had numbered 10,689, a figure subsumed by the 50,495 people counted by census officials in 1870, a number that included both the formerly free and the recently freed.[52]

As Butler's comments indicate, authorities thought of the growing black population of New Orleans as a pre-rational, pre-political mass with no particular consistency and no sense of its own best interests. Blacks occupied public space but were believed to lack the qualifications to participate as citizens in the public sphere of either wartime military efforts or Reconstruction politics. In the terminology of the era, as W. E. B. Du Bois has pointed out, fugitives inched ever so slowly up the status hierarchy from slave to confiscated property—"contraband of war"—to freedmen and later to citizens.[53] Editorials in *l'Union* and the *Tribune*, especially early ones, equivocated over how to position the Creole of color population with respect to the formerly enslaved population. At times the *Tribune* editors offered themselves as exemplars of "Negro" industry and capability: "We hear from every quarter that the Negro is lazy and unable to maintain himself and his family by his own labor. Why: The example of the old free colored population must have shown by this time what are the abilities of the colored race for the civil pursuits of life."[54] However, the editors often stressed how their intelligence set them apart from the larger black population. In an early piece for the French section, the *Tribune* pleaded with the conquering officers to take heed of their former separate status, lamenting, "Although we are of the same race as the unfortunate sons of Africa who have groaned here under the yoke of a cruel and brutal slavery, one could not fairly confuse the newly liberated with our intelligent population whose industry and education has been as useful to society and to the country as any other class of citizens."[55] This tension within their own vision fed on and contributed to the way the city's influential outsiders—army officials, federal authorities, and Reconstruction politicians—viewed the role of Creoles of color.

For Union officers and troops and for newcomers to the city more generally, encounters with the *gens de couleur libre* mediated their visceral disgust with the teeming "contraband" in their midst. Because they were perceived as an intelligent, well-mannered, and cultured population, Creoles of color served a function similar to the mulatto characters of abolitionist literature. Their near-white physical appearance and the presumption of their exceptional mental capabilities and moral qualities elicited empathy from potential allies, making more palatable a sudden proximity to so many black people. In a sense, General Butler's employment of the Native Guard reflected how the in-between status of Creoles of color might render them a useful vanguard. In the summer of 1862 Butler struggled publicly with one of his subordinates, General John Phelps, over the question of conscripting enslaved refugees into the U.S. Army. A staunch abolitionist, Phelps argued for this policy even though its implementation would have devastated Lincoln's plan to reconcile Louisiana's Confederate sympathizers to the Union. Caught between federal policy and Phelps's activism, Butler steered a third course by enlisting *free* people and opened the door for more black participation by refusing to challenge conscripts' descriptions of their status. To justify this policy, Butler accentuated both the appearance and the intellectual abilities of New Orleans' *gens de couleur.* Early in the occupation, he had remarked to Secretary of War Stanton that the city's free blacks "in color, nay, also in conduct . . . had much more the appearance of white gentlemen than some of those who have favored me with their presence claiming to be the 'chivalry of the South.' "[56] After his removal from the Gulf Department, he reflected on the wealth, linguistic talents, and leadership of Major Dumas, "a man," in Butler's estimation, "who would be worth a quarter of a million dollars in reasonably good times. He speaks three languages besides his own, reckoning French and English as his own. . . . He had more capability as a Major than I had as Major General, I am quite sure."[57] By creating battalions in which *gens de couleur* and enslaved refugees (posing as free people) could serve together, Butler also provided the occasion for Creoles of color and the formerly enslaved to develop a common purpose. In perhaps the most dramatic case of wartime vanguardism, Francis Dumas formed a regiment of his former slaves and served as their captain.[58]

As the occupation continued, Creoles of color appeared in accounts and memoirs as mediating figures on the New Orleans social landscape as well as in the military. For example, in a letter to his wife in late September 1862, Captain John William De Forest of Connecticut described his attendance at a dinner party given at the home of the brother of Francis Dumas, presenting a utopia of interracial, intercultural, and intersectional harmony. A shining example of what De Forest termed "a new race," Captain (soon to be Major) Dumas had "the complexion of an Italian and features which remind one of the first Napoleon." Being the "only linguist in the party," De Forest served as translator in the flirtation between his white comrades and two young Creole of color women, "jolly little brunettes with slim figures and lively French manners." An evening among Creoles of color, in particular among the Dumas women, provided De Forest a respite from the legendarily hostile attitudes of other women native to New Orleans. "It was pleasant," he wrote, "to speak to an intelligent woman without being repelled by an angry stare." The Dumas women, two of whom De Forest described as resembling "Jewess[es]," so closely approximated whiteness that De Forest had no trouble considering them "ladies." "Since my arrival here until last evening," he concluded his letter, "I had not uttered a word to one of your sex, barring my charcoal-tinted washerwoman and the cocoanut-brown damsel who waits at our mess table."[59] For De Forest and the other Union soldiers present, the Dumas dinner party provided an entrée into Creole of color society, a unique window onto the moral, intellectual, and social potential of people of African descent.

While the cultural and racial distinctiveness of New Orleans' *gens de couleur* might be considered a bridge to a hypothetical world of wider black inclusion, it also served as a wedge that opponents of radical politics might drive between their group and freedmen. The Creole journalists addressed charges of fraud and self-interest leveled by conservatives as well as by members of the military leadership whose policies they critiqued. Referring to articles in the *Tribune*, "the alleged organ of the free colored Creoles," Major B. Rush Plumly, educational administrator in the regime of Butler's successor, General Nathaniel P. Banks, charged in a letter to the editor of Boston's *Liberator*, "There are not more decided Confederates to be found in the South than may be found among the free colored Creoles of Louisiana. This rebel party is not large, but it is rich, aristocratic, exclusive, and bitterly hostile to the black, except as a slave."[60] In an article supporting the conservative 1864 Louisiana constitution, the *New Orleans Picayune* attempted to attenuate the *Tribune's* opposition by questioning its editors' racial identity and allegiances: "The *Tribune*, a journal ostensibly devoted to the interests of the colored race, but apparently controlled by white men, who seemed to have failed in the struggle for leadership in the work of Reconstruction, says . . . the true course is to vote against the Constitution."[61]

Publishing the charges as well as its responses, the *Tribune's* editors asserted their refusal to be used as a buffer population and the independence of their choice to identify themselves in racial terms. Casting Major Plumly as the true traitor to the cause of the freedmen, the *Tribune* declaimed, "Lord! Save us from our 'friends'!" and reiterated the position that the *Tribune* "fully represents the colored population in spite of all the efforts that some white men have made to divide them." To the local *Picayune*, the *Tribune* staff countered, "The editor of the Picayune is too intelligent and has lived too long in New Orleans to ignore that those who defend in this paper the interest of the colored race belong to that population—a class of people who have never been controlled and shall never be."[62] Here and in their other public interventions, Creole of color journalists embraced inclusion within a "colored race" with its own interests understood over and against those of "white men." "It is not the time to follow in the path of white leaders; it is the time to be leaders ourselves. . . . We gratefully accept the services and assistance of our white brethren. But it is for us, not for them, to decide upon our course of action. Do not let the white men believe that they can do with us what they please. We are able to think for ourselves and to act for ourselves."[63] They articulated an "us" and "them" framework that sought to erase the cultural and status divisions between themselves and the formerly enslaved and to replace it with a racial division between blacks (us) and whites (them), including like-minded white "brethren."

These efforts to discount the sincerity of the newspapermen carried weight because they contained a core of truth. From his vantage point at the *Tribune*, the Belgian Jean-Charles Houzeau often noted the possibly divergent interests of Creoles of color and black Americans. "[Creoles of color] tended to separate their struggle from that of the Negroes," he wrote later. "Some believed that they would achieve their cause more quickly if they abandoned the black to his fate."[64] Even if one disregarded Houzeau's position at the *Tribune*, one could argue that the newspaper was controlled by white men inasmuch as Creoles of color had long placed a value on whiteness by seeking white-skin privilege and asserting their status as slave owners within a racialized slave system. In response to these very real legacies as former slave masters and Confederate sympathizers, the *Tribune* editors sought to refashion their images. In an article that explained the history of "slave labor in Louisiana," the *Tribune* characterized slavery as a social "custom" that had been difficult for wealthy people of any color to resist: "Very often, the poorest among us who could, only by the greatest exertion, procure a few hundred dollars, expended even that in the purchase of a Negro."[65] According to the *Tribune,* Creole of color slaveholding and color prejudice resulted primarily from bequests of property from white ancestors and legal restrictions imposed by the white government. Furthermore, the *gens de couleur libre* had treated their slaves well. Claiming that Major Dumas had been representative of "all colored masters," another article insisted that his slaves had been "treated as freemen, and no one had money enough to buy any of them, for he would not sell them at any price, because he would not give them a master."[66]

During the early spring of 1865, a letter to the editor signed by "Junius, Not a Rich Creole" argued that "The odious Black Code of Louisiana debarred [the slave and the free people of color] from all social intercourse. . . . The *colored people would be a unit* but for the interference in their affairs by irresponsible parties."[67] In the winter and early spring of 1864–65, the *Tribune* and other radicals sought to fulfill the wish for unity and formed the Freedmen's Aid Association to protest the Banks Administration's free labor plan—a plantation management solution that seemed to shore up the institution of slavery.[68] Grounded in utopian socialist principles, the Freedmen's Aid Association hoped to create a new "black phalanx," using the terminology of French socialist Charles Fourier, whose model for communal living had been enormously popular in antebellum America. On radically reorganized plantations, wealthy Creoles of color, a "set of citizens of intelligence, morality, and industry" would oversee the "democratization of capital," and the freedmen would constitute the labor force.[69] The activists hoped to "bring these three elements [capital, intelligence, and labor] to act harmoniously together," and "equally protect the rights of the moneyed men, managers, and laborers, on the basis of individual freedom."[70] Spawning only four midsized plantations, this experiment was not a widespread success: the plantations collapsed amidst widespread confusion over land ownership in the immediate postwar period.[71] Nevertheless the association raised important questions about the course of "black leadership" and the nature of "black solidarity": On what basis might "colored people" act as a unit? Would Creoles of color be able to take on the concerns of the formerly enslaved as their own, or would longstanding cultural, legal, and class privilege undermine their efforts at forging a "black" politics?

The tension among Creoles of color between a vanguard identity and a buffer position emerged clearly in response to the question of universal or partial suffrage, and the consolidation of the *Tribune* group's position for universal manhood suffrage illustrates the evolution of its members' role as black leaders. Initially, the New Orleans *gens de couleur libre* pressed for the suffrage rights of those men of African descent who had been free before the war to the exclusion of the formerly enslaved. When the Constitution of Free State Louisiana was adopted in early 1864, however, the free men of color faced a halfhearted affirmation of their political and civil rights that lacked an enforcement mechanism and the virulent racism of a legislature that sought to banish free blacks from the state.[72] In response, politically active Creoles of color sent a delegation consisting of Jean Baptiste Roudanez—the brother of *l'Union*'s proprietor, Dr. Louis Charles Roudanez—and Arnold Bertonneau, a wine merchant and an ex-Native Guard, to Washington, D.C., to deliver a petition to President Lincoln and members of Congress.[73] Citing the service of their forefathers in 1814–15 and their payment of "taxes on an assessment of more than fifteen millions of dollars," and signed by War of 1812 veterans, loyal union citizens, and one thousand of Louisiana's free men of color, the petition initially requested that "all citizens of Louisiana of African descent, born free before the rebellion, may be . . . directed to the rights and privileges of electors."[74]

Impressed by these francophone activists of color, Lincoln suggested privately to Louisiana governor Michael Hahn that the *gens de couleur* might be an effective buffer. That is, including "the very intelligent and especially those who have fought gallantly in our ranks" in the electorate might help tip the vote toward Republicans without taking the more drastic step of enfranchising freedmen.[75] On the other hand, Senator Charles Sumner criticized the petition for its failure to assume a vanguard role and to provide leadership for blacks more generally. After meeting with Sumner and Congressional radicals, Roudanez and Bertonneau appended a postscript to the original petition before offering it to Lincoln. Conceding the shortcomings of the original petition, they affirmed that "justice and the principles for which [the petitioners] contend require also the extension of [the right of suffrage] to those born slaves, with such qualification as shall affect equally the white and colored citizen."[76]

In the process of mediating their stance, Bertonneau, Roudanez, and the radical fringe of the Creole of color elite forged ties with a national activist community, thus broadening their connections beyond the limited realm of occupied Louisiana. In April 1864 Governor John Andrew of Massachusetts hosted the two *hommes de couleur* at a Boston dinner reception, an event that served as a mutual introduction of the Louisianans and seasoned antislavery advocates. Admitting his embarrassment in "attempting to address such an assembly as the one before him," which included William Lloyd Garrison and Frederick Douglass, Roudanez briefly described their mission to Washington and ceded the floor to Bertonneau. Lavishing praise on the regime of Massachusetts' native son General Butler, the former Native Guard captain rationalized his group's support of the young Confederacy and prayed for the demise of caste and color prejudice. In his speech, Bertonneau cited that touchstone of Biblical wisdom often used by radical abolitionists to refute the claims of racial science: "God created of one blood all nations of men to dwell upon the face of the earth."[77] During the rest of the decade, many African American political figures, previously skeptical or dismissive of the commitment of New Orleans' Creoles of color to blacks more generally, began to recognize them as allies.[78] The *Tribune* group would draw strength from connections such as these to sustain its voice as the most persistently radical newspaper in the darkest depths of early Reconstruction Louisiana.[79]

When the controversy over limited versus universal suffrage emerged again in late 1864 and early 1865, the *Tribune* group expressed unqualified support of extending the suffrage to freedmen as well as *gens de couleur*. In this effort, it opposed renewed efforts by Republican authorities to enfranchise a limited group of educated and propertied men of African descent. Taking center stage in the national debate over the fate of President Lincoln's Reconstruction plan, the question of Louisiana's readmission to the Union hinged on the terms of its constitution, including the role of former secessionists in its government and the nature of Louisiana's policies toward freedmen and blacks who had been free before the war. As a means of demonstrating to Congress the good intentions of Free State Louisiana, federal agents in New Orleans prompted black leaders to petition for limited suffrage. Assuming the position that Bertonneau, Roudanez, and those associated with the *Tribune* had abandoned a year earlier, a group of activists dubbed "memorialists" seized upon this opportunity to expand their political rights. Although the membership of this group cut across cultural lines and included English-speaking black Protestants as well as Creoles of color, the *Tribune* editors took the opportunity to establish the reputations of Creoles of color as a vanguard of black politics.[80] Addressing the issue of Creole ambivalence toward universal suffrage, the *Tribune* group distanced itself from the message of the memorialists at the same time that it tried to persuade them to accept the *Tribune*'s more comprehensive strategy.

In this dual effort, the editors took advantage of the paper's bilingualism. Raising the cry "no distinction; no aristocracy!" and claiming "a broad right for all," the English section of the *Tribune* condemned the memorialists for attempting "to create privileged classes in our midst."[81] The *Tribune* further equated the memorialists with the secessionists for "separating their fortune from that of their brethren . . . [trying] to frame a separate plan of action, and elect a colored Jefferson Davis in opposition to our venerable Mr. [Louis] Banks [the spokesman of the all-black Equal Rights League]."[82] Attempting to bring the "traitors" into a more inclusive fold, the French section of the newspaper addressed them more sympathetically, cautioning Creoles of color to regard universalist rhetoric with suspicion. According to the *Tribune*, the memorialists "have perhaps been seduced by the governor's sweet talk: 'I do not recognize any differences of race.' However, they have forgotten other speeches uttered by this same person . . . 'I am for the liberty of the slaves because I wish to see Louisiana a free state, but I will never admit that the black could have the same privileges as the white.'"[83] On the fiftieth anniversary of the 1815 Battle of New

Orleans, the *Tribune* appealed to the memorialists' sense of national and racial identity in order to wed their cause to that of the freedmen. "Your slave brothers have gotten their liberty and have been made your equals. . . . Could the nation's progress pass you by without your beneficial input? Could it . . . leave you in its shadow and in its memory? It is up to you to raise your own voice."[84] For the *Tribune* group, the political future of Creoles of color rested on the shoulders of the formerly enslaved, and a more complete show of unity with black Americans might stem the threat of their disappearance from social and political life.

Throughout 1865 the *Tribune* redoubled its efforts to convince the *gens de couleur* to widen their narrow interests and support a more comprehensive vision of freedom. In the early fall, for example, the French section of the *Tribune* carried in serialized form a fantastical historical account of the life of Vincent Ogé written by Melvil-Bloncourt, a Guadeloupean writer and activist. A wealthy *homme de couleur* of prerevolutionary Haiti, Ogé would have been familiar to many readers. Two of the heroes of 1815, father and son Charles and Joseph Savary, were alleged to have been related to Ogé.[85] In 1789 Ogé traveled to Paris to petition the French revolutionary government, as Roudanez and Bertonneau would petition Washington seventy-five years later, to enfranchise the colony's free people of color. In his appeal, Ogé made it clear that his sympathies and efforts did not extend to enslaved people. Rebuffed by the National Assembly and thwarted in his efforts to cast a ballot in local elections in Saint Domingue, Ogé and others organized a revolt of Saint Dominguan *gens de couleur libre*, traveling to New Orleans to procure arms and ammunition. Ogé's 1790 rebellion was quickly suppressed by white planters, and after a protracted trial he and his chief co-conspirator were paraded through the public square, brutally broken on the wheel, and finally beheaded, their heads placed on pikes. Within months enslaved Saint Dominguans took up their own cause in a succession of rebellions that eventually culminated in the end of slavery in the colony and Haitian independence.[86]

In his 1789 motion to the Assembly of Colonists in Paris, Ogé pledged that *gens de couleur* might "help ward off the storm [of impending slave revolt] that rumbles over our heads." Dramatizing the investment of his class in the success of the French empire, Ogé advocated that the French consolidate "all our intelligence, all our means, and all our efforts" to ward off the blacks and prevent the destruction of property and the mutilation of "our neighbors, our friends, our wives, [and] our children." Ogé continued, "the slave will raise the standard of revolt, and the islands in the Caribbean Sea will be a vast and baleful conflagration; commerce will be ruined; France will receive a mortal wound, and a multitude of honest citizens will be impoverished and ruined; we will lose everything."[87] Ogé's petition and professed politics clearly indicated his wish to render free people of color a buffer population whose votes would work to insulate the French colonial regime from its enslaved subjects. However, over the course of the nineteenth century, activists in the francophone world and in the United States, eager to forge a more secure union between blacks and mulattoes and between enslaved people and the free black elite more generally, seized upon the story of Ogé in order to highlight the possibilities of a vanguard politics.

For Cyril Bissette, the Martiniquan *homme de couleur* and the publisher of the Paris-based abolitionist journal *Revue des Colonies* from the mid-1830s to the early 1840s, Ogé's exclusion of enslaved people from his conception of citizenship masked his true egalitarian vision, reflecting instead an unfortunate strategy of misguided white advisers. In 1841, at the height of the regime of Haitian president Jean-Pierre Boyer, who hoped to square his mulatto identity with potential *noiriste* critics, the Haitian dramatist Pierre Faubert staged *Ogé, ou le Prejugé de Couleur*, writing the mulatto into the legacy of black nation-building and stressing Ogé's "ardent sympathy for his slave brothers."[88] Having spent three years in Haiti, the mixed-race George Boyer Vashon (no relation to Jean-Pierre Boyer), the first African American graduate of Oberlin College and the first black man admitted to the New York bar, memorialized Vincent Ogé in a multi-stanza poem, ending "Thy coming fame, Ogé! is sure; / Thy name with that of L'Ouverture, / And all the noble souls that stood / With both of you, in times of blood, / Will live to be the tyrant's fear— / Will live, the sinking soul to cheer!"[89] These accounts transform Ogé's expression of mulatto chauvinism into a powerful precursor of Toussaint's rebellion and a decisive show of resistance to the divide-and-conquer practices of the French colonial system with respect to the African-descended population.[90]

From September 21 to September 30, 1865, readers of the French section of the *Tribune* could witness an edifying version of Ogé's story unfold. Casting themselves in the mold of the refashioned Vincent Ogé as "Heros de la Race Africaine (heroes of the African race)," the *Tribune* journalists grappled with the tension in Creole of color politics over whether to assert themselves as an active vanguard of the black population or to serve as a buffer by entering a larger hemispheric debate over the interests of mulattoes in black politics. For the *Tribune*'s French readers, Ogé presented both a model of bold intentions and a warning of how those intentions might be undercut by shortsighted political expediency. In the newspaper, Ogé's moral tale framed announcements for meetings of the Friends of Universal Suffrage, a biracial organization that Houzeau and Trévigne helped found in order to bridge the efforts of the black Equal Rights League and radical whites.[91] In late September this organization embarked on the voluntary registration of disfranchised loyal citizens in a show of opposition to the conservative constitution of 1864. Four and a half years earlier, Madame Couvent's Institute Catholique had been a recruitment center for the Native Guard forming on behalf of the secessionist regime. Now it served the Friends of Universal Suffrage as a registration bureau for the mock elections that would demonstrate black political power and competence.

Within the public spaces of New Orleans, it was increasingly clear that Creoles of color were losing their special privileges and that the racial distinctions of black and white were beginning to trump cultural and linguistic distinctions. In late 1864 the administration of Union general Nathaniel Banks issued passes to be carried by blacks regardless of their prewar status. Ostensibly meant to control the spread of smallpox, this pass system effectively limited the mobility of New Orleans' black population. The *Tribune* protested: "It is an outrage upon the old free colored men, who used that right [of moving at will] during the darkest and most gloomy years of the slave régime and now are deprived of the exercise of their traditional liberties."[92] After Lincoln's assassination, emboldened by Andrew Johnson's amplification of Lincoln's conciliatory policy, the conservative Louisiana legislature continued to ignore the few egalitarian provisions of the state constitution, and a number of ex-Confederates began to surface in the various levels of government, particularly on the police force.[93] Within New Orleans, public life polarized around the former Rebels, now organizing themselves into white supremacist organizations, and a radical contingent that, although interracial and multicultural, increasingly assumed a black identity.[94] The "blackness" of the radicals only intensified when they pursued universal manhood suffrage more urgently.

This racialized political standoff reached its apex in late July 1866 at the Mechanics' Institute, where activists expressly considering extending suffrage to freedmen attempted to reseat the Louisiana Constitutional Convention of 1864. In response, Mayor Monroe, a rebel sympathizer and chief of a secret white supremacist society known as the Southern Cross, and his police force coordinated an apparently planned attack on the assembly that quickly devolved into what one police participant allegedly described as an effort to "exterminate the niggers."[95] L. J. P. Capla, the son of a Battle of 1815 veteran, witnessed the policemen "shooting poor laboring men, men with their tin buckets in their hands, and even old men walking with sticks." Disregarding victims' pleas for mercy, the police-led mob "shot them and when they done that they tramped upon them, and mashed their heads with their boots and shot them after they were down."[96] Demonstrating just how closely black identity and Union identity were yoked together in the public imagination, one "colored man" recalled having overheard two policemen in a grocery store in the days leading up to the riot saying "By God, we are going to hang [Dr. Anthony P.] Dostie and [Governor Michael] Hahn [two prominent white Unionists]. . . . Yes, we are going to shoot down all these God damned niggers."[97] In a similar vein, the nephew of a white conventioneer remembered hearing a barrage of epithets during the riot: "Kill the Yankee nigger," "Shoot the nigger son of a bitch! There goes another nigger. . . . There goes another damned Yankee!"[98] Having escaped through a back door just in time, the *Tribune*'s Belgian editor Jean-Charles Houzeau—described as "colored" in the formal federal investigation of the riot—depicted the episode as "the awful massacre of the blacks and their partisans."[99]

In the heat of the riot, however, phenotype rather than political affiliation served as the ultimate marker of racial identity—the primary arbiter of one's fate. The riot victims were overwhelmingly black: by official count, 3 whites had been killed and 17 wounded, while 119 blacks had been wounded and 34 "colored citizens" had been shot, stabbed, or bludgeoned to death.[100] Those whites who died and suffered the most severe injuries were so well known that there was no mistaking their partisanship, but other whites connected to the convention seemed, because of their racial identity, to have escaped the worst of the violence. In fact, Arnold Bertonneau's white appearance may have saved his life. Under the impression that Bertonneau was a white man, a police officer rescued him from the mob and gave him the option, which Bertonneau did not take, to "run" rather than be taken to the jailhouse for more abuse.[101]

For Creoles of color, the riot demonstrated how completely their partisanship with the blacks would render them outsiders in the eyes of native white New Orleanians. Inaugurating the morning's festivities, a procession of ex-Native Guardsmen wound its way from Marigny through the French Quarter to the Mechanics' Institute on the corner of Canal and Dryades Streets. Marching to the tune of "Yankee Doodle" and bearing the U.S. flag, the ex-soldiers had attracted a "third line" of hundreds of people—mostly black—by the time they reached the convention hall. To the mob of policemen and rebel sympathizers, the sight of so many men of color in Union blue sparked a particularly intense reaction.[102] Spotting in the midst of the fray Charles Gibbons, who had been an officer in the Native Guard, a policeman yelled "There is that damned nigger captain; kill the black son of a bitch."[103] Referring to the nativist violence of the previous decade, a Creole of color army captain, J. B. Jourdan, described a shift in public perception about whose acts of assembly threatened civic identity. According to his testimony, the "thugs" on the police force—a special battalion of "professional killers"—had been "killing foreigners once; now they are killing negroes and loyal men."[104] Those foreigners who had been considered outsiders in the 1850s used the occasion to express their solidarity with other white New Orleanians. According to the testimony of another riot victim, the first shot of the morning had been fired at a member of the procession by an "Irishman" who missed his mark and proceeded to strike the black man with a stick.[105]

Random and brutal violence indoctrinated Creoles of color into the terrorism that had long plagued enslaved people in New Orleans and elsewhere. The police removed a number of people from the scene to the stationhouse lockup, where they were subjected to more abuse. Although a self-described Creole and "well known here," Capla was "miserably mistreated," suffering a gunshot wound and severe body blows after the police dragged him from the institute to the calaboose.

In the fray, Capla was separated from his sixteen-year-old son, who had been shot in the left eye and left in the street for dead.[106] With no regard for the human dignity of the riot victims, teams of whites hauled away carts loaded with the killed and merely wounded. Two days later, twenty-two of these bodies wound up in an unspecified "workhouse," where coroner Charles Delery conducted a rapid "general inquest" on the unidentified victims. Ostensibly to protect workers against the "arising stench" of the corpses, a hot fire had been lit, and Delery determined that "it was the utmost urgency to have the bodies removed."[107] The Creole of color Ludgier Boquille, a French teacher in one of the "Republican schools," spoke of the violation of two close friends who had been murdered in the riot, one whose body was never recovered. The other, Victor Lacroix, the son of tailor François Lacroix, had been shot and killed while presenting his white flag to the encroaching mob. When his body was found, it had been "cut from head to foot, butchered and mutilated in the most shocking and barbarous manner," and robbed of its watch chain and a large sum of money. The murder of Victor Lacroix demonstrates the speed with which white supremacist violence could turn a proud *homme de couleur* "of very light complexion," heir to one of the most extensive real estate fortunes in the city, into a mound of lifeless black flesh.[108]

The *Ancienne Population Libre* Remembers Slavery

As the riot of 1866 demonstrated, public perception increasingly identified Creoles of color, non-native blacks, and freedmen alike as "niggers." However, the *Tribune* sought to substantiate these bonds, to make them more than merely circumstantial and reactive. Speaking across and within lines of language, color, religion, class, and prewar status, the *Tribune* editors faced a "colored population" whose full potential might be undermined by the depths of the various chasms traversing it. In late 1864 they assessed their "peculiar situation":

> Here, the colored population has a twofold origin. There is an old population, with a history and moments of its own, partaking of the feeling and the education of the white. The only social condition known to these men is that of freedom. . . . There is on the other hand, a population of freedmen, but recently liberated from

> the shackles of bondage. All is yet to be done for them. These two populations equally rejected and deprived of their rights, cannot be well estranged from one another. The emancipated will find in the old freemen, friends ready to guide them, . . . But at the same time, the freemen will find in the recently liberated slaves a mass to uphold them.[109]

For the *Tribune* editors, the Creoles of color constituted an active and generative "old population," with the benefits of experience, "a history and moments of their own." In contrast, they saw the freed people, knowing nothing except the "shackles of bondage," as a young, primarily passive population whose best days lay ahead of them. "Recently liberated," they awaited the moment when all might "be done for them." In the only active role envisioned for them, the formerly enslaved would, as a mass, "uphold" the old population of *gens de couleur*. The paternalism of the Creole of color activists toward the recently emancipated did not differ terribly from that of the various missionaries and philanthropists who flocked to the South to oversee the education of the freedmen. Their noblesse oblige also hearkened to a French Romantic tradition that attempted to merge political and artistic expression and that saw in the suffering of the masses a fertile ground for the emergence of the individual Romantic hero.[110]

Part of the difficulty of extracting a consistent political program from the pages of the *Tribune* stems from its efforts to reconcile divergent histories as well as divergent historiographies. In other words, both the Creole of color experience of the past and the ways they interpreted that past—and hence understood the present and future—differed significantly from the historical sensibilities of the newly emancipated and those English-speaking African Americans who had for decades articulated an antislavery political project. When the *Tribune* editors grounded their authority in having "partaken of the feeling and the education of the white," they adopted, at least in part, an understanding of history as progress founded on the "dream of revolutionary transformation" rather than a sense of history as catastrophe founded on the "rupture of the middle passage."[111] Even with their roles as a progressive vanguard of the *ancienne population libre*, the *Tribune* staff members often prioritized their privileges within New Orleans' antebellum society and their cultural ties to a French revolutionary tradition over their own histories of dislocation, dispersal, and disenfranchisement.

The divergent histories experienced by Creoles of color and freedmen under slavery mapped onto differences in poetic and political sensibilities that would prove difficult to assimilate. As late as 1907 the Creole of color activist Rodolphe Desdunes would claim that "The Latin Negro differs radically from the Anglo-Saxon in aspiration and method. One hopes, the other doubts. Thus we often perceive that one makes every effort to acquire merits, the other to gain advantages. One aspires to equality, the other to identity. One will forget that he is a Negro, in order to think that he is a man; the other will forget that he is a man in order to think that he is a Negro. . . . One is a philosophical Negro, the other practical."[112] Desdunes exaggerates for effect, but his sense of the struggle between hope and doubt within an emergent black political sensibility in the early twentieth century bears fruitfully on our understanding of the *Tribune*'s efforts to forge a Reconstruction-era black politics.[113] Arguing from the point of view of a people who had always experienced the "social condition" of freedom—limited though that freedom may have been—Desdunes misreads the skepticism and political tactics of the "Anglo-Saxon Negro" as a dead-end "doubt" and discounts the political legacy of slaves and their representatives. When taking seriously the *Tribune*'s efforts at "passing as black," however, it is important to trace the lineaments of this doubt: its grounding in the experience of the underside of American freedom, its role in formulating an institutional and individual response to a lack of freedom, and its transformation in African American political and religious thought into an expression of prophetic hope. Having imbibed the "feeling and education of the white," the editors of the *Tribune* assumed that they would be perfect guides for the freedmen. However, in the midst of this period of adamant Americanization, the *Tribune* staff would grapple with the slave narrative tradition and African American religious and institutional culture, thus learning how knowledge obtained under the "shackles of bondage" might work to invigorate its own conceptions of freedom and citizenship.

Despite the fact that most of the new Creole of color leaders had not experienced slavery firsthand, other than in some cases as slave owners, their success on the new political scene depended on their ability to share in the memories of enslavement and to imagine the transition from slavery to freedom. Antebellum Creole of color literature such as the poems of *Les Cenelles* bathed in the pathos of the abandoned child's aspirations for legitimacy and legacy within a system of informal *plaçage* and the legal restrictions on interracial families. This expressed melancholia operated as a currency confirming the humanity and refinement of Creoles of color. In this vein, Desdunes's 1911 *Nos Hommes* greets the reader with a preface by "L. M." distinguishing between the Creole of color population and other blacks caricatured as the "common slave." "The common slave does not know the meaning of tears. When he feels the lash of the master's whip falling more and more heavily upon him, he bends his back lower and lower; that is all. This is not so for the Creole of color, for I have seen mothers furtively wipe the tears from their eyes as they told me of sufferings borne by their children because of the injustice of segregation bonds."[114] Having endured "natal alienation," according to Orlando Patterson the most extreme manifestation of "social death," the "common slave" of this portrait not only lacks familial sentiment but, devoid of tears, cannot even feel his own pain.[115] By contrast, the ease with which the Creole of color mother weeps at her child's confrontation with racism confirms the affective capacities of her social and cultural group.

In the context of wartime and Reconstruction Louisiana, the *Tribune* group attempted to turn this sentimental yearning, reserved for elusive white fathers and for those relatives who had disappeared across the color line, toward formerly enslaved people. Thus, the *Tribune* staff instructed fellow French speakers to reevaluate their kinship claims with "white" Louisianans: "In part, the immense interests [of Creoles of color] were annihilated at the moment when the population lent help to General Butler. . . . The population of color has lost all of the sympathy of the secessionists of the state with whom it had lived as a family before the entrance of the Federals."[116] Seeking, then, a familial bond with the freedmen, the *Tribune* staff attempted to conjure a common historical memory by drawing on the tradition of the slave narrative. The Civil War had marked a turning point in the slave narrative convention: an antebellum formula marked by a focus on the individual valor and courage of fugitive slaves gave way to a post-bellum narrative recounting mundane tales of endurance and common suffering.[117] Both forms served the political needs of their moment: The antebellum narrative appealed to abolitionist audiences searching for models of heroic individualism in the experiences of fugitive slaves. The post-bellum narrative voiced the experience of the multitude of those unable to escape or achieve literacy under slavery. The antebellum narrative, exemplified by Frederick Douglass's *Narrative*, employed a Romantic literary style that would appeal to Creoles of color. The post-bellum narrative, which reached its apex with Booker T. Washington's *Up From Slavery*, elicited a proto-realist narration and exhibited the pragmatic outlook that Creole of color elites would find difficult to assimilate.[118]

Reflecting the imperfect convergence of these two narrative projects and the political styles that issued from them, the pages of the *Tribune* staged a meeting between a Romantic politics and a pragmatic politics. In the English section of the first issue of the *Tribune*, the editors covered the proceedings of a political meeting held in a black Protestant church and lingered over the testimony of a newly liberated minister who offered his account to an emotionally supportive audience. "I have not much to say. I am from the back wood. I am not acquainted with societies and the only thing I do know anything about is serving God and telling others to do the same through what I have learned." Here, he emphasizes his humble status and lack of proficiency with words and urbane social settings, claiming his authority from God and experience rather than from institutionalized intellectual training. "I have passed through blood to this land of liberty," he continues. "Where I came from the usual number of stripes was from 500–600 and if you could not stand it, you would have to die."[119] In contrast to the choice between dramatic escape and the social death of slavery offered by most published antebellum narratives, the speaker here details a choice between "stand[ing] it"—slavery's physical humiliation—and actual death. Recounting his journey to freedom, the minister's corporeal testimony makes the passage "through blood" from slavery tangible, inviting the members of his audience who shared memories of these "usual" bodily violations to place themselves in a trajectory from unspeakable suffering to purposeful political activity. Recording rather than partaking of this ritual of transformation, the *Tribune* placed itself beyond the circle of like-minded witnesses. Registering evidence of an experiential barrier, its objective journalistic tone sought to temper its voyeuristic difference from the formerly enslaved person with a respect for the singular nature of the slave experience.[120]

In the French section of the first issue of the *Tribune*, the editors advertised and endorsed a book describing the experience of the Reverend J. Sella Martin, a journey from slavery to freedom that more closely exemplified the antebellum Romantic tradition. As the story goes, Martin was born in 1832 in Charlotte, North Carolina, the son of an enslaved woman named Winifred and a white man to whom she had been given as a concubine by her mistress, a Mrs. Henderson, the man's wealthy aunt. Mrs. Henderson had hoped to occupy her nephew's affections until he grew mature enough to marry sensibly and inherit her fortune, but her plan backfired when he began to show a deeper attachment to Winifred and their children. When young Sella was only six years old, Mrs. Henderson sold him, his mother, and his sister deeper into slavery. Separated by sale from his family, Martin spent the bulk of his enslaved life in Columbus, Georgia, as a *valet de chambre* to a relatively cultured bachelor with failing eyesight. Having become literate over the years through his own efforts, Martin compensated for his master's rapidly deteriorating vision by reading him the papers and carrying on his correspondence. Freed at age eighteen upon the bachelor's death, Martin found himself forced back into slavery by his master's heirs, who sold him farther west. Eventually Martin arrived in New Orleans and was passed among a variety of masters from 1852 to 1855, when he made his daring escape to Chicago aboard a steamboat. Literate, resourceful, and concerned about the plight of those still held in slavery, Martin seemed a perfect candidate for the abolitionist circuit. After a harrowing initial experience on the speaker's podium, which he often likened to being on the auction block, Martin matured into one of the most popular and influential antislavery activists. According to one paper, Martin was a "prodigy," one of the "most interesting and forcible speakers of his age, and of *the* age."[121] Ordained as a Baptist minister in Michigan after a formal tutelage in theology, Martin had by 1864 preached widely in both Old and New England. Regularly the pastor of the famed Joy Street Church, a predominately African American congregation in Boston, Martin also performed stints at predominantly white churches including Boston's Tremont Temple.

On December 2, 1859, the day of John Brown's execution, a day of intense mourning among liberals in Boston, Martin gave a well-received public address casting what many believed to have been the "failure" of John Brown's life in the mold of such grand "failures" as John the Baptist and Jesus Christ. To abolitionist activists who opposed Brown's violence, Martin retorted, "I am prepared, in the light of all human history, to approve of the means; in the light of all Christian principle, to approve of the ends."[122] In 1863, on an extended trip to England, Martin accepted the pastorate of a newly formed nonsectarian church in a working-class neighborhood of London. According to an English antislavery activist, Martin "succeeded in reclaiming a large portion of this barren waste and converting it morally and religiously, if not physically, into a garden." While in England, Martin spent much of his time engaged in heated debate with lobbyists from the Confederate States of America, who had been sent to win the support of the British government, thus "scatter[ing] to the winds the plausible pro-slavery fallacies and popular misapprehensions by which the minds of men had been seduced."[123] Invited to elegant parties, Martin held his own, a noble representative of both his class and his race. "Preeminently the man and the gentleman," Martin refused to perform the role of "fashionable plaything . . . a fine specimen . . . to be lionized and patronized without any recognition of his dignity of a human being." Instead, his presence among English elites represented for English progressives a "vindication of the right of his race to a position of perfect equality with the rest of the progeny of Adam."[124]

Featuring a bold escape and tireless political activism and leadership, Martin's story provided the Creoles of color a point of entry into the discourse of the slave narrative. Heeding the *Tribune* editors' advice and purchasing the biography of Martin, a text they could read at their leisure, the readers of the paper's French section would find parallels between Martin's sensibilities and their own. They would perhaps identify with the white ancestry of Martin and with his mother's "privileged position" among slaves—a "cabin all to herself . . . nominal duties," and "fare . . . from the table of her mistress."[125] They might also identify with Martin's literacy and industry under oppressive conditions, imagining that Martin fled slavery not because of physical abuse but because of his fundamental objection to the injustice of his status. When he realized that his escape might jeopardize the property and freedom of a New Orleans *homme de couleur* who had unwittingly vouched for him, Martin "[overcame] the temptation of getting my freedom at the expense of another's loss and bondage."[126] Such an act of altruism from an enslaved man toward a free man of color would attest to the purity of his intentions. Moreover, Martin's decision to join the abolitionist movement seemed a conscious, selfless choice, similar to one readers might make to enter radical Reconstruction politics on behalf of the formerly enslaved. His acceptance as a leader by numerous interracial religious communities in the United States and abroad indicated an exceptional ability to transcend skin color and achieve desegregation, a chief political goal of New Orleans' *gens de couleur*. Martin's intellectual transnationality and fraternal intimacy with whites would mirror the self-conceptions of many of his Creole of color readers.

Perhaps even more than Sella Martin, John Brown—the famed white abolitionist hero of "Bleeding Kansas" and Harper's Ferry—provided would-be Creole of color activists with a role model that might compel them to marshal the mediating potential of their in-between status on behalf of freed people. In the spring and summer of 1865 the *Tribune* carried a serialized account of the life of John Brown, who had by this time—six years after his martyrdom in Virginia—become an international legend.[127] Written by the French radical exile Pierre Vesinier, "John Brown, Le Christ des Noirs" suffused the memory of Brown with the image of Jesus Christ, demonstrating the heroic and transformative possibilities that lay beyond the boundaries of static social identities. As Emmanuel (God with us), Christ traversed the ground between man and God in a selfless act of love; likewise, Brown collapsed the distinctions between slave and free and between black and white when he "came to bring the good news and to break to chains of the slaves, who were as humble and sober as himself."[128]

Similarly, Creoles of color, situated as they were between black and white, could help illuminate the path to a nonracial democracy. For example, when Louisiana congressman Charles Smith proposed extending the suffrage to quadroons and reclassifying them as white (thus using them as a buffer against black political power), the *Tribune* declared the policy ludicrous because impracticable. According to the *Tribune* editors, lawmakers and law enforcement could not possibly begin to make such distinctions. "There are nearly as many black whites with woolly hair as there are white people of color with silky hair."[129] Furthermore, if the genealogies of New Orleans' *gens de couleur* were any indication, determining "the quality of blood that each of us has in our veins . . . would establish a barrier between the father and the son, between children of the same mother, and would say to some: 'You are white' and to others 'You are people of color.' " In the resulting chaos, the *Tribune* added facetiously, "all would be for the best in the best of all possible Republics!"[130] Christlike in the sense that he took up the burdens of enslaved people as his own, John Brown sacrificed his life for the sake of a colorblind democracy "which had neither slaves nor masters, where men were equal without distinction of color." In their sheer corporeality, Creoles of color might emulate Christ—the original "body that mattered"—in their transcendence of oppositional categories.[131] In the *Tribune's* view, Creoles of color—as a blend (and therefore negation) of the two "pure" races "black" and "white"—embodied the possibility of resolving the racial polarization that plagued the political and social life of the United States.[132]

Exegetical Chosen-ness Meets Metaphysical Transcendence

In the heroic stories of Sella Martin and John Brown, the *Tribune* editors amplified their commitment to eradicating racial barriers and fostering the kinds of alliances Creoles of color had enjoyed in the faubourgs of prewar New Orleans. They seized upon a tradition of abolitionist activism that had long provided the occasion for interracial cooperation and the establishment of long-standing friendships across racial lines. By encouraging "promiscuous audiences" and podiums that failed to segregate listeners and speakers by race or gender, the most radical abolitionists labored against the claims of the new racial science regarding the permanence of racial difference and the inherent inferiority of nonwhites. To critics and supporters, their efforts exemplified both the dire consequences and the regenerative promise of "amalgamation."[133]

However harmonious this alliance, the antebellum struggle against slavery and white supremacy also produced an independent black political tradition investing exclusive racial identities with their own positive revolutionary potential. Whether or not these formulations accompanied the quest for separate territory, they helped shape an emerging black nationalist sensibility that understood black people to be the central actors in sacred and secular historical dramas. Furthermore, they insisted on the importance of institutional autonomy in sustaining an unencumbered "immanent critique" among blacks of various persuasions and in bringing forth the unity necessary to strengthen the bonds of this imagined community. Articulating a nascent black nationalism, institutions such as independent black churches, fraternal organizations, mutual assistance societies, the black press, and the National Negro Convention movement forged a network of African American political organization and sought to provide a connective tissue for various localized efforts.[134] Thus, for the *Tribune* editors, presenting themselves as black leaders was not simply a matter of mining affirmative individual narratives such as those of Martin and Brown. They also had to situate themselves with respect to the emancipatory efforts and nationalist ideologies of African American political structures already in place.

Since the revolutionary period, African American leaders and institutions had engaged in rich dialogical practices and had assumed multiple roles and purposes. For example, after being pulled from their knees during worship service in Philadelphia's white Methodist Episcopal Church in 1787, Richard Allen and Absalom Jones founded the Free African Society, a religious and mutual aid organization that served as an umbrella for a range of fraternal societies and spawned other organizational efforts including, in 1816, the incorporation of the African Methodist Episcopal (AME) Church, the first independent black religious institution. David Walker, the outspoken abolitionist and author of *David Walker's Appeal to the Coloured Citizens of the World* (1829), served as both lay minister in the AME Church and the distribution agent in Boston for the nation's first black newspaper, the New York-based *Freedom's Journal* (1827–1829), published by free blacks Samuel Cornish and John Russworm. In 1830 Allen, the founding AME bishop, and other black Methodists, in conjunction with the black press, inaugurated the National Negro Convention Movement, which Eddie Glaude has called the "secular adjunct of the black church." In semiannual conventions, black representatives met across lines of class, status, profession, region, religious denomination, and (later in the antebellum period) gender.[135] Although delegates engaged in contentious debate often conducted "with gloves off," their overriding goal was to present a unified black position on matters of local and national concern. Individuals meeting together within church groups and literary societies read the proceedings of these conventions, which were published in local and national black newspapers alongside serialized fiction, local news, poetry, opinion pieces, and other items. Taken together, these efforts constituted a multivalent African American public life encompassing both oratory and the written word and combining religious and secular discourses.[136]

The independent and racialized character of African American political, religious, and social institutions presented a particular challenge to Creoles of color, whose own institutional networks traditionally aimed for interracial integration and cooperation. For example, even though the Catholic Church required Sisters of the Holy Family, Henriette Delille's order of Creole of color nuns, to exclude whites, Delille's partner, the Frenchwoman Jeanne d'Aliquot, found her way back to the order, aiding them in their ministry and eventually dying in their convent in 1863 in the midst of the Union occupation.[137] The French priest Claude Paschal Maistre likewise founded a renegade parish, St. Rose of Lima, on the outskirts of Tremé that tended to the needs of his mixed-race neighborhood. His efforts put him in close contact with Creole of color radicals such as André Cailloux, the martyr of the Civil War Battle of Port Hudson. Praised by the *Tribune* for his efforts on behalf of racial cooperation and threatened with censure by the Catholic establishment, Maistre delivered a stirring eulogy before thousands at Cailloux's public funeral.[138] Articles in *l'Union* goaded the Catholic establishment to continue its tradition of inclusiveness in spite of a chastening Americanization. In late 1868 the *Tribune* editors bestowed a gold medal upon Eugène Chassaignac, the leader of Scottish Rite freemasonry in New Orleans, for desegregating fraternal lodges. Spurred on by these events, the *Tribune* renewed *l'Union*'s earlier efforts to desegregate transportation systems, private businesses, and public schools.[139]

Along with the divergence in the character of their respective cultural and religious institutions and circles, Creoles of color and African Americans developed religious practices with somewhat contradictory cosmologies. Resulting in a hybrid perspective at once metaphysical and exegetical, the cultural and political criticism offered by the *Tribune* mined the often-conflicting moral resources of both Creole of color spiritualism and African American Protestant Christianity. In a spiritualist vein, the *Tribune* accessed a realm above the fray of divisive social realities to explore the egalitarian possibilities of transcendence. Simultaneously, following in a Protestant tradition, the newspaper delved beneath the surface of mainstream Biblical interpretation in order to reinvest the displaced legacies of African Americans with historical significance and political purpose.[140] Although spiritualism and Protestant Christianity did not always mesh well, the Creole of color journals drew on both religious traditions, applying a Biblical exegesis and a spiritual metaphysics to their progressive political program.

As many scholars have demonstrated, Biblical exegesis—and readings of Exodus in particular—assumed a primary role for Protestant African American leaders in shaping a politics of emancipation.[141] Placing their community in the role of the ancient Hebrews, God's chosen people, African American leaders incorporated their people into a long-standing American national tradition of chosen-ness; however, they subverted the chosen status of the United States by refiguring America as ancient Egypt rather than as a New Canaan. In configuring a collective identity in this way, they drew upon a national narrative that grounded citizenship in covenantal and genealogical terms reinforced by intertwined narratives of "consent" and "descent."[142] Like the Puritan elect of colonial New England's "city on the hill," America's most conspicuous covenanted community, African Americans figured in their theology as a Christian chosen people and held an external responsibility to provide a "shining example" to other communities of faith and an internal ethical obligation to assess their own moral status on a continual basis.[143]

As one might expect, the themes of Exodus took on a particularly poignant and urgent tone in the upheavals of Civil War and Reconstruction politics.[144] With Louisiana politics assuming center stage in this Biblical drama, the *Tribune* emerged as a key forum for the immanent conversation among African American leaders concerning the moral status and social and political vision of their "people." Throughout its run, the paper culled information and articles from various black newspapers, including the Brooklyn-based *Anglo-African Magazine* and the *AME Christian Recorder*. The pilgrimage of Bertonneau and Roudanez to the North and the good will that passed between them and northern black and white radical Republicans inspired Thomas Hamilton, the editor of the *Anglo-African Magazine*, and his southern correspondent, the fiery Presbyterian minister Henry Highland Garnet, to call a National Convention of Negro leaders—including the Reverend J. Sella Martin—in early October 1864.[145] During the conference, the Reverend P. B. Randolph reminded the assembly of the magnitude of national events: "the overruling father brought out the sons of Abraham from Egyptian bondage 3,000 years ago; and today he leads us—the negro race—with a strong arm from out of the swamps of slavery."[146] Stressing his belief in "a Negro nationality," Garnet cited brave service on the battlefield as an indication of the strength and character of this black nation. The Louisiana delegate James Ingraham, a prominent AME lay leader in New Orleans who had fought alongside the martyred Creole of color André Cailloux at Port Hudson, narrated the battle to great applause. After his speech, the enthusiastic convention moved to hang the battle flag of the First Louisiana Colored Regiment, a symbol of black collective pride, across the speaker's platform.[147]

Back in Louisiana, the *Tribune* published the proceedings of this historic convention and collaborated with Ingraham to organize a Convention of Colored Men of Louisiana. Meeting from early to mid-January 1865, this convention, "the first political move ever made by the colored people of the state acting in a body," according to the *Tribune*, "inaugurated a new era." Describing a mosaic of assembled leaders, the *Tribune* marveled at the way rich and poor delegates, those from city and those from country parishes, French and English speakers, and those born free and those formerly enslaved might work in concert. "There the rich landowner, the opulent tradesmen, seconded motions offered by humble mechanics and freedmen. Ministers of the gospel, officers and soldiers of the U.S. army, men who handle the sword or the pen, merchants and clerks—all the classes of society were represented and united in a common thought: the actual liberation from social and political bondage."[148] Because of the *Tribune*'s demonstrated commitment to social and political equality for blacks and its publication in French and English, the convention leadership recognized it as a natural choice as the "official newspaper" of the convention and the related Negro Equal Rights League, itself an outgrowth of the 1864 National Negro Convention. In the spirit of Exodus politics, the Louisiana Convention also considered the moral and spiritual health of the black community. Outlining the necessary qualities for delegates, the *Tribune* placed a premium on "respectability," the "requisite needed above all others, in order to give weight and force to the Convention, not only among our political enemies, but among ourselves also."[149] In this vein, the AME minister William A. Dove elaborated on the central role of ministers in this political struggle: "every minister of the Gospel has to favor every thing tending to the elevation of his race. . . . If the elders or deacons of the churches do not concur in this move, let them be removed."[150]

Within a week of the assembly's adjournment, seconding Dove's plea for more accountable religious education for the freedmen, the *Tribune* bid "any Reverend or Doctor who feels an interest in this work" to "pay a visit to the office of the *Tribune*."[151] Within days, Dove and the Reverend McCrary had signed on to edit the *Tribune*'s Religious Department. In many ways analogous to the role of the serialized fiction of the *Tribune*'s French section, the material comprising the religious department sought to provide moral instruction for the emergent black political community.[152] In their own commentary and in published speeches and articles from other Christian sources, Dove and McCrary expounded on such varied topics as the moral obligations of husbands to wives, the martial discipline expected of soldiers, and the imitable virtues of the recently assassinated President Lincoln.[153] As one might expect from Exodus politicians, Dove and McCrary expressed the "desire to see our people united religiously as well as politically" and admonished the newly freed and by extension the entire emergent black community to live a strenuous moral life.[154] The saving of souls for God's kingdom—"a thing of difficulty that requires all our diligence"—went hand-in-hand with securing citizenship rights and reinforcing the "ascendant" position of the "African race."[155] When Ethiopia "stretched forth her hands"—to paraphrase, after Dove and McCrary, a favorite Psalm of black intellectuals of the nineteenth century—it would be crucial that this racially, spiritually, and politically defined community exemplify the Christian ethic.[156]

Within the pages of the *Tribune*, the voice of the Religious Department is somewhat out of place. Drawing heavily on Protestant doctrines of preparation, of undertaking and representing a morally exacting wilderness experience as evidence of the sincerity of one's quest for and, thus, one's qualifications for salvation, the Protestant black leadership conveyed a sense of urgency regarding righteous behavior that often registered as prudery. With the Bible as their "guide-book," the "upbuilders of Zion" must testify not only by their faith, but by their "habits and conduct."[157] The Protestants had many occasions to upbraid Catholic and spiritualist Creoles of color. When the *Tribune* group and other Creole of color activists organized a lavish fair for the establishment of an orphanage for formerly enslaved children at Pierre Soulé's mansion, English-speaking Protestant leaders bristled at the presence of alcohol, worried that the charitable raffle constituted gambling, and complained of the fair's failure to suspend operation on the Sabbath. Noting that "the people who did the most for the benefit of the Orphan's Home are Catholics," its organizer Louise de Mortié retorted in the pages of the *Tribune*, "God grant that I may never commit a greater sin than working for the poor on Sundays," referencing St. Matthew for support.[158]

Differences over what constituted morally acceptable behavior strained political relationships between Creoles of color and English-speaking blacks and pointed to deeper divisions in their religious practices and values. For Creoles of color, Reconstruction offered not only the possibility of mobilizing a black political community around the Biblical drama of deliverance from slavery, but it also accelerated their quest for the obliteration of social distinctions of caste and for a reconciliation of terrestrial tensions in a harmonious celestial realm. Under the editorship of Paul Trévigne, who had attended spiritualist séances during the antebellum period, *l'Union* provided a forum for elaborating spiritualist principles and for continuing to oppose a growing conservatism and racism within the local leadership of the Catholic Church.[159] The Native Guard captain and celebrated spiritualist medium Henry Rey contributed a poem, "Ignorance," to the first issue of the journal. In contrast to a Protestant African American perspective, which would have ascribed a more active presence to the forces of evil, Rey portrayed ignorance, the lack of knowledge, as the "true hell of existence / the sole Satan of the Universe," attributing to it the deaths and persecutions of Socrates, Jesus, and Emanuel Swedenborg—whose writings informed spiritualism. In a way, the religious sensibility of the Creole activists had more in common with the transcendentalism of Ralph Waldo Emerson and Henry David Thoreau than it did with the millennial Protestantism of Frederick Douglass and Sella Martin.[160] On the heels of General Butler's decision to conscript soldiers of color into the Union army, Rey described the events of the early Union occupation of New Orleans as the culmination of this "century of enlightenment," where "truth" finally emerged from the darkness, bringing with it "Liberty, universal peace / Human happiness [and] fraternity!"[161]

Another early issue of *l'Union* further grounded the political program of the Creoles of color in the spiritual context of the community. On October 18, 1862, the journal published a letter written by Captain Rey, who was stationed at Camp Strong in the farthest reaches of Tremé toward Lake Pontchartrain. Rey's depiction of the regiment of color presents an incandescent vision of multiracial cooperation and equality: "Mr. editor, come visit our camp . . . You will see crossed a thousand shining bayonets, illumined by the sun, carried by black, yellow and white hands."[162] Creole of color spiritualist leader Paul Huard's exposition on the immortality of the soul immediately follows Rey's letter. For Huard, the human conscience, the "interior sentiment of good and of evil," continually registers its connection to the eternal and omnipresent spirit of God. "Happily for universal harmony in the world, for tranquility and happiness in the family, for religious and public morals," Huard assures his readers, "our soul returns to God from whence it came."[163] As if on cue, one particularly heroic soul returns to the same issue of the journal via spirit communication, offering his "Pensées d'Outre-Tombe (Thoughts from the Other Side of the Grave)." Expressing intense regret for his persecution of enslaved people and his attempted reenslavement of San Dominguans while alive—"savage" and "anomalous" blights on the record of his quest for human liberty—the spirit of Napoleon I revises the popular memory of his grandeur in light of his deeper understanding gained in the afterlife. Napoleon's posthumous admission of guilt and plea for forgiveness allowed the Creole of color community, in need of inspiration, to access his legacy as a particularly noble and charitable expression of the divine spirit.[164]

In the bleaker days ahead, Creoles of color continued to draw resolve from their religious beliefs. Attesting to the existence of a more harmonious realm than occupied and Reconstruction New Orleans, Creole of color martyrs returned as spirit guides. On July 17, 1863, twelve days before his spectacular public funeral, André Cailloux appeared to an entranced Captain Rey, announcing "I have fought, I have succumbed. They have not killed me, but they have made me live."

Urging his compatriots to "Fight on! God demands liberty," Cailloux promised to be the "guiding light that will direct [them] and that [he] will receive [them] in the next world if [they] fall in battle."[165] Likewise, after the demoralizing riot of 1866, the spirit of Victor Lacroix returned to Rey on at least two occasions, days after the riot and then again in February 1869. In his testimony, Lacroix spoke of how the blood of martyrs, which "water[ed] the bricks of the bloody city and mark[ed] the scene [of the 1866 riot] in infamy," would transform itself into a luminescent guiding force that would "chart indelibly a new route for new citizens, called to exercise all the rights and privileges that the Republic accords her children." The blood of martyrs would also bear witness before God: [it] "will speak for you, and He will hear."[166] In a memorial poem, "Ode aux Martyrs," published in the *Tribune* on the first anniversary of the riot, poet Camille Naudin seemed to lament that "*Victor Lacroix est mort, Jeff Davis est vivant* (Victor Lacroix is dead; Jefferson Davis lives)."[167] However, in the context of spiritualist belief—which admonished adherents to regard the death of a friend as "a happy change of condition, a birth into a better world where man, disengaged from the material world, marches unceasingly towards the progress, purity and happiness for which he was created"—Lacroix, in death, served as a beacon of hope for weary leaders and as someone who could testify before the divine spirit on behalf of his compatriots.[168]

Forging the Bonds of Nation and Race

As it did for Americans more generally, the rupture of the Civil War presented the *Tribune* editors with a prime opportunity to reformulate the terms of national identity. On the one hand, they engaged in a racially particularistic rhetoric that sought recognition as a black political voice. On the other hand, they deployed a universalist rhetoric that supported an integrationist racial policy. Not merely an adoption of oppositional rhetorical strategies, these inconsistencies also, and more importantly, reflected confluences and conflicts among the institutional cultures and the spiritual traditions of the developing "black community." For the journalists, bringing about the simultaneous emergence of imagined national and racial communities constituted an unwieldy historiographical project. They drew upon Western nationalist traditions predicated on instituting consistent public practices of memory and forgetting and on forging a shared American legacy. They also adopted the black nationalist and diasporic imperative to remember precisely what other Americans aimed to forget. Juggling divergent national visions, the *Tribune* editors presented ambivalent interpretations of the past, contradictory assessments of the present, and inconsistent prognoses for the future. Each set of ideas and strategies pursued a strand of truth and resisted mutual resolution.

Like other Americans of African descent, the Creole of color journalists practiced what John Ernest has called a "liberation historiography," a critique of and corrective to Western narratives of progress. Assembled from the fragments of personal and collective experience strewn across the Atlantic basin as the result of dehumanizing acts of theft, sale, and rape, African American historical narratives indexed the founding texts and icons of the United States and the memory of Africa as a place of heritage against a transnational, transhistorical fugitive sensibility. For those in the African diaspora, a series of arbitrary displacements confounded attempts to claim any specific place as home. Within a developing African American intellectual tradition, the attempts to express belonging and secure the protections and rights as citizens of somewhere conveyed a profound sense of the historical contingency of seemingly stable and enduring national stories and symbols.[169] Louisiana politics in particular occasioned a thorough reassessment of national stories, and the *Tribune* drew on national, transnational, and diasporic figures such as Victor Hugo, Vincent Ogé, and Sella Martin and claimed territory encompassing the United States, France, the Caribbean, and Africa.

Exemplifying a paradox that Du Bois would later identify as a "double consciousness," a peculiar sensation of "two-ness," the *Tribune* radicals sought to reconcile universalist yearnings with an investment in black racial consciousness. Further anticipating Du Bois, they resisted a total reconciliation, highlighting the ethical duty of the "doubly conscious" citizen, gifted with "second sight," to maintain a position of abstraction from which to critique national directives.[170] Heavily invested in both French and American ideals, they refused to allow race to eclipse culture (or nationality). However—and just as importantly—they also resisted the urge to allow culture (or nationality) to eclipse race.[171] Their nineteenth-century discursive milieu revealed competing notions about the quality of human difference and the basis upon which individuals found themselves categorized by groups, and the journalists made use of all the concepts available to them. They spoke of race in biological terms where the tangible substance, blood, served as a metaphorical tool that expressed degrees of racial purity. They also used a cultural vocabulary of difference with such historicist terms such as *heritage*, *tradition*, and *nation*.[172] In the spirit of the word *Creole*, the journalists—chameleon-like—accessed the constantly shifting usages and intricately interdependent discourses of race *and* nation. They adapted these potentially loaded categories to their particular local uses and articulated their unique vision of American nationhood and intra-racial alliance.

In an article written toward the end of the Civil War, the *Tribune* claimed, "On this free and blessed soil of the United States, we all use one and the same language, we have one interest, one common feeling, the same ideas, same manners, and same patriotism. The blacks are needed as much as the whites for the defense of the country and the tillage of the land. Shall we make two peoples with one people, two nations with one nation? . . . A country can not be powerful unless the people be made into one nation. We want to have one country; let us therefore have one law."[173] These claims, of course, were hardly true in New Orleans, its public culture resonant with overlapping colonial legacies and various linguistic practices, legal traditions, and racial designations. In the face of this complex reality, the *Tribune* editors projected a particularly French ideal of administrative and bureaucratic cohesion as a model for American nationhood.[174] In this vein, they proposed the historical logic by which the United States might achieve multiple kinds of cooperation: racial in the case of black and white, linguistic in the case of Creoles and Americans, sectional in the case of the North and the South, and economic in the case of capital and labor. "One law" for all might work to suture these rifts.

Providing examples from popular European histories, the *Tribune* historicized and demystified national origins, portraying the nation as the resolution of opposing cultural forces: "There is no famous nation which has been formed by a single pure race."[175] In the benighted French past, the Franks had imposed themselves on the Gauls as an "aristocracy," maintaining separate codes for themselves and their Gallic "serfs." According to the *Tribune*, "The brilliant epoch of

French nationality began only when both codes [that of the Franks and that of the Gauls] were blended into one code and the whole people governed by one and the same legislation."[176] So that Americans of all stripes might follow these successful European examples, the Creole of color journals provided history lessons for their readers. The first issues of *l'Union*, for example, reprinted the U.S. Constitution in full. Attempting to salvage the reputations of the founding fathers of the United States, the *Tribune* cherry-picked prime quotations proving their opposition to slavery: "George Washington: 'There is not a man living . . . who wishes more sincerely than I do to see a plan adopted for the abolition of slavery.' Patrick Henry: 'It will rejoice my very soul that every one of my fellow beings was emancipated.' Thomas Jefferson: 'The Almighty has no attribute which could side with us in such a contest [of right and wrong].' "[177] If enemies like the Franks and Gauls could dissolve their dilemmas in the French nation, former slaves and former masters could do the same in America.

A commitment to French and American nationalism aside, the *Tribune* editors by no means rested secure in these traditions. The stories of Vincent Ogé and John Brown recalled the contradictions that slavery and racism brought to bear on revolutionary expressions of equality and freedom in both national contexts, and the *Tribune*'s analysis of current events presupposed the general resistance that its editors' critiques and proposals would meet. Following the example of leaders such as Frederick Douglass, who had delivered his famous address "What to the Slave is the Fourth of July?" on July 5, 1852, the Creole of color journalists expressed deep skepticism and irony about professed national values, invoking memories of the (French and American) founding fathers in order to critique and revise their formulations. *L'Union* used the occasion of July 4, 1863, to publish an ode to Captain Cailloux, a grim reminder that his body and blood-soaked flag had yet to be retrieved from the battlefield where he had fallen on May 27. "We, men of his race, console ourselves, / That, before God alone, he bent his knee. Let Whites and Blacks all follow the noble path / Of the brave André Cailloux."[178] In an earlier issue of *l'Union*, a contributing writer argued that "a new sun . . . must soon appear on our horizon," a sun "*like* the one of" the French Revolution of 1789 but doubly illuminated by the wisdom of critics such as Martiniquan abolitionist Cyrille "Bissette . . . that apostle of liberty in the French colonies," whose journal *Revue des Colonies* pressed for freedom in the relatively conservative French climate of the 1830s and early 1840s.[179] Thus, for Creoles of color, American patriots such as Washington, Henry, and Jefferson resurface in the pages of the *Tribune* as professed abolitionists rather than as wealthy slaveholders, and French heroes like Napoleon I return to the land of the living and use the mouthpiece of the *Tribune* to declare slavery a moral outrage.

Enacting a strategy that Russ Castronovo has called "discursive passing," the *Tribune* editors inhabited a French or American identity with a critical difference.[180] Their particular acts of discursive passing constituted a dual strategy, moving in two directions at once. Not only did they pass as "Americans," occupying forms of national identity for rhetorical purposes, but they also passed as "black Americans," consciously accessing the critical power of racial identity from a position of alterity. In this vein, Vincent Ogé passed not only as French in the pages of the *Tribune*, but also as black. The account of Ogé published there harnessed the energies of this professed and proud *homme de couleur* on behalf of black people more generally, making him an unequivocal "hero of the African race." Likewise, the *Tribune* published Camille Naudin's poem "Le Marseillaise Noir," infusing the French revolutionary anthem with a black critical presence. It also linked the New Orleans' *gens de couleur* with the ethical concerns of a black *(noiriste)* diasporic emancipatory project.[181]

In an article celebrating Africa as the cradle of civilization, the *Tribune* editors suggested that a more thorough consideration of African thought might nourish the moribund cultural practices of the West.[182] Moreover, a quest for the African origins of civilization would correct a "common historical error" indulged by "three different newspapers in this city" that Africans, unchanging and forever locked within a persistent pattern of "barbarism," lacked a historical sense.[183] According to the *Tribune*, Africa's current state of "barbarism and ignorance" should be considered alongside its glorious past. Furthermore, the *Tribune* argued, an appreciation for the African past would revise an understanding of European history, showing that "Europe has similarly had her ages of darkness and barbarism, even after many centuries of civilization and enlightenment."[184]

By fleshing out the African past, the *Tribune* editors engaged in a liberation historiography typical of other African American leaders of the period.[185] At the same time, they claimed an African heritage for themselves, distinct from that of most African Americans, as ancient Egyptians, the middlemen in the transfer of civilization from Africa to the rest of the world. "The Egyptians were a mulatto people, formed by miscegenation between the black and Caucasian race. . . . It was in Egypt, the land of the pyramids that the other nations of the Orient came to learn, for the first time, the sciences and the fine arts."[186] A place of cultural diversity between the rest of Africa and other parts of the world, ancient Egypt represented a crossroads where ideas as well as bloodlines could mingle, and the Egyptians, playing a role similar to that of Creoles of color in Reconstruction New Orleans, served as translators and mediators within this crossroads. As a "mulatto people" the Egyptians, and by extension the Creoles of color, had access to the essential wisdom of a deeper, darker Africa because of their mixed blood as well as their geographical location. Moreover, they would defer the source of genius to "unmixed" Africans. Countering those who would point to the comparative whiteness of the Egyptians as a means of accounting for their civilization, the *Tribune* asked, "Who taught the Egyptians the first rudiments of the useful arts and industry? . . . The Egyptian or mulatto people have received the first elements of their useful knowledge from the Ethiopians—who were pure blacks."[187] Here, the *Tribune* reverses the racial hierarchy of New Orleans, the United States, and Western nations in general. Contrary to conventional wisdom, ancient Egyptians and, by extension, Creoles of color owed their civilized status to their black rather than their white blood. In their discussion of Africa, the Creole of color journalists underscored the extent to which biological race, cultural practices, and geographical positioning all informed national identity.[188]

Thus reinforced, the journalists leveraged their rhetorical commitments both to ancient Africa and to the French republic into a defense of the citizenship rights of people of African descent in the United States of America. In the face of renewed proposals to colonize American blacks elsewhere, these citizenship struggles took on urgency—especially in southeastern Louisiana, which had been captured by federal troops so early in the war. Defying General Butler and higher authorities by freeing and arming the fugitive slaves streaming into his camp on the outskirts of New Orleans, General John Phelps supplemented his wartime abolitionism with the ultimate goal of removing free and freed blacks to Africa, Texas, or points south. Early in the war, Abraham Lincoln had on several occasions proposed relocating African Americans to Chiriqui in present-day Panama.[189]

In one of the early issues of *l'Union*, a contributing writer expressed outrage over President Lincoln's colonization proposal. "Cast[ing] a backward glance on the French Chamber of '48," he portrays an integrated assembly where "the monumental geniuses" Victor Hugo and Alphonse de Lamartine, among others, sat "alongside Pory-Papy, Mazaline, Charles Dain, Louisy Mathieu, Périnen and other celebrated negroes and mulattos," each regarding the others as "fellow citizens."[190] To sentiments such as those expressed by Phelps and Lincoln, the *Tribune*'s editor Jean-Charles Houzeau countered, "Although our ancestors were kidnapped from Africa, we ourselves were born in the United States. Who will deny that we are the children of this country? . . . We do not want to leave our country; and what right do you have to force us to do so?"[191] In response to U.S. officials who refused to admit their common cause with a formerly enslaved population, a New Orleans Creole of color regards his multiracial confreres within a democratic socialist France of 1848 and a white Belgian radical speaks as a kidnapped African and a child of the United States. In the bleak context of the Civil War, the journalists channeled their disparate identities into a vindication of the ideals of the American Union. Their transnational, interracial imaginings made manifest the *Tribune*'s recurring motto: "United we stand, divided we fall!"

The Passing of the *Tribune*

The influence of the *Tribune* and of the radicals in general began to decline at the moment of their triumph when, under the terms of the Reconstruction Acts issued by the U.S. Congress in 1867, General Philip Sheridan, the commander of the military district encompassing Louisiana, removed rebel sympathizers from state and city government and implemented the political reorganization of the state. From November to April, a body composed of roughly equal numbers of black and white delegates crafted a state constitution instituting universal male suffrage and "public rights" for all citizens. Paradoxically, the formal commitment to black social and political rights coincided with a parallel struggle for leadership within the Republican Party, in which moderate political opportunists such as the young rising star, Illinois-born Henry Clay Warmoth, took central stage and courted conservatives more openly.[192] As the true "radical party," the *Tribune* journalists remained outspokenly skeptical of the intentions of the emergent mainstream of the local Republican establishment, which they considered to be a compromised "white man's party."[193] The resulting political standoff reached a crisis in the 1868 state elections. Weathering charges that it wished to "Africanize the state," the *Tribune* faction maintained that the time was ripe for African Americans to "share in all departments of our government," proposing as gubernatorial candidate the ex-Native Guard Major Francis Dumas.[194] Years later, when relating the *Tribune*'s challenge during these "stormy days," Warmoth would raise the specter of Haiti: the "[Pure Radicals] were led by three San Domingo negroes who owned and published the *New Orleans Tribune* and who urged the negroes of Louisiana to assert themselves and follow Hayti, San Domingo, and Liberia, and to make Louisiana an African State."[195]

When the nominating convention voted, Dumas prevailed over Warmoth on the first ballot, only to lose the nomination by five votes on the second. Refusing to accept the party's offer of a lieutenant governorship for Dumas, the *Tribune* group formed a haphazard alternative ticket composed of James Taliaferro, a white ex-slaveholder more conservative than Warmoth, for governor and Francis Dumas for lieutenant governor. Weighing their options, many African American leaders, such as ex-Native Guards James Ingraham and P. B. S. Pinchback, decided to back the politically ascendant and ultimately victorious Warmoth faction. Bolting the convention proved ruinous for the *Tribune* when the Republican Party immediately moved to rescind its financial backing of the paper. Having disagreed with the rest of the staff over the election, the Belgian Jean-Charles Houzeau resigned as coeditor, his viewpoint registering the isolation of the *Tribune*. For Houzeau, the *Tribune* group's refusal to support the mainstream Republican ticket signified a betrayal of a hard-won racial solidarity. "The old aristocratic spirit of the mulatto has reawakened, and today there are three parties: the pro-slavery people, the blacks (with the white radicals) and a little party of mulattoes (with some white malcontents)."[196] Furthermore, Houzeau regarded this blow to the reputations of the *Tribune* and *gens de couleur* associated with it as irreparable—unlike previous challenges to their allegiance to freed people across lines of color, status, and class: "*Parmi les noirs, l'influence de* la Tribune *est naturellement perdue à jamais* (Among the blacks, the *Tribune*'s influence is naturally lost forever)."[197]

With this pronouncement, Houzeau planned his exit, eventually journeying to Jamaica, where he took up residence on a banana plantation with his young "apprentice of color, William Lang," a boy of twelve Houzeau "adopted" in New Orleans. In a letter to his parents, he mapped his trajectory through the Caribbean. From New Orleans, he traversed Cuba from Havana to Santiago on the eastern tip of the island, and from there, he "passed over" to Kingston. Later in the decade, Houzeau returned to Europe, coming full circle by gaining readmittance into the Belgian Royal Academy of Sciences. He spent his later years engaged in the scientific inquiry that his career of activism had put on hold. His final letter to his parents from New Orleans, composed on the brink of this journey, expressed Houzeau's unflagging optimism about the future: "*La saison est magnifique pour mes petites traversées* (It is a magnificent season for my little crossings)."[198]

Given the ease with which Houzeau packed up, pressed on, and returned to his previous pursuits, we are obliged to take his judgments about the rest of the staff with a grain of salt. The arc of his career encompassed various territories, his personae ranging from member of the French proletariat in 1848 Paris to Mexican abolitionist in 1850s Texas to Creole of color radical in Reconstruction Louisiana.[199] The consummate cosmopolitan, Houzeau defied national and racial boundaries at will, participating in Louisiana in what he considered to be one of the greatest revolutions in history. Like Victor Hugo's *passant*, a character type exemplifying the heroic potential of everydayness, Houzeau prided himself on his mobility. He adopted the perspective of one passing by and through various scenes on the same level as the masses, thus grounding his Romantic pursuit of adventure and individual greatness in the plight of the common man.[200] For Houzeau, "the cause that the 'Negro newspaper' was defending," reflected the simultaneous diversity and unity of his lifelong avocation. "[It] was after all only one chapter in the great universal fight of the oppressed of all colors and nations. Whether the victim is called a serf in Russia, peasant in Austria, Jew in Prussia, proletarian in France, pariah in

India, Negro in the United States, at heart is the same denial of justice."[201]

For the Creoles of color in the *Tribune* group who attuned themselves to the particularities suggested by place-based and racial identities, the luxuries of cosmopolitanism and vagaries of universal humanism sustaining Houzeau's sense of purpose could never be an adequate refuge. They would undoubtedly describe their attempts to pass through the complex physical and psychic terrain of post-Civil War New Orleans and their efforts to pass on their memories and legacies to posterity in more fraught terms. In contrast to Houzeau, whose "little crossings" could count on finding a "magnificent season," those of the *gens de couleur* consistently troubled even the most serene of waters. People interested in their story have had difficulty placing it within familiar narrative frames. The editors of the *Tribune* may have failed to consummate the complete union with English-speaking black Americans hoped for by some critics, and they may have abridged their commitment to principles of universal humanism against the wishes of others. Despite their inconsistent approaches and undesirable outcomes, the Creoles of color associated with *l'Union* and the *Tribune* invested themselves fully in the liberating aspects of Creole identity, thus bequeathing to us a particularly substantial and useful legacy. In the midst of occupied and Reconstruction New Orleans—as chaotic, divisive, and unstable a setting as any—the journalists attempted to synthesize a response to violence and opportunity by tending to their deep roots in a city historically traversed by many competing national and diasporic traditions. As Creoles of New Orleans who also aspired to become black leaders, they marshaled the resources of their in-between position, took seriously the experiences of the Sella Martins and the Vincent Ogés, and pressed into public service hard-won intercultural, international, and interracial sensibilities.

Epilogue: No Enviable Dilemma

SPEAKING THROUGH THE MEDIUM Henry Rey in early 1869, the spirit of Victor Lacroix urged his earthbound companion to persevere: "Console yourself, my brother, the triumph of the good cause is assured. Peace will return to the hearth! The turmoil will soon cease, the marks of its passage will disappear little by little."[1] Lacroix's thoughts from beyond the grave inspired his fellow Creoles of color to forge a path for radical politics through the compromised muddle of a series of Republican administrations in New Orleans that had already begun to renege on the egalitarian principles of 1868. The Warmoth-Dunn ticket won the gubernatorial election of 1868, but the ill-fated administration buckled under the weight of internal rivalries in the Republican Party and its futile efforts to reconcile opposing viewpoints within the electorate. The *Tribune* staff had correctly surmised the limits of what Warmoth could achieve, given the unstable nature of his coalition and the intensity of his quest for material gain and personal fame.[2]

Vetoing and otherwise sabotaging civil rights legislation that would enforce the antidiscrimination clause of the 1868 Louisiana constitution, Warmoth alienated his black allies—including his succession of lieutenant governors, Oscar J. Dunn, an English-speaking former slave native to New Orleans, and Pinckney Benton Stewart Pinchback, a Georgia-born, Cincinnati-educated former slave. In a well-publicized letter to the influential New York editor Horace Greeley, Dunn called

Warmoth the "first Ku Klux Governor" of the Republican Party.[3] In late 1871, Dunn died suddenly of a suspected poisoning in one of the unresolved mysteries of Louisiana politics. Pinchback, Dunn's successor and perhaps the most influential black politician in the state, was an indispensable ally of the Warmoth administration, an important bridge to black voters. The son of his former master, Pinchback was as light complexioned as some of his francophone Creole of color counterparts. However, his political sensibilities diverged from the French-speaking radicals of color in many important respects. He eventually signed on to the quest for "public rights" and equal accommodations, but he had not always supported these measures as the radicals had. "I consider myself just as far above coming into company that does not want me, as they are above my coming into an elevation with them," he remarked during the 1867 state constitutional convention, tapping into a separatist strain that had always existed within African American political culture.[4] To the dismay of the *Tribune* group, Pinchback also argued at key moments that the prevailing racism in the North and South would undermine the efficacy of blacks who held high office in state government.[5]

Nevertheless, the power Pinchback sought behind the scenes catapulted him into public prominence, and the extent of his influence became explicit during the contentious 1872 election season.[6] Rather than endorse Governor Warmoth's attempted fusion of conservative elements of the Republican Party and moderate Democrats, Lieutenant Governor Pinchback, leader of an emergent faction within the Republican Party, allied himself with rival William Pitt Kellogg. After a bitter campaign and a hotly contested Kellogg victory, the state House of Representatives impeached Warmoth, a proceeding that Pinchback ultimately supported, citing a "duty to my state, party, and race." After Warmoth's ouster, Pinchback became the first (and until the 1990 ascension of Douglas Wilder of Virginia, the only) African American governor in U.S. history, holding the office for a period of weeks until Kellogg's inauguration.[7] Having proposed the unlikely candidacy of Creole of color radical Aristide Mary as governor, the *Tribune* group regarded the gubernatorial campaign of 1872 with disgust. Rodolphe Desdunes would later malign Pinchback for his "American reasoning," where "the first principle was to succeed," especially when compared to that of francophone activists and politicians such as Mary, whose candidacy had been proposed in a spirit of "enlightened protest."[8]

Against the backdrop of Republican dissolution and diminishing national support for military reconstruction, Warmoth's "Fusionists" and Democratic "redeemers" contested the election of Kellogg and proceeded to seat their own candidate, John McEnery, as governor, citing widespread election fraud and partisanship. In March 1873 McEnery supporters led by former Confederate soldiers clashed violently in Jackson Square with a New Orleans police force headed by Captain Octave Rey, a former Native Guard and a brother of the Creole of color spiritualist medium Henry Rey.[9] In the Red River region of the northern part of the state, McEnery's redeemers killed over one hundred black Republican farmers on April 13, 1873. This event, known as the Colfax Massacre, sparked court proceedings that resulted two years later in the infamous Supreme Court decision *United States v. Cruikshank*. *Cruikshank* effectively eviscerated the Fourteenth Amendment by giving states rather than the federal government the responsibility for prosecuting crimes of individual citizens against one another. Just as Louisiana played a central role in Reconstruction politics—its local struggles demanding national attention and prompting important legislation—the state would also take the lead in helping to engineer a national retreat from assertions of civil, political, and legal equality made during Reconstruction.[10]

As Jean-Charles Houzeau secured his passage through the Caribbean and eventually home to Belgium, his former coworkers at the *Tribune* fought in various ways for their right to pass freely through New Orleans, the southern states, and the nation. Against the tide of enterprising carpetbaggers on the one hand and the forces of "redemption" on the other, Creoles of color held fast to the message delivered by the spirit of Victor Lacroix that "Peace [would] eventually return to the hearth!" Asserting the right to nostalgia and a deep sense of belonging in the city, leading Creoles of color, including Louis Charles Roudanez of the defunct *Tribune* and Aristide Mary, the recently defeated candidate for governor, closed ranks in the late summer of 1873 with former Confederate general P. G. T. Beauregard, whose troops had precipitated the Civil War by firing on Fort Sumter. Deeming themselves "Unifiers," fifty men of color and fifty white men published a manifesto in the *New Orleans Daily Picayune* claiming that Louisiana was "now threatened with Death in every vital organ of her mortal, material, and political being."[11] These "children of her soil . . . whatever race, color, or religion" strained against their differences to reintroduce stability and prosperity in the state. As George Washington Cable's fictional *Grandissime* brothers would do seven years later, the Unifiers reached across the racial, cultural, and political divide to acknowledge a common heritage, resolving that "no distinction should exist among citizens of Louisiana" in places of public accommodation.[12]

With this proclamation, the Unifiers revived the besieged spirit of interracial cooperation and public intimacy that underscored tentative civil rights victories in the late 1860s and early 1870s. In *Sauvinet v. Walker* (1869), Charles Sauvinet, the Native Guard captain and translator who had convinced General Butler to enlist colored troops, gained the right to frequent eating and drinking establishments on an equal footing with whites. In 1872 Josephine Decuir, the sister of Creole of color state treasurer Antoine Dubuclet, insisted on her right to travel from New Orleans to her home plantation in Pointe Coupée parish in the "ladies' cabin," a section reserved for white women. Decuir secured legal victories on the local and state levels in the mid-1870s, only to have them reversed by the U.S. Supreme Court in 1878 after the end of Reconstruction. Describing Decuir as "genteel in her manners, modest in her deportment, neat in her appearance, and quite fair for one of mixed blood," the Louisiana courts modified their distaste for her African blood and lay the groundwork for a solidarity based on class, public demeanor, and appreciation for correct social etiquette. In the process, they accessed the strategies used some twenty years earlier by George Pandelly to temper public perceptions of his dark skin. Pointing, as Pandelly had done, to the legacy of acceptable forms of interracial mixture, the court noted that Decuir's "features are rather delicate with a nose which indicates a decided preponderance of the Caucasian and Indian blood. The blackness and length of the hair, which is straight confirms this idea." Recalling the precedent of *Adele v. Beauregard* (1810) that would read her lightness as a "badge of freedom," the court continued, "[Decuir] never was a slave, nor is she the descendant of a slave. Her ancestors were always free as herself. She has always been respected by those who knew her."[13] The court's sentiments reiterated the arguments of the Unifiers, who attempted as well to merge the interests of the elite regardless of race. The decision also presaged the argument of Cable, whose 1885 "Freedmen's Case in Equity" would contend on behalf of a "just assortment" of citizens into categories of class and comportment rather than those of race.

Upholding the Louisiana State Constitution of 1868, the Unifiers specifically advocated racial integration in "public schools or state institutions of education," calling attention to the difficulties encountered by activists and lawmakers for five years in their attempts to actualize that principle. [14] In the fall of 1867 the city government had assumed control of the public education of "colored" children by incorporating the Freedmen's Bureau schools into its administration. After conducting a survey of questionable objectivity among teachers and principals, the school board established a segregated school system.[15] In May 1868, with disregard for article 135 of the new state constitution, the board exposed five apparently white girls as children of color and expelled them from Bayou Road School in Tremé, thus upholding its commitment to segregation. In the case of one of the girls, the Recorder of Births reassured the committee that he had personally destroyed the "fraudulent" record attesting to her whiteness and had his deputy transfer her name to the "Record for colored children."[16] Despite this official policy, by the early 1870s the school board had capitulated to pressures from the Creole of color elite, integrating roughly one-third of the city's public schools in defiance of mounting white public opinion.

The interracial support of the Unifiers for social integration represented an anomaly on the Louisiana political scene. The *New Orleans Picayune* declared the movement dead only three days after its initial appeal and insisted that white citizens would not suffer such "degradation."[17] A little more than a year later, New Orleans was plunged again into racial violence, prompted by the formation of the White League by many of the same leaders who had supported Unification the year before. In September 1874 the White League staged a violent four-day coup in the streets of New Orleans against the state government, and the public school system, as a perceived bastion of integration, constituted a chief target of the mob. Under the ostensible influence of the organized and militarized White League, local boys took to the streets and forcibly removed pupils of color from their classrooms.[18] In 1877 the school board—loathe to decide whether the "objection to daily social intercourse" between the races in integrated public schools stemmed from premeditated "prejudice" or mere "instinct"—would cite the "turbulent spirit of the white boys" and the "repugnance" of white parents toward blacks as an unacceptable hindrance to public education and a powerful justification for segregation.[19]

Nevertheless, Creoles of color persisted, as martyr of 1866 Victor Lacroix would have them do, in their quest for the "public rights" granted to them by the 1868 constitution.[20] In the late 1870s Paul Trévigne, the former coeditor of the *Tribune*, and Ursin Dellande, a property owner and former broker, brought twin cases against the New Orleans school board that reached the Supreme Court of Louisiana in the early part of 1879. Seeking to prevent the formal division of the public schools along racial lines, Trévigne's case argued that segregation degraded his son "as a citizen" and inflicted upon him "an irreparable injury."[21] Citing article 135 of the 1868 state constitution and the legal victories of Sauvinet and Decuir, Dellande sought the admission of his eleven- and fourteen-year-old sons to the white Fillmore School located 150 feet from his house on St. Claude Street in New Marigny. Assigning Dellande's children instead to a school for the "colored race" six blocks away, the court characterized article 135 of the 1868 constitution as "a 'new policy' of the most startling character, one which upsets the whole order of society, tramples upon the usages of centuries and contains the germ of social war."[22] Meeting with similar hostility from the court, Trévigne failed in his pursuit of civil equality. Formalizing the opposition to civil rights, redeemer politicians issued a new state constitution in December 1879, revoking the 1868 guarantee of "public rights."

As the court battles for equal access to public accommodations and education demonstrated, Creole of color activists held fast to the tenets of the 1868 state constitution, a document infused with the ideals of the American Revolution and the French Revolutions of 1789 and 1848—especially inasmuch as these national traditions incorporated the critiques made by African diaspora figures such as Frederick Douglass and Cyrille Bissette. Throughout the 1880s radical Creoles of color collaborated with revolutionaries from the Caribbean, particularly Cuban activists engaged in their own struggles for emancipation and national independence. The Creole faubourgs provided shelter for Cuban exiles such as Antonio Maceo and facilitated cultural and political exchange among French-, English-, and Spanish-speaking

New Orleanians of color through various networks of mutual aid and fraternal societies. Those with legal training, such as Rodolphe Desdunes and his colleague Louis Martinet, helped bolster these institutional and individual efforts at community and personal uplift, steering people through the rocky and ever-changing course of state and local legislation. Desdunes in particular maintained his commitment to labor equality, supporting and publicizing the efforts of the Knights of Labor to organize rural sugar workers, black and white, against an increasingly oppressive planter regime.[23] In 1889 Martinet founded the *Crusader*, a political newspaper following in the radical footsteps of the *New Orleans Tribune*.

In July 1890, against the considerable opposition of Desdunes, Martinet, and other activists of color, the Louisiana legislature made good on its informal gestures toward segregation and passed the Separate Car Act. According to Creole activists, the proposed act mandating segregation on railroads was "unconstitutional, un-American, unjust, dangerous, and against sound public policy," giving as it would "free license to the evilly disposed that they might with impunity insult, humiliate, and otherwise maltreat inoffensive persons . . . who should happen to have a dark skin."[24] In September 1891 opposition to the segregation law crystallized in the formation of the Citizens' Committee to Test the Constitutionality of the Separate Car Law, which included Desdunes, Martinet, and Aristide Mary, whose "last political act" before his suicide at age seventy was to fund the new effort.[25] In early 1892 the Citizen's Committee found a test case in the attempt of Desdunes's son Daniel to travel between New Orleans and Mobile. When the legality of segregation on interstate carriers was upheld in an unrelated case—thus rendering the Desdunes case irrelevant to the cause—the committee enlisted a local Creole of color activist and shoemaker, Homer A. Plessy, to challenge segregation on an intrastate route from New Orleans to the nearby town of Covington, Louisiana.

For four long years Plessy's case wound its way through the court system within a troubling national climate. From 1892 to 1896 several states instituted segregation laws and disenfranchisement policies; the African American leader Booker T. Washington gave his 1895 "Atlanta Compromise" speech, endorsing social segregation in return for economic cooperation between southern blacks and whites; and conservative political leaders mounted a white supremacist backlash against

Populist attempts to organize black and white workers.[26] Their lonely efforts attesting to the extent to which they had been abandoned by the national Republican Party, the Catholic Church, and local political allies, the Citizen's Committee assailed Democratic attempts to qualify the suffrage, outlaw interracial marriage, and suppress the rights of laborers, to little avail.[27] In May 1896—following what seemed to be the spirit of the times—the Supreme Court handed down its judgment in *Plessy*, asserting the right of whites to be shielded from their repugnance toward blacks over a broad interpretation of the Fourteenth Amendment right to equal protection before the law.[28]

From its conceptualization to the judgment rendered by the Supreme Court, the *Plessy* case exposed the disparities between racial appearance and what was fast becoming racial reality and between social practice and legal principle. The Citizen's Committee had ultimately decided to proceed with Plessy, a plaintiff of light skin color, even though, according to Martinet, such a person might in New Orleans be tolerated by whites in a first-class car, enjoying as he would "a large degree of immunity from [the] accursed privilege" of separate accommodation. Furthermore, Martinet continued, such a strategy might potentially alienate darker-skinned blacks, who were apt to believe that the Citizens' Committee activists "were nearly white or wanted to pass for white." Moving the case forward, however, Plessy's lead attorney, the Ohio-born Albion Tourgée—formerly a Reconstruction politician in North Carolina and one of the few remaining passionate champions of equal rights for blacks—sought to capitalize on the chasm between bodily appearance and racial designation, a paradox that had long been a hallmark of Creole of color identity. In a scattershot argument aimed at the Thirteenth and Fourteenth Amendments, Tourgée's brief to the court revealed some important inconsistencies. On the one hand, the brief insisted on the right of Homer Plessy, described as being "of 7/8ths white blood," to his property in the "reputation of being white," a right that had been taken from him without "due process." However, it also undercut the basis for such a property right in whiteness, arguing further that segregation perpetuated unconstitutional distinctions "of a servile character, coincident with the institution of slavery," a system of caste "separable from the incident of ownership" that unfairly privileged white skin. Tourgée's argument attempted to have it both ways—campaigning for Plessy's property in whiteness while simultaneously contending against the establishment of racial hierarchies. In this sense, the argument in the *Plessy* case reenacted the ambivalent racial sensibilities of New Orleans Creoles of color throughout the previous century evident in the various episodes surveyed in these pages.

As conflicted as their actions and logic have been, however, the Supreme Court's endorsement of "separate but equal" was more insidiously ambiguous, outfitting the wolf of white supremacy in the sheep's clothing of justice and equality. Building on the legal precedent of the reversal of the lower court's decision in *Decuir v. Hall* (1878) and the 1883 civil rights cases that declared the civil rights legislation of the previous decade to be unconstitutional, the majority opinion written by Justice Henry Brown endorsed the distinction between political equality and social equality, shoring up a peculiar loophole in American legal and political discourse. By providing a refuge for racist behavior and legislation, the special domain of the "social" insulated the abstract and pristine notion of "political equality" and the moral status of the privileged "white family" from the virulent racist violence enacted with increasing frequency against black people and their property.[29] Hereafter, the physical and psychological comfort of whites assumed priority in the American legal system. Conceived as a paramount social issue, the "Negro problem" would continue to function as a surrogate for anti-immigrant, antilabor, and gender anxieties along with a host of other concerns.

After the *Plessy* verdict, state efforts to disenfranchise blacks proceeded apace, culminating in the governor's endorsement of the "grandfather clause" as a more "upright and manly" means of disqualifying black voters, especially when compared with the potentially violent and disruptive methods used in other southern states that relied on the discretion and the brawn of poll workers.[30] Desdunes and others struggled to achieve an adequate spiritual stance heading into the "nadir" of African American history. Lynching would become commonplace in Louisiana and the rest of the South, and race riots would destabilize southern urban areas, including Wilmington, North Carolina (1898), New Orleans (1900), and Atlanta (1906). Amidst these dispiriting developments, Desdunes called for an attitude of "forlorn hope and noble despair."[31] Eventually blinded by a 1911 accident incurred on the wharf as a U.S. customs agent, his family partially dispersed after the relocation of son Daniel to Boystown, Nebraska, Rodolphe Desdunes labored to prepare the hearth for the sense of peace that Victor Lacroix's spirit had promised would return.

In 1907 a weary Desdunes entered the fray of a rapidly polarizing struggle over the course of black leadership. Two years before, W. E. B. Du Bois had joined public forces with Booker T. Washington's most outspoken black critics, formalizing a split between Washington's politics of accommodation to Jim Crow and what was seen to be a radical insistence on political and social rights.[32] In a short pamphlet, "A Few Words to Dr. DuBois 'with Malice Towards None,'" Desdunes responded to press reports of a recent speech in which Du Bois "expressed himself very freely about the lack of book knowledge in the Southern Negroes and also about their inefficiency in the industrial line."[33] Desdunes's exasperation over the shrinking platform for African American assessments of the so-called Negro problem is palpable in the pamphlet even as he seems to accept at face value and publicize a caricature of Du Bois's position. The pamphlet presents a curiously conflicted agenda culled from the experiences of New Orleanians of color and the history of the French empire.

Desdunes rushes to the defense of the masses: they lack book knowledge simply because "they are busy" and the conditions under which they labor "suggest charity and discreetness on the part of sociologists, ethnologists, and anthropologists."[34] He also moves to expand the pantheon of black heroes—exemplary figures from which African Americans might draw inspiration. "Speaking for Louisiana, with such names as Séjour, Cailloux, Crowder, Arsene, Dunn, Dubuclet, Roudanez, Mary, Lafon, we have nothing to fear from the judgment of posterity."[35] Indeed, "our object is to remind our eminent sociologist that . . . we sacrifice no prestige by increasing the company [of leaders] from well chosen examples."[36] With these suggestions, Desdunes sows the seeds of his portraits of representative Creole lives in *Nos Hommes et Notre Histoire* (1911). Striking a provocative note, he suggests that Toussaint L'Ouverture, whom Du Bois had cited as a paragon of black independence, had been the "Booker T. Washington of San Domingo." Instead, Desdunes recommends Jacques Dessalines, who, by killing whites and expelling them from the island, actively created Haiti as a black nation. With a hint of sarcasm undercut by a genuine appreciation of Dessalines's legacy, Desdunes advises, "If it be necessary to point to one model only, we had better be correct as well as consistent, and give this place of honor to the one who has earned it—Dessalines."[37] With these gestures of pride and independence, Desdunes points toward his charge in the closing pages of *Nos Hommes:* rather than "show a passive attitude of resignation" or "suffer in silence," his "people" should take the "noble and dignified" course and "fight, no matter what."[38]

Even so, Desdunes's "Few Words" constitutes a curious retreat from Creole of color activism for "public rights," activism that presaged the Du Boisian political program. His insistence on "patience and conciliation" rather than "unseasonable aggression" carries the hallmarks of a Washingtonian philosophy, albeit tempered by the memory of radical politics in New Orleans. "We have had the educated Negro; we have had the voting Negro. We have had all the power of a friendly administration to support them and they did nothing but pass away."[39] In the place of scholarly and enfranchised upstarts, "the moral Negro is the type we need, the Negro who appreciates the sense of duty and dignity of conviction."[40] He also cites the remarks of President Theodore Roosevelt at Washington's Tuskeegee Institute: "Negroes . . . should cease to be Negroes, in order to live, think, feel and act as true Americans, just as Brown, Garrison, Lovejoy, Phillips, Lincoln, and Longworth, ceased to be whites, that they might become the instruments of loving humanity."[41] The memory of the famous meal shared by Roosevelt and Washington at the White House had begun to lose luster among black Americans, many of whom most recently expressed outrage over Roosevelt's 1906 "dishonorable discharge" of black soldiers in Brownsville, Texas, amid dubious charges of their riotous behavior. In light of these developments, Desdunes's generous adoption of Roosevelt's rhetoric strikes an incongruous chord. Nonetheless, Desdunes expresses an abiding faith in "the ultimate triumph of white man's charity over the white man's inhumanity," and, at points, he echoes Roosevelt, urging black leaders to do away with racial affiliation: "to be Negroes at all, when dealing with fundamental ideals is . . . a most erroneous doctrine."[42]

We might attribute Desdunes's mood to an overarching investment—consistent with what we have seen of the Creole of color intellectual tradition—in the progress of race relations from the shadows of intolerance to the light of mutual respect. Accordingly, Desdunes's response to

Du Bois naturalizes rather than politicizes the forces of white supremacy: the "prevailing notions against Negro demonstration of any sort" is "part of nature in our latitudes and must so manifest itself until the coming of a mysterious transformation."[43] In language reminiscent of the spiritualism of the *Tribune* group, Desdunes attempts to access a metaphysical realm of harmonious union above the commotion of divisive racial politics. "We have entered the age of atonement. We have nothing to recommend our prayers, but the achievements and sufferings of our heroes, martyrs and patriots . . . we shall have to conjure with their names that we might keep open the 'door of hope.' "[44] Desdunes and his cohort may have looked for comfort in the spirit communiqués of Victor Lacroix and others, preserved as they were in sturdy binding befitting their status as both sacred text and practical reference.[45] Again, Lacroix's assurance echoed from the once-bloody vestibule of the Mechanics' Institute: "The turmoil will soon cease, the marks of its passage will disappear little by little."[46]

We might also attribute Desdunes's defensive and somewhat reactionary tone to an intense pride of place, his sense of himself as a southerner and a New Orleanian. By 1907 Du Bois himself had lived in the South for ten years and—with the death in 1899 of his eighteen-month-old son under a segregated medical system and with the mob violence threatening his neighborhood in the 1906 Atlanta riot—had endured white supremacy on both intimate and public levels.[47] Yet for Desdunes, Du Bois would always be a son of New England, a carpetbagger of sorts having descended on the benighted South to bestow a foreign wisdom. Desdunes was necessarily suspicious of the promises of outsiders in an era of federal retreat from local matters in southern states. "The conflict between Hamiltonian and Jeffersonian theories is not settled," Desdunes reminds Du Bois, referring to the clash between federal jurisdiction and states' rights, "and until it is settled, the feelings of our [white] neighbors must enter into our calculation."[48] Raising a special standard for New Orleans' Creoles of color, Desdunes prompts Du Bois to consider how this francophone population might influence American race leadership. "As little as we may surmise about it, there are two distinct schools of politics among the Negroes. The Latin Negro differs radically from the Anglo-Saxon in aspiration and method. One hopes, the other doubts. . . . One aspires to equality, the other to identity. One will forget that he is a Negro in order to think that he is a man; the other will forget that he is a man in order to think that he is a Negro. . . . One is a philosophical Negro, the other practical." A merger of the two sensibilities would produce, according to Desdunes, a productive fusion "that could not find a parallel in the history of the black race."[49]

Desdunes's critique of him notwithstanding, Du Bois had already considered and implemented a number of his recommendations. In 1905 he and other black professionals and academics had launched the Niagara Movement. Its "Declaration of Principles" called for equal accommodation and universal manhood suffrage, but it also addressed the plight of the laboring classes and, in the spirit of atonement and self-help, outlined specific duties for "race men" and their families. The efforts of Du Bois and his cohort would culminate in the formation of the interracial National Association for the Advancement of Colored People (NAACP) and provide institutional support for radicals of all races. As a result of NAACP legal efforts, the Supreme Court's decision in *Brown v. Board of Education of Topeka* (1954) eventually overturned the *Plessy* verdict. Tactics aside, Du Bois and his cohort had imbibed the spirit of the Creole of color protest tradition. The fathers of both Desdunes and Du Bois had been sons of Saint Domingue/Haiti, and Alfred Du Bois seemed to have practiced a ethic of vagabondage that, even while it encouraged him to abandon his young family—including two-year-old William—also seemed to convey to his famous son a sense of movement beyond and above the twin veils of race and nation.[50] In *The Souls of Black Folk* (1903), Du Bois picked up the mantle of the Creole of color quest for meaningful legacy and public redress waged during the long nineteenth century and found it sullied but not destroyed by the humiliating defeat of *Plessy v. Ferguson.* His *Souls* took up the question that New Orleans' Creoles of color had been grappling with in their literary expression, in the courtroom, and in their political journals for decades: "What does it *feel* like to be a problem?"[51] In response, Du Bois weighed the psychological costs and benefits of living within the "veil," paying special regard to the "soul" of the "American Negro." Defying strictures of genre and boundaries of race and nation, Du Bois distilled the essential features of this maligned entity and retrofitted black culture and history for future battles. If "the problem of the twentieth century" was to be "the problem of the color-line," then those "darker races of men" needed a compelling sense of their past and their purpose if they meant to demand national legacy and defend their claims to civilization.[52]

The spirit of the martyr Lacroix spoke of a peace returning to the hearth, but Du Bois would not have expected it to appear soon. To Lacroix's extended claim, he would have countered, "What if the turmoil unleashed by white supremacy proved to be ceaseless and its marks permanent?" Over the course of the nineteenth century, from the Haitian Revolution to *Plessy v. Ferguson*, Creoles of color had accumulated many physical, legal, and psychological souvenirs of racism and imperialism, marks they bore unsuspectingly, ambivalently, or defiantly as the context dictated. With *Plessy*, the U.S. Supreme Court had told them that their (discursively if not actually) dark bodies were to be a badge of slavery and a source of shame. In response, Du Bois scoured history and his prodigious imagination for the voices of those exiles from national recognition, hoping to discern the gift of their "second sight." What he found there presented the gamut of experience and conveyed a complex emotional landscape. There was Josie, a "thin homely girl of twenty," a budding young student of "unconscious moral heroism" who died unceremoniously, overworked and brokenhearted, in the Tennessee countryside; Booker T. Washington, "the most distinguished Southerner since Jefferson Davis" whose "Gospel of Work and Money" had "shift[ed] the burden of the Negro problem to the Negro's shoulders;" the emancipated slave woman, a "form hovering dark and mother-like," having survived the evils of rape and bondage "only to see her dark boy's limbs scattered to the winds by midnight marauders;" Alexander Crummell, the Episcopal priest who, having suffered the "deep death" of doubt, humiliation, and despair on three continents, returned to America "[bringing] within his wide influence all that was best of those who walk within the Veil;" the tenant farmers and convicts of the Georgia black belt who testified in myriad ways that "this land was a little Hell;" black John, the field hand "ruined" by schooling, who avenged his sister's assault by white John, declared "I'm going to be free," and went to face certain death at the hands of the lynch mob; and Du Bois's own son Burghardt, his funeral procession mocked by the "pale faced" denizens of Atlanta—"they did not say much—they only glanced and said 'Niggers!' "[53]

In their abjection, endurance, submission, and vehemence, this motley assembly recalled Camille Thierry's cast of dispossessed, displaced, suicidal, haunting, vengeful, and resilient vagabonds. As Thierry had done in his 1874 collection of poems and the *Cenelles* poets had done in 1845, Du Bois demonstrated how a focus on the perspective of exiles could bring the range of human expression into sharp relief and could light a path to self-consciousness for those lacking the shelter of a national narrative. His powerful metaphor of duality and in-betweenness has shored up African American identity and the African American quest for justice for more than a century: "It is a peculiar sensation, this double-consciousness. . . . One ever feels his two-ness—an American, a Negro; two souls, two thoughts, two unreconciled strivings; two warring ideals in one dark body, whose dogged strength alone keeps it from being torn asunder."[54] Du Bois portrays the African American consciousness as a Creole terrain, a tension-filled place where competing formulations of racial and national identity vie for relevance. On this middle ground, the spiritual strivings of "black folk" yield both triumph and sorrow, and they provoke swift and decisive action as often as they prompt deep and abiding resignation.

Abbreviations

AHR	*American Historical Review*
AJMS	*American Journal of the Medical Sciences*
ARC	Amistad Research Center, Tulane University Library
BPOC	Benjamin F. Butler, *Private and Official Correspondence of Gen. Benjamin F. Butler during the Period of the Civil War* (Norwood, Mass., 1917)
CCR	New Orleans Civil Court Records
Census	U.S. Federal Census, Orleans, Louisiana
CM	*Century Magazine*
[SMS1]CRC	Charles Roussève Collection
DBR	*De Bow's Review*
HNMM	*Harper's New Monthly Magazine*
HR	House Reports, 39th Congress, 2nd Session, Number 16
HWM	*Harper's Weekly Magazine*
JAH	*Journal of American History*
JSH	*Journal of Southern History*
JSML	*Journal de la Société Medical de la Louisiane*
LaC	*Louisiana Courier / Courier de la Louisiane*
LaHist	*Louisiana History*
[SMS2]LSCR	Louisiana Supreme Court Records
LSU	Special Collections, Hill Memorial Library, Louisiana State University
MCC	Marcus Christian Collection
NAR	*North American Review*
NOB	*New Orleans Bee / L'Abeille de la Nouvelle Orleans*
NODC	*New Orleans Daily Crescent*
NODD	*New Orleans Daily Delta*

NODP	*New Orleans Daily Picayune*
NOMSJ	*New Orleans Medical and Surgical Journal*
NONARC	New Orleans Notarial Archive Research Center
NOPL	Louisiana Division, New Orleans Public Library
NOPSSR	New Orleans Public Schools Superintendent Records
NOTD	*New Orleans Times-Democrat*
PCR	Parish Court Records
RGCSR	René Grandjean Collection, Series IX, Spiritualism Records; Subseries IX.1, Séance Registers
SCR	*New Orleans Sanitary Commission Report* (New Orleans, 1854)
SCT	Special Collections Division, Tulane University Library
UNO	Manuscripts and Special Collections, Earl K. Long Library, University of New Orleans
WOR	U.S. War Department, *War of the Rebellion: A Compilation of the Official Records of the Union and Confederate Armies* (Washington, D.C., 1880–1901)

Notes

Prologue: Passing as American

1. *NOB*, May 29, 1858.

2. *Anastasie Desarzant v. P. LeBlanc and E. Desmaziliere, his wife*, No. 5868, 14 La Ann. xii, unreported. (December 1859), LSCR, UNO, witness Ménard. Case cited as *Desarzant v. LeBlanc* hereafter. The names of those involved, especially that of Desmaziliere, are not spelled consistently in the court record. For clarity, I use the names above throughout.

3. Arthé Anthony, "'Lost Boundaries': Racial Passing and Poverty in Segregated New Orleans," in Sybil Kein, ed. *Creole: The History and Legacy of Louisiana's Free People of Color* (Baton Rouge: Louisiana State University Press, 2000), p. 296, n. 1.

4. Louis F. Tasistro, *Random Shots and Southern Breezes, Containing Critical Remarks on the Southern States and Southern Institutions, with Semi-Serious Observations on Men and Manners* (New York: Harper and Brothers, 1842), p. 51.

5. A. Oakey Hall, *The Manhattaner in New Orleans; or, Phases of "Crescent City" Life* (New York: J. S. Redfield, 1851), p. 27.

6. See John S. Kendall, "The Municipal Election of 1858," *LHQ* 5 (1922). See also Frank Towers, *The Urban South and the Coming of the Civil War* (Charlottesville: University of Virginia Press, 2004), pp. 146–148; Mary P. Ryan, *Civic Wars: Democracy and Public Life in the American City during the Nineteenth Century* (Berkeley: University of California Press, 1997), pp. 146–151; *NOB*, May 27, 1858; May 28, 1858; May 29, 1858; June 3, 1858; *NODP*, June 3, 1858. Some courts did indeed adjourn because of the violence, see *NOB*, June 7, 1858.

7. *Desarzant v. LeBlanc*, witness Roach, p. 58; witness Parker, pp. 59–60.

8. *Desarzant v. LeBlanc*, witness Ménard, p. 70.

9. Thomas Jefferson, quoted in Norman Walker, "Advantages of New Orleans," in Henry Rightor, ed., *Standard History of New Orleans* (Chicago: Lewis Publishing Company, 1900), p. 57.

10. George Dargo, *Jefferson's Louisiana: Politics and the Clash of Legal Traditions, Studies in Legal History* (Cambridge, Mass.: Harvard University Press, 1975); John Davis, *Travels in Louisiana and the Floridas, in the Year 1802, Giving a Correct Picture of Those Countries. Tr. from the French, with Notes, &C* (New York: I. Riley & Co., 1806); Paul F. Lachance, "The 1809 Refugees to New Orleans: Reception, Integration, and Impact," *LaHist* 29, no. 2 (1988); Adam Rothman, *Slave Country: American Expansion and the Origins of the Deep South* (Cambridge, Mass.: Harvard University Press, 2005). On tensions over French and English dancing, see Ned Sublette, *The World that Made New Orleans: From Spanish Silver to Congo Square* (Chicago: Lawrence Hill Books, 2008), pp. 240-244.

11. Lachance, "1809 Refugees"; Claiborne quoted in Caryn Cossé Bell, *Revolution, Romanticism, and the Afro-Creole Protest Tradition in Louisiana, 1718–1868* (Baton Rouge: Louisiana State University Press, 1997), p. 39.

12. *Moniteur*, June 24, 1809, quoted in Lachance, "1809 Refugees," p. 251; see pp. 245–253 on the initial reception of refugees.

13. *Desarzant v. LeBlanc*, judgment, Louisiana Supreme Court.

14. M. Christine Boyer, *The City of Collective Memory: Its Historical Imagery and Architectural Entertainments* (Cambridge, Mass.: MIT Press, 1994), pp. 321–343.

15. Brent Hayes Edwards, *The Practice of Diaspora: Literature, Translation, and the Rise of Black Internationalism* (Cambridge, Mass.: Harvard University Press, 2003); Paul Gilroy, *The Black Atlantic: Modernity and Double Consciousness* (Cambridge, Mass.: Harvard University Press, 1993); and Earl Lewis, "To Turn as on a Pivot: Writing African Americans into a History of Overlapping Diasporas," *AHR* 100, no. 3 (1995) all explore the possibilities of diasporic thought for racial politics and experiences of modernity. Also see James Clifford, *Routes: Travel and Translation in the Late Twentieth Century* (Cambridge, Mass.: Harvard University Press, 1997), pp. 244–277; Brent Hayes Edwards, "The Uses of *Diaspora*," *Social Text* 66, vol. 19, no. 1 (Spring 2001), pp. 45–73; and Tiffany Ruby Patterson and Robin D. G. Kelley, "Unfinished Migrations: reflections on the African Diaspora and the Making of the Modern World," *African Studies Review* 43, no. 1, pp. 11–45 stress the historical context of the term "diaspora" as arising during the 1950s and 1960s, and yet they attempt to discern a useful meaning of the term that can be applied in various historical contexts. Thomas Bender, *The Unfinished City: New York and the Metropolitan Idea* (New York: New Press, 2002) describes urban identities as similarly situated between the local and the global. Also see James Clifford, *Routes: Travel and Translation in the Late Twentieth Century* (Cambridge, Mass.: Harvard University Press, 1997), pp. 244–277.

16. See contributors to Arnold Hirsch and Joseph Logsdon, eds., *Creole New Orleans: Race and Americanization* (Baton Rouge: Louisiana State University Press, 1992); Sybil Kein, ed.,*Creole;* the articles collected in the special issue of the *Journal of American Folklore* 116, no. 459; Thomas Fiehrer, "From Quadrille to Stomp: The Creole Origins of Jazz," *Popular Music* 10, no. 1 (1991); and Roger D. Abrahams et al., *Blues for New Orleans: Mardi Gras and America's Creole Soul* (Philadelphia: University of Pennsylvania Press, 2006).

17. On the racial and national strictures on "Creole" places, see Benedict R. O'G Anderson, *Imagined Communities: Reflections on the Origin and Spread of Nationalism*, rev. and extended ed. (London and New York: Verso, 1991), pp. 47–65; Chris Bongie, "Resisting Memories: The Creole Identities of Lafcadio Hearn and

Edouard Glissant," *SubStance* 26, no. 3 (1997). On "Creole" as a continuum from essentialism to relationality, see Chris Bongie, *Islands and Exiles: The Creole Identities of Post/Colonial Literature* (Stanford, Calif.: Stanford University Press, 1998), pp. 42–75. On the role of Creolization in upholding absolutism in an earlier period, see Herman L. Bennett, *Africans in Colonial Mexico: Absolutism, Christianity, and Afro-Creole Consciousness, 1570–1640* (Bloomington: Indiana University Press, 2003), pp. 2–3.

18. The term *Americanization* has been used as a synonym for *assimilation* and refers to individuals and groups immigrating to the United States. Neil Cowan, *Our Parent's Lives: The Americanization of Eastern European Jews* (New Brunswick, N.J.: Rutgers University Press, 1996); David A. Richards, *Italian-American: The Racializing of an Ethnic Identity* (New York: New York University Press, 1999). The term also describes an imperial process of spreading American values in the wake of conquest. See Peter J. Kastor, *The Nation's Crucible: The Louisiana Purchase and the Creation of America* (New Haven: Yale University Press, 2004) and more generally the essays collected in Amy and Donald E. Pease Kaplan, ed., *Cultures of United States Imperialism* (Durham, N.C.: Duke University Press, 1993).

19. Or on common water: Ira Berlin has described the hybrid cultural practices, cosmopolitan sensibility, and intermediary function of a charter generation of "Atlantic Creoles." Ira Berlin, "From Creole to African: Atlantic Creoles and the Origins of African-American Society in Mainland North America," *The William and Mary Quarterly* 53, no. 2 (1996); and Ira Berlin, *Generations of Captivity: A History of African-American Slaves* (Cambridge, Mass.: Belknap Press of Harvard University Press, 2003), pp. 23–49. On language, see Grey Gundaker, *Signs of Diaspora; Diaspora of Signs: Literacies, Creolization, and Vernacular Practice in African America* (New York: Oxford University Press, 1998). On the application of recent linguistic theory in the field of folklore, see the special issue devoted to Creolization of the *Journal of American Folklore* 116, no. 459.

20. On the meaning of the word *Creole* in Louisiana, see Joseph G. Tregle, Jr., "Creoles and Americans," in Hirsch and Logsdon, eds., *Creole New Orleans*; Carl A. Brasseaux, *French, Cajun, Creole, Houma: A Primer on Francophone Louisiana* (Baton Rouge: Louisiana State University Press, 2005) pp. 85–115; Joseph G. Tregle, Jr., "On That Word 'Creole' Again: A Note," *LaHist* 23, no. 2 (1982).

21. J. Hector St. John de Crèvecoeur, *Letters from an American Farmer* (Oxford and New York: Oxford University Press, 1998), pp. 43–44. On melting pots in the American imagination, see Werner Sollors, *Beyond Ethnicity: Consent and Descent in American Culture* (New York: Oxford University Press, 1986), pp. 66–101.

22. Grace Elizabeth King, *New Orleans: The Place and the People* (New York and London: The Macmillan Company, 1904), p. 268.

23. On self-making in the slave trade, see Walter Johnson, *Soul by Soul: Life inside the Antebellum Slave Market* (Cambridge, Mass.: Harvard University Press, 1999). On Martin, see John W. Blassingame, *Slave Testimony: Two Centuries of Letters, Speeches, Interviews, and Autobiographies* (Baton Rouge: Louisiana State University Press, 1976), pp. 702–735. On Walker and self-making, see Amy S. Greenberg, *Manifest Manhood and the Antebellum American Empire* (Cambridge and New York: Cambridge University Press, 2005), pp. 170–196. See Shelley Streeby, *American Sensations: Class, Empire, and the Production of Popular Culture* (Berkeley: University of California Press, 2002), pp. 152–155, on New Orleans as a popular

site for filibustering in the American imagination. On Walker's trial in New Orleans, see *NOB*, June 1, 2, 3, 1858.

24. Waging "whiteness" entailed a number of different strategies: legal, literary, rhetorical, performative, and scientific. David R. Roediger, *The Wages of Whiteness: Race and the Making of the American Working Class* (London: Verso, 1991); Cheryl I. Harris, "Whiteness as Property," *Harvard Law Review* 106, no. 8 (1993); Ian Haney-López, *White by Law: The Legal Construction of Race* (New York: New York University Press, 1996). On this vast scholarship, see Shelley Fisher Fishkin, "Interrogating Whiteness, Complicating Blackness: Remapping American Culture," *American Quarterly* 47 (1995).

25. See statutes in the section "Slaves and Free Persons of Color," in Henry Jefferson Leovy, *The Laws and General Ordinances of the City of New Orleans* (New Orleans: E. C. Wharton, 1857), p. 258; David C. Rankin, "The Forgotten People: Free People of Color in New Orleans, 1850–1870" (Ph.D. dissertation, Johns Hopkins University, 1976), pp. 63–4; Judith Kelleher Schafer, *Becoming Free, Remaining Free: Manumission and Enslavement in New Orleans, 1846–1862* (Baton Rouge: Louisiana State University Press, 2003).

26. See Carol Wilson, *The Two Lives of Sally Miller: A Case of Mistaken Racial Identity in Antebellum New Orleans* (New Brunswick, N.J.: Rutgers University Press, 2007).

27. On Anatole Broyard, see Henry Louis Gates, *Thirteen Ways of Looking at a Black Man* (New York: Random House, 1997), pp. 180–214; Anatole Broyard, *Kafka Was the Rage: A Greenwich Village Memoir* (New York: Carol Southern Books, 1993); and Bliss Broyard, *One Drop: A True Story of Family, Race, and Secrets: A Memoir* (New York: Little, Brown and Co., 2007).

28. In nineteenth-century New Orleans as elsewhere, family law reflected broader cultural and racial currents. See Lawrence Meir Friedman, *Private Lives: Families, Individuals, and the Law* (Cambridge, Mass.: Harvard University Press, 2004), introduction, esp. p. 12, for a discussion of law as a product of society.

29. On marriage in nineteenth-century America, see Nancy F. Cott, *Public Vows: A History of Marriage and the Nation* (Cambridge, Mass.: Harvard University Press, 2000); and Friedman, *Private Lives*. For an exploration of family law in the slave South, see Michael Grossberg, *Governing the Hearth: Law and the Family in Nineteenth-Century America* (Chapel Hill: University of North Carolina Press, 1985). These texts generally deal with the common law states, which Louisiana was not.

30. See Kimberly S. Hanger, *Bounded Lives, Bounded Places: Free Black Society in Colonial New Orleans, 1769–1803* (Durham: Duke University Press, 1997), pp. 89–108; and Jack D.L. Holmes, "Do It! Don't Do It!: Spanish Laws on Sex and Marriage," in Edward F. Haas, ed., *Louisiana's Legal Heritage* (Pensacola, Fla.: Perdido Bay Press, 1983). See Judith Kelleher Schafer, *Slavery, the Civil Law, and the Supreme Court of Louisiana* (Baton Rouge: Louisiana State University Press, 1994), pp. 180–200 on antebellum views on "open and notorious concubinage."

31. *Plaçage* is a somewhat contested term. In the early nineteenth century, the term described unmarried cohabiting couples regardless of race, prompting some to argue that the stigma attending the relationship comes largely from visitors to New Orleans. However, as we will see in chapter 4, the Louisiana Civil Code and the courts began to adopt this language of stigma from 1825 onward.

32. *Desarzant v. LeBlanc,* witness Drouet, p. 80.

33. *Desarzant v. LeBlanc,* witness Ménard, p. 71.

34. See Christopher E. G. Benfey, *Degas in New Orleans: Encounters in the Creole World of Kate Chopin and George Washington Cable* (New York: Knopf, 1997), pp. 122–139 on the interracial Rillieux family, including painter Edgar Degas and Creole of color scientist Norbert Rillieux.

35. Charles Gayarré, "The Creoles of History and the Creoles of Romance, A Lecture Delivered in the Hall of the Tulane University" (New Orleans, 1885), pp. 2–3. See Edward Larocque Tinker, *Toucoutou* (New York: Dodd Mead & Co., 1928); Lafcadio Hearn, "Los Criollos," in Lafcadio Hearn and S. Frederick Starr, *Inventing New Orleans: Writings of Lafcadio Hearn* (Jackson: University Press of Mississippi, 2001), pp. 30–38.

36. Alice Dunbar-Nelson, "People of Color in Louisiana, Part I," *Journal of Negro History* 1, no. 4 (October 1916), p. 367; Charles B. Roussève, *The Negro in Louisiana: Aspects of His History and His Literature* (New York: Xavier University Press, 1937), pp. 22–24. This usage closely parallels contemporary usage. See the various essays in Kein, ed., *Creole.*

37. Rodolphe Lucien Desdunes, *Our People and Our History,* trans. Sister Dorothea Olga McCants (Baton Rouge: Louisiana State University Press, 1973); on Castra see pp. 3–5; on Delille see pp. 97–99.

38. Ibid., p. 21.

39. See Gwendolyn Midlo Hall, *Africans in Colonial Louisiana: The Development of Afro-Creole Culture in the Eighteenth Century* (Baton Rouge: Louisiana State University Press, 1992), and "The Formation of an Afro-Creole Culture," in Hirsch and Logsdon, eds., *Creole New Orleans,* pp. 58–87, on Creole slaves. See Richard Tansey, "Out-of-State Free Blacks in Late Antebellum New Orleans," *LaHist* 22, no. 4 (1981), pp. 369–386 on African Americans from elsewhere. I use *Creole of color* to describe the group that David Rankin characterizes as the "Forgotten People." See his "The Forgotten People." "L.M.," the author of the preface to Rodolphe Lucien Desdunes, *Nos Hommes et Notre Histoire* (Montréal: Arbour & Dupont, 1911), pp. 3–4, refers to "le Créole de couleur." (It is not clear who L.M. was. He has been alternatively identified as "L. Martin" and "a French Canadian." See Desdunes, *Our People and Our History,* trans. McCants, p. xxviii.) I use "Creole of color" despite Joseph Tregle's objections to it as racist. See his "Creoles and Americans," in Hirsch and Logsdon, eds., *Creole New Orleans,* pp. 138–139.

40. Rankin, "The Forgotten People," pp. 105–106.

41. See Hanger, *Bounded Lives,* pp. 26–51 for a statistical account of manumission by phenotype, age, sex, and other characteristics in the Spanish period. *Adelle v. Beauregard,* 1 Mart. La. 183 (Fall 1810), cited in Helen T. Catterall, ed., *Judicial Cases Concerning American Slavery and the Negro, Volume III, Cases from the Courts of Georgia, Florida, Alabama, Mississippi, and Louisiana* (New York: Octagon Books, 1968), p. 447. *Sally Miller v. Belmonti,* 11. Rob. La. 339 (July 1845), cited in Catterall, p. 571.

42. See Werner Sollors, *Neither Black nor White yet Both: Thematic Explorations of Interracial Literature* (New York: Oxford University Press, 1997), pp. 255–262 on these two related forms of passing.

43. David C. Rankin, "The Impact of the Civil War on the Free Colored Community of New Orleans," *Perspectives in American History* XI (1977–1978), p. 396.

44. Gary B. Mills, *The Forgotten People: Cane River's Creoles of Color* (Baton Rouge: Louisiana State University Press, 1977); Rankin, "The Forgotten People."

45. *Desarzant v. LeBlanc*, witness Dupré, p. 78.

46. W. E. B. Du Bois, Henry Louis Gates, and Teri Hume Oliver, *The Souls of Black Folk: Authoritative Text, Contexts, Criticism* (New York: W. W. Norton, 1999), p. 5. Creoles of color experienced an invisibility similar to that of Ralph Ellison's "Invisible Man": "When they approach me, they see only my surroundings, themselves, or figments of their imagination—indeed, everything and anything except me." Ralph Ellison, *Invisible Man* (New York: Vintage International, 1995), p. 3. This ontological problem recalls that of "marking" in Thomas Holt, "Marking: Race, Race-Making, and the Writing of History," *The American Historical Review* 100, no. 1 (1995).

47. Du Bois, Gates, and Oliver, *Black Souls*, p. 127.

48. My notion of the ambivalent effects this perspective draws from Michel de Certeau's description of "bridge" or "frontier" narration. See Michel de Certeau, *The Practice of Everyday Life* (Berkeley, Calif.: University of California Press, 1984), pp. 122–129. See also Edouard Glissant's categories of *retour* and *détour* (reversion and diversion) in Edouard Glissant and J. Michael Dash, *Caribbean Discourse: Selected Essays* (Charlottesville: University Press of Virginia, 1989), p. 26. In contrast, some scholars view "creolity" as "nothing but revolutionary." See Robert and Ana C. Cara Baron, "Introduction: Creolization and Folklore—Cultural Creativity in Process," *Journal of American Folklore* 116, no. 259 (2003), p. 5.

49. On documents regarding the *Plessy* case, see Otto H. Olsen, *The Thin Disguise: Turning Point in Negro History; Plessy v. Ferguson; a Documentary Presentation, 1864–1896* (New York: Humanities Press, 1967). Recent work on *Plessy* includes Saidiya V. Hartman, *Scenes of Subjection: Terror, Slavery, and Self-Making in Nineteenth-Century America* (New York: Oxford University Press, 1997), pp. 189–206; and Stephen Michael Best, *The Fugitive's Properties: Law and the Poetics of Possession* (Chicago: University of Chicago Press, 2004), pp. 237–256. Joseph R. Roach, *Cities of the Dead: Circum-Atlantic Performance* (New York: Columbia University Press, 1996), pp. 233–237 calls Plessy's act of passing "whiteface minstrelsy."

50. See Mark Golub, "Plessy as 'Passing': Judicial Responses to Ambiguously Raced Bodies in Plessy v. Ferguson," *Law & Society Review* 39, no. 3 (2005) and for an interpretation portraying *Plessy* as less ambiguous.

51. The phrase comes from Tourgée's and Walker's "Brief of Relator" to the Criminal District Court of New Orleans. *Plessy v. Ferguson*, Acc 106. Docket #11134, *Ex Parte* Homer A. Plessy. New Orleans. January 1893. 45 La. Ann. 80. Item 10, LSCR, UNO. Both Justice Brown and Justice Harlan repeat the concept as a "badge of slavery."

52. Joseph R. Roach, "Deep Skin: Reconstructing Congo Square," in Harry Justin and David Krasner Elam, eds., *African American Performance History* (New York: Oxford University Press, 2001), 102–103. 1910 Census, Roll T624_521, p. 2A, district 98; 1920 Census, Roll T625_620, p. 8A, district 103; January 20, 1922, Voter Registration Books, 1922–1926, NOPL.

53. W. E. B. Du Bois, "Criteria of Negro Art," *Crisis* 32 (October 1926), p. 290.

54. The phrase is from Sollors, *Neither Black nor White.*

55. Du Bois, "Criteria of Negro Art," pp. 290–291.

56. Ralph Ellison, "Change the Joke and Slip the Yoke" (1958), in Ralph Ellison and John F. Callahan, *The Collected Essays of Ralph Ellison* (New York: Modern Library, 1995), pp. 100–112.

57. These efforts perhaps culminated in the International Olympic Committee's decision to stage the 1996 Olympic Games in the Atlanta, Georgia of both Margaret Mitchell (of *Gone With the Wind* fame) and Martin Luther King, Jr.

58. Sybil Kein, "Toucoutou," *An American South: Poems* (East Lansing: Michigan State University Press, 1996), pp. 25–26.

59. On the notion that the dead or apparently dead bear witness, see Joan Dayan, *Haiti, History, and the Gods* (Berkeley: University of California Press, 1995), pp. 36–37. See Sharon Patricia Holland, *Raising the Dead: Readings of Death and (Black) Subjectivity* (Durham, N.C.: Duke University Press, 2000); and Roach, *Cities of the Dead*, p. 37 on the "intense experiences" of the ritual of dying. On another haunted landscape, see Judith Richardson, *Possessions: The History and Uses of Haunting in the Hudson Valley* (Cambridge, Mass.: Harvard University Press, 2003). See Vincent Brown, *The Reaper's Garden: Death and Power in the World of Atlantic Slavery* (Cambridge, Mass.: Harvard University Press, 2008), p. 5 for a discussion of "mortuary politics," the ways in which people employ meanings derived from death and death-related activities within struggles toward political ends.

60. Henry C. Castellanos, *New Orleans as It Was: Episodes of Louisiana Life* (Baton Rouge: Louisiana State University Press, 1978), pp. 80–83.

61. Camille Thierry, "Les Vagabondes: Poésies Americaines" (Paris: 1874); on responses to Mariquita in Charles Gayarré's *Fernando de Lemos*, see H. Garland Dupre, "Fernando de Lemos," *Proceedings Louisiana Historical Society* (March 1906), p. 29.

62. On how power shapes sources, repositories, narratives, and histories, see Michel-Rolph Trouillot, *Silencing the Past: Power and the Production of History* (Boston: Beacon Press, 1995), especially pp. 48–53.

63. George Washington Cable, "How I Got Them, 1882-1889," in *Strange True Stories of Louisiana* (Gretna, La.: Pelican Publishing Co., [1889] 1994), p. 4.

64. For a description of Christian's efforts and the discrimination he faced, see Marilyn Hessler, "Marcus Christian: The Man and His Collection," *LaHist* 28, no. 1 (1987), pp. 37–41 and Jerah Johnson, "Marcus B. Christian and the WPA History of Black People in Louisiana," *LaHist* 21, no. 1 (1979), pp. 113–115. If black and white southerners have indeed formed divergent memories of their collective heritage, as W. Fitzhugh Brundage has recently noted, racism in the archive may have played at least a small role in shaping this disparity. W. Fitzhugh Brundage, *The Southern Past: A Clash of Race and Memory* (Cambridge, Mass.: Belknap Press of Harvard University Press, 2005).

65. Virginia R. Domínguez, *White by Definition: Social Classification in Creole Louisiana* (New Brunswick, N.J.: Rutgers University Press, 1986), pp. 36–45; James O'Byrne, "Many Feared Naomi Drake and Powerful Racial Whim," *New Orleans Times-Picayune*, August 16, 1993, A7.

66. Melissa Nobles, *Shades of Citizenship Race and the Census in Modern Politics* (Stanford, Calif.: Stanford University Press, 2000), appendix, pp. 187–190.

67. 1850 Census, Roll M432_238, p. 131.

68. On the allure of the archive, see Carolyn Steedman, *Dust: The Archive and Cultural History* (New Brunswick, N.J.: Rutgers University Press, 2002); and

Jacques Derrida, *Archive Fever: A Freudian Impression, Religion and Postmodernism* (Chicago: University of Chicago Press, 1996); the phrase "quintessence of dust" is from William Shakespeare, *Hamlet*, Act II, Scene 2.

69. Du Bois, Gates, and Oliver, *Souls*, p. 127.

70. See Edwards, *Practice of Diaspora*, pp. 84–89 on the role of translation in expressions of black internationalism in the twentieth century, and Best, *Fugitive's Properties*, p. 124, on the "fugitive" or "excess" meaning produced by translation.

1. Seeking Shelter under White Skin

1. See doctors' testimony from *SCR* for details on the course of the disease. See also *"Traitment de la Fièvre Jaune: Methode du Docteur Dufour"* in *NOMSJ* (March 1857), pp. 640–648, on symptoms and various courses of treatment, and "History and Incidents of the Plague in New Orleans," *HNMM*, 7 (Nov. 1853), p. 799.

2. *NODP*, June 23, 1853. Many accounts consider the epidemic a man-made rather than a natural disaster. See John Duffy, *Sword of Pestilence: The New Orleans Yellow Fever Epidemic of 1853* (Baton Rouge: Louisiana State University Press, 1966), especially pp. 129–145. See also Ari Kelman, *A River and Its City: The Nature of Landscape in New Orleans* (Berkeley: University of California Press, 2003), pp. 16, 94–99.

3. "History and Incidents of the Plague," *HNMM*, p. 798; *Orleanian*, quoted in "Plague in the Southwest" *DBR* 15, no. 1 (Dec. 1853), pp. 602–605.

4. *NODP*, July 30, 1853.

5. *NODC*, August 22, 1853.

6. "Marie (Fontenay) de Grandfort (Mme Manoèel de Grandfort)," *L'Autre Monde*, 2, âed. ed. (Paris: Librairie nouvelle, 1857), p. 64.

7. *NODC*, August 11, 1853.

8. *NODC*, August 11, 1853; August 22, 1853.

9. *NODC*, August 9, 1853.

10. *NODC*, August 9, 1853.

11. George Washington Cable, *The Creoles of Louisiana* (New York: Charles Scribner's Sons, 1884), p. 301.

12. Official tally from *SCR*, p. 461 (chart). See Grace King, *New Orleans: The Place and the People* (New York: Macmillan, 1920), pp. 280–290, for a figure of 111 per thousand people (p. 287). This death count is probably low due to the number of unreported cases. See Cable, *Creoles of Louisiana*, p. 302.

13. Charles E. Rosenberg, *The Cholera Years: The United States in 1832, 1849, and 1866* (Chicago: University of Chicago Press, 1987) on how epidemics expose wider concerns over immigration, urbanity, and a changing American identity. For a discussion of the relationship between disease and culture over a longer time, see William Hardy McNeill, *Plagues and Peoples* (Garden City, N.Y.: Anchor Press, 1976).

14. Although it had been proposed as early as 1881 that the mosquito was the vector of yellow fever, the theory was not generally accepted until 1900. See Jean Slosek, "*Aedes Aegypti* Mosquitoes in the Americans: A Review of Their Interactions with the Human Population," *Social Science and Medicine* 23, no. 3 (1986), p. 289.

15. On the genre of "medical topography" in the nineteenth-century South, see Stephen Stowe, *Doctoring the South: Southern Physicians and Everyday Medicine in the Mid-Nineteenth Century* (Chapel Hill: University of North Carolina Press, 2004), pp. 201–207. Erasmus Darwin Fenner, *History of the Epidemic Yellow Fever: At New Orleans, La., in 1853* (New York: Hall, Clayton, 1854) is a classic example of a medical topography, as is the *SCR*. See Kelman, *River and Its City*, pp. 91–96.

16. Alternatively, John Duffy takes the overwhelming optimism of the New Orleans press at face value. Duffy, *Sword of Pestilence*, p. 172.

17. *NODP*, August 1, 1853.

18. See Kelman, *River and Its City*, pp. 91–92 on the debate over "miasms" or importation as a source of yellow fever. Also see *SCR*, p. 395. Others blamed the epidemics of 1853 and 1858 on the port. See Charles Faget, *JSML*, August 1859.

19. Duffy, *Sword of Pestilence*, pp. 21–24.

20. *NOB*, August 9, 1853.

21. The *Orleanian*, quoted in "Plague in the Southwest," *DBR*, pp. 608, calls attention to the various preoccupations of the Board—including their consideration of Pandelly's plight. There is a passing mention of the well-known "Pandelly affair" in Arnold R. Hirsch and Joseph Logsdon, *Creole New Orleans: Race and Americanization* (Baton Rouge: Louisiana State University Press, 1992), p. 98. Also, Marcus Christian's "Blacks in Louisiana," MCC, UNO, briefly outlines the episode.

22. Alexander Dimitry, the chief architect of the public school system, in the tradition of Horace Mann, was one of Pandelly's uncles. For more information on Dimitry, see Donald E. DeVore and Joseph Logsdon, *Crescent City Schools: Public Education in New Orleans, 1841–1991* (Lafayette: Center for Louisiana Studies, University of Southwestern Louisiana, 1991). This election was lamented in the Whig press as a triumph for Democrats, especially those with explicit ties to the emerging immigrant community. *NOB*, March 29, 1853.

23. *Pandelly v. Wiltz* (Nov. 1853), Fourth District Court, New Orleans, Docket # 7021, CCR, NOPL. The spelling of *Pandelly* is inconsistent within the document.

24. For allegations of Pandelly's membership in the Clay Club, see *Pandelly v. Wiltz*, witness Lévé. For information on the Clay Club, see Mary Gehman, *The Free People of Color of New Orleans: An Introduction* (New Orleans: Margaret Media, 1994), pp. 70–71.

25. Quotes from Pandelly's petition in *Pandelly v. Gillmore*, Fourth District Court, Docket # 6721 (July 1853), CCR, NOPL. Emphasis on *status* present in the original. This word is often highlighted by italicizing or underlining.

26. *NOB*, October 31, 1853.

27. Cable, *Creoles of Louisiana*, p. 303, emphasis mine.

28. See Rosenberg, *Cholera Years*, on rapid Americanization in the wake of cholera epidemics.

29. *NOB*, February 3, 1854 (emphasis mine).

30. Norman Walker, "Municipal Government," in Henry Rightor, ed., *Standard History of New Orleans* (Chicago: Lewis Publishing Company, 1900), p. 98. On the breakdown of the separate municipality system, Robert C. Reinders, *End of an Era: New Orleans, 1850–1880* (New Orleans: Pelican, 1964), pp. 51–61. See also Joseph G. Tregle, Jr., "Creoles and Americans," in Hirsch and Logsdon, eds., *Creole New Orleans*, p. 163.

31. Duffy, *Sword of Pestilence,* p. 7.

32. *NODP,* May 29, 1853.

33. *NODP,* July 21, 1853.

34. Duffy, *Sword of Pestilence,* pp. 105–106; *NODP,* August 24, 1853.

35. "History and Incidents of the Plague in New Orleans," *HNMM,* 7 (November 1853), p. 799.

36. Duffy, *Sword of Pestilence;* Kelman, *River and Its City.*

37. Kelman, *River and Its City,* p. 117. On the 1793 yellow fever epidemic as simultaneously signaling an opportunity for racial resistance and a crisis over racial representation, see Joanna Brooks, *American Lazarus: Religion and the Rise of African-American and Native American Literatures* (New York: Oxford University Press, 2003), pp. 152–178.

38. Kelman, *River and Its City,* p. 108.

39. On cultural implications of disease, see Susan Sontag, *Illness as Metaphor, and AIDS and Its Metaphors* (New York: Picador USA, 2001), and Sander L. Gilman, *Disease and Representation: Images of Illness from Madness to AIDS* (Ithaca: Cornell University Press, 1988).

40. *SCR,* p. 461 (chart).

41. A. Oakey Hall, *The Manhattaner in New Orleans; or, Phases of "Crescent City" Life* (New York, 1851), p. 69. Hall probably suffered from yellow fever during the mid- to late 1840s, shortly after arriving in New Orleans from New York City in 1844 or 1845. See Henry Kmen, "Introduction," Hall, *Manhattaner,* pp. xiii–xxviii for biographical information on Hall. The association between yellow fever and residential status is a useful narrative strategy in New Orleans' fiction. In George Washington Cable's *The Grandissimes,* published in 1880, a yellow fever epidemic gains his character Joseph Frowenfeld access to the complicated and multilayered world of the Creoles and precipitates his choosing pharmacy as an occupation. Cable, *The Grandissimes: A Story of Creole Life* (New York: Penguin Books, 1988), pp. 8–13.

42. Ludwig von Reizenstein and Steven W. Rowan, *The Mysteries of New Orleans* (Baltimore: Johns Hopkins University Press, 2002), pp. 530–531. On German-language urban mysteries in the United States, see Werner Sollors, "Emil Klauprecht's Cincinnati, Oder Geheimnisse Des Westens (1854–55) and the Beginnings of Urban Realism in America," *In Their Own Words* 3, no. 2 (1986). On urban anxiety in European cities in the 1830s and 1840s and the genre of urban mysteries more generally, see Richard Maxwell, *The Mysteries of Paris and London* (Charlottesville: University Press of Virginia, 1992). On the development of the genre in the American context, see Michael Denning, *Mechanic Accents: Dime Novels and Working-Class Culture in America,* rev. ed. (London and New York: Verso, 1998), and Shelley Streeby, *American Sensations: Class, Empire, and the Production of Popular Culture* (Berkeley: University of California Press, 2002). On Reizenstein and his novel's publication, see "Introduction" Reizenstein and Rowan, *Mysteries.* French immigrant Charles Testut (*Les mystères de la Nouvelle-Orleans,* 1852–54) also applied the urban mystery genre to New Orleans, although apparently not as successfully or coherently as Reizenstein.

43. Theodore Clapp, *Autobiographical Sketches and Recollections, during a Thirty-Five Years' Residence in New Orleans* (Boston: Phillips Sampson and Company, 1857), p. 71.

44. Ibid., p. 207.

45. "History and Incidents of the Plague in New Orleans," *HNMM*, VII (1853), p. 846.

46. Samuel Cartwright, "Prevention of Yellow Fever." *NOMSJ*, November 1853, pp. 317.

47. See Cable, *Creoles of Louisiana*, p. 299; *NOB*, August 22, 1853. See also *SCR*, especially p. 251, where Dr. Edward Barton confessed that the 1853 epidemic was the only time he witnessed a case of yellow fever in a black person.

48. See Joseph Logsdon, "Immigration through New Orleans," in M. Mark Stolarik, ed., *Forgotten Doors: The Other Ports of Entry to the United States* (Philadelphia: Balch Institute Press, 1988), pp. 105–125.

49. Reizenstein and Rowan, *Mysteries*, p. 179.

50. See *NOB*, March 29, 1853. On the breakdown of the American party system around sectional lines and the issue of slavery, see David Morris Potter, *The Impending Crisis, 1848–1861* (New York: Harper and Row, 1976).

51. For details see Leon Cyprian Soulé, *The Know Nothing Party in New Orleans: A Reappraisal* (Baton Rouge: Louisiana Historical Association, 1962). Frank Towers, *The Urban South and the Coming of the Civil War* (Charlottesville: University of Virginia Press, 2004) charts developments in New Orleans alongside those in St. Louis and Baltimore. Mary Ryan marks the height of nativism in New Orleans from 1854 to 1858 in *Civic Wars: Democracy and Public Life in the American City during the Nineteenth Century* (Berkeley: University of California Press, 1997), pp. 146–151.

52. On the distinction between the Catholicism of the Creoles (characterized by anticlericalism) and that of immigrants, see Towers, *Urban South*, pp. 105–106, and Roger Baudier, *The Catholic Church in Louisiana* (New Orleans: A. W. Hyatt Stationery mfg. co. ltd., 1939), pp. 327–344. Caryn Cossé Bell, *Revolution, Romanticism, and the Afro-Creole Protest Tradition in Louisiana, 1718–1868* (Baton Rouge: Louisiana State University Press, 1997), pp. 145–186, attributes the Creole anticlericalism to the prevalence of free masonry and its attendant republican ideals. The Louisiana delegates to the 1855 national Know-Nothing convention in Philadelphia proposed that the anti-Catholic clause be taken out of the national platform; see Charles Gayarré, "Address on the 'Religious Test' to the Convention of the American Party Assembled in Philadelphia on the Fifth of June, 1855," Houghton Library, Harvard University.

53. Gayarré, "Address on the 'Religious Test."

54. Charles Gayarré, "Address to the People of Louisiana on the State of Political Parties" (New Orleans, 1855). With more compassion for the newcomers, the famous pro-slavery physician Samuel Cartwright suggested that the immigration problem and the problem of yellow fever could be eliminated by scattering "republican comforts" among the immigrant victims of the disease. Samuel Cartwright, "Prevention of Yellow Fever," *NOMSJ*, November 1853, p. 317. On linking nativism and disease, see Alan M. Kraut, *Silent Travelers: Germs, Genes, and the "Immigrant Menace"* (New York: Basic Books, 1994), and Judith Walzer Leavitt, *Typhoid Mary: Captive to the Public's Health* (Boston: Beacon Press, 1996).

55. *NODD*, June 3, 1856; Ryan, *Civic Wars*, pp. 146–151; Towers, *Urban South*, pp. 146–148.

56. Towers, *Urban South*, pp. 122–124, 145–148, and 193–196.

57. Ryan depicts nativist violence in the urban areas during the 1850s as anti-Catholic or anti-Irish, anti-German, etc., and urban violence in the 1860s forward as typically racial, i.e., anti-black. See Ryan, *Civic Wars*, p. 180.

58. Josiah Nott, "The Mulatto a Hybrid: Probable Extermination of the Two Races if the Whites and Blacks Are Allowed to Intermarry," *AJMS* 6, 1843. For biographical information on Nott, see Reginald Horsman, *Josiah Nott of Mobile: Southerner, Physician, and Racial Theorist* (Baton Rouge: Louisiana State University Press, 1987).

59. See Josiah Clark Nott, "Two Lectures on the Natural History of the Caucasian and Negro Races" (1844) reprinted in Drew Gilpin Faust, *The Ideology of Slavery: Proslavery Thought in the Antebellum South, 1830–1860* (Baton Rouge: Louisiana State University Press, 1981), pp. 208–238. See also George M. Fredrickson, *The Black Image in the White Mind: The Debate on Afro-American Character and Destiny, 1817–1914* (Middletown, Conn.: Wesleyan University Press, 1987), pp. 75–82.

60. The alleged immunity of blacks has historically been widely taken for granted. There is still some debate about whether the statistically lower susceptibility of blacks to yellow fever is due to innate or acquired protection. See K. David Patterson, "Yellow Fever Epidemics and Mortality in the United States, 1693–1905," *Social Science and Medicine* 34, no. 8 (1992), pp. 861–862, and Kenneth F. Kiple and Virginia H. Kiple, "Black Yellow Fever Immunities, Innate and Acquired, as Revealed in the American South," *Social Science History* 1, no. 4 (1977).

61. Faget, *JSML*, April 1860. See Edward Larocque Tinker, *Les Écrits des Langue Française en Louisiane* (Paris: Librarie Ancienne Honoré Champion, 1931), entries on Délery, pp. 114–125, and on Faget, pp. 197–201, for further elaboration of the debate. The claim that biological differences between the races caused the difference in diseases suffered by blacks and whites was unusual for southern doctors; see Stowe, *Doctoring the South*. Even Cartwright argued that these differences were based on social conditions; see Grier, "The Negro and His Diseases," *NOMSJ*, May 1853; also Cartwright, "Prevention of Yellow Fever," *NOMSJ*, November 1853.

62. See David Lowenthal, *The Heritage Crusade and the Spoils of History* (Cambridge: Cambridge University Press, 1998) on the prominence of kinship and lineage in identity (chapters 2 and 3) and the competing importance of biology and race (chapter 9).

63. Maurice Halbwachs and Lewis A. Coser, *On Collective Memory* (Chicago: University of Chicago Press, 1992), pp. 68–74; Raphael Samuel et al., *Theatres of Memory*, volume 1 (London: Verso, 1994), pp. 227–241.

64. The oldest document that Wiltz presents is dated February 1, 1756. See *NODC*, August 4, 1853. The documents were not bundled with the court records. The account here is from Wiltz's publication of the documents in the August 4, 1853, issue of the *Crescent*.

65. Throughout these documents, names often switched arbitrarily between their French and Spanish versions.

66. I refer to the marriage in terms of "impropriety" rather than "illegality" because interracial marriages were permitted, although discouraged, during the Spanish period. See Kimberly S. Hanger, *Bounded Lives, Bounded Places: Free Black Society in Colonial New Orleans, 1769–1803* (Durham: Duke University Press, 1997), p. 93.

67. Wiltz's interpretation is taken from *NODC*, August 4, 1853. All emphasis is his.

68. See Drew Gilpin Faust, *A Sacred Circle: The Dilemma of the Intellectual in the Old South, 1840–1860* (Baltimore: Johns Hopkins University Press, 1977); John McCardell, *The Idea of a Southern Nation: Southern Nationalists and Southern Nationalism, 1830–1860* (New York: Norton, 1979).

69. For an elaboration of this role, see Faust, *Sacred Circle*, pp. 87–111.

70. *NODC*, August 9, 1853.

71. See Faust, *Sacred Circle*, pp. 105–111 on southern apologists' disdain for political corruption, and pp. 122–127 on white racial superiority as an essential feature of the pro-slavery argument.

72. Charles Gayarré, *The School for Politics: A Dramatic Novel* (New York: Appleton, 1854), pp. 26, 150. Embittered by his failure to win reelection to the state legislature and to secure an appointment as U.S. ambassador to Spain, Gayarré vilified his political rivals—chiefly French-born Pierre Soulé—in this drama. See Tinker, *Les Écrits*, pp. 226–227, and Towers, *Urban South*, pp. 99–100.

73. This southern pastoral has roots in Jefferson's republicanism. On the pastoral in southern nationalists of the late antebellum period, see McCardell, *Idea of a Southern Nation*. See Towers, *Urban South*, on the challenges southern urbanism posed for southern nationalism.

74. *NODC*, August 9, 1853.

75. *NOB*, February 6, 1854.

76. Wiltz was, in effect, contributing to the creation of a southern collective identity, a historical memory that naturalized questions of race and ideologies of white supremacy. See W. Fitzhugh Brundage, *The Southern Past: A Clash of Race and Memory* (Cambridge, Mass.: Belknap Press of Harvard University Press, 2005), p. 4.

77. "Introduction," *SCR*, p. ix.

78. "Report of Doctor Edward H. Barton on the Sanitary Condition of New Orleans," ibid., p. 394.

79. "Dedication," ibid., p. ii.

80. *NODC*, August 9, 1853.

81. Hall, *Manhattaner*, p. 78. See Judith Schafer's reconstruction of the Presbytere from Hall and newspaper accounts; Judith Kelleher Schafer, *Becoming Free, Remaining Free: Manumission and Enslavement in New Orleans, 1846–1862* (Baton Rouge: Louisiana State University, 2003), pp. xviii–xix.

82. *NOB*, February 3, 1854.

83. *LaC*, February 8, 1854.

84. The reportage of the Pandelly affair, a "human interest story," confirms Benedict Anderson's sense of the importance of newspapers in creating the "imaginative linkage" among various members of any extended community and depicts the "personal life" as a "representative body." The spectacular nature of the Pandelly affair seems to have intensified and highlighted the process of bonding the "imagined community." See Benedict R. O'G Anderson, *Imagined Communities: Reflections on the Origin and Spread of Nationalism* (London: Verso, 1991), pp. 32–33.

85. *LaC*, February 5, 1854.

86. *Cauchoix v. Dupuy*, 3 La 206, No. 2125 (January1831); *Bollumet v. Phillips*, 2 Rob. La 365, No. 10,856 (June 1842); *Dobard et al. v. Nuñez*, 6 La. Ann. 294, No.

1944 (April, 1851), LSCR, UNO. On the wider antebellum southern legal setting, see Ariela J. Gross, "Litigating Whiteness: Trials of Racial Determination in the Nineteenth Century South," *Yale Law Journal*, October 1998.

87. Cheryl I. Harris, "Whiteness as Property," *Harvard Law Review* 106, no. 8 (1993).

88. *Cauchoix v. Dupuy* (January 1831).

89. This is how he is portrayed. As became evident in the trial, the definition of Creole as descending from the French and Spanish colonists does not completely apply to Pandelly. What is important to note is that his Creoleness was taken for granted, a fiction that people were willing to accept without reservation.

90. *NOB*, February 3, 1854 (emphasis mine).

91. *NOB*, February 4, 1854.

92. *LaC*, February 5, 1854.

93. *NOB*, February 4, 1854.

94. Hanger, *Bounded Lives;* Jennifer M. Spear, "Colonial Intimacies: Legislating Sex in French Louisiana," *The William and Mary Quarterly* 60, no. 1 (2003).

95. *LaC*, February 5, 1854.

96. *Pandelly v. Wiltz*, witness Montamat.

97. Ibid., witness Paimpare.

98. Ibid., witness Adam.

99. See DeVore and Logsdon, *Crescent City Schools.*

100. *NOB*, February 2, 1854.

101. See *NOB*, February 6, 1854 on Dimitry's school and *NOB*, February 10, 1854 on Dimitry's lectures. See Joseph Tregle, "Creoles and Americans" in Hirsch and Logsdon, eds., *Creole New Orleans*, p. 179 on the Dimitry-Gayarré friendship.

102. *Pandelly v. Wiltz*, witness Portier.

103. See *Forstall and Forstall v. Dimitrys*, New Orleans Parish Court, No. 6382, 1832, PCR, NOPL, and the defendant's exception filed in the *Forstalls v. M. and Mme Dimitry* case. The bulk of this case is now filed with *Pandelly v. Wiltz.* This judgment anticipates Cheryl Harris's argument in "Whiteness as Property."

104. *Pandelly v. Wiltz*, plaintiff's petition.

105. Joseph R. Roach, *Cities of the Dead: Circum-Atlantic Performance* (New York: Columbia University Press, 1996), p. 39.

106. I draw on Bernard Hibbitts's discussion of non-Western cultures in "'Coming to Our Senses': Communication and Legal Expression in Performative Cultures," *Emory Law Journal* 41 (1992), pp. 873–960. See also Milner S. Ball, "The Play's the Thing: An Unscientific Reflection of Courts under the Rubric of Theater," *Stanford Law Review* 28, no. 81 (1975). Ariela Gross, *Double Character: Slavery and Mastery in the Antebellum Southern Courtroom* (Athens, Ga.: University of Georgia Press, 2006) argues that social relationships between masters and slaves were revealed in courtroom litigation. More generally, see Robert A. Ferguson, *The Trial in American Life* (Chicago: University of Chicago Press, 2007).

107. Gross, "Litigating Whiteness," considers case law *and* the courtroom drama to understand how communities defined and enacted of racial identity. See especially pp. 110–112 and pp. 133–135.

108. *LaC*, February 8, 1854.

109. Marigny testimony cited in *NOB*, February 2, 1854.

110. Ibid.

111. From plaintiff's petition, *Pandelly v. Wiltz.*

112. See Claudio Saunt, *A New Order of Things: Property, Power, and the Transformation of the Creek Indians, 1733–1816* (Cambridge: Cambridge University Press, 1999), and Daniel H. Usner, *Indians, Settlers and Slaves in a Frontier Exchange Economy: The Lower Mississippi Valley before 1783* (Chapel Hill: University of North Carolina Press, 1992).

113. See Adam Rothman, *Slave Country: American Expansion and the Origins of the Deep South* (Cambridge, Mass.: Harvard University Press, 2005), pp. 37–70 on the remarkable diversity of the colonial and early national southwestern frontier and on overlapping national and tribal jurisdictions.

114. Historians have cited cultural and demographic factors as the reason for métissage in Louisiana. See Gwendolyn Midlo Hall, *Africans in Colonial Louisiana: The Development of Afro-Creole Culture in the Eighteenth Century* (Baton Rouge: Louisiana State University Press, 1992), and Hanger, *Bounded Lives.* Thomas N. Ingersoll, *Mammon and Manon in Early New Orleans: The First Slave Society in the Deep South, 1718–1819* (Knoxville: University of Tennessee Press, 1999) downplays the importance of interracial sexual relationships. See Spear, "Colonial Intimacies," pp. 75–98, on the official and vernacular discourse of métissage in the French Atlantic World and on the differences between policies involving Indians and those involving Africans. Spear also provides an extensive historiography of métissage.

115. *NOB,* February 7, 1854.

116. See Shari M. Huhndorf, *Going Native: Indians in the American Cultural Imagination* (Ithaca, N.Y.: Cornell University Press, 2001). Ironically, contemporary New Orleanians—in the city and in the post-Katrina diaspora—have "gone native" in order to bolster their "blackness" in various parades and ritual performances of the "Mardi Gras Indians." See George Lipsitz, *Time Passages: Collective Memory and American Popular Culture* (Minneapolis: University of Minnesota Press, 1990), pp. 233–253; Roach, *Cities of the Dead,* pp. 192–198; Michael P. Smith, "Behind the Lines: The Black Mardi Gras Indians and the New Orleans Second Line," *Black Music Research Journal* 14, no. 1 (1994). For a discussion of recent attempts to recover Native American identities within black and white Creole contexts, see Andrew J. Jolivétte, *Louisiana Creoles: Cultural Recovery and Mixed-Race Native American Identity* (Lanham, Md.: Lexington Books, 2007).

117. *Boullemet v. Phillips,* 2 Rob. La 365, No. 10, 856 (June 1842). See Gross, "Litigating Whiteness," p. 121. Boullemet was able to make a convincing claim of his "Indianness" even though his family had come from Saint Domingue. Many witnesses seemed skeptical that his darker ancestors were Indian rather than African. For Saint Dominguans, claims to whiteness would be harder to make in the increasingly racially fraught decade of the 1850s.

118. George Washington Cable, *The Grandissimes: A Story of Creole Life* (New York: Penguin Books, 1988), pp. 18.

119. See Philip Joseph Deloria, *Playing Indian* (New Haven, Conn.: Yale University Press, 1998), pp. 20–21.

120. From Cable, *Grandissimes,* pp. 17–24.

121. On "feathered peoples," see Roach, *Cities of the Dead,* pp. 119–178, and Smith, "Behind the Lines," pp. 49–55.

122. Tinker, *Les Écrits,* p. 404.

123. John H. B. Latrobe and Samuel Wilson, *Southern Travels: Journal of John H. B. Latrobe, 1834* (New Orleans: Historic New Orleans Collection, 1986), p. 71.

124. Tinker, *Les Écrits*, p. 400; on details of Rouquette's life, see pp. 400–414. See also Thomas F. Haddox, *Fears and Fascinations: Representing Catholicism in the American South* (New York: Fordham University Press, 2005), pp. 34–36.

125. See Robert F. Berkhofer, *The White Man's Indian: Images of the American Indian from Columbus to the Present* (New York: Knopf, 1978), pp. 86–96, 145–166; Richard Slotkin, *Regeneration through Violence: The Mythology of the American Frontier, 1600–1860* (Middletown, Conn.: Wesleyan University Press, 1973), especially chaps. 13 and 14; Deloria, *Playing Indian*, especially chaps. 2 and 3; Jill Lepore, *The Name of War: King Philip's War and the Origins of American Identity* (New York: Knopf, 1998), pp. 191–226; Philip Fisher, *Hard Facts: Setting and Form in the American Novel* (New York: Oxford University Press, 1985), pp. 22–86.

126. Fredrickson, *Black Image*, pp. 97–129; Eric Lott, *Love and Theft: Blackface Minstrelsy and the American Working Class* (New York: Oxford University Press, 1993).

127. See Circe Sturm, *Blood Politics: Race, Culture, and Identity in the Cherokee Nation of Oklahoma* (Berkeley: University of California Press, 2002) on language of blood quanta in determining native identification. Also see Lowenthal, *Heritage Crusade*, pp. 202–204 on blood as one of many biological features determining heredity and belonging and pp. 206–219 on blood as an important trope in debates over purity and racial mixture. See Bertram Wyatt-Brown, *Southern Honor: Ethics and Behavior in the Old South* (New York: Oxford University Press, 1982), pp. 119–125 on blood as an important metaphor for family patrimony. On the widespread anxiety over blood as a possible racial contaminant, see Keith Wailoo, *Drawing Blood: Technology and Disease Identity in Twentieth-Century America* (Baltimore: Johns Hopkins University Press, 1997).

128. Reginald Horsman, *Race and Manifest Destiny: The Origins of American Racial Anglo-Saxonism* (Cambridge, Mass.: Harvard University Press, 1981); Amy S. Greenberg, *Manifest Manhood and the Antebellum American Empire* (Cambridge: Cambridge University Press, 2005).

129. Melissa Nobles, *Shades of Citizenship Race and the Census in Modern Politics* (Stanford, Calif.: Stanford University Press, 2000), p. 52. On the development of the racial science of ethnology, see William Stanton, *The Leopard's Spots: Scientific Attitudes toward Race in America, 1815–59* (Chicago: University of Chicago Press, 1960), and Fredrickson, *Black Image*, pp. 71–96.

130. Theda Perdue, *"Mixed Blood" Indians: Racial Construction in the Early South* (Athens: University of Georgia Press, 2003), chap 2. Of course, as Perdue reminds us in chapter 3, a mixed racial identity could also be used as evidence of Indian degeneracy and treachery. See also Thomas N. Ingersoll, *To Intermix with Our White Brothers: Indian Mixed Bloods in the United States from Earliest Times to the Indian Removals* (Albuquerque: University of New Mexico Press, 2005). On the mixed-race African, see Fredrickson, *Black Image*, pp. 120–124, and Werner Sollors, *Neither Black nor White yet Both: Thematic Explorations of Interracial Literature* (New York: Oxford University Press, 1997), pp. 220–245 on multivalence of the tragic mulatta figure.

131. Walter Johnson, *Soul by Soul: Life inside the Antebellum Slave Market* (Cambridge, Mass.: Harvard University Press, 1999), pp. 113–115, and Roach, *Cities of the Dead*, pp. 215–217.

132. *Pandelly v. Wiltz*, witness Bonneral.
133. Roselius cited in *LaC*, February 3, 1854.
134. *Pandelly v. Wiltz*, witness Portier.
135. Ibid.
136. Roselius cited in *LaC*, February 3, 1854.
137. *Pandelly v. Wiltz*, witness Portier.
138. Roach, *Cities of the Dead*, p. 2.
139. Ibid., p. 3.
140. See Phelan, *Unmarked*, pp. 2–13.
141. *NOB*, February 3, 1854.
142. *LaC*, February 3, 1854.
143. *NOB*, February 7, 1854.
144. Incidentally, Grace King's short story "The Little Convent Girl," *Balcony Stories* (1893; New Orleans: L. Graham Co., 1914), pp. 340–356, uses the Mississippi River as a metaphor for the uncontainable force of racial identity. See also Ann Laura Stoler, *Carnal Knowledge and Imperial Power: Race and the Intimate in Colonial Rule* (Berkeley: University of California Press, 2002), pp. 179–183 for a parallel consideration of the role of native women in the French colonial context.
145. *Pandelly v. Wiltz*, questions for witness St. Jean, Baton Rouge. The headdress called a *tignon* was an indication that the wearer was a woman of color who had been required by Spanish colonial law to keep her hair covered. See Violet Harrington Bryan, "Marcus Christian's Treatment of the *Gens de Couleur Libre*" in Sybil Kein, *Creole: The History and Legacy of Louisiana's Free People of Color* (Baton Rouge: Louisiana State University Press, 2000), pp. 47–48.
146. From *Forstalls v. Dimitrys*, cited in *Pandelly v. Wiltz*. Another witness echoed this sentiment in French, saying of Marianne, *"les cheveux etaient longs, droits, et plaits en ses traits la faisaient reconnaitre facilement pout une descendante de sauvegesse et de blanc."*
147. *Pandelly v. Wiltz*, witness Piquene and witness Lévé. When Lévé gave this description—black as *"le cul d'un chaudiere"*—there was considerable commotion in the courtroom; see *NOB*, February 8, 1854.
148. *Pandelly v. Wiltz*, witness Courcelle.
149. Charles Patton Dimitry, in Stanley Clisby and George Campbell Huchet de Kernion Arthur, eds., *Old Families of Louisiana* (New Orleans: Harmanson, 1931), pp. 17–20.
150. This genre would culminate in Grace Elizabeth King, *Creole Families of New Orleans* (New York: The Macmillan Company, 1921).
151. Cable, *Creoles of Louisiana*, pp. 305–306. In telling this story, Cable countered the notion that purity descended on New Orleans from the outside with the massive urban planning campaign of the Union general Benjamin Butler.
152. Conversation with Greg Osborn at NOPL in the summer of 1999.

2. Failing to Become White

1. *Anastasie Desarzant v. P. LeBlanc and E. Desmaziliere, his wife*, No. 5868, 14 La Ann. xii, unreported (December 1859), LSCR, UNO. Hereafter, case cited as *Desarzant v. LeBlanc*. Portions of this chapter appeared as Shirley E. Thompson,

"'*Ah, Toucoutou, Ye Conin Vous*': History and Memory in Creole New Orleans," *American Quarterly* 53, no. 2 (2001).

2. This mutual aid society paid for Justine Bacquié's burial in 1854.

3. See Act before Notary A. Abat, May 14, 1853, NONARC.

4. See Mary Bernard Deggs, Virginia Meacham Gould, and Charles E. Nolan, *No Cross, No Crown: Black Nuns in Nineteenth-Century New Orleans* (Bloomington: Indiana University Press, 2001), p. 210, fn. 30.

5. Edward Larocque Tinker, *Gombo, the Creole Dialect of Louisiana, Together with a Bibliography* (Worcester, Mass.: no publisher, 1936), p. 117. Tinker's text "reprinted from the April, 1935, Proceedings of the American Antiquatian Society."

6. *Abat v. Mourier*, Parish Court of New Orleans, No. 9727 (May 1, 1854), CCR, NOPL.

7. See Henry Edward Khrebiel, *Afro-American Folk-Songs* (Portland, Maine: Longwood Press, [1914] 1974), pp. 140–155 on "satirical songs of the Creoles." Joseph Beaumont (1820–1872) was the first president of Les Francs Amis, an association of men of color started in February 1860. See Edward Larocque Tinker, *Les Écrits des Langue Française en Louisiane* (Paris: Librarie Ancienne Honoré Champion, 1931), pp. 31–32.

8. Rodolphe Desdunes (1849–1928) was one of the organizers of the Comité des Citoyens that brought the *Plessy v. Ferguson* case to trial. See Charles O'Neill, "Forward," in Rodolphe Lucien Desdunes, *Our People and Our History*, trans. Sister Dorothea Olga McCants (Baton Rouge: Louisiana State University Press, 1973).

9. New York-born Edward Larocque Tinker (1881–1968) was a bibliophile, collector, and historian of Louisiana. He moved to New Orleans in 1916. His most popular work is *Creole City: Its Past and Its People* (New York: Longmans, 1953).

10. In this sense, Toucoutou has become what Pierre Nora has called a "*lieu de memoire*": "Between Memory and History: Les Lieux De Memoire," *Representations*, no. 26 (1989), p. 7. My discussion of the Toucoutou affair benefits from recent critiques of Nora's approach: Joseph R. Roach, "Deep Skin: Reconstructing Congo Square," in Harry Justin and David Krasner Elam, eds., *African American Performance History* (New York: Oxford University Press, 2001), p. 101; the contributors to Geneviève Fabre and Robert G. O'Meally, *History and Memory in African-American Culture* (New York: Oxford University Press, 1994); Wulf Kansteiner, "Finding Meaning in Memory: A Methodological Critique of Collective Memory Studies," *History and Theory* 41 (2002); Kerwin Lee Klein, "On the Emergence of Memory in Historical Discourse," *Representations* 69 (2000).

11. On New Orleans' multi-genre performance cultures, see Joseph R. Roach, *Cities of the Dead: Circum-Atlantic Performance* (New York: Columbia University Press, 1996); George Lipsitz, *Time Passages: Collective Memory and American Popular Culture* (Minneapolis: University of Minnesota Press, 1990); Gavin Roger Jones, "Signifying Songs: The Double Meaning of Black Dialect in the Work of George Washington Cable," *American Literary History* 9 (1992).

12. *Desarzant v. LeBlanc*, witness.

13. On nineteenth-century anxiety over women in public and gender roles in marriage, see Mary P. Ryan, *Women in Public: Between Banners and Ballots, 1825–1880* (Baltimore: Johns Hopkins University Press, 1990), pp. 58–95; Nancy F. Cott, *Public Vows: A History of Marriage and the Nation* (Cambridge, Mass.: Har-

vard University Press, 2000), especially pp. 60–67. In Louisiana law, a wife was barred from appearing in court without the authority of her husband (Louisiana Civil Code, Book I, Title IV, chap. 5, art. 123). However, she could conduct business and make her will without his authority. (art. 128, 132).

14. 1850 Census, Roll M432_238, p. 131 and p. 128.

15. On *Macarty v. Mandeville* (1847) and related cases, see chapter 4.

16. See Paul F. Lachance, "The 1809 Refugees to New Orleans: Reception, Integration, and Impact," *LaHist* 29, no. 2 (1988). See also Thomas Fiehrer, "Saint-Domingue/Haiti: Louisiana's Caribbean Connection," *LaHist* 30, no. 4 (1989), pp. 428–431, on an earlier wave of immigration by way of Jamaica in 1803–1804. For a sustained scholarly investigation of the migrations from Saint Domingue, see the collection of essays in Carl A. Brasseaux, Glenn R. Conrad, and David Cheramie, eds., *The Road to Louisiana: The Saint-Domingue Refugees, 1792–1809* (Lafayette, La.: Center for Louisiana Studies, University of Southwestern Louisiana, 1992). Also see Ned Sublette, *The World that Made New Orleans: From Spanish Silver to Congo Square* (Chicago: Lawrence Hill Books, 2008), especially pp. 248-261. Nathalie Dessens, *From Saint-Domingue to New Orleans: Migration and Influences* (Gainesville: University Press of Florida, 2007) synthesizes relevant research. On the course of the Haitian Revolution more generally, see Laurent Dubois, *Avengers of the New World: The Story of the Haitian Revolution* (Cambridge, Mass.: Belknap Press of Harvard University Press, 2004); David Patrick Geggus, *Haitian Revolutionary Studies* (Bloomington: Indiana University Press, 2002).

17. In 1842 Stephen Boullemet, a native of Saint Domingue, convinced the court of his white identity in a slander case against a fellow militia officer accusing him of having African blood. However, by 1859 racial anxieties were so intense that claims such as these were more difficult to make. See chapter 1 for a discussion of "Indian blood" as a mediator in Boullemet's case and that of Pandelly. *Boullemet v. Phillips* 2 Rob. La 365, No. 10,856 (June 1842).

18. Fiehrer, "Saint-Domingue/Haiti," pp. 423–425. Carolyn E. Fick, *The Making of Haiti: The Saint Domingue Revolution from Below* (Knoxville: University of Tennessee Press, 1990), pp. 17–22.

19. See Werner Sollors, *Neither White Nor Black Yet Both: Thematic Explorations of Interracial Literature* (Cambridge, Mass.: Harvard University Press, 1997), pp. 120-121 on Médéric-Louis-Élie Moreau de Saint-Méry's "racial calculus."

20. See David Nicholls, *From Dessalines to Duvalier: Race, Colour and National Independence in Haiti* (Cambridge and New York: Cambridge University Press, 1979), pp. 4–5, on the Haitian constitution. See also Joan Dayan, *Haiti, History, and the Gods* (Berkeley: University of California Press, 1995), pp. 3–5, 24–27. See Geggus, *Haitian Revolutionary Studies*, pp. 207–220, on the complex politics on the ground.

21. Alfred N. Hunt, *Haiti's Influence on Antebellum America: Slumbering Volcano in the Caribbean* (Baton Rouge: Louisiana State University Press, 1988), pp. 37–83 on the varied receptions of the refugees and their impact on the institutional culture of their host communities. Althéa de Puech Parham, *My Odyssey; Experiences of a Young Refugee from Two Revolutions* (Baton Rouge: Louisiana State University Press, 1959) describes a particular animosity of Americans in Philadelphia toward the incoming "French."

22. On the general impact of the Haitian Revolution in the Atlantic world, see essays in Geggus, *Impact of the Haitian Revolution*; Laurent Dubois, *A Colony of*

Citizens: Revolution and Slave Emancipation in the French Caribbean, 1787–1804 (Chapel Hill: University of North Carolina Press, 2004); and David Brion Davis, *Inhuman Bondage: The Rise and Fall of Slavery in the New World* (Oxford and New York: Oxford University Press, 2006), pp. 157–174.

23. These include African American activists David Walker, Henry Highland Garnett, and William Wells Brown; the white American journalist James Redpath; and the French Romantic writer Victor Hugo. See Hunt, *Haiti's Influence*, pp. 84–101, on Toussaint's image in antebellum America.

24. See Sibylle Fischer, *Modernity Disavowed: Haiti and the Cultures of Slavery in the Age of Revolution* (Durham, N.C.: Duke University Press, 2004), pp. 41–57 and Matt Childs, "A Black French General Arrived to Conquer the Island: Images of the Haitian Revolution in Cuba's 1812 Aponte Rebellion," in Geggus, *Impact of the Haitian Revolution*, pp. 135–156, on the Aponte Conspiracy, and other essays in the Geggus volume for additional context. See Gwendolyn Midlo Hall, *Africans in Colonial Louisiana: The Development of Afro-Creole Culture in the Eighteenth Century* (Baton Rouge: Louisiana State University Press, 1992), pp. 343–374 on the Pointe Coupée uprising. See James Sidbury, *Ploughshares into Swords: Race, Rebellion, and Identity in Gabriel's Virginia, 1730–1810* (Cambridge and New York: Cambridge University Press, 1997), pp. 39–48, 87, 97, and Douglas R. Egerton, *Gabriel's Rebellion: The Virginia Slave Conspiracies of 1800 and 1802* (Chapel Hill: University of North Carolina Press, 1993), pp. 45–48, 160–172, on the impact of Saint Domingue on Gabriel's Rebellion. On Vesey's case and the controversy over the nature of the uprising, see Michael P. Johnson, "Denmark Vesey and His Co-Conspirators," *The William and Mary Quarterly* 58, no. 4 (2001). See responses in *The William and Mary Quarterly* 59, no. 1 (2002), and Davis, *Inhuman Bondage*, pp. 222–223.

25. On the scope of this immigration, see essays in Geggus, *Impact of the Haitian Revolution*, especially pp. 193–246. Some refugees managed to preserve their wealth and status in their new homes; see Geggus, "The Caradeux and Colonial Memory," in *Haitian Revolutionary Studies*, pp. 231–247.

26. On the relief effort, see Lachance, "1809 Refugees," pp. 248–252, and Fiehrer, "Saint-Domingue/Haiti," p. 431. The "enslaved" refugees were of dubious slave status, considering slavery had never been reinstated in Haiti after being abolished throughout the French empire in 1794. Rebecca Scott has called attention to the reenslavement of a bulk of the refugee population as part of the terms of admittance to various asylum countries.

27. Claiborne to U.S. Secretary of State Smith, July 29, 1809, quoted in Lachance, "1809 Refugees," p. 252.

28. Cited in David C. Rankin, "The Forgotten People: Free People of Color in New Orleans, 1850–1870" (Ph.D. dissertation, Johns Hopkins University, 1976), p. 62.

29. City councilor quoted in Adam Rothman, *Slave Country: American Expansion and the Origins of the Deep South* (Cambridge, Mass.: Harvard University Press, 2005), p. 104.

30. Caryn Cossé Bell, *Revolution, Romanticism, and the Afro-Creole Protest Tradition in Louisiana* (Baton Rouge: Louisiana State University Press, 1997), p. 39; H. E. Sterkx, *The Free Negro in Antebellum Louisiana* (Rutherford, N.J.: Fairleigh Dickinson University Press, 1972), pp. 92–94.

31. Quoted in Charles Gayarré, *History of Louisiana*, 2nd ed. (New York: W.J. Widdleton, 1867), Vol. 4, pp. 226–227.

32. See Rothman, *Slave Country*, pp. 106–117, on the 1811 rebellion.

33. Bell, *Revolution, Romanticism*, pp. 48–51. Claibourne, quoted in Gayarré, *History of Louisiana*, IV, p. 336; Jackson to Claiborne, September 21, 1814, in John Spencer Bassett, ed., *Correspondence of Andrew Jackson, Volume II* (Washington, D.C.: Carnegie Institution of Washington, 1926-35), p. 57. Jackson, Address "To the Free Coloured Inhabitants of Louisiana," September 21, 1814, in Bassett, ed., *Correspondence of Andrew Jackson, Volume II*, pp. 58–59.

34. See Frantz Fanon, *Black Skin, White Masks* (New York: Grove Press, 1967), p. 43 on financial or status "whitening" in the French Caribbean. See also Carl N. Degler, *Neither Black nor White: Slavery and Race Relations in Brazil and the United States* (New York: Macmillan, 1971), pp. 207–264 on a similar phenomenon in Brazil.

35. The "duplicity of names" makes it difficult to discuss the case with clarity. While Desarzant was called Toucoutou, Anastasie Desarzant, and Madame Maurice Antoine Abat, I use Desarzant most frequently. I use Toucoutou when it is appropriate to the context. Likewise, Desarzant's mother was known as Justine Bacquié, Françoise Bacquié, Justine Martin, and Françoise Martin. I use Justine Bacquié most frequently unless the context demands otherwise.

36. See Dessens, *From Saint-Domingue to New Orleans*, pp. 46–66 on the sense of community among refugees in the early period and on the resurgence of a "symbolic ethnicity" of Saint Dominguan identity in the 1830s and 1840s.

37. Bell, *Revolution, Romaniticism*, pp. 60–64.

38. On efforts from the 1820s to the 1850s to send American blacks to Haiti, see Hunt, *Haiti's Influence*, pp. 147–188. On maroonage in Haiti, see Geggus, *Haitian Revolutionary Studies*, pp. 69–81.

39. Claiborne to Jackson, October 28, 1814, in Dunbar Rowland, ed., *Official Letter Books of W. C. C. Claiborne, 1801-1816, Volume VI* (Jackson Miss.: State Department of Archives and History, 1917), p. 294.

40. *Desarzant v. LeBlanc*, witness Ménard.

41. *Desarzant v. LeBlanc*, witness Dupré.

42. Houston A. Baker, *Turning South Again: Re-Thinking Modernism/Re-Reading Booker T* (Durham, N.C.: Duke University Press, 2001), p. 15.

43. *Desarzant v. LeBlanc* (my emphasis).

44. Frederick Merk, *Manifest Destiny and Mission in American History: A Reinterpretation* (New York: Vintage Books, 1966), pp. 202–214; Amy S. Greenberg, *Manifest Manhood and the Antebellum American Empire* (Cambridge and New York: Cambridge University Press, 2005), pp. 41, 170–196 on filibusters William Walker and Narcisco Rodriguez; Shelley Streeby, *American Sensations: Class, Empire, and the Production of Popular Culture* (Berkeley: University of California Press, 2002), pp. 152–155 on New Orleans as a popular site for filibustering in the American imagination.

45. *NOB*, June 1, 1858.

46. John C. Calhoun, *Cong. Glob*, 30 Cong., 1 Sess., 98 (January 4, 1848), quoted in Merk, *Manifest Destiny and Mission*, p. 162.

47. On the active silencing of events comprising the Haitian Revlution in history and historiography, see Michel-Rolph Trouillot, *Silencing the Past: Power and the Production of History*, (Boston: Beacon Press, 1995), pp. 70–107.

48. Ira Berlin, *Slaves without Masters: The Free Negro in the Antebellum South* (New York: Pantheon Books, 1975), pp. 369–380; Thomas D. Morris, *Southern Slavery and the Law, 1619–1860* (Chapel Hill: University of North Carolina Press, 1996), pp. 371–423; Michael P. Johnson and James L. Roark, *Black Masters: A Free Family of Color in the Old South* (New York: Norton, 1984), pp. 233–288. On the Louisiana context, see Judith Kelleher Schafer, *Becoming Free, Remaining Free: Manumission and Enslavement in New Orleans, 1846–1862* (Baton Rouge: Louisiana State University, 2003), and Walter Johnson, "The Slave Trader, the White Slave, and the Politics of Racial Determination in the 1850s," *The Journal of American History* 87, no. 1 (2000).

49. See "Slaves and Free Persons of Color," General Ordinances, 1857; *Register of Free Persons of Color Allowed to Remain in the State*, 1841–1860, Mayors Office; Richard Tansey, "Out-of-State Free Blacks in Late Antebellum New Orleans," *LaHist* 22, no. 4 (1981); "An Act to Permit Free Persons of African Descent to Select a Master and Become Slaves for Life," March 17, 1859, *Louisiana Acts*, 1859, pp. 214–215. See Morris, *Southern Slavery and the Law*, pp. 17–36; Victoria E. Bynum, *Unruly Women: The Politics of Social and Sexual Control in the Old South* (Chapel Hill: University of North Carolina Press, 1992), pp. 88–110; Richard Clement Wade, *Slavery in the Cities: The South, 1820–1860* (London and New York: Oxford University Press, 1967), pp. 80–110; Martha Elizabeth Hodes, *White Women, Black Men: Illicit Sex in the Nineteenth-Century South* (New Haven, Conn.: Yale University Press, 1997), pp. 116–122. On how people of color used the court to secure freedom, see Schafer, *Becoming Free*, and Ariela Julie Gross, *Double Character: Slavery and Mastery in the Antebellum Southern Courtroom* (Princeton, N.J.: Princeton University Press, 2000).

50. Ariela J. Gross, "Litigating Whiteness: Trials of Racial Determination in the Nineteenth Century South," *Yale Law Journal*, October 1998.

51. See John Bailey, *The Lost German Slave Girl: The Extraordinary True Story of Sally Miller and Her Fight for Freedom in Old New Orleans* (New York: Atlantic Monthly Press, 2005), pp. 20–47 on the plight of German immigrants to Louisiana during the 1810s. See also Carol Wilson, *The Two Lives of Sally Miller: A Case of Mistaken Racial Identity in Antebellum New Orleans* (New Brunswick, N.J.: Rutgers University Press, 2007) for a thorough discussion of the case and its reception.

52. In a duplicity of names that would have made Justine Bacquié proud, Bridget Wilson was Mary Wilson, Mary Briggers, Mary Miller, Salmomé Müller, and Sally Miller depending on her "marriages," the whims of her owners, and what her campaign for freedom demanded.

53. See George Washington Cable, "Salome Müller, the White Slave, 1818-1845," in *Strange True Stories of Louisiana* (Gretna, La.: Pelican Publishing Co., 1994), pp. 145–191. Cable's account first appeared in the 1889 *Century Magazine*. J. Hanno Deiler, a professor at Tulane, wrote a similar account and published it in a German-language newspaper in 1888. See Louis Voss, "Sally Mueller, the German Slave," *Louisiana Historical Quarterly* 12 (1929), p. 447. See *Sally Miller v. Louis Belmonti and John Miller*, Docket 5623, LSCR, UNO, 11 Rob. 339, and *Miller v. Miller et al.*, Docket 1114, LSCR, UNO, 4 La An 354. The transcripts and notes of both trials reveal the possibility of mistaken identity in the case, even though Cable's and Deiler's accounts do not. See Bailey, *The Lost German Slave Girl*, pp. 222–254.

54. On the fancy trade, see Monique Guillory, "Under One Roof: The Sins and Sanctity of the New Orleans Quadroon Balls," in Judith Jackson Fossett and Jeffrey A. Tucker, eds. *Race-Consciousness: African-American Studies for the New Century* (New York: New York University Press, 1997), pp. 82–87; Monique Guillory, "Some Enchanted Evening on the Auction Block: The Cultural Legacy of the New Orleans Quadroon Balls," Ph.D. dissertation, New York University, 1999; Walter Johnson, *Soul by Soul: Life inside the Antebellum Slave Market* (Cambridge, Mass.: Harvard University Press, 1999), pp. 113–115; Roach, *Cities of the Dead*, pp. 215–217; Johnson, "Politics of Racial Determination," pp. 16–20. On the crisis over women's sexuality in the antebellum period, see Hodes, *White Women, Black Men*, especially chap. 5; Bynum, *Unruly Women;* Nancy F. Cott, "Passionlessness: An Interpretation of Victorian Sexual Ideology, 1790–1850," *Signs* 4, no. 2 (1978). On the southern conception of women's courtship role, see Anne Firor Scott, *The Southern Lady: From Pedestal to Politics, 1830–1930* (Chicago: University of Chicago Press, 1970), and Steven M. Stowe, *Intimacy and Power in the Old South: Ritual in the Lives of the Planters* (Baltimore: Johns Hopkins University Press, 1987), pp. 50–121. See Ryan, *Women in Public*, pp. 95–129 on the "politicization of sexuality" in the urban areas of New York and New Orleans, and Wyatt-Brown, *Southern Honor*, pp. 226–253 for women's "place" and man's "world" more generally. On gender issues in colonial Virginia, see Kathleen M. Brown, *Good Wives, Nasty Wenches, and Anxious Patriarchs: Gender, Race, and Power in Colonial Virginia* (Chapel Hill: University of North Carolina Press, 1996). On southern ideas about black women's sexuality, see Deborah G. White, *Ar'n't I a Woman? Female Slaves in the Plantation South*, rev. ed. (New York: W.W. Norton, 1999), chap. 1. On black women's sexuality more generally, see Hazel V. Carby, *Reconstructing Womanhood: The Emergence of the Afro-American Woman Novelist* (New York: Oxford University Press, 1987), chap. 2, and Michele Mitchell, *Righteous Propagation: African Americans and the Politics of Racial Destiny after Reconstruction* (Chapel Hill: University of North Carolina Press, 2004), pp. 108–140. On how class status shaped opinions about white women's sexual availability, see Hodes, *White Women, Black Men*, pp. 4–5, and Johnson, "Politics of Racial Determination," pp. 32–34.

55. Johnson, "Politics of Racial Determination," p. 17.

56. Ibid., pp. 36–37 on attitudes of working-class white men on the lower court jury.

57. See *Miller v. Miller et al.*, 1849 La, 4 La An 354.

58. Johnson, "Politics of Racial Determination," pp. 36.

59. Ibid., p. 20. See Morris, *Southern Slavery and the Law*, pp. 21–36 on presumptions of whiteness and blackness in southern law.

60. See *Constance Bique Perrine v. City of New Orleans, Edward Planchard, appellant and als.* no. 6036, 15 La. Ann. 133, 1859, LSCR, UNO.

61. State law designated whipping as a type of punishment reserved for enslaved people. See Henry Jefferson Leovy, *The Laws and General Ordinances of the City of New Orleans* (New Orleans, 1857), pp. 179 (No. 548) and 257 (No. 750).

62. *Perrine v. City of New Orleans* (my emphasis).

63. *Desarzant v. LeBlanc.*

64. See Guillory, "Under One Roof," on the slippage between the status of the *placée* and the fancy girl.

65. *Desarzant v. LeBlanc*, witness Ménard.

66. *Desarzant v LeBlanc*, witness Dupré.

67. *Desarzant v. LeBlanc*, witness Prados.

68. The testimony is written in English translation and then again in French at this point. *Desarzant v LeBlanc*, witness Prados.

69. This is yet another example of how intimate relationships across racial lines trouble the distinction between the public and the private. See Carole Pateman, *The Disorder of Women: Democracy, Feminism, and Political Theory* (Stanford, Calif.: Stanford University Press, 1989), especially chap. 6, "Feminist Critiques of the Public/Private Dichotomy," pp. 118–140, and essays in Dorothy O. Helly and Susan Reverby, eds., *Gendered Domains: Rethinking Public and Private in Women's History* (Ithaca, N.Y.: Cornell University Press, 1992). See Lawrence Meir Friedman, *Private Lives: Families, Individuals, and the Law* (Cambridge, Mass.: Harvard University Press, 2004), especially chaps. 1 and 2; Michael Grossberg, *Governing the Hearth: Law and the Family in Nineteenth-Century America* (Chapel Hill: University of North Carolina Press, 1985); and Cott, *Public Vows*, on the penetration of the family, marriage, and domestic relations by the law and the state. See Judith Kelleher Schafer, *Slavery, the Civil Law, and the Supreme Court of Louisiana* (Baton Rouge: Louisiana State University Press, 1994), pp. 180–200 on the threat posed by "open and notorious concubinage." Friedman, *Private Lives*, p. 30 cites a the 1825 Louisiana Civil Code (Book I, Title V, art. 137) granting a woman the right to divorce her husband if he has brought his "concubine" into their common dwelling—a veiled reference to conspicuous *plaçage*—as an example of a double-standard in divorce law (compare with La Civil Code, Book I, Title V., art. 136). See also Wyatt-Brown, *Southern Honor*, pp. 307–311 on southern social norms in general.

70. See *NOB*, October 15, 1850.

71. See *Desarzant v. LeBlanc*, documents presented by plaintiff.

72. *Desarzant v. LeBlanc.*

73. The Friends of the Cabildo, *New Orleans Architecture, Vol. IV: The Creole Faubourgs* (Gretna, La.: Pelican, 1996), p. 123 includes a photograph and architectural inventory of the creole cottage in which Toucoutou was born.

74. *Desarzant v. LeBlanc*, witness Prados.

75. *Desarzant v. LeBlanc.*

76. *Virginie Laizer, wife of Jean Lacaze v. Her Husband*, Fifth District Court of New Orleans, March 24, 1856, Docket # 10,842, CCR, NOPL.

77. *Desarzant v. LeBlanc*, witnesses Lazard and Williams. Gross, "Litigating Whiteness," discusses this strategy in trials throughout the South. See chapter 1 for discussion of a similar strategy in the Pandelly trial.

78. *Desarzant v. LeBlanc*, witness Ménard.

79. See "Ordinance Concerning Free Persons of Color," *Digest of Acts of the Legislature and Decisions of the Supreme Court of Louisiana Relative to the General Council of the City of New Orleans* (New Orleans, 1847), 80.

80. Nora, "Between Memory and History: Les Lieux De Memoire," *Representations* 26 (Spring, 1989), p. 24.

81. Desdunes, *Our People*, p. 64. Relevant folklore studies include Khrebiel, *Afro-American Folk-Songs;* Alcée Fortier, *Louisiana Folk-Tales: In French Dialect and English Translation* (Millwood, N.Y.: Kraus, 1976); George Washington Cable, "Creole Slave Songs [and] the Dance in Congo Square" *Century Magazine* (February 1886), pp. 807–828.

82. Desdunes, *Our People*, pp. 61, 63.

83. See Lyle Saxon et al., *Gumbo Ya-Ya: A Collection of Louisiana Folktales* (Cambridge, Mass.: Riverside Press, 1945), p. 428.

84. Creole version in Rodolphe Lucien Desdunes, *Nos Hommes et Notre Histoire* (Montréal: Arbour & Dupont, 1911), pp. 58–59. English translation in Desdunes, *Our People*, pp. 63–64.

85. Another version of this verse is "*Yé va fé vous jist délogé* (They will just put you out)" "Jacdeloge" may refer to a character that has been ejected from a box at the theater. See Saxon, *Gumbo Ya-Ya*, p. 428.

86. Desdunes, *Our People*, pp. 62–63. The implications of this filial relationship are discussed in chapter 4 below.

87. Reid Mitchell, *All on a Mardi Gras Day: Episodes in the History of New Orleans Carnival* (Cambridge, Mass: Harvard University Press, 1995); Michael P. Smith, "Behind the Lines: The Black Mardi Gras Indians and the New Orleans Second Line," *Black Music Research Journal* 14, no. 1 (1994).

88. Elizabeth A. McAlister, *Rara! Vodou, Power, and Performance in Haiti and Its Diaspora* (Berkeley: University of California Press, 2002); Dayan, *Haiti, History, and the Gods;* Richard D. E. Burton, *Afro-Creole: Power, Opposition, and Play in the Caribbean* (Ithaca, N.Y.: Cornell University Press, 1997).

89. I draw on Henry Louis Gates, *The Signifying Monkey: A Theory of Afro-American Literary Criticism* (New York: Oxford University Press, 1988). See especially his discussion of the *loa* Legba's importance to the African American literary tradition in chap. 1.

90. Dustin H. Griffin, *Satire: A Critical Reintroduction* (Lexington: University Press of Kentucky, 1994), chap. 3, pp. 71–94.

91. Cable, *Creole Slave Songs [and] the Dance in Congo Square*, p. 808. On the notion of "double meaning," see Jones, "Signifying Songs," pp. 244–267.

92. See Griffin, *Satire*, chap. 4, pp. 95–114 on the problem of satiric closure. More generally, see Frank Kermode, *The Sense of an Ending; Studies in the Theory of Fiction* (New York: Oxford University Press, 1967), and Barbara Herrnstein Smith, *Poetic Closure: A Study of How Poems End* (Chicago: University of Chicago Press, 1968). On closure and "indeterminacy" in the African American literary tradition, see Gates, *Signifying Monkey*, pp. 227–237.

93. Gates, *Signifying Monkey*, especially p. 22 on the tension between the literal and figurative in the African American critical tradition; Griffin, *Satire*, pp. 115–132 on the complicated relationship between satirists and historians in that satirists entice historians to search for what is real in their parodies. That describes the effect of Beaumont's song on Tinker and on me.

94. On the "dozens," see Gates, *Signifying Monkey*, pp. 71–88, and on politics and pleasure, see Griffin, *Satire*, chaps. 6 and 7.

95. Gates, *Signifying Monkey*, p. 70 on the cultural work happening on the meta level (third space) of discourse. Reference to a third term or third person breaks up the two-dimensional relationship between signifier and signified, allows for interpretive flexibility, and occasions the display of linguistic dexterity. See also Mel Watkins, *On the Real Side: Laughing, Lying, and Signifying: The Underground Tradition of African-American Humor That Transformed American Culture, from Slavery to Richard Pryor* (New York: Simon & Schuster, 1994).

96. Amy Robinson, "It Takes One to Know One," *Critical Inquiry* 20, no. 4 (1994), pp. 715–736, on passing as a triangulated act. See also Judith Butler's

discussion of Nella Larsen's *Passing* (1928) in *Bodies That Matter: On the Discursive Limits of "Sex"* (New York: Routledge, 1993), pp. 167–185.

97. Sally Kittredge Evans, "Free Persons of Color," in Friends of the Cabildo, *New Orleans Architecture Vol. IV: The Creole Faubourgs*, p. 31, and The Friends of the Cabildo, *New Orleans Architecture, Vol. VI: Faubourg Tremé and the Bayou Road* (Gretna, La.: Pelican, 1980), pp. 92–93.

98. See Cheryl I. Harris, "Whiteness as Property," *Harvard Law Review* 106, no. 8 (1993), and Ian Haney-López, *White by Law: The Legal Construction of Race* (New York: New York University Press, 1996).

99. As a member of the Comité des Citoyens, Desdunes helped stage the *Plessy v. Ferguson* case. His son, Daniel Desdunes, was plaintiff in a test case for that suit. Charles A. Lofgren, *The Plessy Case: A Legal-Historical Interpretation* (New York: Oxford University Press, 1987), pp. 33–41.

100. See Roach, *Cities of the Dead*, pp. 233–237.

101. Rebecca J. Scott, *Degrees of Freedom: Louisiana and Cuba after Slavery* (Cambridge, Mass.: Belknap Press of Harvard University Press, 2005); Rodolphe Lucien Desdunes, "A Few Words to Dr. Dubois, with Malice Towards None" (New Orleans: 1907) pamphlet in CRC, ARC; Desdunes, *Our People*.

102. Kevin Kelly Gaines, *Uplifting the Race: Black Leadership, Politics, and Culture in the Twentieth Century* (Chapel Hill: University of North Carolina Press, 1996).

103. Desdunes, "A Few Words."

104. Desdunes, *Our People*, p. 62. Matthew John Caldwell Hodgart, *Satire* (New York: McGraw-Hill, 1969), pp. 35–39 suggests that searching for a moral is a limited way to read satire.

105. Desdunes, *Our People*, p. 62.

106. Ibid., p. 61.

107. See Tinker, *Les Écrits*.

108. George Washington Cable, *Strange True Stories of Louisiana* (Gretna, La.: Pelican, [1888] 1994), p. 1.

109. I explore the Cable controversy in detail in chapter 3.

110. The racist cultural context of early twentieth-century Louisiana may explain Tinker's failure to cite the Desarzant case. Perhaps Tinker was trying to protect the identities of people whose ancestors were involved in the case.

111. Cable, "How I Got Them, 1882-89" in *Strange True Stories*, p. 2.

112. Edward Larocque Tinker, *Toucoutou* (New York: Dodd Mead and company, 1928), p. 8.

113. On the features of the genre of melodrama, see Peter Brooks, *The Melodramatic Imagination: Balzac, Henry James, Melodrama, and the Mode of Excess* (New Haven, Conn.: Yale University Press, 1976), especially chap. 1. See also Ben Singer, *Melodrama and Modernity: Early Sensational Cinema and Its Contexts* (New York: Columbia University Press, 2001) on melodrama and the early cinema, a popular form among many of Tinker's readers.

114. Tinker, *Toucoutou*, p. 191.

115. Ibid., p. 278.

116. Ibid., pp. 111–112.

117. Gilman, "Black Bodies, White Bodies"; Brenda Gayle Plummer, *Haiti and the United States: The Psychological Moment* (Athens: University of Georgia Press,

1992); Hans Schmidt, *The United States Occupation of Haiti, 1915–1934* (New Brunswick, N.J.: Rutgers University Press, 1971).

118. For early interest in the Creole language, see Alcée Fortier, "The French Language in Louisiana and the Negro-French Dialect," *Transactions of the Modern Language Association of America* II (1884–85), pp. 96–111; Alcée Fortier, *Louisiana Studies: Literature, Customs and Dialects, History and Education* (New Orleans: F. F. Hansell, 1894). See also Lafcadio Hearn, "A Sketch of the Creole Patois," in *An American Miscellany* (New York: Dodd, Mead and Co., 1924), pp. 154–158.

119. Edward Larocque Tinker, "Gombo: The Creole Dialect of Louisiana," *Proceedings of the American Antiquarian Society* 45 (April 1935), p. 101."

120. Charles Gayarré, "Mr. Cable's Freedmen's Case in Equity," *New Orleans Times Democrat* (January–February, 1885).

121. The most protracted example of this is *Le Carillon*, a journal edited by J. M Durel or P. Durel from 1869 to 1875.

122. On dialect, literature, and the politics of local color writing, see Gavin Jones, *Strange Talk: The Politics of Dialect Literature in Gilded Age America* (Berkeley: University of California Press, 1999), especially pp. 98–133 on Cable. In the hands of Cable or his friend Mark Twain, dialect could support a progressive racial vision; see Shelley Fisher Fishkin, *Was Huck Black? Mark Twain and African-American Voices* (New York: Oxford University Press, 1993). On Lafcadio Hearn's use of New Orleans Creole as a means of avoiding Americanization, see Lafcadio Hearn and S. Frederick Starr, *Inventing New Orleans: Writings of Lafcadio Hearn* (Jackson: University Press of Mississippi, 2001). On dialect as a conundrum for black authors in particular, see Eric J. Sundquist, *To Wake the Nations: Race in the Making of American Literature* (Cambridge, Mass.: Harvard University Press, 1993), pp. 271–454. In its various guises, dialect literature, like blackface minstrelsy, has elicited a dual reaction of "love and theft": Eric Lott, *Love and Theft: Blackface Minstrelsy and the American Working Class* (New York: Oxford University Press, 1993).

123. Abbé Adrien [E. Junius] Rouquette, "Critical Dialogue between Aboo and Caboo on a New Book; or, a Grandissime Ascension" (New Orleans: 1880), pp. 20–23.

124. Tinker, "Gombo," p. 104.

125. Tinker, *Toucoutou*, pp. 87–88.

126. Tinker, "Gombo," p. 104.

127. On Congo Square in New Orleans culture, see Roach, *Cities of the Dead*, p. 63–68; Jerah Johnson, "New Orleans' Congo Square: An Urban Setting for Early Afro-American Culture Formation," *LaHist* (1991); Roach, "Deep Skin"; Edward C. Carter, *The Papers of Benjamin Henry Latrobe: Journals 1799–1820*, Vol. III (New Haven, Conn.: Yale University Press, 1980), pp. 202–203.

128. Daniel E. Walker, *No More, No More: Slavery and Cultural Resistance in Havana and New Orleans* (Minneapolis: University of Minnesota Press, 2004); Roach, "Deep Skin"; Johnson, "New Orleans' Congo Square." Sublette, *The World that Made New Orleans*, pp. 271–286 explores the impact of various African and Caribbean influences on the music and dances of Congo Square.

129. Benjamin Henry Latrobe and John H. B. Latrobe, *The Journal of Latrobe: Being the Notes and Sketches of an Architect, Naturalist and Traveler in the United States from 1797 to 1820* (New York: D. Appleton, 1905), pp. 179–182.

130. Descriptions from George Washington Cable, *The Grandissimes: A Story of Creole Life* (New York: Penguin Books, 1988), pp. 189. Cable also composed an ethnographical account of Congo Square in *Century Magazine* (February 1886). On how these performances worked to confirm the whiteness of onlookers, see Roach, "Deep Skin," and Bryan Wagner, "Disarmed and Dangerous: The Strange Career of Bras-Coupé," *Representations*, no. 92 (2005), pp. 117–151. On how white identity is confirmed and constructed in the spectacle of black performance in a slave context, see Saidiya V. Hartman, *Scenes of Subjection: Terror, Slavery, and Self-Making in Nineteenth-Century America* (New York: Oxford University Press, 1997), pp. 32–36.

131. Tinker, *Toucoutou*, pp. 103–104. See Sander L. Gilman, "Black Bodies, White Bodies: Toward an Iconography of Female Sexuality in Late Nineteenth Century Art, Medicine, and Literature," in Henry Louis Gates, ed., *"Race," Writing, and Difference* (Chicago: University of Chicago Press, 1986) on the iconography of black women's bodies. Tinker's description conforms to the standard depiction exemplified by the transnational fascination with the body of Saartjie Baartman, "The Hottentot Venus."

132. Tinker, *Toucoutou*, p. 104.

133. Ibid., p. 23.

134. Ibid.

135. Ibid., p. 25.

136. On "The Legend of Laveau in the Stories People Tell," see Barbara J. Eckstein, *Sustaining New Orleans: Literature, Local Memory, and the Fate of a City* (New York: Routledge, 2006), pp. 22–29. For an account of the lives of the Marie Laveaus, see Martha Ward, *Voodoo Queen: The Spiritied Lives of Marie Laveau* (Jackson, Miss.: University of Mississippi Press, 2004).

137. Henry C. Castellanos, *New Orleans as it Was: Episodes of Louisiana Life* (New Orleans: L. Graham and Son, 1895), p. 100.

138. 1860 Census, Roll M653_422, p. 152 and Roll M653_421, p. 423.

139. Succession of Anastasie Desarzant, Second District Court, Orleans Parish, February 10, 1872. Probate Records, NOPL. Act before notary O. Drouet, February 10, 1872, NONARC.

140. 1930 Census, Stratford, Fairfield, CT, Roll 260, p. 24B, district 216.

141. See "An Act Relative to Marriages," *Acts Passed by the General Assembly of the State of Louisiana at the First Session of the First Legislature, Begun and Held in the City of New Orleans, June 29, 1868* (New Orleans, 1868), pp. 278–279.

142. Whitelaw Reid, *After the War: A Southern Tour, May 1, 1865, to May 1, 1866* (Cincinnati and New York: Moore, Wilstach & Baldwin, 1866), pp. 243–245.

3. Claiming Birthright in the Creole City

1. Notary Christoval Morel drew up this inventory of Lacroix's personal belongings after his death on April 15, 1876. Christoval Morel, April 19, 1876–May 3, 1876, NONARC. On shipments of Parisian fabrics, see succession of Francois Lacroix, New Orleans Civil District Court No. 9804, Box 1, Folder 28, CCR, NOPL. On artistry of Cordeviolle and Lacroix, see *NODP*, September 9, 1874. *Cohen's New Orleans and Southern Directory*, 1853 for advertisment. Juliet E. K. Walker, *The History of Black Business in America: Capitalism, Race, Entrepreneurship* (New York: Macmillan Library Reference, 1998), pp. 109–110 on the tailoring practices of Lacroix and others in New Orleans.

2. Louis F. Tasistro, *Random Shots and Southern Breezes, Containing Critical Remarks on the Southern States and Southern Institutions, with Semi-Serious Observations on Men and Manners* (New York: Harper and Brothers, 1842), Vol. II, p. 54.

3. Charles Baudelaire and Wallace Fowlie, *Flowers of Evil and Other Works—Les Fleurs du Mal et Oeuvres Choisies, A Dual-Language Book* (New York: Dover Publications, 1992), pp. 193, 197.

4. See Martin Robison Delany, *The Condition, Elevation, Emigration, and Destiny of the Colored People of the United States* (New York: Arno Press, 1968), pp. 99–100 on Cordeviolle's international reputation.

5. *NODP*, September 9, 1874. See testimony of Theodule Drouet, succession of François Lacroix, Box 1, Folder 15, CCR, NOPL.

6. On hygienic conditions of New Orleans in the mid-nineteenth century, see Christina Vella, *Intimate Enemies: The Two Worlds of the Baroness de Pontalba* (Baton Rouge: Louisiana State University Press, 1997), pp. 255–257, and Judith Kelleher Schafer, *Becoming Free, Remaining Free: Manumission and Enslavement in New Orleans, 1846–1862* (Baton Rouge: Louisiana State University, 2003), p. xvii. On the living and dead dog problem, see *NODP*, September 14, 1842; September 14, October 20, November 3, 1847; May 28, 1854.

7. My understanding of Lacroix incorporates aspects of Baudelaire's *flâneur*, or dandy, and Michel de Certeau's transgressive "walker" in the city. Lacroix as *flâneur* achieves mastery over his city by holding himself aloof from it and maintaining an aristocratic ethos within an emerging democratic culture. See "The Dandy" in Baudelaire and Fowlie, *Flowers of Evil*, pp. 192–199. See also Michel de Certeau, *The Practice of Everyday Life* (Berkeley: University of California Press, 1984), pp. 91–110, especially his characterization of walking as an "exilic activity" on p. 107.

8. Schafer, *Becoming Free*.

9. See Notary Christoval Morel, May 19, 1876–May 20, 1876, inventory of succession of Mrs. Cecile Edouary, deceased wife of Francois Lacroix, NONARC. Also see succession of François Lacroix, Box 1, Folder 6, CCR, NOPL for the 1856 figure and Notary Christoval Morel, May 3, 1876, NONARC for Lacroix's net worth at his death.

10. Virginia R. Domínguez, *White by Definition: Social Classification in Creole Louisiana* (New Brunswick, N.J.: Rutgers University Press, 1986) details this process; see chap. 3, "Properties of Blood," pp. 56–89. See also Loren Schweninger, "Property Owning Free African-American Women in the South, 1800–1870," in Wilma King, Darlene Clark Hine, and Linda Reed, eds., *We Specialize in the Wholly Impossible: A Reader in Black Women's History* (Brooklyn, N.Y.: Carlson Publishing Co., 1995).

11. See Sheldon S. Wolin, *The Presence of the Past: Essays on the State and the Constitution* (Baltimore: Johns Hopkins University Press, 1989).

12. Ibid. pp. 139–140. The results of these competing labors resonate in city places—in the lay of the land, in architecture, and in movement through space. See Andreas Huyssen, *Present Pasts, Urban Palimpsests, and the Politics of Memory* (Stanford, Calif.: Stanford University Press, 2003) on cities as palimpsests. For a consideration of New Orleans in particular, see M. Christine Boyer, *The City of Collective Memory: Its Historical Imagery and Architectural Entertainments* (Cambridge, Mass.: MIT Press, 1994), especially p. 322.

13. "Point of entanglement" is Edouard Glissant's term; Edouard Glissant and J. Michael Dash, *Caribbean Discourse: Selected Essays* (Charlottesville: University Press of Virginia, 1989), p. 26.

14. Here I refer to Esau's inheritance of "a mess of pottage" (Genesis 25: 19–34; 26: 34, 35). James Weldon Johnson raised the analogy in the context of racial passing, referring to the final predicament of his ex-colored musician who ends up living as a white businessman as "a mess of pottage." See the final line of Anonymous (James Weldon Johnson), *The Autobiography of an Ex-Coloured Man* (Boston: French and Company, 1912).

15. On making meaning of place, see Yi-fu Tuan, *Space and Place: The Perspective of Experience* (Minneapolis: University of Minnesota Press, 1977), and Boyer, *City of Collective Memory*, especially pp. 321–343.

16. Violet Harrington Bryan, *The Myth of New Orleans in Literature: Dialogues of Race and Gender* (Knoxville: University of Tennessee Press, 1993); Boyer, *City of Collective Memory.*

17. Henry Louis Gates, Jr., and Nellie McKay make swift mention of *Les Cenelles* as the "first anthology of African American poetry" compiled by the "black New Orleans writer Armand Lanusse." The anthology fits awkwardly in an African American literary tradition grounded in resistance to slavery and the struggle for literacy. See Henry Louis Gates and Nellie Y. McKay Gates, eds., *The Norton Anthology of African-American Literature* (New York: W. W. Norton and Co., 1997), p. 286. This rubric also guides the analysis of the most recent translation of *Les Cenelles* into English: Régine Latortue and Gleason R. W. Adams, eds., *Les Cenelles: A Collection of Poems of Creole Writers of the Early Nineteenth Century* (Boston: G. K. Hall, 1979). On the legacy of this anthology, see Floyd Cheung, "*Les Cenelles* and Quadroon Balls: 'Hidden Transcripts' of Resistance and Domination in New Orleans, 1803–1845," *Southern Literary Journal* 29, no. 2 (1997), and Thomas F. Haddox, "The 'Nous' of Southern Catholic Quadroons: Racial, Ethnic, and Religious Identity in *Les Cenelles*," *American Literature* 73, no. 4 (2001).

18. A *cenelle* comes from a hawthorn bush—a thorny bush with delicate flowers—an appropriate metaphor for Creole of color identity. Rodolphe Lucien Desdunes, *Our People and Our History*, trans. Sister Dorothea Olga McCants (Baton Rouge: Louisiana State University Press, 1973) p. 11.

19. Henry Renshaw, "Charles Gayarré," Proceedings of Louisiana Historical Society, Wednesday December 20, 1905, *Publications* III (March 1906).

20. Charles Gayarré, *Essai Historique sur la Louisiane* (New Orleans, 1830); Gayarré, *Histoire de la Louisiane*, (New Orleans, 1846–1847); Gayarré, *Histoire de la Louisiane: La Domination Française*, 2 vols., and *Histoire de la Louisiane: La Domination Espagnole* (New York, 1854); Gayarré, *Histoire de la Louisiane: La Domination Américaine* (New York, 1866); Gayarré, *History of Louisiana*, 4 vols. (New York, 1866). Edward Larocque Tinker, *Les Écrits de Langues Française en Louisiane* (Paris: Librairie Ancienne Honoré Champion, 1932), pp. 218–245; see pp. 236–245 for a complete bibliography of Gayarré's writing.

21. Grace Elizabeth King, *New Orleans: The Place and the People* (New York: The Macmillan Company, 1904), pp. 268–272.

22. Quoted in Boyer, *City of Collective Memory*, p. 479.

23. Records of financial cooperation and intermarriage between "Creoles" and white "Americans" complicate the notion of their separate and conflicting identi-

ties. However, the perception of this breach remains a defining feature of New Orleans' historiography and lore due in large part to Gayarré and his school of thought. See Joseph Tregle, Jr., "Creoles and Americans," in Arnold R. Hirsch and Joseph Logsdon, *Creole New Orleans: Race and Americanization* (Baton Rouge: Louisiana State University Press, 1992), pp. 131–132; Robert C. Reinders, *End of an Era: New Orleans, 1850–1880* (New Orleans: Pelican, 1964), p. 9. See Norman Walker, "Municipal Government," in Henry Rightor, ed., *Standard History of New Orleans* (Chicago: Lewis Publishing Company, 1900), p. 79 for an account that concurs with Gayarré's distinction. Recent scholarship on Creoles of color reproduces the cultural saga, focusing on their kinship with other French speakers and reinforcing their cultural difference from black Americans. See Caryn Cossé Bell, *Revolution, Romanticism, and the Afro-Creole Protest Tradition in Louisiana, 1718–1868* (Baton Rouge: Louisiana State University Press, 1997), and Sybil Kein, *Creole: The History and Legacy of Louisiana's Free People of Color* (Baton Rouge: Louisiana State University Press, 2000).

24. This is especially true of the city commons. However, private disputes between neighbors and family members also produced confusion over ownership. See The Friends of the Cabildo, *New Orleans Architecture, Vol. VI: Faubourg Tremé and the Bayou Road* (Gretna, La.: Pelican, 1980), pp. 3–85 on the development of what is now called Tremé from various land claims, emphasizing these problems of conveyance. See also Ari Kelman, *A River and Its City: The Nature of Landscape in New Orleans* (Berkeley: University of California Press, 2003).

25. On the Romantic notion of the social value of literature and art, see David Owen Evans, *Social Romanticism in France, 1830–1848: With a Selective Critical Bibliography* (Oxford: Clarendon Press, 1951), and Ellie Nower Schamber, *The Artist as Politician: The Relationship between the Art and the Politics of the French Romantics* (Lanham, Md.: University Press of America, 1984). On the cultural implications of this schism, see Walker, "Municipal Government," p. 79, and Grace King, *New Orleans*, pp. 268–272. Kelman, *River and Its City*, pp. 69–78 details events leading up to this schism, a battle for improvements to the levee system that broke down along cultural (American versus Creole) lines.

26. Gayarré invoked the Romantic nationalist historian Walter Scott, that "wonderful magician of [Scotland's] romantic hills." Charles Gayarré, *History of Louisiana* (New York: Redfield, 1854), p. vii. See Hugh Trevor-Roper, "The Invention of Tradition: The Highland Tradition of Scotland" in E.J. Hobsbawm and T.O. Ranger, *The Invention of Tradition* (Cambridge: Cambridge University Press, 1983), pp. 15–41.

27. Gayarré, *History of Louisiana*, Vol. I (1854), p. 13.

28. See Raymond Williams, *The Country and the City* (New York: Oxford University Press, 1973) for the distinction between land (that which is to be worked) and landscape (a vista to be enjoyed from a distance and a distinct class—and racial—position). On the iconography and techniques of landscape, see Denis Cosgrove, "Prospect, Perspective and the Evolution of the Landscape Idea," *Transactions of the Institute of British Geographers* 10, no. 1 (1985), especially p. 46; Denis E. Cosgrove, *Social Formation and Symbolic Landscape* (London: Croom Helm, 1984); Stephen Daniels, *Fields of Vision: Landscape Imagery and National Identity in England and the United States* (Cambridge: Polity Press, 1993). On the function of landscape in nineteenth-century America, see Angela L. Miller, *The Empire of the Eye: Landscape*

Representation and American Cultural Politics, 1825–1875 (Ithaca: Cornell University Press, 1993).

29. Roulhac Toledano, *Richard Clague, 1821–1873*, New Orleans Museum of Art, Exhibition Catalogue, 1974.

30. Richard Slotkin, *Regeneration through Violence: The Mythology of the American Frontier, 1600–1860* (Middletown, Conn.: Wesleyan University Press, 1973); Jill Lepore, *The Name of War: King Philip's War and the Origins of American Identity* (New York: Knopf, 1998).

31. Biographical information on Gayarré in Tinker, *Les Écrits*, pp. 218–245. At $30,000, the statue by "Mills" is the first equestrian statue in the United States with its entire weight supported by the hind legs of the horse. See also Edward Larocque Tinker, "Charles Gayarré, 1805–95," *Biographical Society of America* 27, no. 1 (1933), p. 36.

32. To the extent that the Cable-Gayarré debate is also one about the right to claim New Orleans as home, Cable comes up short. While he was born in the city, his parents were immigrants from Virginia and New England, and he was a staunch Presbyterian. This pedigree was no match for that of Gayarré, whose parentage on both sides stemmed from the colonial period.

33. George Washington Cable, *The Silent South* (Montclair, N.J.: Patterson Smith, 1969), pp. 41–43. On the myriad uses of Lee in the post-bellum popular imagination, see the essays in Peter Wallenstein and Bertram Wyatt-Brown, *Virginia's Civil War* (Charlottesville: University of Virginia Press, 2004), Part I, pp. 9–59. See David W. Blight, *Race and Reunion: The Civil War in American Memory* (Cambridge, Mass.: Belknap Press of Harvard University Press, 2001), especially pp. 140–210, 255–299; W. Fitzhugh Brundage, *The Southern Past: A Clash of Race and Memory* (Cambridge, Mass.: Belknap Press of Harvard University Press, 2005), especially pp. 12–54; and Bertram Wyatt-Brown, *The Shaping of Southern Culture: Honor, Grace, and War, 1760s–1890s* (Chapel Hill: University of North Carolina Press, 2001), especially Part III, pp. 177–293 on the post Civil War struggle over the soul of the South and the imperatives driving commemoration in the South.

34. Cable's political writings consisted of "The Freedman's Case in Equity," *CM* 29, no. 3 (January 1885), pp. 409–419; "The Silent South," *CM* 30, no. 5, pp. 674–692 (a reply to Henry Grady's "In Plain Black and White" response to his "Freedmen's Case," also published in *CM* 29, no. 6 (April 1885), pp. 909–918); shorter letters to the editors, less-extensive articles; and numerous addresses later published. See George Washington Cable, *The Negro Question: A Selection of Writings on Civil Rights in the South* (Garden City, N.Y.: Doubleday, 1958), and *Silent South*. On Cable's political activity, see Lucy Leffingwell Cable Bikle, *George W. Cable: His Life and Letters* (New York: C. Scribner's Sons, 1928), pp. 154–165.

35. Cable, "The Freedman's Case"; *Silent South*, pp. 22–23.

36. Cable, "The Freedman's Case." p. 23.

37. On Cable as dialect writer, see Gavin Roger Jones, *Strange Talk: The Politics of Dialect Literature in Gilded Age America* (Berkeley: University of California Press, 1999), pp. 115–133.

38. On Cable's career and his debates with Grady in *Century* magazine, see Edward L. Ayers, *Southern Crossing: A History of the American South, 1877–1906* (Oxford and New York: Oxford University Press, 1995), pp. 202–210.

39. Charles Gayarré, "The Creoles of History and the Creoles of Romance, a Lecture Delivered in the Hall of the Tulane University, by Hon. Charles Gayarré,

on the 25th of April, 1885" (New Orleans: C. E. Hopkins, 1885). Other New Orleanians also responded to Cable. See the pamphlet: Abbé Adrien [E. Junius] Rouquette, "Critical Dialogue between Aboo and Caboo on a New Book; or, a Grandissime Ascension" (New Orleans: 1880).

40. Gayarré, "Creoles of History," pp. 2, 6; Tregle, "Creoles and Americans," on Gayarré's capitulation to Americanization.

41. Gayarré, "Creoles of History," p. 11.

42. Ibid., p. 6.

43. His protégé Grace King, for example, whitens Creole history by excising relatives of color from "great" families. See her *Creole Families of New Orleans* (New York: The Macmillan Company, 1921).

44. See Christopher E. G. Benfey, *Degas in New Orleans: Encounters in the Creole World of Kate Chopin and George Washington Cable* (New York: Knopf, 1997), p. 261.

45. Gayarré, "Creoles of History," p. 32.

46. In addition to *Grandissimes*, works that use this device include Charles Waddell Chesnutt, *Paul Marchand, F.M.C* (Jackson: University Press of Mississippi, 1998), and Mark Twain, *Pudd'nhead Wilson and Those Extraordinary Twins* (1893). In *Absalom, Absalom!* (1936), William Faulkner moves beyond the context of New Orleans to Mississippi, where his Creole of color character Charles Bon and the white heir Henry Sutpen struggle over birthright. See Eric Sundquist on this motif more broadly, especially the chapter on Mark Twain and Homer Plessy in *To Wake the Nations: Race in the Making of American Literature* (Cambridge, Mass.: Harvard University Press, 1993), pp. 225–270.

47. George Washington Cable, *The Grandissimes: A Story of Creole Life* (New York: Penguin Books, 1988), p. 38.

48. Ibid., pp. 41–42.

49. Ibid., pp. 36, 41.

50. Homi K. Bhabha, *The Location of Culture* (London and New York: Routledge, 1994), p. 76.

51. On Cable's preference for a "just assortment" of people according to their refinements and manners, see Saidiya V. Hartman, *Scenes of Subjection: Terror, Slavery, and Self-Making in Nineteenth-Century America* (New York: Oxford University Press, 1997), pp. 164–171.

52. Cable, *The Grandissimes*, p. 268; Gayarré, "Creoles of History," p. 31.

53. The fate of Honoré f.m.c. is similar to that of the chased and doomed "Convent Girl" of Grace King's creation. Grace Elizabeth King, "The Little Convent Girl," *Balcony Stories* (Ridgewood, N.J.: Gregg Press, 1968).

54. See *Historical Sketch Book and Guide to New Orleans and Environs, with Map* (New York, 1885), especially pp. 293–299, an entry written by Lafcadio Hearn, and illustrations throughout.

55. See George M. Fredrickson, *The Black Image in the White Mind: The Debate on Afro-American Character and Destiny, 1817–1914* (Middletown, Conn.: Wesleyan University Press, 1987) on the romantic racialist's ability to hold both positive and negative views of blacks.

56. See also his unpublished manuscript, "Essay on the Quadroons" (1890), and his article for the *NOTD*, "Blacks in Louisiana," October 17–December 5, 1880. Draft in Gayarré Papers, Special Collections, Tulane University.

57. Charles Gayarré, "The Southern Question," *NAR* 1877, p. 492.

58. Ibid.

59. Charles Gayarré, *Fernando de Lemos Truth and Fiction; a Novel* (New York, 1872), pp. 36–77.

60. Gayarré, "Creoles of History," p. 17. The New Orleans branch of the family of French artist Edgar Degas had changed its name to de Gas. Apparently, this was a common practice. See Benfey, *Degas in New Orleans*, p. 12.

61. On narrative implications of exile, see Glissant and Dash, *Caribbean Discourse*, pp. 16–26.

62. The veterans of color of 1815 remained a cohesive interest group throughout antebellum New Orleans, forming clubs and mutual aid and literary societies. See Bell, *Revolution, Romanticism*, pp. 89–90. On their formation of the Association of Colored Veterans for parading purposes, see Mary Gehman, *The Free People of Color of New Orleans: An Introduction* (New Orleans: Margaret Media, 1994), p. 71.

63. See Desdunes, *Our People*, p. 5.

64. *"Bosquet fleuri. Témoin de notre flame, / Je te revois, ce n'est point une erreur, / Ruisseau chéri, c'est à toi que mon âme / veut en ce jour confier son bonheur."* Nelson Desbrosses, "Le Rétour au Village aux Perles ("The return to the Village of Pearls") in Armand Lanusse, ed., *Les Cenelles: Choix de Poesies Indigenes* (New Orleans: H. Lauve, 1845), pp. 118-119. Author's translations throughout unless otherwise noted. The comment about the area's young women appears as a footnote in the original text.

65. Kimberly S. Hanger, *Bounded Lives, Bounded Places: Free Black Society in Colonial New Orleans, 1769–1803* (Durham, N.C.: Duke University Press, 1997); Friends of the Cabildo, *New Orleans Architecture, Vol VI: Faubourg Tremé and the Bayou Road.*

66. *"Banni du monde entire, . . . / Je suis seul, toujours seul dans le champ des tombeaux, / Où le saule éploré balance ses rameaux."* Bo . . . rs, "The Orphan of the Tombs," *Les Cenelles*, p. 73.

67. On the various registers—legal, contractual, conceptual, and metaphorical—ascribing meaning to property and landscape, see David Delaney, *Race, Place, and the Law, 1836–1948* (Austin: University of Texas Press, 1998), pp. 1–28.

68. Sally Kittredge Evans, "Free Persons of Color," in The Friends of the Cabildo, *New Orleans Architecture, Volume IV: The Creole Faubourgs* (Gretna, La.: Pelican Publishing Complany, 1996), p. 26 suggests that property transfers in the notarial archives is the "key to a more personal documentation of this group." H. E. Sterkx, *The Free Negro in Antebellum Louisiana* (Rutherford, N.J.: Fairleigh Dickinson University Press, 1972), and John W. Blassingame, *Black New Orleans, 1860–1880* (Chicago: University of Chicago Press, 1973) note the general prevalence of black landholders without exploring their sense of place.

69. Wolin, *Presence of the Past*, pp. 139–140.

70. After serving five years for shooting and killing a neighbor's slave and witnessing the seizure of all of his property to cover court costs in the suit against him, Claude Tremé, a native Frenchman, married Julie Moreau and inherited the plantation directly lakeward from the French Quarter. Four years later, he began to parcel it out—creating Faubourg Tremé. See Friends of the Cabildo, *New Orleans Architecture, Col VI: Faubourg Tremé and the Bayou Road*, pp. 13-15.

71. Richard Campanella, *Time and Place in New Orleans: Past Geographies in the Present Day* (Gretna, La.: Pelican, 2002), pp. 66–70.

72. Ludwig von Reizenstein and Steven W. Rowan, *The Mysteries of New Orleans* (Baltimore: Johns Hopkins University Press, 2002), p. 534.

73. Friends of the Cabildo, *New Orleans Architecture, Vol VI: Faubourg Tremé and the Bayou Road,* p. 63.

74. Claiborne, the "main street of Black New Orleans," continued to be a major thoroughfare well into the twentieth century, when residential segregation was more widespread. During the late 1960s, the famously resented I-10 project decimated this stretch of North Claiborne, effectively segmenting what had once been a cohesive neighborhood. Campanella, *Time and Place in New Orleans,* p. 69.

75. See Estate inventory of François Lacroix, Notary Christoval Morel, April 19, 1876–May 3, 1876, and that of Julien Lacroix, Notary, Onesiphore Drouet, January 6, 1869, NONARC.

76. See Board of Health citation, September 10, 1973; succession of François Lacroix, Box 1, Folder 2, CCR, NOPL.

77. Friends of the Cabildo, *New Orleans Architecture, Vol VI: Faubourg Tremé and the Bayou Road,* pp. 56–59.

78. Ibid., p. 63.

79. See Alecia P. Long, *The Great Southern Babylon: Sex, Race, and Respectability in New Orleans, 1865–1920* (Baton Rouge: Louisiana State University Press, 2004), pp. 102–147; Al Rose, *Storyville, New Orleans, Being an Authentic Illustrated Account of the Notorious Red-Light District* (Tuscaloosa: University of Alabama Press, 1974).

80. Paxon's *New Orleans Registry and Directory,* cited in Friends of the Cabildo, *New Orleans Architecture, Vol VI: Faubourg Tremé and the Bayou Road,* p. 65.

81. On the cultural and racial importance of Congo Square, see George Washington Cable, "The Dance in Place Congo," *CM,* February 1886; Daniel E. Walker, *No More, No More: Slavery and Cultural Resistance in Havana and New Orleans* (Minneapolis: University of Minnesota Press, 2004), pp. 2–3; Harry Justin Elam and David Krasner, *African-American Performance and Theater History: A Critical Reader* (Oxford and New York: Oxford University Press, 2001); Jerah Johnson, "New Orleans' Congo Square: An Urban Setting for Early Afro-American Culture Formation," *LaHist* (1991).

82. Lacroix's properties and the neighborhoods surrounding them performed a heterotopic function in New Orleans in "suspect[ing], neutraliz[ing], or invert[ing]" social, political, and cultural practices emanating from the center. See Michel Foucault, "Of Other Spaces," *Diacritics* 16 (1986).

83. Friends of the Cabildo, *New Orleans Architecture, Vol VI,* pp. 101–103.

84. See Ibid., pp. 93–94.

85. On struggles between French- and English-speaking Catholic constituencies over freemasonry, see Roger Baudier, *The Catholic Church in Louisiana* (New Orleans: H. W. Hyatt Stationery mfg. co. ltd.,1939), pp. 249–324, and Bell, *Revolution, Romanticism,* pp. 146–155.

86. Friends of the Cabildo, *New Orleans Architecture, Vol. VI,* pp. 68–69.

87. Bell, *Revolution, Romanticism,* pp. 265–268.

88. Stephen J. Ochs, *A Black Patriot and a White Priest: André Cailloux and Claude Paschal Maistre in Civil War New Orleans* (Baton Rouge: Louisiana State University Press, 2000), pp. 2–5; *HWM.* August 29, 1863.

89. On the early history of the Sisters of the Holy Family, see O. S. B. Cyprian Davis, *Henriette Delille: Servant of Slaves, Witness to the Poor* (New Orleans: Archdio-

cese of New Orleans in Cooperation with the Sisters of the Holy Family, 2004), pp. 35–58; Virginia Meacham Gould and Charles E, Nolan, "Introduction," in Mary Bernard Deggs, Virginia Meacham Gould, and Charles E. Nolan, *No Cross, No Crown: Black Nuns in Nineteenth-Century New Orleans* (Bloomington: Indiana University Press, 2001), pp. xxiii–xxxvi; and Bell, *Revolution, Romanticism*, pp. 127–134.

90. Emily Clark and Virginia Meacham Gould, "The Feminine Face of Afro-Catholicism in New Orleans, 1727–1852," *William and Mary Quarterly* 59, no. 2 (2002) describes how women of African descent came to participate in organized Catholicism, focusing on Henriette Delille and her ancestors.

91. Tracy Fessenden, "The Sisters of the Holy Family and the Veil of Race," *Religion and American Culture* 10, no. 2 (2000) maintains that the "veil of race" facilitated these revolutionary actions under the eyes of authorities, with or without sanction. See especially pp. 202–205.

92. *Soard's New Orleans City Directory* (New Orleans, 1875).

93. See David C. Rankin, "The Impact of the Civil War on the Free Colored Community of New Orleans," *Perspectives in American History* XI (1977–1978).

94. This inventory of Julien Lacroix's house and store was notarized by Onesiphore Drouet at the request of the widow, Ursuline Jean. See O. Drouet, March 20, 1868, NONARC.

95. 1850 Census, Slave Schedule, p. 292.

96. See "Architectural Inventory" in Friends of the Cabildo, *New Orleans Architecture Vol IV*, p. 149.

97. See, for example, Delaney, *Race, Place, and the Law*, pp. 93–116, and Hale, *Making Whiteness*, especially her chapter on consumption and the market, pp. 121–197. See also Steven Hoelscher, "Making Place, Making Race: Performances of Whiteness in the Jim Crow South," *Annals of the Association of American Geographers* 93, no. 3 (2003).

98. Howard N. Rabinowitz, *Race Relations in the Urban South, 1865–1890* (Athens: University of Georgia Press, 1996) brackets New Orleans, emphasizing its difference from the typical southern city.

99. See David C. Rankin, "The Forgotten People: Free People of Color in New Orleans, 1850–1870" (Ph.D. dissertation, Johns Hopkins University, 1976) on how the reluctance of Creoles of color to identify with blacks has rendered them a "forgotten people." See Arthé Anthony, "The Negro Community in New Orleans, 1880–1920: An Oral History" (Ph. D. dissertation, University of California, Irvine, 1978), and Arthé Anthony, "'Lost Boundaries': Racial Passing and Poverty in Segregated New Orleans," *LaHist* 36, no. 3 (1995) on the sense of cultural uniqueness in isolation for Creoles of color. See Bell, *Revolution, Romanticism* on mutual affiliations of Creoles of color and whites. Other recent studies of Creole of color intimacy with whites include Ochs, *Black Patriot and a White Priest* and Diana I. Williams, "'They Call It Marriage': The Interracial Louisiana Family and the Making of American Legitimacy," (Ph. D. dissertation, Harvard University, 2007).

100. See Bell, *Revolution, Romanticism*, p. 183, and Charles B. Roussève, *The Negro in Louisiana: Aspects of His History and His Literature* (New York: Xavier University Press, 1937), p. 41.

101. See Bell, *Revolution, Romanticism*, p. 183, and Patricia Brady, "Black Artists in Antebellum New Orleans," *LaHist* (1991), pp. 20–23. Warbourg did a bas relief of scenes from Stowe's *Uncle Tom's Cabin*, a work commissioned in London.

102. See 1840 mayor's office rolls, and Richard Tansey, "Out-of-State Free Blacks in Late Antebellum New Orleans," *LaHist* 22, no. 4 (1981).

103. My sense of an "alternative public" draws on such revisions of the theories of Jürgen Habermas as Nancy Fraser, "Rethinking the Public Sphere: A Contribution to the Critique of Actually Existing Democracy" and Mary Ryan, "Gender and Public Access: Women's Politics in Nineteenth-Century America," both in Craig J. Calhoun, *Habermas and the Public Sphere* (Cambridge, Mass.: MIT Press, 1992), pp. 109–142, 259–289; the articles in Black Public Sphere Collective, *The Black Public Sphere: A Public Culture Book* (Chicago: University of Chicago Press, 1995); and Evelyn Brooks Higginbotham, *Righteous Discontent: The Women's Movement in the Black Baptist Church, 1880–1920* (Cambridge, Mass.: Harvard University Press, 1993), pp. 7–13.

104. See Rankin, "Impact of the Civil War," pp. 382–383 and real estate inventories in Friends of the Cabildo, *New Orleans Architecture Vol. IV and New Orleans Architecture, Vol VII.*

105. See Roulhac Toledano, Sally Kittredge Evans, and Mary Louise Christovich, "Types and Styles," in Friends of the Cabildo, *New Orleans Architecture, Vol. IV,* pp. 41–55 on the Creole cottage and 63–70 on the American townhouse. Also see Benjamin Henry Latrobe et al., *The Journals of Benjamin Henry Latrobe, 1799–1820: From Philadelphia to New Orleans* (New Haven: Yale University Press, 1980), p. 266 (entry of March 22, 1819).

106. Toledano, Evans, and Christovich, "Types and Styles," pp. 63–70.

107. Benjamin Henry Latrobe and John H. B. Latrobe, *The Journal of Latrobe: Being the Notes and Sketches of an Architect, Naturalist and Traveler in the United States from 1797 to 1820* (New York: D. Appleton, 1905), pp. 209–211.

108. On the more lax climate for urban slaves, see Richard Clement Wade, *Slavery in the Cities: The South, 1820–1860* (London: Oxford University Press, 1967), pp. 143–179, 209–226. See also my discussion of fugitive J. Sella Martin in chapter 5 of this book.

109. Henry Jefferson Leovy, *The Laws and General Ordinances of the City of New Orleans* (New Orleans, 1857), pp. 257–268 on comprehensive legislation passed by the Louisiana legislature in early 1857. See also Wade, *Slavery in the Cities,* pp. 180–208 on punitive measures taken against enslaved people in cities.

110. Solomon Northup, *Twelve Years a Slave* (London: 1853), pp. 79–80. See Walter Johnson, *Soul by Soul: Life inside the Antebellum Slave Market* (Cambridge, Mass.: Harvard University Press, 1999), pp. 2–3; also see Joseph R. Roach, *Cities of the Dead: Circum-Atlantic Performance* (New York: Columbia University Press, 1996), pp. 211–216 on the slave auction as performance.

111. Louisiana Civil Code of 1825, art. 461. For laws pertaining to the housing of slaves, see Leovy, *The Laws and General Ordinances of the City of New Orleans,* pp. 257–258, Nos. 750, 751, 752.

112. For a discussion of this phenomenon, see Hartman, *Scenes of Subjection,* pp. 5–6, 17–48.

113. Succession of François Lacroix, Box 1, Folder 7, CCR, NOPL. According to the U.S. Census, Lacroix owned two slaves in 1850, a mulatto female aged forty and a black female aged thirty-eight. In 1860, he owned three (apparently different) women, all listed as black, ages sixty, thirty-five, and sixteen.

114. See John Churchill Chase, *Frenchmen Desire Goodchildren: And Other Streets of New Orleans* (New York: Collier Macmillan, 1979), p. 86, and Edward Larocque

Tinker, *Creole City: Its Past and Its People* (New York: Longmans Green, 1953), p. 9 for accounts of the naming of streets.

115. Diana I. Williams, "'They Call It Marriage'" details interracial marriages in nineteenth-century Louisiana, particularly legal marriages from 1868 to 1892. In a paper given at the 2002 Berkshire Conference of Women Historians, Williams used the union of Sarah and Victor Lacroix as a foil for the later period of her study. The 1868 Louisiana legislature legalized interracial marriage when it abolished the racial restrictions governing the drawing up of civil contracts.

116. This Reconstruction-era riot, discussed in chapter 5, was one of two (the other in Memphis) often cited as evidence that Johnson's policies were not working and was a major catalyst for Radical Congressional Reconstruction. See Eric Foner, *Reconstruction: America's Unfinished Revolution, 1863–1877* (New York: Harper and Row, 1988), pp. 262–264; Gilles Vandal, *The New Orleans Riot of 1866: Anatomy of a Tragedy* (Lafayette: Center for Louisiana Studies University of Southwestern Louisiana, 1983); and Chase, *Frenchmen Desire Goodchildren.*

117. From Succession of François Lacroix, Box 1, Folder 4, CCR, NOPL.

118. On the reputation of Gasquet Street, see Long, *Great Southern Babylon*, p. 23.

119. From the succession of Victor Lacroix, Second District Court, No 2853678. December 8, 1866, CCR, NOPL.

120. Although her study brackets New Orleans, Martha Hodes argues that white communities often tolerated these liaisons when the woman was of lower-class status. See Martha Elizabeth Hodes, *White Women, Black Men: Illicit Sex in the Nineteenth-Century South* (New Haven, Conn.: Yale University Press, 1997), pp. 4–5. This seems to be somewhat true in this case, but the class status of Sarah Brown seems to have provoked François Lacroix's intolerance.

121. Mary Gehman, "Visible Means of Support: Businesses, Professions, and Trades of Free People of Color," in Sybil Kein, ed., *Creole: The History and Legacy of Louisiana's Free People of Color* (Baton Rouge: Louisiana State University Press, 2000), p. 213.

122. Succession of François Lacroix, Box 1, Folder 4, CCR, NOPL.

123. 1870 Census, Roll M593_521, p. 129. *Soards's New Orleans Directory* (1875).

124. See succession of François Lacroix and inventory of Lacroix estate, Christopher Morel, April 19, 1876–May 3 1876, NONARC.

125. In contrast, David Rankin reads the postwar pitfalls of Lacroix and three other Creoles of color—Aristide Mary, John Racquet Clay, and Jean Baptiste Jourdain—as examples of what Émile Durkheim termed "egoistic suicides." (Although Lacroix's death was due to natural causes, the other three men killed themselves.) See Rankin, "Impact of the Civil War," p. 407.

126. François Lacroix to Major General Nathaniel P. Banks, September 5, 1864; see Ibid., p. 403. On the issue of Yankee proprietors in the South, see Lawrence N. Powell, *New Masters: Northern Planters during the Civil War and Reconstruction* (New Haven: Yale University Press, 1980). The issue of Creole of color political and social identity during Reconstruction is taken up more fully in chapter 5. Here it forms the backdrop for a consideration of the common struggles of Lacroix and other Louisianans for proprietorship and birthright in this period.

127. 1870 Census, Roll M593_521, p. 103. See Foner, *Reconstruction*, pp. 205–207 on taxation policy during Reconstruction and pp. 588–589 on tax reform as a political issue for Redeemers after Reconstruction.

128. *NODP*, September 9, 1874.

129. The *Picayune* enacts a "toponalysis" of François Lacroix, offering a "systematic psychological study of [his] intimate [life]" based on the disarray of his home and his "misuse" of interior space. See Gaston Bachelard, *The Poetics of Space* (Boston: Beacon Press, 1969), p. 8.

130. Roach, *Cities of the Dead*, p. 40 on René Girard's notion of sacrifice and the "monstrous double."

131. Succession of François Lacroix, Box 1, Folder 15, CCR, NOPL.

132. Gayarré, "The Southern Question," pp. 491–492.

133. See Tinker, *Les Écrits*, p. 231 on Gayarré's insolence with Seward.

134. See Boyer, *City of Collective Memory*, pp. 323–343 on how New Orleans courted tourism by emphasizing its Creole past in ruins.

135. Gayarré, *Fernando de Lemos*, p. 152.

136. Tinker, *Les Écrits*, p. 236.

137. My understanding of exile draws on Judith N. Shklar and Stanley Hoffmann, *Political Thought and Political Thinkers* (Chicago: University of Chicago Press, 1998), especially pp. 38–72. Shklar distinguishes among different levels of emotion for the exile—personal, familial, political, racial—that also fluctuate according to the degree of choice one has had over one's exile.

138. Delany, *Condition, Elevation, Emigration*, p. 100.

139. The *New Orleans Annual and Commercial Directory for 1843* (New Orleans, 1842) lists Lacroix and Cordeviolle at 123 Chartres and Dumas and Colvis at 124 Chartres.

140. Act before T. Guyol, March 3 1846, minors Colvis, Vol. 3, No 130, NONARC.

141. Act before T. Guyol, January 9, 1846, Vol. 3, Act 4, January 25, 1846, NONARC.

142. Enslaved people also attempted to capitalize on the French abolition of slavery in 1848 and a 1791 statute that automatically freed any enslaved person that set foot on its soil. Judith Kelleher Schafer, *Slavery, the Civil Law, and the Supreme Court of Louisiana* (Baton Rouge: Louisiana State University Press, 1994).

143. See Michel Fabre, "New Orleans Creole Expatriates in France: Romance and Reality," and Lester Sullivan, "Composers of Color of Nineteenth Century New Orleans: The History behind the Music," in Kein, *Creole*, pp. 179–195, 71–100, respectively. See also Brady, "Black Artists."

144. On the crisis in Attapakas, see Bell, *Revolution, Romanticism*, pp. 85–87. See Desdunes, *Our People*, pp. 112–114 on his father's role as emigration agent; chapters 2 and 4 for accounts of Anastasie Desarzant and Patrice Macarty, who maintained ties to or reinvested in Cuba. On the role of Creoles of color in the Mexican Revolution, see Bell, *Revolution, Romanticism*, 57–64, and on Fouché's plans for Eureka, see *Documens Relatifs à la Colonie d'Eureka, dans l'état de Veracruz* (New Orleans, 1857), SCT.

145. See table in Walker, *History of Black Business*, pp. 93–94.

146. Ibid., p. 93.

147. "*Adieu! Je ne crains pas que les jours de l'absence / Me fassent t'oublier: / J'aime à me souvenir, et j'aurai souvenance. De toi, près du foyer.*" Camille Thierry, "Adieu (Farewell)," *Les Cenelles*, p. 117.

148. The phrase is René Depestre's. He suggests that the culture of the Antilles derives more from Africa than France. See his interview with Aimé Césaire conducted at

the Cultural Congress of Havana in 1967 and translated and reprinted in Césaire, *Discourse on Colonialism*, trans. Joan Pinkham (New York: Monthly Review Press, 2000), p. 83. The Cuban context of this conversation between Haitian Depestre and Martiniquan Césaire echoes an itinerant sensibility also operating for New Orleans' nineteenth-century *gens de couleur.* Here I emphasize the francophone influences; however, they also maintained ties with the remnants of their settlement in Santiago de Cuba and elsewhere in the Spanish-speaking world. See Rebecca J. Scott, *Degrees of Freedom: Louisiana and Cuba after Slavery* (Cambridge, Mass.: Belknap Press of Harvard University Press, 2005), especially pp. 75–77. Sibylle Fischer, *Modernity Disavowed: Haiti and the Cultures of Slavery in the Age of Revolution* (Durham, N.C.: Duke University Press, 2004) delineates a culture of disavowal that emerges in nineteenth-century Cuba, Haiti, and the Dominican Republic as a critique of Western modernity and a response to Haitian revolutionary practices and ideals. It is instructive to consider New Orleans' Creoles of color against this backdrop.

149. Bell, *Revolution, Romanticism*, p. 94.

150. For biographical information on Bissette, see Lawrence C. Jennings, "Cyril Bissette, Radical Black French Activist," *French History* 9 (1995). For two recent assessments of Bissette's influence, see Brickhouse, *Transamerican Literary Relations and the Nineteenth-Century Public Sphere* (Cambridge UK and New York: Cambridge University Press, 2004), pp. 89–125, and Chris Bongie, *Islands and Exiles: The Creole Identities of Post/Colonial Literature* (Stanford, Calif.: Stanford University Press, 1998), pp. 266–287.

151. *Revue des Colonies*, first edition, July 1834, p. 8. Published monthly, the journal typically ran between thirty and forty pages and carried opinion pieces and news reports from various colonies and nations—particularly though not always located in the Caribbean. In November 1834 the journal began to print fiction, poetry, and other imaginative works. See Brickhouse, *Transamerican Literary Relations*, pp. 113–117, and Bongie, *Islands and Exiles*, pp. 267–279.

152. J. Michael Dash, *Literature and Ideology in Haiti, 1915–1961* (Totowa, N.J.: Barnes & Noble Books, 1981), p. 9 on Nau's idea of productive "fusion." See also Brickhouse, *Transamerican Literary Relations*, pp. 113–117.

153. On the emergence of the notion of "negritude" in the 1930s and 1940s, see Brent Hayes Edwards, *The Practice of Diaspora: Literature, Translation, and the Rise of Black Internationalism* (Cambridge, Mass.: Harvard University Press, 2003).

154. Epitaph cited in Charles O'Neill, *Victor Séjour: Parisian Playwright from Louisiana* (Lafayette: University of Southwestern Louisiana Press, 1995), p. 161.

155. Hobsbawm and Ranger, *The Invention of Tradition.*

156. *"Ah! Quand, seul et pensif, debout sur Sainte-Hélène, / Ses regards se tournaient vers la France lointaine, / Comme vers une étoile d'or: / Son front s'illuminait d'un souvenir de flame; / It s'écriait: 'Mon Dieu, je donnerais mon âme, / Pour la revoir encore."* Victor Séjour, "Le Retour de Napoléon," *Les Cenelles*, p. 57.

157. See Rodolphe Lucien Desdunes, "A Few Words to Dr. Dubois, with Malice Towards None" (New Orleans: 1907), pp. 8–9. The portrayal of Napoleon III as a return of Napoleon I would have countered assertions—made most famously by Karl Marx in "The Eighteenth Brumaire of Louis Napoleon Bonaparte" (1852)—that the nephew's reign and character played as "farce" to the uncle's "tragedy."

158. Henry Louis Gates, Jr., and Nellie McKay, eds., *The Norton Anthology of African American Literature* (New York: Norton, 1997), pp. 286–299 call Séjour an

African American. Marc Shell and Werner Sollors, eds., *The Multilingual Anthology of American Literature* (New York: New York Univ. Press, 2000), pp. 146–181 place the text in its francophone context and include the original French text.

159. See Shell and Sollors, *Multilingual Anthology*, p. 149. Charles O'Neill, *Séjour: Parisian Playwright from Louisiana* (Lafayette: University of Southwestern Louisiana, Center for Louisiana Studies, 1995), pp. 7–8 gives 1834–1836 as the range of possible dates of Séjour's departure from New Orleans.

160. Séjour's life and subject matter traversed boundaries that have frustrated anthologists intent upon establishing a coherent, consistent, national African American literary tradition. The first recent anthology to include "Le Mulâtre" as an American text, implicitly criticizes Séjour for his expatriate status. See Gates and McKay, *Norton Anthology*, p. 286. Although Séjour and his family owned, bought, sold, and sometimes manumitted slaves throughout the antebellum period, he may have had plans for two plays on race and/or slavery, a dramatic portrayal of the life of John Brown and a lost manuscript, *L'Esclave*. See O'Neill, *Séjour*, pp. 111–114, and Sollors, "The First African-American Short Story" in Shell and Sollors, *The Multilingual Anthology*, pp. 146–147. Some of his best dramas, recently reissued, focused on Jews, giving Séjour the opportunity to explore themes of dispossession, passing, misplaced children, and racial and religious persecution. See Victor Séjour, Norman R. Shapiro, trans., and M. Lynn Weiss, ed., *The Fortune Teller* (Urbana: University of Illinois Press, 2002) and *The Jew of Seville* (Urbana: University of Illinois Press, 2002).

161. As politician, Lamartine penned the text of the law finally abolishing slavery in the French empire in 1848. *Bug-Jargal* (1824), a tale of the heroism of Toussaint and the Haitian Revolution, was Victor Hugo's earliest fiction. Soon to be exiled themselves, Lamartine and Hugo were ideological brothers to the exile Séjour. Alexandre Dumas *père et fils*, Parisians of African descent, served as role models for displaced Africans across the diaspora.

162. On the moral, political, and symbolic value of exile for French Romantics, see Deborah Elise White, "Victor Hugo's Romantic Exile," *European Romantic Review* 16, no. 2 (2005).

163. Bell, *Revolution, Romanticism* details this collaboration in such venues as fraternal organizations, spiritualist clubs, newspapers, and other literary organizations; see especially chapters 5 and 6.

164. See ibid., pp. 208–215.

165. Russ Castronovo, *Necro Citizenship: Death, Eroticism, and the Public Sphere in the Nineteenth-Century United States* (Durham, N.C.: Duke University Press, 2001), especially chapter 4, and Bell, *Revolution, Romanticism*, pp. 187–221.

166. Bell, *Revolution, Romanticism*, pp. 206–207 on Valmour, pp. 198–199 on Barthet.

167. *Le Spiritualiste de la Nouvelle Orleans*, September-October 1858. Quoted in ibid., p. 214.

168. On the lives of Marie Laveau, mother and daughter, see Martha Ward, *Voodoo Queen: The Spirited Lives of Marie Laveau* (Jackson: University Press of Mississippi, 2004).

169. *New Orleans Times*, June 26, 1872.

170. Robert Tallant, *Voodoo in New Orleans* (New York: The Macmillan Company, 1946), p. 54.

171. See Ward, *Voodoo Queen*, pp. 140–153 on the hoax of 1874 and pp. 3–20 on the difficulty of distinguishing between the women. Also see Tallant, *Voodoo in New Orleans*, p. 75.

172. On the twentieth-century rise of "Spritual Churches" in New Orleans and how they combine aspects of Catholicism, spiritualism, and voodoo, see Claude F. Jacobs and Andrew J Kastow, *The Spiritual Churches of New Orleans: Origins, Beliefs, and Rituals of an African American Religion* (Knoxville, Tenn.: University of Tennessee Press, 1991).

173. *"Il est des moments, dans la vie d'un peuple qui souffre, oú il serait bon pour lui de changer de climat."* Desdunes, *Nos Hommes*, p. 152.

174. Blassingame, *Black New Orleans*, p. 75. On Thierry's dissatisfaction with Sidney Thezan, see succession of Camille Thierry, Second District Court, Parish of Orleans, No 38,009, CCR, NOPL, especially testimony of A Brieugne and letters from Thierry to Thezan that were entered into evidence. See also succession of Sidney Thezan, Second District Court, Parish of New Orleans, No. 37,326, CCR, NOPL. Several of Thezan's friendships—including those with Thierry and Francis Dumas (Joseph Dumas's son)—seemed to turn sour as a result. There is some indication that Thezan's business dealings played a role in his death, which may have been a suicide. The nearly illegible handwriting of the person who recorded his succession proceedings obscures much of this drama.

175. See especially "Mariquita la Calentura," "Le général Magloire d'Hoquincourt," and "Haricot," in Camille Thierry, *Les Vagabondes: Poesies Americaines* (Paris, 1874), pp. 15–16, 47–48, 85–86, respectively.

176. See Gayarré, *Fernando De Lemos*, pp. 44–48. For an account of Mariquita as a "half-crazed negress," see H. Garland Dupre, "Fernando de Lemos," *Proceedings*, Louisiana Historical Society, March 1906, p. 29.

177. *"Pauvre, pauvre Mariquita! . . . / Que m'avais-tu fait, vieille femme? / Avais-tu jété dans mon âme / Les tristesses de l'avenir?"* Thierry, "Mariquita la Calentura," p. 15 [author's translation].

178. *"Et lá, fatigue, mais sublime, / chercher dans ta pensée intime / quelque plan nouveau, surhumain, / pour la lutte lendemain."* Thierry, "Abd-el-Kader," in ibid., p. 31 [author's translation].

179. *"L'exil, ami, je le redoute, / Mais dois-je rester ici? . . . Non!" "Courage! Il est une autre rive."* Thierry, "La chanson de l'exilé," in ibid., p. 41 [author's translation].

180. The exile "[authorizes] by diversion," in the words of Glissant, "the necessary return to the point where our problems lay in wait for us." Glissant and Dash, *Caribbean Discourse*, p. 25.

181. See succession of Joseph Dumas, Civil District Court, Parish of Orleans, No. 211, CCR, NOPL, (December 1880), testimony of P. Alcée Dumas, p. 16. One of the key concerns of his succession was whether Dumas was born in Louisiana, Canada, or France. As other native proprietors had to do, Dumas may have been taking his "oath of allegiance" to the U.S. government. A non-U.S. birth also would have voided his citizenship and perhaps put his New Orleans property in jeopardy.

182. Colonel N. U. Daniels quoted in Joseph T. Wilson, *The Black Phalanx: A History of the Negro Soldiers of the United States in the Wars of 1775–1812, 1861–65* (Hartford, Conn.: American Publishing Company, 1888), p. 211.

183. Bell, *Revolution, Romanticism*, p. 263.

184. 1910 Census, Roll T624_524, p. 6B, district 205; 1930 Census, Roll 811, p. 26B, district 231. Cecilia Lacroix is listed as white, her father hailing from France or Louisiana and her mother from New York or Ireland, depending on the year.

185. I thank Emily Landau for alerting me to former Lacroix holdings that became brothels in the late nineteenth century.

186. On Storyville, see Long, *Great Southern Babylon*, and Rose, *Storyville.*

4. Establishing Propriety in the City of Sin

1. George Washington Cable, "Madame Delphine," *Old Creole Days: A Story of Creole Life* (Gretna, La.: Pelican Publishing Co., [1879] 1997), p. 20.

2. Ibid., p. 23.

3. Ibid., p. 28.

4. For an example of masquerade in literature, see George Washington Cable, *The Grandissimes: A Story of Creole Life* (New York: Penguin Books, 1988), chap. 1. See Monique Guillory, "Some Enchanted Evening of the Auction Block: The Cultural Legacy of the New Orleans Quadroon Balls" (Ph.D. dissertation, New York University, 1999), pp. 142–147 on legislative efforts against masked balls.

5. Loren Schweninger, "Property Owning Free African-American Women in the South, 1800–1870," in Darlene Clark Hine, Wilma King, and Linda Reed, eds., *We Specialize in the Wholly Impossible: A Reader in Black Women's History* (Brooklyn, N.Y.: Carlson Publishing, 1995), pp. 253–279; see chart on p. 269. In Louisiana, 427 black women held property worth more than $1,500,000 in 1850. Virginia ranked a distant second with 234 black women owning $25,600 worth of property. See also David C. Rankin, "The Forgotten People: Free People of Color in New Orleans, 1850–1870" (Ph.D. dissertation, Johns Hopkins University, 1976), pp. 115–121. On antebellum black businesswomen, see Juliet E. K. Walker, *The History of Black Business in America: Capitalism, Race, Entrepreneurship* (New York: Macmillan, 1998), pp. 127–149.

6. See Vernon V. Palmer, *The Louisiana Civilian Experience: Critiques of Codification in a Mixed Jurisdiction* (Durham, N.C.: Carolina Academic Press, 2005), especially pp. 3–18; Ferdinand Stone, "The Law with a Difference and How it Came About," in Hodding Carter, ed., *The Past as Prelude: New Orleans, 1718–1968* (New Orleans: Tulane University, 1968), pp. 42–70.

7. Virginia R. Domínguez, *White by Definition: Social Classification in Creole Louisiana* (New Brunswick, N.J.: Rutgers University Press, 1986), chap. 3, especially pp. 62–79. This echoes Michael Grossberg's claim regarding the stigma of "bastardy" in the United States more generally in the first half of the nineteenth century. See Michael Grossberg, *Governing the Hearth: Law and the Family in Nineteenth-Century America* (Chapel Hill: University of North Carolina Press, 1985), pp. 196–233. Louisiana, following a civil law tradition, had a relatively benign stance on white bastards. After the implementation of the Civil Code of 1825, children of color were explicitly barred from the terms under which white bastards could achieve legitimacy. For both white children and children of color born out of wedlock, the category of "natural" child further commuted the stigma attached to illegitimacy.

8. Cable, "Madame Delphine," p. 3.

9. Ibid.

10. I am thinking of a model akin to Linda Kerber's "republican mother." See Linda K. Kerber, *Women of the Republic: Intellect and Ideology in Revolutionary America* (Chapel Hill: University of North Carolina Press, 1980). For people of African descent who aspired to American citizenship and middle-class status, women's propriety and ability to serve as models for children was especially urgent. See Michele Mitchell, *Righteous Propagation: African Americans and the Politics of Racial Destiny after Reconstruction* (Chapel Hill: University of North Carolina Press, 2004).

11. John Blassingame, *Black New Orleans, 1860–1880* (Chicago: University of Chicago Press, 1973), pp. 57, 128–129, and Caryn Cossé Bell, *Revolution, Romanticism and the Afro-Creole Protest Tradition* (Baton Rouge: Louisiana State University Press), especially chaps. 4 and 5, emphasize the experience of men.

12. Military service has been a dominant theme of Creole of color historiography from the beginning, buttressing the claims of free people of color to the rights and privileges of citizenship. See Kimberly Hanger's *Bounded Lives, Bounded Places: Free Black Society in Colonial New Orleans, 1789–1803* (Durham, N.C.: Duke University Press, 1997), chap. 4, pp. 109–135 for a discussion of the free *pardo* and *moreno* militia during the Spanish colonial period. See Roland McConnell, *Negro Troops in Antebellum Louisiana: A History of the Battalion of Free Men of Color* (Baton Rouge: Louisiana State University Press, 1968), pp. 15–33, and Rodolphe Lucien Desdunes, *Our People and Our History*, trans. Sister Dorothea Olga McCants (Baton Rouge: Louisiana State University Press, 1973), pp. 5–6 for a discussion of Creole of color participation in the War of 1812. See also Mary F. Berry, "Negro Troops in Blue and Gray: The Louisiana Native Guards, 1861–1863" *LaHist* 8, no. 2 (Spring 1967), pp. 185–190, and Roland McConnell, "Louisiana's Black Military History," in Robert MacDonald, John R. Kemp, and Edward F. Haas, eds., *Louisiana's Black Heritage* (New Orleans: Louisiana State Museum, 1979), pp. 49–53. Military service was a springboard to political leadership and thus more historiographic representation. See David C. Rankin, "The Origins of Black Leadership in New Orleans during Reconstruction," *Journal of Southern History* 40 (1974); also Charles Vincent, *Black Legislators in Louisiana during Reconstruction* (Baton Rouge: Louisiana State University Press, 1976).

13. Desdunes, *Our People*, p. 98.

14. I allude to the operation of a "separate spheres" ideology, well aware of scholarly revision to the idea of a hard distinction between the public (male) realm of work and politics and the private (female) realm of the home and family life. I follow Nancy Cott's identification of Christian and spiritual reform as an arena of public concern for women that both grows out of separate sphere ideology and also potentially subverts the strict consignment of women to the domestic sphere. See Nancy F. Cott, *The Bonds of Womanhood: "Woman's Sphere" in New England, 1780–1835* (New Haven, Conn.: Yale University Press, 1977); see especially "Preface to the Second Edition: Then and Since," (1997) for an assessment of the "cult of domesticity" from a later vantage point. On separate spheres, see Linda Kerber, "Separate Spheres, Female Worlds, Women's Place: The Rhetoric of Women's History," *Journal of American History* 75 (1988), pp. 9–39. On the notion of domesticity for nonwhite women, see Carla L. Peterson, *Doers of the Word: African-American Women Speakers and Writers in the North (1830–1880)* (New York: Oxford University Press, 1995), pp. 14–17. On the cult of domesticity in the social

outlook of the black "aspiring class" of Desdunes's day, see Mitchell, *Righteous Propagation.* For a discussion of the activism of free women of color in another Catholic context, see Diane Batts Morrow, *Persons of Color and Religious at the Same Time: The Oblate Sisters of Providence, 1828–1860* (Chapel Hill: University of North Carolina Press, 2002).

15. See Bell, *Revolution, Romanticism,* pp. 125–134, especially pp. 133–134 on her resistance to *plaçage.* See also Sister Audrey Marie Detiege's pamphlet, "Henriette Delille, Free Woman of Color: Foundress of the Sisters of the Holy Family" (New Orleans, 1976) in Howard-Tilton Memorial Library, and Sister Mary Francis Borgia Hart, *Violets in the King's Garden: A History of the Sisters of the Holy Family of New Orleans* (unpublished paper, 1976), Louisiana Division, Earl K. Long Library, University of New Orleans. Emily Clark and Virginia Meacham Gould speak of the "symbolic conjoining of a French priest and a pious woman of African descent" in Emily Clark and Virginia Meacham Gould, "The Feminine Face of Afro-Catholicism in New Orleans, 1727–1852," *William and Mary Quarterly* 59, no. 2 (2002). Delille is being considered for sainthood. See Mary Bernard Deggs, Virginia Meacham Gould, and Charles E. Nolan, *No Cross, No Crown: Black Nuns in Nineteenth-Century New Orleans* (Bloomington: Indiana University Press, 2001), p. xxi.

16. Hart, "Violets in the King's Garden," p. 21. See also Tracy Fessenden, "The Sisters of the Holy Family and the Veil of Race," *Religion and American Culture* 10, no. 2 (2000), pp. 187–188 on the veil as a metaphor of concealment, allowing the Sisters of the Holy Family wide latitude for their various activities. The Sisters also function as a veil for Desdunes, shielding the legacy of his Creoles from the "sin" associated with the quadroon balls.

17. See will of Veuve Bernard Couvent, November 12, 1832, filed before L. P. Caire, July 10, 1837, New Orleans Probate Records, Louisiana Division, New Orleans Public Library. See *Prospectus de l'Institution Catholique des Orphelins dans l'Indigence* (New Orleans, 1847), Special Collections, Howard-Tilton Memorial Library, Tulane University.

18. On Madame Couvent, see Desdunes, "Mme Bernard Couvent," trans. Raoul Pérez, *Negro History Bulletin,* 8 (October 1943); Charles B. Roussève, *The Negro in Louisiana: Aspects of His History and His Literature* (New York: Xavier University Press, 1937), pp. 43–44; Caryn Cossé Bell, *Revolution, Romanticism, and the Afro-Creole Protest Tradition in Louisiana, 1718–1868* (Baton Rouge: Louisiana State University Press, 1997), pp. 123–125; and McCants's notes to Desdunes, *Our People,* pp. 101–107.

19. Desdunes, *Our People,* p. 102.

20. Ibid., pp. 101–102. The fact that the Couvents did not have any children of their own may contribute to their obscurity for him.

21. Ibid., p. 107.

22. Al Rose, *Storyville, New Orleans, Being an Authentic Illustrated Account of the Notorious Red-Light District* (Tuscaloosa: University of Alabama Press, 1974), pp. 131, 208. For a more recent appraisal of Storyville, see Alecia P. Long, *The Great Southern Babylon: Sex, Race, and Respectability in New Orleans, 1865–1920* (Baton Rouge: Louisiana State University Press, 2004).

23. Joseph G. Tregle, Jr., "Early New Orleans Society: A Reappraisal," *The Journal of Southern History* 18, no. 1 (1952), p. 34. For the most part, Tregle reads the opinions of the popular press of New Orleans regarding free people of color as "fact."

24. Ibid., p. 35. "Housewife" seems a somewhat incongruous term—more applicable to the 1950s than the 1820s.

25. Joseph Roach and Monique Guillory liken the "attendants" of quadroon balls to "fancy girls," nearly white slave women who commanded a high price at auction. See Monique Guillory, "Under One Roof: The Sins and Sanctity of the New Orleans Quadroon Balls," in Judith Jackson Fossett and Jeffrey A. Tucker, eds., *Race-Consciousness: African-American Studies for the New Century* (New York: New York University Press, 1997), pp. 69–75, and Joseph Roach, *Cities of the Dead: Circum-Atlantic Performance* (New York: Columbia University Press, 1996), pp. 2–3.

26. Bernhard and Heinrich Luden, *Travels through North America, during the Years 1825 and 1826* (Philadelphia: Carey, Lea & Carey, 1828), Vol. II, p. 62.

27. See Guillory, "Under One Roof," pp. 67–92. Also see Fessenden, "Sisters of the Holy Family," pp. 204–205.

28. See Sterling Brown, "Negro Characters as Seen by White Authors," *Journal of Negro Education* 2 (1933), pp. 179–203; reprinted in James A. Emanuel and Theodore L. Gross, eds., *Dark Symphony: Negro Literature in America* (New York: Free Press, 1968), pp. 139–171. On the overdetermination of the tragic mulatta figure by the political and moral strictures of abolitionist literature and by a context of legalized racial binarism, see Werner Sollors, *Neither Black nor White*, pp. 224–245. On the "mulattarroon" as a conceptual space from which to challenge either-or categories of race, gender, and morality, see Jennifer DeVere Brody, "The Yankee Hugging the Creole: Reading Dion Boucicault's *The Octoroon*," in Sybil Kein, ed. *Creole: The History and Legacy of Louisiana's Free People of Color* (Baton Rouge: Louisiana State University Press, 2000), p. 116, and Hortense Spillers, "Notes on an Alternative Model: Neither/Nor," in Elizabeth Meese and Alice Parker, eds., *The Difference Within: Feminism and Critical Theory* (Philadelphia: J. Benjamins, 1989). On the multivalence of the stereotype, see Sollors's "excursus" on the tragic mulatto in *Neither Black nor White*, pp. 221–245. For a more limited and less flexible assessment, see Anna Shannon Elfenbein, *Women on the Color Line: Evolving Stereotypes and the Writings of George Washington Cable, Grace King, Kate Chopin* (Charlottesville: University Press of Virginia, 1989), pp. 1–24. There is a masculine tragic mulatto as well—that mixed-race man who is too intelligent for his position and thus becomes rebellious and potentially revolutionary, as for example Stowe's character George Harris in *Uncle Tom's Cabin.*

29. Cable, " 'Tite Poulette," *Old Creole Days*, p. 243. Anonymous letter sent to Cable, reprinted in the introduction to "Madame Delphine" in the 1893 edition of *Old Creole Days* and quoted in Monique Guillory, "Some Enchanted Evening of the Auction Block," p. 161. Cable continued to insist that 'Tite Poulette was a white girl assumed to be a person of color. See Elfenbein, *Women on the Color Line*, p. 46.

30. See Sollors, *Neither Black nor White*, pp. 142–161 for a discussion of racial calculus.

31. See Brown, "Negro Characters as Seen by White Authors," pp. 162–163.

32. On the destabilizing effects of beauty, see Plato, *Phaedrus;* Dante, *Vita Nuova.* On the distinction between the beautiful and the sublime, see Edmund Burke, *A Philosophical Enquiry into the Origin of Our Ideas of the Sublime and Beautiful*, and Immanuel Kant, *Observations on the Feeling of the Beautiful and Sublime.* On critics of beauty, see Elaine Scarry, *On Beauty and Being Just* (Princeton, N.J.: Princeton University Press, 1999), pp. 71–86.

33. The hair of the mixed-race woman has often functioned as a symbol of her exotic beauty, as, for example, in Charles Baudelaire's poem "La Chevelure (Her Hair)" in *Fleurs du Mal/Flowers of Evil.*

34. See Walter Johnson, "The Slave Trader, the White Slave, and the Politics of Racial Determination in the 1850s," *The Journal of American History* 87, no. 1 (2000), p. 26, fn. 28 on the number of interlocutors who inquired of the beauty of a mixed-race woman whose case he was researching.

35. John H. B. Latrobe, *Southern Travels: Journal of H. B. Latrobe, 1834* (New Orleans: Historic New Orleans Collection, 1986), p. 78.

36. Albert Emile Fossier, *New Orleans, the Glamour Period, 1800–1840: A History of the Conflicts of Nationalities, Languages, Religious, Morals, Cultures, Laws, Politics and Economics during the Formative Period of New Orleans* (New Orleans: Pelican, 1957), p. 356.

37. Desdunes, *Our People,* p. 98.

38. Gustave de Beaumont, "Forward," *Marie, or Slavery in the United States: A Novel of Jacksonian America,* trans. Barbara Chapman (Stanford, Calif.: Stanford University Press, 1958), p. 5.

39. Lydia Maria Child, *Romance of the Republic* (Boston: Tincknor and Fields, 1867), p. 5.

40. William Faulkner, *Absalom, Absalom!* (New York: Vintage, [1936] 1986), p. 91.

41. Lydia Maria Child, *An Appeal in Favor of That Class of Americans Called Africans* (Boston, 1833) p. 210. On Child, see Carolyn L. Karcher, *The First Woman in the Republic: A Cultural Biography of Lydia Maria Child* (Durham, N.C.: Duke University Press, 1994).

42. Lydia Maria Child, "The Quadroons," in *Liberty Bell* (Boston: The American Anti-Slavery Fair, 1842), pp. 116–117. The story appeared on pp. 115–141.

43. Ibid., p. 118.

44. Ibid., p. 120.

45. Ibid., p. 141. For a similarly tragic tale, see Cassy's story in Harriet Beecher Stowe, *Uncle Tom's Cabin; or, Life among the Lowly* (New York: Norton, [1852] 1994), pp. 310–319.

46. Alice Dunbar-Nelson, "Sister Josepha" from *The Goodness of St. Rocque and Other Stories* reprinted in Gloria T. Hull, ed., *The Works of Alice-Dunbar Nelson, Volume 1* (New York: Oxford University Press, 1988), pp. 160; 161; 172; 170–171.

47. Alice Dunbar-Nelson, "Odalie" from *The Goodness of St. Rocque and Other Stories* reprinted in Hull, ed., *Works of Alice Dunbar-Nelson,* pp. 186; 189.

48. On Dunbar-Nelson's conflicts over traditional women's roles and skin color in her personal life and fiction, see Violet Harrington Bryan, *The Myth of New Orleans in Literature: Dialogues of Race and Gender* (Knoxville: University of Tennessee Press, 1993), pp. 62–78. Other women writers wrestling with gender expectations include Kate Chopin, Charlotte Perkins Gilman, and white racial purist Grace King. See Bryan, pp. 42–78 on King, Chopin, and Dunbar-Nelson. See Elfenbein, *Women on the Color Line,* pp. 74–116 on King and pp. 117–157 on Chopin. For a general discussion, see Jennifer Fleissner, *Women, Compulsion, Modernity: The Moment of American Naturalism* (Chicago: University of Chicago Press, 2004).

49. The physical representations of Creole of color women as near white (or impossibly white) and disarmingly beautiful need not accompany progressive politics in

order to provoke a meditation on female purity and chastity and to outline the ethical dimensions of life under institutions such as *plaçage* for all involved. In *Absalom, Absalom!* (p. 93), William Faulkner describes them as "not whores. Not even courtesans." Instead, they are the "only true chaste women, not to say virgins in America." This characterization accompanies Quentin Compson's initiation into white southern manhood, and the morality of the mixed-race woman emerges as a central concern for a local, regional, and national identity. See also Bryan, *Myth of New Orleans*, pp. 79–94.

50. Gustave de Beaumont, *Marie, or, Slavery in the United States: A Novel of Jacksonian America* (Baltimore: Johns Hopkins University Press, 1999), pp. 40–41.

51. Armand Lanusse, "Un Mariage de Conscience," in *L'Album Littéraire: Journal des Jeunes Gens Amateurs de Litterature*, August 1843, pp. 130–137, CRC, ARC.

52. Alice Dunbar-Nelson, "By the Bayou St. John" from *The Goodness of St. Rocque and Other Stories* reprinted in Hull, ed. *The Works of Alice Dunbar Nelson*, pp. 92; 91.

53. See Karen Halttunen, *Confidence Men and Painted Women: A Study of Middle-Class Culture in America, 1830–1870* (New Haven, Conn.: Yale University Press, 1982), p. xv. As in New Orleans' culture, "masking" plays an important role in the social processes Halttunen describes; see pp. 153–190.

54. George Washington Cable, *The Grandissimes: A Story of Creole Life* (New York: Penguin Books, 1988), p. 57. Alternatively, Anna Elfenbein reads Cable's Palmyre as a reinscription of the tragic mulatta stereotype in *Women on the Color Line*, pp. 53–65. Grace King has a more despicable character of the same name in her short story "Madrilène; or, the Festival of the Dead"; see Bryan, *Myth of New Orleans*, pp. 51–53.

55. Cable, *Grandissimes*, p. 60.

56. Ibid.

57. Ludwig von Reizenstein and Steven W. Rowan, *The Mysteries of New Orleans* (Baltimore: Johns Hopkins University Press, 2002), p. 11.

58. Ibid., p. 14. As the name Lucy Wilson and the ethnicity of Emil demonstrate, Reizenstein, in the German-language press, is much more attuned to the multiplicity of cultures and linguistic communities comprising New Orleans in the 1850s. His cultural categories don't sort into "French Creole" and "American" categories as do Gayarré's, for example. Even so, the form of *plaçage* practiced here mirrors closely that of the more paradigmatic French Creole practice.

59. Ibid., pp. 533–534.

60. Most histories of Creoles of color invite such a reading even if they do not fully follow up on its implications. For example, the anthology of Creole of color poetry *Les Cenelles* (1845) forms a touchstone of Creole of color history even though, for most historians, literary themes serve as a mere reflection of the historical context. See Desdunes, *Our People*, pp. 25–59; Roussève, *Negro in Louisiana*, pp. 67–91; Bell, *Revolution, Romanticism*, pp. 114–123.

61. Edward Larocque Tinker, *Creole City: Its Past and Its People* (New York: Longman's Green and Co., 1953), p. 268. Régine Latortue and Gleason R.W. Adams, "Preface," *Les Cenelles: A Collection of Poems of Creole Writers of the Early Nineteenth Century* (Boston: G.K. Hall, 1979), pp. xiii–xiv compare the poetry unfavorably with both the Haitian poetry of Coriolan Ardouin and Ignace Nau and

the antislavery poetry of (black and white) Anglo-Americans, most notably Emerson, Whittier, Longfellow, and George Moses Horton. Alternatively, see Charles Hamilton Good, "The First American Negro Literary Movement," *Opportunity*, March 1932, 76–79.

62. George Washington Cable, *Creole Slave Songs [and] the Dance in Congo Square* (New York: 1886), p. 808. Cable also interprets the meanings of "cocodrie" and "trouloulou."

63. Cable, *The Grandissimes*, chap. 50, p. 291; Tregle, "Early New Orleans Society," p. 36.

64. Recent scholars have viewed *Les Cenelles* in a more favorable light. Floyd Cheung, "*Les Cenelles* and Quadroon Balls: 'Hidden Transcripts' of Resistance and Domination in New Orleans, 1803–1845," *Southern Literary Journal* 29, no. 2 (1997) employs James C. Scott's concept of "hidden transcripts" to the poems and places the Creole of color poets squarely within the blues tradition of primarily anglophone black Americans, a reading that I find difficult to support since *Les Cenelles* does not formally alter the tradition of French Romantic poetry. Thomas Haddox reads *Les Cenelles* in light of the religious experiences of Creoles of color within the Catholic Church. Thomas F. Haddox, *Fears and Fascinations: Representing Catholicism in the American South* (New York: Fordham University Press, 2005), and Thomas F. Haddox, "The 'Nous' of Southern Catholic Quadroons: Racial, Ethnic, and Religious Identity in Les Cenelles," *American Literature* 73, no. 4 (2001).

65. Haddox, *Fears and Fascinations*, p. 26.

66. Cheung underestimates the conservatism of the poets' view of women as their "symbolic prize." Cheung, "*Les Cenelles* and Quadroon Balls," p. 7. For his part, Haddox presents a compelling argument for Lanusse and other poets' ambivalent stance toward *plaçage* (especially considering the status of some of them as children of such arrangements) in "Southern Catholic Quadroons," p. 772.

67. Nicholas Osmond, "Rhetoric and Self-Expression in Romantic Poetry" in John Cruickshank, ed., *French Literature and Its Background* 4 (Oxford: Oxford University Press, 1969), pp. 24–26. See also Naomi Judith Andrews, *Socialism's Muse: Gender in the Intellectual Landscape of French Romantic Socialism* (Lanham, Md.: Lexington Books, 2006). The Romantic gesture to nature also reinforces the conservatism of the *Cenelles* poets. See, for example, L. Boise, "Au Printemps" (To Spring*)*, *Les Cenelles*, p. 109.

68. " '*Je vais, à ta prière, / Veiller sur te chemin: / Tu seras sur la terre / A l'ombre de ma main.*' " Questy, "Vision," in *Les Cenelles*, p. 35.

69. Sibylle Fischer, *Modernity Disavowed: Haiti and the Cultures of Slavery in the Age of Revolution* (Durham, N.C.: Duke University Press, 2004), pp.77–106 describes the poetry and politics of the nineteenth-century Cuban poet, mulatto Plácido, in terms of a psychology of the abject. Plácido continually disrupts generic conventions. While the *Cenelles* poets occupy a similar abject position with respect to the United States, they seem to find more positive use for French Romanticism. The barber Joseph Beaumont discussed in chapter 2 comes closer to Plácido in spirit.

70. A. K. Thorlby, "The Concept of Romanticism," in *French Literature* 4, p. 6.

71. See Tinker, *Creole City*, pp. 268–270. Tinker calls *Les Cenelles* "a significant milestone in the Negro's long road toward education" (p. 270). Armand Lanusse, *Creole Voices: Poems in French by Free Men of Color First published in 1845*, ed. Edward

Maceo Coleman (Washington, D.C.: Associated Publishers, 1945) is compiled and presented in this vein; see Coleman's "Preface," pp. xvii–xx. See Bell, *Revolution, Romanticism*, pp. 93–94, 105–123 for a discussion of the harsh publishing climate.

72. Armand Lanusse, dedication page, *Les Cenelles*, p. 7.

73. *"Veuillez bien accepter ces modestes Cenelles / Que notre coeur vous offre avec sincérité; / Q'un seul regard tombé de vos chastes prunelles / Leur tienne lieu de gloire et d'immortalité."* Ibid., p. 7.

74. Lanusse, "Introduction," *Les Cenelles* p. 14. The poets are aware that nations need monuments, particularly of the chaste and virtuous feminine kind. See Andrews, *Socialism's Muse*, pp. 117–137; Lynn Avery Hunt, *The Family Romance of the French Revolution* (Berkeley: University of California Press, 1992), pp. 82–84.

75. Lanusse, "Introduction," *Les Cenelles*, p. 14. *"Ces poètes y verront comment pensaient ceux qui les auront précédés, et comment on chantait ces charmantes Louisianaises dont la beauté, les grâces et l'amabilité se conserveront sans doute dans toute leur merveilleuse pureté chez celles qui leur succèderont."*

76. Cheung, "*Les Cenelles* and Quadroon Balls," p. 7.

77. *"Mircé si vous m'aimez, si vous êtes ma soeur, / Ecoutez les conseils d'un frère qui vous aime; / Je suis un pauvre diable, et puis un grand parleur, / Puis autre chose encor, vous le savez vous-même!"* Questy "Causerie (Chat)," in *Les Cenelles*, p. 165.

78. *"Pensez un seul instant à l'amour qui nous lie . . . / Eh! Savez-vous, Mircé, ma pauvre chère enfant, / Ce que c'est que cet homme? et vous savez, cruelle, / Ce qui se passe en moi, dans ma coeur, dans mon sang, / Lorsqu'à mes yeux l'un d'eux quelquefois se révèle!)"* Ibid.

79. Sollors, *Neither Black nor White*, pp. 286–287, 324–335 on the proximity of themes of incest and miscegenation in a wide variety of literary, legal, and psychological material. On the "tension between the condemnation of incest and the commitment to patriarchy" and the reluctance of southern judges to disturb hierarchies within the household, see Peter Winthrop Bardaglio, *Reconstructing the Household: Families, Sex, and the Law in the Nineteenth-Century South* (Chapel Hill: University of North Carolina Press, 1995), pp. 39–48. Hunt, *The Family Romance of the French Revolution*, pp. 84–85 notes that in the French revolutionary imagination, incest is sometimes understood as a virtue. I am not claiming that Creole of color men and women were *actually* involved in incestuous relationships. I am merely suggesting that the prevalence of this theme in their imaginative work opens up a space for addressing the viability of their vulnerable group.

80. Louisiana Civil Code of 1825, Book I, Title IV, Chapter 2, Articles 95, 96, and 97. Bertram Wyatt-Brown, *Southern Honor: Ethics and Behavior in the Old South* (New York: Oxford University Press, 1982), pp. 312–314 cites a nineteenth-century Mississippi intellectual: "The same law which forbids consanguineous amalgamation forbids ethnical amalgamation. Both are incestuous. Amalgamation is incest" (p. 312).

81. On the French nation as a nation of metaphorical siblings, or more precisely as a nation of orphans and, thus, potential siblings, see Marc Shell's discussion of Racine and Rousseau in *Children of the Earth: Literature, Politics, and Nationhood* (New York: Oxford University Press, 1992), pp. 124–128 and 142–145, respectively.

82. Bo . . . rs, "L'Orphelin des Tombeaux," in *Les Cenelles*, pp. 70–74. Haddox focuses on the father-son dynamic of this poem to the exclusion of the spectral sister-lover-mother figure. Haddox, *Fears and Fascinations*, pp. 21–23.

83. According to Virginia Domínguez, marriages between adopted siblings was sometimes permitted. See Domínguez, *White by Definition*, p. 59.

84. *"Tenir entre mes bras cette vierge timide! / M'enivrer du regard de sa prunelle humide!"* Bo . . . rs, "L'Orphelin des Tombeaux," p. 73.

85. See Mitchell, *Righteous Propagation*, for an exploration of this dynamic in the context of a turn-of-the-nineteenth-century black nationalist ethos and eugenics-inflected concern with "racial destiny." Shell also points to a codification of rigid gender roles and misogyny within discourses of universal equality, noting that if the *fraternité* were to include women, it could not propagate itself without resorting to incest. *Children of the Earth*, pp. 183–184.

86. Auguste Populus, "A Mon Ami, P.," in *Les Cenelles*, p. 53.

87. Armand Lanusse, "Le Dépit (Spite)," in ibid., p. 37.

88. *"Que vous fuyez l'hymen et son sévère code / Pour en adopter un moins sûr mais plus commode."* Lanusse, "A Elora," in ibid., p. 101.

89. *"En vain dans des palais déployant leur splendeur, / Voudraient-elles cacher cette horrible laideur, / Celles qui vivent même au sein de la richesse, / Font lire sur leurs fronts: indignité, bassesse!"* Ibid., p. 102.

90. *"c'est cette vertu qui s'oppose sans crainte / Aux volontés d'un coeur impudique et vénal, / Cette douce candeur, cette innocence empreinte / Sur ton front virginal."* M. F. Liotau, "A Ida" (To Ida), in *Les Cenelles*, p. 134.

91. *"Vierge, c'est toujours toi qui vis dans ma pensée, / Qui fais battre mon coeur, / Qui ramènes l'espoir en mon âme affaissée / Sous le faix du malheur.)"* P. Dalcour, "Le Chant d'Amour (Love Song)," in ibid., p. 21.

92. See P. Dalcour's "La Foi, l'Espérance, et la Charité (Faith, Hope, and Charity)" and "Acrostiche (Acrostic)," in ibid., pp. 103; 120.

93. *"Parfois confiante au serment / Que je lui fais d'être constant, / Je vois faiblir simple fillette; / Je ris . . . toujours fidèle aux plaisirs, / Mon feu dure autant que mes désirs; / Je vole à nouvelle amourette."* Valcour B., "L'Heureux Pélerin (The Happy Wanderer)," in ibid., p. 24; P. Dalcour, "Caractère (Character)," in ibid., p. 172.

94. *"Par nos jeunes danseurs ta main est réclamée, / Va voltiger, Emma, je te suivrai des yeux.— / L'archet a résonné!!"* Lanusse, "Le Jeune Fille au Bal," in ibid., p. 122.

95. *"Tes sens sont accablés et tu valses encore!— / Oh! qu'a donc cette enfant? Elle est folle, mon Dieu! . . . "* Ibid.

96. *"Près de cette bougie où la douleur l'enchaîne, / Il périt consumé, faute d'attention." "Viens, viens auprès de moi te reposer un peu."* Ibid.

97. Cheung indicates that the values of Catholic Church and those of Creoles of color overlap. See Cheung, "*Les Cenelles* and Quadroon Balls," p. 13. Haddox cautious against this easy elision, suggesting that Creoles of color adopt the forms of Catholic ritual and alter the content to fit their needs as a politically and economically compromised population. See Haddox, *Fears and Fascinations*, p. 26. I bridge these positions, arguing that the *Cenelles* poets ultimately put great stock in the religious and moral virtue of their women in spite of the ambiguities presented by *plaçage*. These are tensions that Catholics have been wrestling with for a long time. See Shell, *Children of the Earth*, pp. 139–142.

98. *"Eglise Saint-Louis, vieux temple, reliquaire, / Te voilà maintenant désert et solitaire! / Ceux qui furent commis ici bas à tes soins, / Du tabernacle saint méprisant les besoins, / Ailleurs ont etrainé la phalange chrétienne."* M. F. Litou, "Une Impression (An Impression)," in *Les Cenelles*, p. 162.

99. Armand Lanusse, "Un Mariage de Conscience," in *L'Album Littéraire: Journal des Jeunes Gens Amateurs de Litterature*, August 1843, pp. 130–137, CRC, ARC.

100. *"Que ne puis-je, Pasteur—Quoi donc?* placer *ma fille . . ."* Armand Lanusse, "Epigramme (Epigram)," in *Les Cenelles*, p. 48.

101. *"Cette enfant, sans sa mère, eût peut-être été sage. / Epouse, à son époux elle eût donné ses soins; / Mère, de ses enfants prévenu les besoins."* Lanusse, "A Elora (To Elora)," in *Les Cenelles*, p. 100.

102. *"Pour que l'on abusât de sa simplicité, / Se mère, sans remords, fut de complicité."* Ibid.

103. Ann Laura Stoler describes a similar bias against native mothers of mixed-race children in French colonial societies in *Carnal Knowledge and Imperial Power: Race and the Intimate in Colonial Rule* (Berkeley: University of California Press, 2002), pp. 87–96. Hunt, *The Family Romance of the French Revolution*, pp. 89–123, discusses the ambivalent iconography of motherhood in the context of the French Revolution.

104. Harriet Martineau, *Retrospect of Western Travel*, vol. 2 (London: Saunders and Ottley, 1838), p. 142. The most famous version of the story is that of George Washington Cable, "The Haunted House in Royal Street, 1831–82" in *Strange True Stories of Louisiana* (Gretna, La.: Pelican, [1889] 1994), pp. 192–219. For a tourist-driven account, see *Picayune's Guide to New Orleans* (New Orleans, 1904). Christopher Benfey relates the story of the haunted house in *Degas in New Orleans: Encounters in the Creole World of Kate Chopin and George Washington Cable* (Berkeley: University of California Press, 1997), pp. 31–46. Madame Lalaurie has taken the brunt of the blame for these atrocities, having been characterized by the local papers as a "demon in the shape of a woman" (*Bee*, April 11, 1834). However, the condition of some of the victims seemed to suggest their subjection to the various surgical experiments of her husband, Doctor Lalaurie. More research needs to be done on the Lalaurie affair, but medical experimentation on enslaved people was common in the antebellum United States. See Harriet A. Washington, *Medical Apartheid: The Dark History of Medical Experimentation on Black Americans from Colonial Times to the Present* (New York: Doubleday, 2006).

105. Grace Elizabeth King, *Creole Families of New Orleans* (New York: The Macmillan Company, 1921), p. 374.

106. On the early provenance of the Macarty family, see ibid., pp. 368–382. Augustin Macarty served as mayor of New Orleans from 1815 to 1820. See Domínguez, *White by Definition*, p. 279, appendix. Augustin Macarty is listed as "August."

107. Charles Gayarré, "The Creoles of History and the Creoles of Romance, a Lecture Delivered in the Hall of Tulane University" (New Orleans, 1885), p. 15.

108. King, *Creole Families*, p. 373.

109. Ibid., p. 368.

110. Grace Elizabeth King, *New Orleans: The Place and the People* (New York: The Macmillan Company, 1904), p. 348.

111. Stanley Clisby Arthur, *Old Families of Louisiana* (New Orleans: Harmanson Publishers, 1931), p. 333.

112. Grace Elizabeth King, "Madrilène, or the Festival of the Dead," *HNMM*, 81, no. 486 (1890), pp. 879–880.

113. Guillory, "Some Enchanted Evening," pp. 65–71; Rankin, "Forgotten People," pp. 81–105. It is important to underscore that these were not common-

law marriages. Louisiana was a mixed jurisdiction where such matters were adjudicated with reference to a civil code. Also, common-law marriages were common elsewhere in the United States in the antebellum period and enjoyed protection under the law. See Grossberg, *Governing the Hearth*, pp. 73–75. See also Lawrence Meir Friedman, *A History of American Law* (New York: Simon & Schuster, 1985), pp. 17–24. Grossberg also points out that courtship was fair game for common-law judges, and throughout the early nineteenth century, judges ruled against parties for "broken promises" of engagement (Grossberg, chap. 2).

114. John S. Whitaker, *Sketches of Life and Character in Louisiana*, quoted in Tregle, "Early New Orleans Society," p. 26.

115. Charles Olivier in *Nicholas Theodore Macarty v. Eulalie Mandeville, f.w.c.* No. 626, 3 La. Ann. 239 June, 1847, LSCR, UNO.

116. *Macarty v. Mandeville*, witness Marigny.

117. Ibid.

118. Kimberly S. Hanger, *Bounded Lives, Bounded Places: Free Black Society in Colonial New Orleans, 1769–1803* (Durham, N.C.: Duke University Press, 1997); on interracial and interstatus relationships in the French colonial period, see Jennifer M. Spear, "Colonial Intimacies: Legislating Sex in French Louisiana," *The William and Mary Quarterly* 60, no. 1 (2003), pp. 75–98.

119. *Macarty v. Mandeville*, witness Blanchard.

120. *Macarty v. Mandeville*, witness Charbenet.

121. Walker, *History of Black Business*, p. 132.

122. *Macarty v. Mandeville*, witness Bermudez.

123. *Badillo et al. v. Francisco Tio*, No. 1745, 6 La. Ann. 129, January 1851, LSCR. UNO.

124. Business partners Jean Baptiste Azereto and Francisco Cheti devised a scheme to donate Azereto's property to his mistress of color, Eugenie Glesseau, while he was still living. Azereto effectively "laundered" a series of real estate transactions to Glesseau and their minor children through Cheti. See The Friends of the Cabildo, *New Orleans Architecture, Vol. IV: The Creole Faubourgs* (Gretna, La.: Pelican, 1974), p. 29. Paul F. Lachance, "The Formation of a Three-Caste Society: Evidence from Wills in Antebellum New Orleans," *Social Science History* 18, no. 2 (1994) surveys various methods of circumventing the inheritance laws, including appointing a testamentary executor. The overall claim of Lachance's article, that interracial unions seem to have declined over the course of the antebellum period, does not seem to follow from his method of looking at wills of white men to determine the extent of their financial obligations to women of color. It fails to address men who had no money or property, those who made no will, those who did not care to provide for a "wife" of color, and those who found other ways to secure their legacies to their families of color.

125. I am not aware of any kinship relation between Victoria Wiltz and Victor Wiltz of chapter 1, but I would not be surprised if one existed.

126. *Louisiana Civil Code*, 1825, Article 227.

127. *Badillo v. Tio*, judge's opinion.

128. See Shael Herman, *The Louisiana Civil Code: A European Legacy for the United States* (n.p.: Louisiana Bar Foundation, 1993) on joint property and family property. See also David W. Grunning, *Family and Obligation: The Louisiana Code of Persons* (Austin, Tex.: Butterworth Legal Publishers, 1990). Frederick William

Swain, Jr., and Kateryn Venturatos Lorio, *Louisiana Successions and Donations: Materials and Cases* (Austin, Tex.: Butterworth Legal Publishers, 1985), pp. 1–9, gives an overview of family law in relation to successions.

129. Domínguez, *White by Definition*, pp. 72–89. Article 1468 had drastic effects for slave mistresses who inherited their freedom from their masters-lovers. They were technically considered to be "immovables" under Louisiana law, often valued at more than 10 percent of movables. Therefore, they were rarely able to "inherit" themselves. See also Judith Kelleher Schafer, *Slavery, the Civil Law, and the Supreme Court of Louisiana* (Baton Rouge: Louisiana State University Press, 1994), pp. 180–200.

130. See Hanger, *Bounded Lives*, pp. 92–102 on laws governing interracial marriage during the Spanish period. See Carl A. Brasseaux, "The Moral Climate of French Colonial Louisiana, 1699–1763," *Louisiana History* 27 (1986) on the French period.

131. On Père Antoine's reputation, see Guillory, "Some Enchanted Evening," pp. 89–90; Bell, *Revolution, Romanticism*, pp. 66–72; Fessenden, "Sisters of the Holy Family," pp. 198–199.

132. Gayarré, "Creoles of History," p. 11.

133. *Badillo v. Tio*, judgment.

134. *Macarty v. Mandeville*, judgment.

135. *Badillo v. Tio*, judgment.

136. Louisiana Civil Code, Article 226.

137. *Badillo v. Tio*, concurring opinion.

138. See Wyatt-Brown, *Southern Honor*. See also Orlando Patterson, *Slavery and Social Death: A Comparative Study* (Cambridge, Mass.: Harvard University Press, 1982), pp. 10–14 describing the master-slave relationship as one hinging on honor.

139. A slave society such as the American South, and antebellum Louisiana in particular, may have maintained patriarchal family arrangements long after Victorian social codes encouraged more egalitarian and affectionate sentiments in what Michael Grossberg calls the "republican household" elsewhere in the nineteenth-century United States. See Bardaglio, *Reconstructing the Household*, pp. 23–34 on southern patriarchy, and Grossberg, *Governing the Hearth*, pp. 4–9 on the "republican family." See Steven M. Stowe, *Intimacy and Power in the Old South: Ritual in the Lives of the Planters* (Baltimore: Johns Hopkins University Press, 1987) on how formalized ritual culture and expectations shaped southern sentiment and feeling. The limitations patriarchy seems to have imposed on practices of affection and sentiment may have been one of the reasons for the sentiment attaching to *plaçage*, a domestic arrangement without the burdens of marriage.

140. *Badillo v. Tio*, judgment.

141. *Macarty v. Mandeville*, judgment.

142. Ibid.

143. Ibid.

144. See succession of Eulalie Mandeville, Second District Court, New Orleans #1,999, 1849, probate records, NOPL.

145. See testimony of François Victor, succession of Céleste Perrault, Second District Court of New Orleans #11,255, 1859–1860, probate records, NOPL. See also testimony of François Lacroix. Paris seems to have offered this shelter for other free women of color. Marie Boulard, for example, married her white husband John Dupré in 1835, and they managed a business and properties in New Orleans

from France. See my "Mon Cher Dupré: Managing the Legitimacy of Love and Property in the Antebellum Black Francophone Atlantic," unpublished paper presented at Southern Association of Women Historians Annual Conference, June 2003, Athens, Ga., and Bernhard, *Travels*, p. 62.

146. See Schafer, *Slavery, the Civil Law*, pp. 250–288 on the Louisiana Supreme Court's overwhelming tendency under Judge George Eustis (chief justice from 1846–1853) to rule on behalf of enslaved people who journeyed to free states or countries. See Paul Finkelman, *An Imperfect Union: Slavery, Federalism, and Comity* (Chapel Hill: University of North Carolina Press, 1981), especially pp. 206–216, on the question of slave law and comity among states.

147. Schafer, *Slavery, the Civil Law*, pp. 276–280. In *Eugénie, f.w.c., v. Préval* (1847) and *Arsène, alias Cora, f.w.c., v. Pignéguy* (1847), both plaintiffs won their freedom after returning to Louisiana from France. However, in *Couvent, f.m.c., v. Guesnard* (1859), the minor Mary did not receive her freedom because she had resided in France after the passage of the 1846 Louisiana law, and in *Liza v. Puissant* (1852), the court applied the terms of the 1846 law retroactively, again denying Liza and her seven children freedom.

5. Choosing to Become Black

1. B. F. Butler to Edwin M. Stanton, Secretary of War, May 25, 1862, BPOC, Vol. I, p. 520.

2. *NOPD*, April 21, 1861.

3. *NODP*, April 23, 1861.

4. *NODD*, April 28, 1861.

5. Loren Schweninger, "Ante-bellum Free Persons of Color in Postbellum Louisiana," *LaHist* 30 no. 4 (Fall 1989), pp. 348–357.

6. *NODP*, April 27, 1861, and April 28, 1861. See James G. Hollandsworth, *The Louisiana Native Guards: The Black Military Experience during the Civil War* (Baton Rouge: Louisiana State University Press, 1995), pp. 1–11 on the service of the Native Guards to the Confederacy.

7. *WOR*, Series IV, Vol. I, p. 869. See *WOR*, Vol. XV, p. 557 for Governor Moore's orders to reinstate the Native Guards on March 24. See Hollandsworth, *Native Guards*, chap. 1, especially pp. 6–11 on the mutual ambivalence of the state militia and the Native Guards.

8. Kate Mason Rowland and Mrs. Morris L. Croxall, eds., *Journal of Julia LeGrand: New Orleans 1862–1863* (Richmond: Everett Waddey Co., 1911), p. 40.

9. Benjamin Butler, *Butler's Book* (Boston, 1892), pp. 373–374.

10. See Butler to Stanton, August 14, 1862, BPOC, Vol. II, p. 192. Butler's testimony before the American Freedman's Inquiry Commission, November 28, 1863, cited in Hollandsworth, *Native Guards*, p. 16.

11. *WOR*, Series III, Vol. 2, pp. 436–438.

12. See Roland McConnell, *Negro Troops in Antebellum Louisiana: A History of the Battalion of Free Men of Color* (Baton Rouge: Louisiana State University Press, 1968); Christopher Leslie Brown and Philip D. Morgan, *Arming Slaves: From Classical Times to the Modern Age* (New Haven, Conn.: Yale University Press, 2006).

13. See United States Adjutant-General's Office, *Official Army Register of the Volunteer Force of the United States Army for the Year 1861, '62, '63, '64, '65* (Washington,

D.C.: Government Printing Office, 1865), Part 8, pp. 246–248, 246–254 for lists of colored Louisiana regiments.

14. On Port Hudson, see Hollandsworth, *Native Guards*, pp. 48–69, and William F. Messner, *Freedmen and the Ideology of Free Labor: Louisiana 1862–1865* (Lafayette: University of Southwestern Louisiana Press, 1978), pp. 132–137; George H. Hepworth, *The Whip, Hoe, and Sword; or, the Gulf-Department in '63* (Boston: Walker Wise and Co., 1864), pp. 187–194.

15. Banks is supposed to have said that there "were no Union dead in that sector" of the battlefield where Cailloux had been stuck down. Hollandsworth, *Native Guards*, pp. 59–60. Stephen J. Ochs, *A Black Patriot and a White Priest: André Cailloux and Claude Paschal Maistre in Civil War New Orleans* (Baton Rouge: Louisiana State University Press, 2000), pp. 2–5; *HWM*, August 29, 1863; Rodolphe Lucien Desdunes, *Our People and Our History*, trans. Sister Dorothea Olga McCants (Baton Rouge: Louisiana State University Press, 1973), p. 125.

16. See Ira Berlin, Joseph P. Reidy, and Leslie S. Rowland, *The Black Military Experience: Freedom, a Documentary History of Emancipation, 1861–1867*, Ser. 2 (Cambridge: Cambridge University Press, 1982), pp. 321–328.

17. *New Orleans Tribune*, October 31, December 5, 1865. On the Friends of Universal Suffrage, see Charles Vincent, *Black Legislators in Louisiana during Reconstruction* (Baton Rouge: Louisiana State University Press, 1976), pp. 38–40.

18. See Peyton McCrary, *Abraham Lincoln and Reconstruction: The Louisiana Experiment* (Princeton, N.J.: Princeton University Press, 1978); Ted Tunnell, *Crucible of Reconstruction: War, Radicalism, and Race in Louisiana, 1862–1877* (Baton Rouge: Louisiana State University Press, 1984), pp. 1–7.

19. On 1866 riot, see Gilles Vandal, *The New Orleans Riot of 1866: Anatomy of a Tragedy* (Lafayette: Center for Louisiana Studies, University of Southwestern Louisiana, 1983); James G. Hollandsworth, *An Absolute Massacre: The New Orleans Race Riot of July 30, 1866* (Baton Rouge: Louisiana State University Press, 2001); James Keith Hogue, *Uncivil War: Five New Orleans Street Battles and the Rise and Fall of Radical Reconstruction* (Baton Rouge: Louisiana State University Press, 2006), pp. 31–52; Eric Foner, *Reconstruction: America's Unfinished Revolution, 1863–1877* (New York: Harper and Row, 1988), pp. 261–264.

20. See Vincent, *Black Legislators*, chap. 1, and Hollandsworth, *Native Guards*, pp. 104–116.

21. Butler's testimony before the American Freedman's Inquiry Commission, Boston, May 1, 1863, in Berlin, Reidy, and Rowland, *The Black Military Experience*, p. 313.

22. *The Liberator*, April 15, 1864.

23. HR, Testimony, 124–126.

24. Critical accounts include Mary F. Berry, "Negro Troops in Blue and Gray: The Louisiana Native Guards, 1861–1863," *LaHist* 8, no. 2 (1967); David C. Rankin, "The Origins of Black Leadership in New Orleans during Reconstruction," *JSH* 40 (1974). More positive assessments include Manoj K. and Joseph Reidy Joshi, "'To Come Forward and Aid in Putting Down This Unholy Rebellion': The Officers of Louisiana's Free Black Native Guard during the Civil War Era," *Southern Studies* 21, no. 3 (1982), and Caryn Cossé Bell, "Un Chimère: The Freedmen's Bureau in Creole New Orleans," in Paul A. Cimbala and Randall M. Miller, eds., *The Freedmen's Bureau and Reconstruction* (New York: Fordham Univer-

sity Press, 1999). Hollandsworth, *Native Guards*, offers a relatively balanced account. For an evocative poetic portrayal of the Native Guard, see Natasha D. Trethewey, *Native Guard* (Boston: Houghton Mifflin, 2006).

25. Caroline Senter, "Creole Poets on the Verge of a Nation," in Sybil Kein, *Creole: The History and Legacy of Louisiana's Free People of Color* (Baton Rouge: Louisiana State University Press, 2000), pp. 276-294 on the *Tribune*'s political project as an acknowledgement of the constructed nature of race. However, Senter fails to link this project to a larger strategy of black American political leadership. See Eddie S. Glaude, *Exodus! Religion, Race, and Nation in Early Nineteenth-Century Black America* (Chicago: University of Chicago Press, 2000). See also Evelyn Brooks Higginbotham, "African-American Women's History and the Metalanguage of Race," *Signs* 17, no. 2 (1992) on how race has been a discourse of both oppression and liberation.

26. This is true whether the scholar is sympathetic to the Creole of color leadership or not. See Rankin, "Origins of Black Leadership"; Caryn Cossé Bell, *Revolution, Romanticism, and the Afro-Creole Protest Tradition in Louisiana, 1718–1868* (Baton Rouge: Louisiana State University Press, 1997); Caryn Cossé Bell and Joseph Logsdon, "The Americanization of Black New Orleans, 1850–1900," in Arnold R. Hirsch and Joseph Logsdon, *Creole New Orleans: Race and Americanization* (Baton Rouge: Louisiana State University Press, 1992); and Senter, "Creole Poets on the Verge."

27. Glaude, *Exodus!* pp. 160–167. See Cornel West, *Prophesy Deliverance! An Afro-American Revolutionary Christianity* (Philadelphia: Westminster Press, 1982), especially pp. 15–24 on the sources of Afro-American thought, pp. 27–36 on the particular predicament of blacks in the United States, and pp. 69–91 on the variety of African American responses to racism.

28. See Edward Larocque Tinker, *Les Écrits des Langue Française en Louisiane* (Paris: Librarie Ancienne Honoré Champion, 1931) and *Bibliography of the French Newspapers and Periodicals of Louisiana* (Worcester, Mass.: Proceedings of the American Antiquarian Society, 1942) on the *Tribune* and *l'Union.*

29. See *l'Union*, *"Un Mot sur la Population de Couleur,"* October 1, 1862.

30. See Desdunes, *Our People*, pp. 133–138, and Charles B. Roussève, *The Negro in Louisiana: Aspects of His History and His Literature* (New York: Xavier University Press, 1937). See Maurice Agulhon, *Les Quarante-Huitards:* [*Documents*] (Paris: Gallimard/Julliard, 1975) on the French revolutionaries of 1848.

31. These groups included the National Brotherhood Union, the National Equal Rights League, the Freedmen's Aid Association, and the Friends of Universal Suffrage.

32. On the influence of the *Tribune* in Washington, see Jean-Charles Houzeau and David C. Rankin, *My Passage at the New Orleans Tribune: A Memoir of the Civil War Era* (Baton Rouge: Louisiana State University Press, 1984), pp. 84–88. See also Foner, *Reconstruction*, p. 66. A *Tribune* article, "Is There Any Justice for the Black?" in French on December 15, 1864, and in English on December 20, 1864, was quoted extensively in Congress by Pennsylvania Representative William D. Kelley.

33. In Philadelphia, Houzeau was working on a monograph comparing the mental faculties of humans and other animals from data gathered in Texas and Mexico. See Rankin, "Introduction," Houzeau and Rankin, *My Passage*, pp. 8–11.

Houzeau wrote his memoir in 1868 and published in as a pamphlet in 1870 under the title "Mon Passage à la Tribune de la Nouvelle Orléans." Two years later it was published in two parts in as "Le Journal Noir, aux États Unis, de 1863 à 1870," *Revue de Belgique*, 9 (May 15 and June 15, 1872). Also see his obituary in *Ciel et Terre: Revue Populaire d'Astronomie, de Météorologie et de Physique du Globe*, IX–X (1888–1889).

34. Houzeau and Rankin, *My Passage*, p. 83.

35. Ibid. For another example of passing as black in wartime New Orleans, see Bliss Broyard, *One Drop: My Father's Hidden Life—A Story of Race and Family Secrets* (New York: Little, Brown and Company, 2007), pp. 189-204.

36. Joseph R. Roach, *Cities of the Dead: Circum-Atlantic Performance* (New York: Columbia University Press, 1996), pp. 211–215.

37. Two works dealing directly with the *Tribune*—William P. Conner, "Reconstruction Rebels: The *New Orleans Tribune* in Post-War Louisiana," *LaHist* 21, no. 2 (1980), pp. 159–181, and Finnean Leavens, "*L'Union* and the *New Orleans Tribune* and Louisiana Reconstruction" (masters thesis, Louisiana State University, 1966)—see the newspapers in this "vanguard" paradigm.

38. Benedict R. O'G Anderson, *Imagined Communities: Reflections on the Origin and Spread of Nationalism* (London: Verso, 1991) on the role of print media in marking calendrical time and promoting the nationalist programs of Creoles in the Americas. Following Brent Edwards's modification of Anderson's work, I emphasize the *Tribune* editors' insistence on "translation" and "reciprocity" in mediating among multiple constituencies. See Brent Hayes Edwards, *The Practice of Diaspora: Literature, Translation, and the Rise of Black Internationalism* (Cambridge, Mass.: Harvard University Press, 2003), pp. 115–118. Drawing on Edwards's terminology, I would characterize the political project of the *Tribune* as a particularly well-articulated "joint" within diasporic politics. See Edwards, "The Uses of *Diaspora*," *Social Text* 66, vol. 19, no. 1, (Spring 2001), p. 77.

39. Houzeau and Rankin, *My Passage*, pp. 80–81.

40. See Rankin, "Introduction," p. 27. Also see John W. Blassingame, *Black New Orleans, 1860–1880* (Chicago: University of Chicago Press, 1973), p. 77, and Roussève, *Negro in Louisiana*, p. 119.

41. Rankin, "Introduction," pp. 30–31.

42. Roussève, *Negro in Louisiana*, p. 119.

43. *L'Union*, November 1, 1862, French. (All citations from the French section of *L'Union* and *la Tribune* are the author's translation.)

44. *Tribune*, July 21, 1864, English. Among the Republican newspapers of the South and in the nation, the *Tribune* was one of the most radical. Richard H. Abbott and John W. Quist, *For Free Press and Equal Rights: Republican Newspapers in the Reconstruction South* (Athens: University of Georgia Press, 2004).

45. *L'Union*, November 8, 1862, French; *l'Union*, November 1, 1862, French.

46. Though their rhetoric seems to suggest that the editors undertook a Habermasian project concerned with the development of a rational public sphere of sustained and enlightened debate among citizens, the journalists shaped their vision to confront the irrationality of racism. See Evelyn Brooks Higginbotham, *Righteous Discontent: The Women's Movement in the Black Baptist Church, 1880–1920* (Cambridge, Mass.: Harvard University Press, 1993), pp. 7–13. On African American journalists, see the essays collected in Todd Vogel, *The Black Press: New Literary and Historical Essays* (New Brunswick, N.J.: Rutgers University Press, 2001).

47. Desdunes, *Our People*, p. 67.

48. W. E. B. Du Bois, Henry Louis Gates, and Terri Hume Oliver, *The Souls of Black Folk: Authoritative Text, Contexts, Criticism* (New York: W.W. Norton, 1999), pp. 11, 17.

49. Benjamin F. Butler to his wife, July 28, 1862, in BPOC, p. 117.

50. Blassingame, *Black New Orleans*, p. 221, table 1.

51. James Parton, *General Butler in New Orleans* (New York: Mason Brothers, 1864), p. 492.

52. See David C. Rankin, "The Impact of the Civil War on the Free Colored Community of New Orleans," *Perspectives in American History* XI (1977–1978), p. 401. The population of free people of color included out-of-town free blacks as well.

53. Benjamin Butler came up with the term *contraband* to characterize the fugitive slaves who fled to his camps. See Du Bois, *Souls*, pp. 17–33.

54. *Tribune*, February 4, 1865, English.

55. "La Population de Couleur et les Yankees," *Tribune*, August 4, 1864, French.

56. BPOC, Vol. 1, p. 520.

57. Testimony of Butler before the Freedman's Inquiry Commission, November 28, 1863, quoted in Hollandsworth, *Native Guards*, pp. 26–27.

58. *Tribune*, July 2, 1867.

59. John William De Forest and James H. Croushore, *A Volunteer's Adventures; a Union Captain's Record of the Civil War* (New Haven, Conn.: Yale University Press, 1946), pp. 47–48. On attitudes of white women to occupying forces see Mary P. Ryan, *Women in Public: Between Banners and Ballots, 1825–1880* (Baltimore: Johns Hopkins University Press, 1990), pp. 143–147.

60. *Tribune*, December 6, 1864, English.

61. *Tribune*, September 6, 1864, English.

62. *Tribune*, December 6, 7, 1864, English.

63. *Tribune*, February 1, 1865, English.

64. Houzeau and Rankin, *My Passage*, pp. 81–82.

65. *Tribune*, August 13, 1864, English.

66. *Tribune*, July 2, 1867, English. This explanation anticipates Carter G. Woodson's thesis that black slaveholders were more benevolent than whites and tended to be related to those they enslaved. See Carter G. Woodson, "Free Negro Owners of Slaves in the United States," *Journal of Negro History* 9 (1924).

67. *Tribune*, March 31, 1865, English (my emphasis).

68. On the alternative plantation plan, see *Tribune*, January 28, 29, 1865. Also see advertisements for meetings of the Freedmen's Aid Association throughout February, March, and April 1865. See Conner, "Reconstruction Rebels," pp. 159–180 for an account of the *Tribune's* involvement with the Freedmen's Aid Association. In this effort, the *Tribune* staff spoke to the overlapping concerns of race and labor in Republican politics; see Heather Cox Richardson, *The Death of Reconstruction: Race, Labor, and Politics in the Post-Civil War North, 1865–1901* (Cambridge, Mass.: Harvard University Press, 2001).

69. The *Tribune* group and its allies resurrected some of the teachings of socialist Charles Fourier, the French utopian socialist who had influenced a number of communities in the United States in the 1840s and early 1850s. On Fourierism

in general, see Carl Guarneri, *The Utopian Alternative: Fourierism in Nineteenth-Century America* (Ithaca, N.Y.: Cornell University Press, 1991). See Bell, *Revolution, Romanticism*, pp. 168–171 on the Louisiana context. Messner, *Freedmen*, pp. 109–111 discusses some of the goals of the Freedman's Aid Association without getting into its socialist principles. On *Tribune* ally Thomas J. Durant and his socialist ideals, see Joseph G. Tregle, Jr., "Thomas J. Durant, Utopian Socialism and the Failure of Presidential Reconstruction in Louisiana," *JSH* 45, no. 4 (1979), pp. 487–512. *Tribune*, January 28, 1865, English.

70. *Tribune*, January 28, 1865, English. The plan was utopian because, like earlier Fourierist experiments, it declined to regard class conflict as inevitable. The association's alternative plantation scheme attempted as well to reconcile the communal logic of socialism with individualist impulses of democracy in the construction of the harmonious society.

71. The utopian vision of the Freedmen's Aid Association may have also conflicted in important respects with grassroots rural challenges to the Banks plan. See Rebecca Scott, *Degrees of Freedom: Louisiana and Cuba after Slavery* (Cambridge, Mass.: Belknap Press of Harvard University Press, 2005), pp. 30–60, and John C. Rodrigue, *Reconstruction in the Cane Fields: From Slavery to Free Labor in Louisiana's Sugar Parishes, 1862–1880* (Baton Rouge: Louisiana State University Press, 2001). The *Tribune's* coverage of the Black Convention of January 1864 suggested a dissonance between urban and rural delegates, admonishing city-dwelling leaders not to "fall behind" those from the parishes who often expressed more radical views than their urban counterparts. See *Tribune*, January 14, 1865, English.

72. Tunnell, *Crucible of Reconstruction*, p. 78; *New Orleans Times*, November 6, 1863.

73. See Foner, *Reconstruction*, p. 49; Caryn Cossé Bell and Joseph Logsdon, "The Americanization of Black New Orleans," in Hirsch and Logsdon, *Creole New Orleans*, pp. 224–229.

74. Petition printed in *Boston Liberator*, April 1, 1864. Original petition dated January 5, 1864.

75. Abraham Lincoln to Michael Hahn, March 13, 1864, in Ray P. Basler, ed., *The Collected Works of Abraham Lincoln* (New Brunswick, N.J.: Rutgers University Press, 1953–1955), Vol. VII, p. 243.

76. *The Liberator*, April 1, 1864. Original postscript signed March 10, 1864.

77. Acts 17:26. Cited in *The Liberator*, April 15, 1864.

78. Bell and Logsdon, "The Americanization of Black New Orleans," pp. 226–227.

79. Abbott and Quist, *For Free Press;* Tunnell, *Crucible of Reconstruction*, pp. 66–91; Conner, "Reconstruction Rebels"; Bell and Logsdon, "The Americanization of Black New Orleans."

80. On the memorialist controversy, see Tunnell, *Crucible of Reconstruction*, pp. 80–83; McCrary, *Abraham Lincoln and Reconstruction*, pp. 207–210, 232–233, 293–302; James M. McPherson, *The Struggle for Equality: Abolitionists and the Negro in the Civil War and Reconstruction* (Princeton, N.J.: Princeton University Press, 1964), pp. 308–310.

81. *Tribune*, February 5, 1865, English.

82. *Tribune*, February 14, 1865, English.

83. *Tribune*, February 3, 1865, French.

84. *Tribune*, February 3, 1865, French.

85. Rothman, *Slave Country: American Expansion and the Origins of the Deep South* (Cambridge, Mass.: Harvard University Press, 2005), p. 105.

86. On Ogé's role in Haitian history, see C. L. R. James, *The Black Jacobins: Toussaint L'Ouverture and the San Domingo Revolution* (New York: Vintage Books, 1989), pp. 68–76; Carolyn E. Fick, *The Making of Haiti: The Saint Domingue Revolution from Below* (Knoxville: University of Tennessee Press, 1990), pp. 82–84; and Aimé Césaire, *Toussaint Louverture; La Révolution Française et le Problème Colonial* (Paris: Présence Africaine, 1962), pp. 90–103. On Ogé's death, see James, p. 74.

87. Vincent Ogé, "Motion to the Assembly of Colonists, 1789," in Lynn Avery Hunt, *The French Revolution and Human Rights: A Brief Documentary History* (Boston: Bedford Books of St. Martin's Press, 1996), p. 103.

88. Anna Brickhouse, *Transamerican Literary Relations and the Nineteenth-Century Public Sphere* (Cambridge: Cambridge University Press, 2004), p. 231 on Faubert's use of Haiti's racial politics to critique those of the United States. On the regime of Boyer, see Ludwell Lee Montague, *Haiti and the United States, 1714–1958* (Durham, N.C.: Duke University Press, 1940), pp. 16–23, and Michel-Rolph Trouillot, *Haiti, State against Nation: The Origins and Legacy of Duvalierism* (New York: Monthly Review Press, 1990), pp. 50–56.

89. Julia Griffiths, *Autographs for Freedom* (Boston: J. P. Jewett, 1853), p. 60. See William Wells Brown, *The Black Man: His Antecedents, His Genius, and His Achievements* (New York, 1863), pp. 223–227 on Vashon.

90. See Chris Bongie, *Islands and Exiles: The Creole Identities of Post/Colonial Literature* (Stanford, Calif.: Stanford University Press, 1998), pp. 268–269 on the "mulatto vision" of history. On Ogé as a symbol of mulatto elitism, see Leon Francis Hoffman, "Haitian Sensibility," in A. James Arnold, Julio Rodríguez-Luis, and J. Michael Dash, *A History of Literature in the Caribbean* (Amsterdam and Philadelphia: J. Benjamins, 1994), Vol. 1, p. 368.

91. See Mary P. Ryan, *Civic Wars: Democracy and Public Life in the American City during the Nineteenth Century* (Berkeley: University of California Press, 1997), pp. 262–263 on the National Equal Rights League. (Ryan mistakenly refers to the *New Orleans Tribune* as the *Louisiana Tribune.*)

92. *Tribune*, April 30, 1865. See also "*Le Droit d'Aller et de Venir* (The Right to Come and Go)," *Tribune*, December 2, 1864, French.

93. Vandal, *New Orleans Riot;* Hollandsworth, *Absolute Massacre;* Hogue, *Uncivil War.*

94. Ryan, *Civil Wars*, pp. 260–271.

95. Testimony of Charles Gibbons, *HR*, p. 124. W. E. B. Du Bois, *Black Reconstruction in America* (New York: Russell and Russell, 1964), p. 465 on Monroe's membership in the Southern Cross.

96. Capla testimony, *HR*, p. 120.

97. Gibbons testimony, *HR*, p. 124.

98. Fish testimony, *HR*, p. 37.

99. Houzeau to his parents, July 31, 1866, in Hossam Elkhadem, Anenette Félix, and Liliane Wellens-De Donder, eds., *Jean-Charles Houzeau, Lettres Adressées des États-Unis à Sa Famille*, (Bruxelles: Centre National d'Histoire des Sciences, 1994), p. 395. Author's translation of "*l'affreux massacre de noirs et de leurs partisans.*"

100. *HR*, p. 12.

101. Hollandsworth, p. 107; Bertonneau testimony, August 4, 1866, *House Executive Documents*, Thirty-Ninth Congress, Second Session, Vol. 10, no. 68, p. 130.

102. See Hogue, *Uncivil War*, pp. 48–52 on comparisons of the riot to the Fort Pillow Massacre of black POWs by Confederate troops.

103. Gibbons testimony, *HR*, p. 124.

104. Jourdan testimony, *HR*, p. 206; also see Capla testimony, *HR*, p. 121.

105. John Sidney testimony, *HR*, p. 401.

106. Capla testimony, *HR*, p. 120.

107. Coroners report, *HR*, p. 12.

108. Boquille testimony, *HR*, p. 384. See also excerpts from a speech given on the first anniversary of the massacre by Rufus Waples, Esq., quoted in Emily Hazen Reed, *Life of A. P. Dostie; or, the Conflict of New Orleans* (New York: W. P. Tomlinson, 1868), p. 338.

109. *Tribune*, December 29, 1864, English.

110. Ellie Nower Schamber, *The Artist as Politician: The Relationship between the Art and the Politics of the French Romantics* (Lanham, Md.: University Press of America, 1984). On "politics, fantasy, and identity" in the 1848 revolution, see Jerrold E. Seigel, *Bohemian Paris: Culture, Politics, and the Boundaries of Bourgeois Life, 1830–1930* (New York: Viking, 1986), pp. 59–96; on how the phenomenon cut across national boundaries, see Adam Zamoyski, *Holy Madness: Romantics, Patriots, and Revolutionaries, 1776–1871* (New York: Viking, 2000); on how gender intersects with the Romantic political and social project, see Naomi Judith Andrews, *Socialism's Muse: Gender in the Intellectual Landscape of French Romantic Socialism* (Lanham, Md.: Lexington Books, 2006).

111. Paul Gilroy, *The Black Atlantic: Modernity and Double Consciousness* (Cambridge, Mass.: Harvard University Press, 1993), p. 197. See also M. Jacqui Alexander, *Pedagogies of Crossing: Meditations on Feminism, Sexual Politics, Memory, and the Sacred* (Durham, N.C.: Duke University Press, 2005). I argue that the antebellum blacks' experience of the terrors of enslavement and racism charged their activism with a tragic sense of the limits of America's promise, a mindset that their white allies did not usually share. Occasionally whites—most notably, John Brown—transcended these barriers of perspective. See John Stauffer, *The Black Hearts of Men: Radical Abolitionists and the Transformation of Race* (Cambridge, Mass.: Harvard University Press, 2002), pp. 1–7.

112. Rodolphe Lucien Desdunes, "A Few Words to Dr. Du Bois, with Malice towards None," New Orleans, 1907.

113. Desdunes was undoubtedly exasperated by the polarization of early-twentieth-century African American politics around the approaches of W. E. B. Du Bois and Booker T. Washington—both articulating versions of an American grain of pragmatism. On Washington, see Houston A. Baker, *Turning South Again: Re-Thinking Modernism/Re-Reading Booker T* (Durham, N.C.: Duke University Press, 2001). On Du Bois as pragmatist, see Cornel West, *The American Evasion of Philosophy: A Genealogy of Pragmatism* (Madison, Wisc.: University of Wisconsin Press, 1989).

114. Desdunes, *Our People*, p. xxvii.

115. Orlando Patterson, *Slavery and Social Death: A Comparative Study* (Cambridge, Mass.: Harvard University Press, 1982), pp. 5–9.

116. *Tribune*, August 4, 1864, French.

117. On the shift in voice over the nineteenth century, see William L. Andrews, "The Representation of Slavery and the Rise of Afro-American Literary Realism,

1865–1920," in Deborah E. McDowell and Arnold Rampersad, *Slavery and the Literary Imagination* (Baltimore: Johns Hopkins University Press, 1989), pp. 62–80. On romanticism and slave narratives, see Andrews's "The 1850s: The First Afro-American Literary Renaissance," in William L. Andrews, *Literary Romanticism in America* (Baton Rouge: Louisiana State University Press, 1981), pp. 38–60 and *To Tell a Free Story: The First Century of Afro-American Autobiography, 1760–1865* (Urbana: University of Illinois Press, 1986).

118. See Eric Sundquist's discussion of Douglass's *My Bondage and My Freedom* in Eric J. Sundquist, *To Wake the Nations: Race in the Making of American Literature* (Cambridge, Mass.: Harvard University Press, 1993), pp. 82–112. On Washington and the post-bellum narrative, see Andrews, "Rise of Afro-American Literary Realism."

119. *Tribune*, July 19, 1864, English.

120. On "voyeurism" in abolitionist activism, see Saidiya V. Hartman, *Scenes of Subjection: Terror, Slavery, and Self-Making in Nineteenth-Century America* (New York: Oxford University Press, 1997), pp. 17–23.

121. The story of Martin's life is from Brown, *The Black Man*, pp. 241–245 and from Martin's *Autobiography of Sella Martin*, in John W. Blassingame, *Slave Testimony: Two Centuries of Letters, Speeches, Interviews, and Autobiographies* (Baton Rouge: Louisiana State University Press, 1976), pp. 702–735.

122. See *The Liberator*, December 9, 1859.

123. "Return of the Reverend J. Sella Martin to the United States," letter from W. Farmer, London, March 18, 1864. Printed in *The Liberator*, April 8, 1864.

124. *The Liberator*, April 8, 1864.

125. *Autobiography of Sella Martin*, p. 703.

126. Ibid., p. 731.

127. On John Brown's international renown, see Seymour Drescher, "Servile Insurrection and John Brown's Body in Europe," *JAH* 80, no. 2 (1993), pp. 499–524.

128. *Tribune*, May 14, 1865, French. The story continued until the end of July. See Werner Sollors, *Beyond Ethnicity: Consent and Descent in American Culture* (New York: Oxford University Press, 1986), pp. 50–55 on importance of Christ imagery to American identity.

129. *Tribune*, October 23, 1864, French. See Tunnell, *Crucible of Reconstruction*, p. 80 on the episode. The Smith Bill was swiftly voted down. See also *Tribune* (French) November 10, 12, and 16, 1864.

130. See "Colored Politics," *Tribune*, May 29, 1867, and "Has the Time Come to Drop the Words 'White' and 'Black'?" *Tribune*, June 18, 1867, English.

131. Phrase from Judith Butler, *Bodies That Matter: On the Discursive Limits of "Sex"* (New York: Routledge, 1993).

132. In the early twenty-first century, Barack Obama has made a similar argument in his 2008 campaign for the presidency of the United States. See especially his speech "A More Perfect Union," delivered March 18, 2008, Philadelphia, Pa.

133. See Stauffer, *Black Hearts of Men*, and Richard S. Newman, *The Transformation of American Abolitionism: Fighting Slavery in the Early Republic* (Chapel Hill: University of North Carolina Press, 2002).

134. In describing the language of the *Tribune* as "nationalist," I echo Eddie Glaude's "ironic" description of an African American political tradition using "nation language." Those who enter into this discourse do not generally seek separate territory for African Americans, but rather believe in the political efficacy of

claiming and pursuing a positively defined racial solidarity. See Glaude, *Exodus!* pp. 162–163. See also Tommie Shelby, *We Who Are Dark: The Philosophical Foundations of Black Solidarity* (Cambridge, Mass.: Belknap, 2005). John Ernest, *Liberation Historiography: African American Writers and the Challenge of History, 1794–1861* (Chapel Hill: University of North Carolina Press, 2004), p. 57 describes the black imagined community as a "nation within the nation."

135. Glaude, *Exodus!* p. 113.

136. On black public and institutional culture, see ibid.; Elizabeth McHenry, *Forgotten Readers: Recovering the Lost History of African American Literary Societies* (Durham, N.C.: Duke University Press, 2002); the essays in Vogel, *Black Press;* Ernest, *Liberation Historiography;* Joanna Brooks, *American Lazarus: Religion and the Rise of African-American and Native American Literatures* (Oxford and New York: Oxford University Press, 2003).

137. Mary Bernard Deggs, Virginia Meacham Gould, and Charles E. Nolan, *No Cross, No Crown: Black Nuns in Nineteenth-Century New Orleans* (Bloomington: Indiana University Press, 2001).

138. On Maistre, his radical stewardship of free people of color, slaves, and poor immigrants, his friendship with Cailloux, and Callioux's funeral, see Ochs, *Black Patriot.* See also Desdunes, *Our People*, pp. 121–122 on Maistre and pp. 124–125 on Cailloux.

139. Logsdon and Bell, "The Americanization of Black New Orleans," pp. 232–236; Bell, *Revolution, Romanticism;* Roger A. Fischer, *The Segregation Struggle in Louisiana, 1862*–77 (Urbana: University of Illinois Press, 1974). On the desegregation of fraternal lodges, see *Tribune*, June 18, 23, July 25, 26, 1867, January 5, 1869. On *l'Union*'s criticism of Catholic leadership, see *l'Union* November 15, December 2, 1862, May 31, 1864.

140. I draw the distinction between the metaphysical and the exegetical from the exchange between Robert Penn Warren ("Nigger, your breed ain't metaphysical," from "Pondy Woods," 1928) and Sterling Brown ("Cracker, your breed ain't exegetical," 1973 interview). See Mark A. Sanders, "Sterling Brown and the Afro-Modern Moment," *African American Review*, Fall 1997, pp. 393–397. Penn Warren suggests the inherent inability of blacks to transcend the limits of the physical world and engage in rarefied abstract thought. Brown counters that whites lack the critical skills necessary to make intellectual sense of their own and others' historical experience. He reveals that the metaphysical yearnings of the white American depend on the permanence of black racial inferiority implied by the epithets "Nigger" and "breed." Russ Castronovo, *Necro Citizenship: Death, Eroticism, and the Public Sphere in the Nineteenth-Century United States* (Durham, N.C.: Duke University Press, 2001) makes a similar argument to Brown's in his discussion of antebellum American spiritualism.

141. See James H. Cone, *A Black Theology of Liberation* (Philadelphia: Lippincott, 1970), West, *Prophesy Deliverance! An Afro-American Revolutionary Christianity*, C. Eric Lincoln and Lawrence H. Mamiya, *The Black Church in the African American Experience* (Durham, N.C. and London: Duke University Press, 1990), Peter J. Paris, *The Social Teaching of the Black Churches* (Philadelphia: Fortress Press, 1985), Brooks, *American Lazarus*, and Glaude, *Exodus!* on black theology and black religious leadership; Mark A. Noll, *America's God: From Jonathan Edwards to Abraham Lincoln* (Oxford: Oxford University Press, 2002), pp. 417–421, and E. Brooks Ho-

lifield, *Theology in America: Christian Thought from the Age of the Puritans to the Civil War* (New Haven, Conn.: Yale University Press, 2003), pp. 306–318 on African American theology in the context of an evolving American theology.

142. Sollors, *Beyond Ethnicity*. See Sacvan Bercovitch, *The American Jeremiad* (Madison: University of Wisconsin Press, 1978) on chosen-ness. See Robert H. Abzug, *Cosmos Crumbling: American Reform and the Religious Imagination* (New York: Oxford University Press, 1994), pp. 30–57 on a rhetoric of chosen-ness in nineteenth-century American Protestantism. See Sollors, *Beyond Ethnicity*, pp. 40–65 on the centrality of Biblical typology to American identity, especially pp. 42–50 for a discussion of chosen-ness. Glaude, *Exodus!* pp. 46–53 recasts Bercovitch's frame for the African American context.

143. Glaude, *Exodus!* pp. 80–81.

144. See David W. Blight, *Race and Reunion: The Civil War in American Memory* (Cambridge, Mass.: Belknap Press of Harvard University Press, 2001), chap. 9, especially pp. 319–324 on black millennialism and the Civil War in African American memory.

145. Bell and Logsdon, "The Americanization of Black New Orleans," p. 231.

146. See George L. Ruffin Committee on Publication, John S. Rock, and William Howard Day, "Proceedings of the National Convention of Colored Men, Held in the City of Syracuse, N.Y., October 4, 5, 6, and 7, 1864; with the Bill of Wrongs and Rights, and the Address to the American People," 1864, pp. 20–21. P. B. Randolph subsequently traveled to New Orleans and challenged Creole of color leadership. Soon driven from the scene by the *Tribune* radicals, Randolph later repudiated his African heritage and joined a spiritualist "free thought" community. See Bell and Logsdon, "The Americanization of Black New Orleans," pp. 239–240.

147. Ruffin, Rock, and Day, "Proceedings of the National Convention of Colored Men," pp. 12–13.

148. *Tribune*, January 15, 1965, English.

149. *Tribune*, January 4, 1865, English.

150. *Tribune*, January 14, 1865, English.

151. *Tribune*, January 21, 1865, English.

152. Tunnell, *Crucible of Reconstruction*, pp. 86–89, attributes many of these recommendations to the middle-class elitism of Dove, McCrary, and the *Tribune* staff. Saidiya Hartman, *Scenes of Subjection*, pp. 125–163 understands these moral dictates to be part of the "encumbered freedom" of formerly enslaved people, and the *Tribune*'s Religious Department makes use of "The Freedman," one of the key instruments indoctrinating freed people into a middle-class morality. However, as Glaude points out, the elaboration of a communal moral standard is central to a political project of chosen-ness. See Glaude, *Exodus!* pp. 123–125. For a discussion of "politics of respectability" in another religious-political context, see Higginbotham, *Righteous Discontent.*

153. *Tribune*, March 9, May 7, 1865, English.

154. *Tribune*, January 31, 1865, English.

155. *Tribune*, February 1, March 9, 1865, English.

156. Psalms 68:31. On the political and religious ideology of Ethiopianism to black nationalist thought, see Albert J. Raboteau, "'Ethiopia Shall Soon Stretch Forth Her Hands': Black Destiny in Nineteenth Century America," in Albert J. Raboteau, *A Fire in the Bones: Reflections on African-American Religious History*

(Boston: Beacon Press, 1995). See Wilson J. Moses, "Assimilationist Black Nationalism, 1890–1925," in Wilson Jeremiah Moses, *The Wings of Ethiopia: Studies in African-American Life and Letters* (Ames: Iowa State University Press, 1990), pp. 95–105.

157. *Tribune,* January 31, 1865.

158. *Tribune,* June 14, 1865. On the continuing orphanage controversy and on religion as a source of division between Creoles of color and Protestant blacks, see Bell and Logsdon, "The Americanization of Black New Orleans," pp. 234–241. Also see *Tribune,* June 14, October 25, November 23, December 5, 1865; November 24, 1866; May 21, 1867.

159. See Bell, *Revolution, Romanticism,* pp. 187–221 on spiritualists as Catholic dissidents.

160. See Castronovo, *Necro Citizenship,* pp. 183–187 on Douglass's novella "The Heroic Slave" as a response to the spiritualist vogue among his friends and colleagues.

161. Henry Rey, "L'Ignorance," *l'Union,* September 27, 1862. *"C'est l'enfer vrai de l'existence, Le seul Satan de l'univers."*

162. Rey, Letter to the Editor, *l'Union,* October 18, 1862. *"Monsieur le redacteur, venez visiter notre camps . . . vous verrez croiser mille baïonnettes blanches reluisant au soleil, tenues par des mains noires, jaunes et blanches."*

163. Huard, *l'Union,* October 18, 1862. *"Heureusement pour l'harmonie universelle du monde, pour la tranquillité et le bonheur de la famille, pour la morale religieuse et publique" . . . "notre âme retourne à Dieu, d'où elle vient. . ."*

164. *L'Union,* October 18, 1862.

165. André Cailloux as spirit guide, Henry Rey medium, July 17, 1863, RGCSR, 85–30, UNO.

166. Victor Lacroix as spirit guide, Henry Rey medium, February 21, 1869, RGCSR, 85–31, UNO.

167. *Tribune,* July 30, 1867. Caroline Senter, "Creole Poets on the Verge of a Nation," pp. 288–289 reads this poem as a lament over the eclipse of Creole of color racial in-between-ness by the Anglo-American racial binary.

168. Spirit communication from "*Un*" to medium Henry Rey, February 16, 1869, RGCSR, 85–31, UNO. On spiritualism, mesmerism, and related practices as a de-radicalizing influence on American politics, see Castronovo, *Necro Citizenship.* For Creoles of color, spiritualism, especially via the periodical *Le Spiritualiste,* was a powerful vehicle for political dissent. See Bell, *Revolution, Romanticism,* pp. 213–221. For another account of the relationship among African American protest, abolitionism, and spiritualism—in particular as these relate to the theatricality of Henry "Box" Brown, see Daphne A. Brooks, *Bodies in Dissent: Spectacular Performances of Race and Freedom, 1850-1910* (Durham, N.C.: Duke University Press, 2006), pp. 14–22; 120–126.

169. Ernest, *Liberation Historiography,* especially pp. 1–37.

170. Du Bois, Gates, and Oliver, *Souls,* p. 11; Sollors, *Beyond Ethnicity,* p. 49 emphasizes the benefits of being born within the veil.

171. The historiography of the Civil War and Reconstruction experience of New Orleans' Creoles of color has been polarized around those who seem to wish they had taken on a more forceful role as racial heroes (see especially Rankin, "The Forgotten People" and "Origins of Black Leadership") and those who celebrate

their attempts to rise above race and embrace their cultural heritage instead (see especially, Bell and Logsdon, "The Americanization of Black New Orleans" and Bell, *Revolution, Romanticism*).

172. On the dichotomy between phenotype (Gobineau) and history (Renan) in French thought, see Tzvetan Todorov, *On Human Diversity: Nationalism, Racism, and Exoticism in French Thought* (Cambridge, Mass.: Harvard University Press, 1993), pp. 90–170. Anthony Appiah, *In My Father's House: Africa in the Philosophy of Culture* (New York: Oxford University Press, 1992), pp. 28–46 elaborates on this ambiguity in his discussion of W. E. B. Du Bois's essay "Conservation of Races." See Glaude, *Exodus!* pp. 63–81 on the intertwined languages of race and nation. See David Theo Goldberg, *The Racial State* (Malden, Mass.: Blackwell, 2002) on the features of national cultures and state practices predicated on race, and Russ Castronovo, *Fathering the Nation: American Genealogies of Slavery and Freedom* (Berkeley: University of California Press, 1995) on genealogies of race and nation in the antebellum United States.

173. *Tribune*, February 23, 1865, English.

174. On the idea of the unitary state as the defining feature of French nationalist thought, see John M. Murrin, "The French Revolution and the Emergence of the Nation Form," in Michael A. Morrison and Melinda S. Zook, *Revolutionary Currents: Nation Building in the Transatlantic World* (Lanham, Md.: Rowman and Littlefield, 2004), and Ernest Gellner, *Nations and Nationalism* (Ithaca, N.Y.: Cornell University Press, 1983). In contrast, the United States has emphasized an expansionist ideal and has maintained a commitment to a dual citizenship of individuals to the federal and state governments. Madison's Federalist 51, for example, expounds on the benefits of a "compound government."

175. *Tribune*, June 7, 1865, French. This formulation anticipates Ernest Renan's classic 1882 lecture "*Qu'est-ce qu'un nation?* (What is a nation?)", where he attempted to establish narrative and consensus (memory and forgetting) rather than race and language as a basis for nationhood.

176. *Tribune*, February 21, 1865, French; February 23, 1865, English.

177. *Tribune*, February 22, 1865, English.

178. *L'Union*, July 4, 1863.

179. *L'Union*, October 18, 1862 (my emphasis). On Bissette, see Brickhouse, *Transamerican Literary Relations*, pp. 89–117; Bongie, *Islands and Exiles*, pp. 266–287; Lawrence C. Jennings, "Cyril Bissette, Radical Black French Activist," *French History* 9 (1995).

180. See Castronovo, *Fathering the Nation*, pp. 190–228 on "discursive passing."

181. See Edwards, *Practice of Diaspora*, pp. 25–38 on the distinction between *nègre* (derogatory) and *noir* (triumphalist) and the subsequent reclamation of the term *Nègre* in the twentieth century. Senter, "Creole Poets on the Verge," pp. 290–292 discusses how Naudin rescued *La Marseillaise* from the Confederates, among whom the anthem was also popular.

182. In contrast, David Rankin argues that Creoles of color systematically repudiated their African heritage. David C. Rankin, "The Forgotten People: Free People of Color in New Orleans, 1850–1870" (Ph.D. dissertation, Johns Hopkins University, 1976), p. 135.

183. This perspective echoed that of G. W. F. Hegel, who characterized Africans as an ahistorical people in his *The Philosophy of History* first published in 1837 from lectures given in 1830–1831.

184. *Tribune*, August 13, 1865, English.

185. Phrase is from Ernest, *Liberation Historiography.*

186. *Tribune*, August 13, 1865, English.

187. *Tribune*, August 13, 1865, English. See Gayraud S. Wilmore, *Black Religion and Black Radicalism: An Interpretation of the Religious History of African Americans*, 3rd ed. (Maryknoll, N.Y.: Orbis Books, 1998), pp. 125–162, and Ernest, *Liberation Historiography*, pp. 68–78. Both Wilmore and Ernest stress the importance of Africa as a racial home and a place of religious origin (via Moses in Egypt). Also see Sibylle Fischer, *Modernity Disavowed: Haiti and the Cultures of Slavery in the Age of Revolution* (Durham, N.C.: Duke University Press, 2004), pp. 48–54 on Egypt as an important touchstone for Haitian revolutionaries and those they inspired.

188. Ethnological debates raged regarding the racial character of the ancient Egyptians. See Samuel George Morton, *Crania Aegyptiaca* (Philadelphia: J. Penington, 1844) for the racist view. See Mia Bay, *The White Image in the Black Mind: African-American Ideas about White People, 1830–1925* (New York: Oxford University Press, 2000), pp. 26–30, 67–71 for John Russworm's and Frederick Douglass's counterclaims.

189. See Messner, *Freedmen*, pp. 9–20 on General Phelps's Anglo-Saxonism, his colonization plans, and his impact on Butler's confiscation program. On Republican support of colonization, see Foner, *Free Soil, Free Labor, Free Men*, pp. 267–280. On Lincoln and colonization, see Benjamin Quarles, *Lincoln and the Negro* (New York: Oxford University Press, 1962). Also see Cox, *Lincoln and Black Freedom*, pp. 23–24, and Mark E. Neely, Jr., "Abraham Lincoln and Black Colonization: Benjamin Butler's Spurious Testimony," *Civil War History*, XXV (March 1979), pp. 77–83, which stress Lincoln's wavering support of colonization.

190. *L'Union*, October 18, 1862.

191. Houzeau and Rankin, *My Passage*, p. 109.

192. Tunnell describes this paradox in *Crucible of Reconstruction*, chap. 6, especailly pp. 134–135.

193. See, for example, "The White Man's Party and the Radical Party," *Tribune*, October 30, 1867, English.

194. *Tribune*, October 25, 1867.

195. Henry Clay Warmoth, *War, Politics, and Reconstruction; Stormy Days in Louisiana* (New York: The Macmillan Company, 1930), p. 51.

196. Houzeau to his parents, April 2, 1868, *Lettres*, p. 428. "*Le viel esprit aristocratique du mulatre s'est réveillé, et aujourd'hui il y a trois partis: les esclavagistes, les noirs (avec les blancs radicaux), et un petit parti de mulâtres (avec quelques blancs mécontents)*" (author's translation).

197. Ibid.

198. Houzeau to his parents, May 9, 1868, *Lettres*, p. 430.

199. David Rankin, "Introduction," Houzeau and Rankin, *My Passage*, pp. 7, 24 on Houzeau's passing. On Houzeau's escape from Texas, see Jean-Charles Houzeau, "La Terreur Blanche au Texas et Mon Evasion" (Bruxelles: Ve Parent et Fils, 1862). The House Reports, 39th Congress, Second Session, no. 16, Report of the Select Committee on the New Orleans Riots (1867) lists Houzeau as "colored."

200. C. W. Thompson, *Walking and the French Romantics: Rousseau to Sand and Hugo* (Oxford and New York: P. Lang, 2003), pp. 107–127.

201. Houzeau and Rankin, *My Passage*, p. 76.

Epilogue: No Enviable Dilemma

1. Spirit of Victor Lacroix to Rey medium, February 21, 1869, RGCSR, 85–31, UNO.

2. On Warmoth as a "whipping boy" of the right and left, see Ted Tunnell, *Crucible of Reconstruction: War, Radicalism, and Race in Louisiana, 1862–1877* (Baton Rouge: Louisiana State University Press, 1984), pp. 151–172; Henry Clay Warmoth, *War, Politics, and Reconstruction; Stormy Days in Louisiana* (New York: The Macmillan Company, 1930).

3. Oscar J. Dunn to Horace Greeley in Tunnell, *Crucible of Reconstruction*, p. 165.

4. Pinchback's support for the *Tribune* group's policies fluctuated according to the political context. As lieutenant governor and state senator, he often supported equal accommodation bills in spite of his initial distaste for sharing social space with whites. Joe Gray Taylor, *Louisiana Reconstructed* (Baton Rouge: Louisiana State University Press, 1974), p. 211. Pinchback's grandson, Harlem Renaissance-era writer Jean Toomer, fashioned—as had francophone Creoles of color—an influential literary expression of and response to racial ambiguity.

5. Tunnell, *Crucible of Reconstruction*, p. 145. Tunnell argues that Pinchback's position constituted an expedient deferral to white leadership. I maintain that his position was a cautious but complex response to the realities of American racism, with a long-standing tradition in African American politics.

6. Although I have referred to Pinchback as a supporter of Warmoth, this alliance, like many during Reconstruction, was short-lived and strategic. For an overview of Pinchback's life, see James Haskins, *Pinckney Benton Stewart Pinchback* (New York: Macmillan, 1973).

7. Pinchback to Warmoth, December 9, 1872, in Tunnell, *Crucible of Reconstruction*, p. 171. See Tunnell, pp. 169–172 on the course of the 1872 election. On Warmoth's ouster from office, see Taylor, *Louisiana Reconstructed*, pp. 209–252. On the often bitter and contested nature of Louisiana elections under Reconstruction, see Tunnell, pp. 160–161.

8. On Creole of color animosity toward Pinchback and Southern University, see Joseph and Caryn Cossé Bell Logsdon, "The Americanization of Black New Orleans," in Arnold R. and Joseph Logsdon Hirsch, eds., *Creole New Orleans: Race and Americanization* (Baton Rouge: Louisiana State University Press, 1992), pp. 210–204, 251–254. For a comparison of Pinchback and Mary, see Rodolphe Lucien Desdunes, "Hommage Rendu à la Mémoire de Alexandre Aristide Mary," New Orleans, 1893, pp. 5–9, A. P. Tureaud Collection, ARC. See Rodolphe Lucien Desdunes, *Our People and Our History*, trans. Sister Dorothea Olga McCants (Baton Rouge: Louisiana State University Press, 1973), p. 140 on Mary's role in the 1872 election.

9. Desdunes, *Our People*, pp. 114–123 on Rey, and James Keith Hogue, *Uncivil War: Five New Orleans Street Battles and the Rise and Fall of Radical Reconstruction* (Baton Rouge: Louisiana State University Press, 2006), pp. 91–115 on the riot in general.

10. In addition to *Cruikshank*, significant Louisiana cases include the *Slaughter-House Cases* (1873), which put section 1 of the Fourteenth Amendment to the test; *Decuir v. Hall* (1878), a segregation case discussed below; and *Plessy v. Ferguson* (1896). Also, the deadlock in the contested 1876 presidential election hinged on results in Louisiana.

11. Unification Papers, LSU.

12. Unification Papers; Christopher E. G. Benfey, *Degas in New Orleans: Encounters in the Creole World of Kate Chopin and George Washington Cable* (New York: Knopf, 1997), pp. 180–183, p. 206 on Cable.

13. *Decuir v. Benson*, Docket #4829, LSCR, UNO.

14. Unification Papers, LSU.

15. See survey of teachers conducted on September 16, 1867, NOPSSR, UNO.

16. NOPSSR, UNO, 5th Military District, June 15, 1868. See interview with B. Aggeret, a white Freedmen's Bureau teacher. Interviewees perhaps sensed the biased nature of the survey. Creole of color principals such as Ludger Boquille of the Republican School and Armand Lanusse of the Couvent Institute declined to offer opinions.

17. *NODP*, July 18, 1873.

18. Roger A. Fischer, *The Segregation Struggle in Louisiana, 1862–77* (Urbana: University of Illinois Press, 1974); Tunnell, *Crucible of Reconstruction*, pp. 119–120. See Benfey, *Degas in New Orleans*, pp. 215–226 on the attack on the schools. In a curious coincidence, Madame Lalaurie's Haunted House (discussed in chapter 4 of this book) was a girl's school in 1874, a site of this racist assault. Cable, "The Haunted House in Royal Street, 1831–82," in *Strange True Stories of Louisiana* (Gretna, La.: Pelican, [1889] 1994), pp. 219–232.

19. Board of School Directors, Public School Superintendent Report, June 22, 1877, NOPSSR, UNO.

20. *State of Louisiana, Ex. Relator Ursin Dellande v. City School Board No. 7500*, 33 La Ann. 1469 (1881), and *Paul Trévigne v. The School Board of New Orleans et als. No. 6832*, 31 La Ann. 105 (January 1879), LSCR, UNO.

21. *Trévigne v. School Board*, plaintiff's brief.

22. *State of Louisiana ex Rel. Ursin Dellande v. City School Board*, opinion of the court.

23. Rebecca J. Scott, *Degrees of Freedom: Louisiana and Cuba after Slavery* (Cambridge, Mass.: Belknap Press of Harvard University Press, 2005), pp. 77–87. See John C. Rodrigue, *Reconstruction in the Cane Fields: From Slavery to Free Labor in Louisiana's Sugar Parishes, 1862–1880* (Baton Rouge: Louisiana State University Press, 2001) on the rural quest for rights. See Rebecca J. Scott, "Se Battre pour Ses Droits," *Cahiers du Brésil Contemporain* 53/54 (2003) on antisegregation activism of Creoles of color. See James B. Bennett, *Religion and the Rise of Jim Crow in New Orleans* (Princeton, N.J.: Princeton University Press, 2005) on interracial cooperation in the New Orleans Methodist Episcopal Church.

24. May 24, 1890, memorial to the state legislature cited in C. Vann Woodward, "The Case of the Louisiana Traveler," in John A. Garraty, ed. *Quarrels that have Shaped the Constitution* (New York: Harper and Row, 1962), p. 147.

25. Charles A. Lofgren, *The Plessy Case: A Legal-Historical Interpretation* (New York: Oxford University Press, 1987); Scott, *Degrees of Freedom;* Woodward, "Louisiana Traveler"; Desdunes, *Our People*, p. 141 on Mary.

26. Scott, "Se Battre pour Ses Droits"; Nell Irvin Painter, *Standing at Armageddon: The United States, 1877–1919* (New York: W.W. Norton, 1987). For a recent assessment of Booker T. Washington's political, social, and educational sensibility, see Houston A. Baker, *Turning South Again: Re-Thinking Modernism/Re-Reading Booker T* (Durham, N.C.: Duke University Press, 2001).

27. Scott, *Degrees of Freedom*, pp. 88–91.

28. Argument of the defendant is that of *contract-répugnant*. Desdunes, *Our People*, p. 147.

29. See Saidiya V. Hartman, *Scenes of Subjection: Terror, Slavery, and Self-Making in Nineteenth-Century America* (New York: Oxford University Press, 1997), pp. 157–171 on how the "social" encompassed the "racial" in the last decades of the nineteenth century.

30. *Louisiana Senate Journal*, 1898, p. 33.

31. Rayford W. Logan, *The Negro in American Life and Thought: The Nadir, 1877–1901* (New York: Dial Press, 1954). Desdunes, "Forlorn Hope and Noble Despair," cited in Scott, *Degrees of Freedom*, pp. 91–92.

32. On the crisis in black leadership, see W. E. B. Du Bois, Henry Louis Gates, and Terri Hume Oliver, *The Souls of Black Folk: Authoritative Text, Contexts, Criticism* (New York: W.W. Norton, 1999), pp. 34–45; David L. Lewis, *W. E. B. Du Bois—Biography of a Race, 1868–1919* (New York: H. Holt, 1993), pp. 297–342.

33. Rodolphe Lucien Desdunes, "A Few Words to Dr. Du Bois, with Malice Towards None," (New Orleans, 1907) CRC, ARC, p. 1.

34. Ibid., p. 2.

35. Ibid., p. 13.

36. Ibid.

37. Ibid., pp. 5–6.

38. Desdunes, *Our People*, pp. 147–148.

39. Desdunes, "A Few Words," p. 11.

40. Ibid., p. 7.

41. Ibid., p. 5.

42. Ibid., pp. 9, 4–5.

43. Ibid., p. 3.

44. Ibid., p. 11.

45. Caryn Cossé Bell, *Revolution, Romanticism, and the Afro-Creole Protest Tradition in Louisiana, 1718–1868* (Baton Rouge: Louisiana State University Press, 1997), p. 217.

46. Victor Lacroix as spirit guide, Henry Rey medium, February 21, 1869, RGCSR, 85–31, UNO.

47. On these tragedies and Du Bois's Atlanta years more generally, see Lewis, *W. E. B. Du Bois*, pp.226–228; 333–337; 343–385.

48. Desdunes, "A Few Words," p. 12.

49. Ibid., p. 13.

50. On Alfred Du Bois's heritage and W. E. B. Du Bois's complex feelings about his father, see Lewis, *W. E. B. Du Bois*, pp. 21–23; 52.

51. Du Bois, Gates, and Oliver, *Souls*, p. 9.

52. Ibid., p. 17.

53. Ibid., pp. 47; 35, 40, 45; 27; 140–141; 82; 153; 133.

54. Ibid., p. 11.

Acknowledgments

A NUMBER OF PEOPLE HAVE read part or all of this manuscript and have offered invaluable advice. The shortcomings of the book are due to my failure to heed all of it. Evelyn Brooks Higginbotham's historian's eye for both detail and the larger picture of African American and women's history helped me immensely as I shaped early drafts. I am in permanent debt to Garnette Cadogan, who has read and reread countless versions of the entire book. Even though his sharp critical eye and astute suggestions have been a constant source of frustration, his bold imagination and enthusiasm for my work have buoyed me throughout. Our mutual love of New Orleans and its history, culture, and people has provided the impetus for our friendship but, happily, has not imposed limits on it. Julia Mickenberg has also been a font of encouragement and support. She has not only brought her inimitable critical sensibilities to drafts of various chapters, but she has even helped conjure some of them into being.

Judith Schafer read the entire manuscript early on and subsequently guided me through many of the particularities of Louisiana's legal culture. I also thank Janet Davis, Carolyn Eastman, Steven Hoelscher, Nhi Lieu, Stephen Marshall, Jolie Olcott, Werner Sollors, and Jennifer Wilks for reading drafts of various chapters. The anonymous readers for Harvard University Press offered extensive and invaluable comments.

I have benefited immensely from the openness, curiosity, and energy that thrive in the American Studies Department at the University of Texas (UT) at Austin. UT's John L. Warfield Center for African and African American Studies has been an important intellectual home, and I continue to be grateful to Edmund T. Gordon and Omi Olomo (Joni L. Jones) for their commitment to fostering a politically progressive atmosphere for historical, cultural, and activist scholarship. I presented a portion of this work at the Center's Diaspora Talks and benefited immensely from participants' comments. Fellow members of the Black Diaspora Consortium have encouraged me to think more broadly about the practical and theoretical aspects of diaspora. During the spring of 2007, I was a Humanities Institute Faculty Fellow at UT. Though, technically, I brought another project to this seminar, our wonderfully thought-provoking discussions shaped my final revisions for this book.

I could never have conducted this research without generous financial support. I would like to thank the Ford Foundation for fellowship in every sense of the word. I am grateful as well to the Harvard Graduate Society, the Charles Warren Center for American History, and the History of Civilization Committee for funding research travel. The Faculty Development Program and the Center for African and African American Studies at UT Austin have provided much-appreciated support for summer research.

New Orleans has a plethora of rich archives that would be useless without its passionately dedicated archivists. Bruce Raeburn at the Hogan Jazz Archives at Tulane University is a font of knowledge about the New Orleans performance culture and graciously introduced me to pertinent recordings by Edward "Kid" Ory. I would also like to acknowledge Brenda Square at the Amistad Research Center; Sally Reeves of the New Orleans Notarial Archives; Greg Osborn, Irene Wainwright, and Wayne Everard at the New Orleans Public Library; Lester Sullivan of Xavier University; and John Kelley and Marie Windell of the Earl K. Long Library of the University of New Orleans (UNO). Marie Windell, in particular, transformed long hours of research at UNO into an enchanted journey through time and space. In the post-Katrina period, UNO archivists James Lien, Sean Benjamin, and Florence Jumonville helped me fill some important research gaps from afar. Thomas Lanham of Louisiana State Museum and Sally

Stassi of the Historic New Orleans Collection have been patient and helpful in locating maps and illustrations for me.

On one of my first research trips to New Orleans, I met my "big brother" Garnette, who has over the years hosted (in his physical space and his intellectual engagement) an ever-evolving and delightfully sprawling interrogation of American culture. I am grateful for his friendship, food, and fellowship. I would also like to acknowledge Roseanne Adderley, Caryn Cossé Bell, Samuel Du Bois Cook, Sylvia Cook, Monique Guillory, Sybil Kein, the late Joseph Kennedy, Emily Landau, Michael Lomax, Jasmine Mir, Lawrence Powell, Bruce Raeburn, Don Richmond, Judith Schafer, Felipé Smith, Teresa Toulouse, and Sherrie Tucker who extended themselves to me in various ways. I thank Brita, Roberto, and Lilias Bonechi; the staff and residents of Adams House circa 1997–2001; Araya and Denise Haile and family; Maya Browne; Maria Franklin; Asale Angel-Ajani; Joanna Brooks, David Kamper, and family; the congregation of Mt. Olive Baptist Church, and especially the Reverend Richard Carter, who exemplifies African American Biblical exegesis; and Jason, Angie, and the whole crew at Flightpath Coffee House, my office away from the office.

I express gratitude to my father, Joseph E. Thompson, Sr., for being my role model and hero and for reading significant portions of this work. I am grateful to my mother, Shirley W. Thompson, for pushing me to do more than I ever believe I can. My brother, Joseph E. Thompson, Jr., has helped me maintain a sense of humor and has been a source of sanity and wisdom. My sister, Amber G. Thompson, assisted me in the archives but, more importantly, forced me to keep my eyes open to the sights and sounds around me. In recent years, my familial circle has expanded to include a wealth of in-laws whose prayers have sustained me and whose talent and creativity have inspired me. I would like to express my gratitude to my parents; my mother-in-law, Christine Marshall; and my nephew Bjorn Hannibal for stepping in at crucial moments to help with childcare.

Stephen and Solomon Marshall have transformed my life and my sense of what is possible. Though this book is in many respects a meditation on the prospects of cultural and literal death, Steve and Solo have been an unambiguous source of life and light. I dedicate this book to them.

Index